MUSKIE
ON THE FLY

MUSKIE
ON THE FLY

ROBERT S. TOMES

Photography by Eric Engbretson, Ted Fauceglia,
James Linehan, Thomas R. Pero, and many others

Illustrations by Chris Armstrong

Library of Congress Cataloging-in-Publication Data
Tomes, Robert S.
      Muskie on the fly./Robert S. Tomes.—1st ed.
        p. cm.
      ISBN 9780974642758 (hardcover)
Muskie. 2. Fly fishing. I. Title.

Library of Congress Control Number 2007940619

Book and jacket design by Gregory Smith Design

Published by Wild River Press, Post Office Box 13360, Mill Creek, Washington 98082 USA

Wild River Press Web site address: www.wildriverpress.com

Printed in China through Four Colour Imports, Ltd.

10 9 8 7 6 5 4 3 2 1

DEDICATION

THIS BOOK IS DEDICATED TO MY WIFE, CYNTHIA, for her love, patience, and encouragement. To my mother, Joann, and father, James, for nurturing my early fishing passion. To Andy Burrows, for giving me a chance to fulfill my fly fishing dreams. To Jim Chapralis, for encouraging me to share my experiences with others. And finally, to all the dedicated fly fishers and muskie anglers around the country who make this such a wonderful sport. Thank you.

ACKNOWLEDGMENTS

THE BOOK YOU HOLD IN YOUR HANDS REPRESENTS SEVERAL DECADES of personal experience exhaustively recorded, photographed, organized, and condensed during the last three years into several hundred pages of ink, paper, photos, and illustrations. In this self-publishing, digital age an undertaking of this magnitude may seem like an anachronism. For me, however, it was the only way to thoroughly cover this new and rather arcane subject matter with the depth and quality I desired. It also follows in a long, and, I think, important tradition of fly-fishing—and muskie-fishing— books that pay deep respect to both the reader and the great game fish that is the muskellunge. Compared to my normal freelance-writing endeavors, writing this book has been a monumental but nonetheless satisfying undertaking. A project of this quality and substance is certainly not possible without advice and guidance from others. Hidden between these pages are the unique talents and knowledge of many fine and dedicated individuals who share my passion and have played a significant role in the creation of *Muskie on the Fly*.

I am most thankful to the three principal architects who brought this book to life: publisher and editor Tom Pero for embracing and directing my vision and giving me the opportunity to write the first book ever published on fly fishing for muskies; graphic designer Greg Smith for his brilliant design skills, technical expertise and patience in creating the stunning layout; and our gifted illustrator Chris Armstrong for vividly capturing the essence of this sport and fish in ways I never thought possible. Thank you all for making my dream a reality.

A core group of conventional and fly-fishing experts who served as motivators, consultants, and advisors also deserve my utmost gratitude for their individual contributions and dedication to this book: muskie fly-fishing guides Troy Anderson, Brad Bohen, Pat Ehlers, "Musky Joe" Flater, Steve Kunnath, Don Larson, Dan Legere, Mike Lazarus, Mark Meritt, Mike Mladenik, and Tom Schenk; muskellunge historian Larry Ramsell; fly tier extraordinaire Jon Uhlenhop; northern pike fly-fishing expert Barry Reynolds; fishing authority Don Dubin; photographers Eric Engbretson, Ted Fauceglia, Jim Linehan, Paul Melchior, and Lisa Meritt; outdoor writer Dale Bowman; proof readers Cameron Derbyshire, Jethro Felton, Clay Stauffer, Robert Swan, and John Van Vleet.

I am also thankful for the support, encouragement and camaraderie (and free coffee!) provided over the years by a number of fly-fishing establishments around the country including the Trout & Grouse in Northfield, Illinois; Chicago Fly Fishing Outfitters and Orvis Chicago in Chicago, Illinois; One More Cast in Countryside, Illinois; Hayward Fly Fishing Company in Hayward, Wisconsin; Tight Lines Outfitters in De Perre, Wisconsin; The Fly Fishers in Milwaukee, Wisconsin; The Fly

Angler in Fridley, Minnesota; Lost River Outfitters and Silver Creek Outfitters in Ketchum, Idaho; Front Range Anglers in Boulder, Colorado; Davidson River Outfitters in Pisgah Forest, North Carolina; Maine Guide Fly Shop in Greenville, Maine; and the Urban Angler in New York, New York.

The same heartfelt thanks goes out to my many friends and supporters in fly-fishing clubs, muskie-fishing clubs, fishing organizations, fly-fishing and muskie publications, Web sites, television, radio, and fly-fishing shows around the country that have provided exposure, support, and encouragement over the past several years: The Anglers' Club of Chicago; Rick Bannerot and The Anglers' Club of New York; Muskies Inc.; Muskies Canada; Zachary Arnold and the members of Chicagoland Muskie Hunters; Bob Jennings and *Muskie* Magazine; Jim Saric and Steve Heiting of *Musky Hunter* Magazine; Jack Burns, formerly of *Esox Angler* magazine; Tom Helgeson of *Midwest Fly Fishing* Magazine and The Great Waters Fly Fishing Expo; Chuck Furimsky and Barry Serviente of The Fly Fishing Show; Crispin and Bill Battles, Chris Major, and Dudley Hall of *Fly Fish America* Magazine; John Randolph and Ross Purnell of *Fly Fisherman* Magazine; Dick Wentz of Keokee Publications and *The Fly Fisher* Magazine published by the Federation of Fly Fishers; Marshall Cutchin of MidCurrent Flyfishing News; Nick Amato of Amato Publications; Pete McDonald of *Boating* Magazine; Dave Carlson's *Northland Adventures* television show; Mike Mladenik's *Fishing with Northwood's Guide Mike Mladenik* television show and *Northwoods Adventures* Magazine; Mike Jackson's Outdoors radio show; Emmett Brown of the National Freshwater Fishing Hall of Fame; the International Game Fish Association; outdoor writer Bill Barbee; and John Field of the American Casting Association.

For technical and research assistance, advice and direction regarding muskie biology, habitat and behavior in Chapter 2, my sincere appreciation to Wisconsin Department of Natural Resources Fisheries Biologists Frank Pratt, Jr., Tim Simonson, John Kubisiak, Steve Timler, and Maine Department of Inland Fisheries and Wildlife Public Relations Specialist Bill Pierce—thank you for your dedication and hard work on behalf of muskie fishers everywhere. A note of gratitude as well to Minnesota's Cass County Historical Society for use of the Leech Lake photo included in Chapter 3, and to the International Game Fish Association and the National Freshwater Fishing Hall of Fame for the use of their fly-rod muskie world record data.

For product support, technical advice and assistance, a special note of gratitude to Jon Bauer and Jim Andras of Bauer Reels; James Shaughnessy of Beulah Fly Rods; Charles Sander of Charlie's Specialties; Matt Cassel of Cliff Outdoors; Norman Hartman, Gregg Thorne, and Nate Dablock of Cortland Line Company; Enrico Puglisi of Enrico Puglisi Flies Ltd.; Steve Rajeff of G.Loomis;

Glenn Young of Gamakatsu hooks; Chris Conaty and Hogan Brown of Idylwilde Flies; Barry Stokes of Islander Reels; Shinichiro Asano of Little Presents; Tom Rosenbauer, T.J. Roy, Tony Mort, Joe Owens, Nate Jenkins, Lee Robinson and Paul Kearney of Orvis; Chris Callanan and Troy Cooley of Outcast Sporting Gear; Tim Rajeff of Rajeff Sports; Rainy Riding and the staff of Rainy's Flies; Marlin Roush of Rio Products; Jeff Wieringa, Tim Pommer and John Mazurkiewicz of 3M Scientific Anglers; Moose Hofer of Scott Fly Rods; Jeff Schluter and Brad Wright of St. Croix; Jim Teeny and the staff of Teeny Lines; Lefty Kreh and Jim Shulin of Temple Fork Outfitters; Bruce Olsen of Umpqua Feather Merchants; Ryan Harrison and Jennifer Lavigne of Waterworks-Lamson and many others.

My appreciation as well to the following talented muskie and fly-fishing guides and friends for their insights, encouragement and support in the creation of this book: Tom Anderson, Nathaniel Axtell, Mark Aspinall, Brad Befus, Chad Cain, John Chlebowski, Mike Clancy, Rich Clarke, Jon Cullen, Phil Cusey, Jerry Darkes, Paul Dixon, Thomas Drysdale, Kevin Feenstra, Andy Flater, Austin Flater, Ernie French, William "Dal" Frost, Kelly Galloup, Tim and Dan Garry, Rusty Gates, Steven Gomberg, Ben Hall, John and Terri Herzer, Thad Hinshaw, Dec Hogan, Jim Klug, Ben Kuneg, Andy Kurkulis, Peter Kraeger, Joey Lin, Daryl and Mary Lorberter, Brendan McCarthy, Brian Meszaros, Joseph Meyer, Jody Mills, Jack Mitchell, Mark Newhouse, John O'Hearn, Todd Polacek, Gary and Connie Pierce, Eve Reilly, Curt Schlesinger, Nikki Seger, Victor Shawe, Jon Spiegel, Peter Sykes, Kip Vieth, Tanner Wildes, Mark Whitehead, and David Wood.

A very special note of thanks to all those muskie fly-fishing fanatics throughout North America who have waited patiently (and not so patiently) for the long-awaited release of this book—your kind letters, emails, and phone calls were a constant source of inspiration, encouragement, and motivation.

And, finally, to all the professional fly-fishing guides, and special fishing friends and associates, living and deceased, around the globe I've had the honor of fishing with and who generously shared their time, passion, and unique talents (and single-malt and flies!) with me on and off the water from Montauk Point to New Zealand and from Patagonia to Alaska: Thank you sincerely for making me a better fisherman and a better person.

ROBERT S. TOMES
CHICAGO, ILLINIOS
January 2008

CONTENTS

FOREWORD 1

FRONTIS 4

CHAPTER 1 Hooked for Life 10

CHAPTER 2 The Magnificent Muskie 20

CHAPTER 3 The Mind Game 42

CHAPTER 4 The Right Stuff 58

CHAPTER 5 Big Flies for Big Fish 84

CHAPTER 6 Essential Fly-Rod Skills 122

CHAPTER 7 Proven Presentation Techniques 140

CHAPTER 8 Converting Follows 172

CHAPTER 9 Getting Hooked Up 188

CHAPTER 10 A Season on the Water 212

CHAPTER 11 Muskie Guides 238

CHAPTER 12 Great Fly-Rod Muskie Waters 256

CREDITS 275

INDEX 276

FOREWORD

IT WAS AT THE ORIGINAL TROUT AND GROUSE FLY SHOP, then in Wilmette, Illinois, where I first met an enthusiastic, 14-year-old youngster named Robert Tomes. As I recall, he worked part time in Andy Burrows's shop, famous for Saturday morning get-togethers, when anglers of all experience levels congregated to drink coffee, exchange stories, share new techniques, and even flash a few photos of trophy fish. Bright-eyed, always helpful and alert, young Tomes listened and absorbed all the useful information he could—filing it away in his memory bank for future use. Clearly, he was fascinated with everything that concerned angling: species, tackle, challenges— and, of course, the best fishing places.

We stayed in touch through much of his adult life. As he became more and more successful in his professional career, his angling horizons expanded around the globe as he sought to satisfy his insatiable appetite for angling adventure. Robert was interested in fishing new places as well as for new species wherever they took him.

"How else do you know if you really like a certain species or fishing destination unless you take a chance, go out and experience them firsthand?" he would say. Makes sense. So he attacked his fly fishing with lessons first learned from his formative days at the Trout and Grouse: Listen. Research. Absorb. Analyze. Plan. Strategize.

And, most importantly, never ever give up!

From a young age he succeeded with just about every species he sought, including permit on a fly, perhaps the most difficult of all angling games we've learned to play. Bonefish? Tarpon? He's pursued them all with consistent success. In fact, he's one of the few I know who accomplished a coveted grand slam very early in his saltwater career. All these species and experiences helped to fashion a mind set for future challenges.

I also found it remarkable that no matter what fish he targeted, Tomes was not only successful, but also usually landed specimens that were as big or bigger than anyone had caught. Talk about "bragging rights." His probable world-record steelhead from British Columbia comes to mind, but equally as impressive were (and are) his incredible results from heavily fished waters around the Midwest.

Okay, not every trip was a success. Weather conditions and other variables can foil the best of angling plans. Tomes learned to deal with that, too. His most important motto—"don't give up"— served him well. More often than not his last cast (or last half-dozen casts) converted a poor fishing day into a good one.

Through the years I knew of Robert's unique obsession with muskie on the fly. I understood and shared his addiction having quit my job in my late twenties and spent an entire season on an Ontario island chasing one big muskie. Never went to town. Got my hair cut by a native guide. Just muskie fished. To be sure, I know all about the attraction of muskie fishing. I'm also well acquainted with the frustrations, the hard work, and the physical and mental drain that one may experience day after day while other "normal" anglers are out enjoying themselves catching easier species.

No one, to my mind, is more qualified to tackle muskies on the fly than Robert Tomes. Clearly, he is the man to write the first comprehensive book on this emerging sport. He has paid his dues. He casts and retrieves. Casts and retrieves. Hundreds of times. All day long. From dawn to night. And then some. His five-hundredth cast is delivered with the same confidence and optimism as his first dozen. He does not stop. True, he is a powerful caster who possesses unusual endurance. Believe me, friends, you need that to succeed in any type of muskie fishing, let alone with a fly rod.

But persistence isn't everything. Robert always fishes smart. With each and every cast he probes the water constantly searching for clues and, in his mind, clicking off years of previous experiences that might help him convert a slow day into a successful one. He changes flies. He alters his retrieves. He shortens or lengthens his average cast. And if things don't go exactly according to plan? There's always another spot to check out. Or another day. Same energy. Same determination. Same confidence.

Over several decades of pursuing these legendary freshwater monsters, Robert Tomes has consistently taken fish that should make conventional muskie anglers stop and re-think their time-honored approach. His unique fly-fishing techniques, strategies, and flies add another dimension to the sport and open entirely new worlds for like-minded fly anglers who seek a new, exciting adventure.

Muskie on the Fly is for all anglers reaching for that new challenge, exploring a facet of angling that has a limited fraternity, but is bound to multiply with the popularity of this book. Pay close attention to what Tomes says. About muskies. About tackle. About strategy. About perseverance. He has been there. He knows his subject better than anyone. He may well be the best there is in the sport and is certainly the best authority for writing the very first book on the subject.

JIM CHAPRALIS
EVANSTON, ILLINIOS
May 2007

A note from the Publisher.

Jim Chapralis pioneered international fishing travel and assisted in publicizing sport fishing in a number of Latin American countries. He fished in 40 countries for most of the important gamefish and was fortunate to fish with many of world's top anglers. Jim wrote five fishing books and numerous articles and produced a monthly international newsletter for 25 years. He competed in international and national casting championships and won four gold metals in distance fly casting (senior division). In recognition of his significant contributions to the sport of fishing, he was recently inducted into the National Freshwater Fishing Hall of Fame in Hayward, Wisconsin. Sadly, Chapralis passed away in November 2007, shortly before this book went to press. He was 76.

"*I am haunted by waters.*"
—NORMAN MACLEAN

"*Fishing for muskellunge is like writing love letters that are never mailed. Your chances of success are limited but there is pleasure in the ritual.*"

—NELSON BRYANT

The New York Times

YAK ATTACK

FIRE TIGER

Overall Length: Ten to 15 inches.

HOOK: Gamakatsu SC15-2H size 4/0 to 5/0.

THREAD: UTC 140 red.

RATTLE: Large rattle inside EZ Body Braid.

TAIL: (tying order) 1. Red yak hair, 2. orange yak hair, 3. orange Ice Wing Fiber.

WING: (tying order) 1. Yellow Big Fly Fiber high tied, 2. chartreuse yak hair hollow tied, 3. green yak hair hollow tied.

CHEEKS: Opal mirage Flashabou.

TOPPING: Emerald green Ice Wing Fiber.

EYES: Doll eyes (15mm).

HEAD: Thread coated in 5-Minute epoxy.

BARRING: Black waterproof marker.

HOOKED FOR LIFE

"No man is born an artist or an angler."
—Issac Walton

I AM OBSESSED WITH A FISH. Not just any fish: A giant piscatorial predator with teeth like a barracuda and the disposition of a pit bull. It's a fish so dominant in its position at the very top of the food chain that it normally eats other game fish, various waterfowl, and small mammals. Sometimes it even bites people. In truth, this fish is so hard to catch that many who try—even for just a day—eventually give up out of boredom, frustration, or sheer physical pain.

This fish is definitely not your typical fly-rod quarry. It does not move gently through the water sipping little insects, nor does it inspire thoughts of solitude and inner peace. Rather, it is a moody, unpredictable fish with an enormous and seemingly insatiable appetite. This denizen of lakes and rivers routinely makes the most jaded anglers angry, excited, elated, and even a little bit scared, all at the same time.

Like the eternal hunt for the Loch Ness Monster or Big Foot, some who have pursued this special fish begin to question their own sanity and, on slower days, whether it actually exists. Those who are fortunate enough to finally hook or simply glimpse this mysterious aquatic beast find themselves with a compulsive desire to catch one—regardless of the chances for success. As if divinely cursed by the Greek gods, they will do just about anything for an opportunity at a muskie: risking financial ruin; traveling far and wide on a moment's notice; often forsaking jobs, friends, and family. My personal pursuit of this fish also knows no limits. It is satisfied only when I'm on the water, fly rod in hand, casting a big fly for hours on end.

This is the life of a serious muskie fly fisher. I love every moment of it.

As a reminder of my first encounter with a muskie, I keep an old photo on my office desk. It shows my mother and me at the foot of a well-weathered boat dock. I have a grin on my face from ear to ear; my mom is looking pretty pleased, too. In one hand I'm proudly holding up my first-ever muskie, a fish literally as long as my leg. I caught this trophy up in northern Wisconsin, near Boulder Junction, one of two towns self-proclaimed as "Muskie Capital of the World" in that muskie-obsessed state. I was using the appropriately named Mepps Musky Killer, an enormous bucktail spinner with a huge silver blade and a 5/0 treble hook.

I was only 14. I'll never forget this fish and the fleeting fame it brought me that great day. My dad,

who took the photo, never fails to remind me that even after catching this fish I begged and pleaded with him to go out again and try for an even bigger one. I reluctantly decided to relish my early success after an old-timer stopped by the dock to congratulate me on my big fish, remarking that he'd fished his entire lifetime for a "keeper" muskie (30 inches at the time) and had yet to accomplish his elusive goal.

To be accurate, my fishing obsession started many years prior to my first muskie. I'd been a confirmed fishing addict for as long as anyone could remember, wetting a line wherever and whenever I could. As a kid growing up in the suburbs of Chicago near Lake Michigan, I had discovered a surprising number of good fishing opportunities close to home. On any given summer afternoon I could be found riding my Sting-Ray bike, tenuously balancing my rod and tackle box on the handlebars, the few blocks down to the lake to catch anything that was biting: yellow perch, carp, coho salmon, even steelhead. The Great Lakes salmonid fishery was emerging quickly and I was making the most of it. And I didn't even have a boat or a driver's license.

Dad, who didn't quite understand my fishing obsession, nevertheless did his best to encourage me. He wasn't a fisherman himself but I'm sure he figured this was a lot better than some of the other stuff teens got involved with those days. After several years of wondering what the hell had gotten into me, he bought us a small boat with an outboard and we started making short fishing forays around the Midwest. Our first trips were strictly do-it-yourself affairs but after a

Boulder Junction, Wisconsin—my first muskie with Mom: An indelible experience that marked the beginning of a life-long obsession.

Legendary Wisconsin guide Ray Kennedy nets a hefty walleye during an early fishing foray with my father. Learning experiences such as this provided the foundation to hone my skills for future pursuits.

few disappointing outings with limited success, we realized the value of hiring a professional fishing guide to show us the way.

One of our first real fishing guides was the legendary Ray Kennedy of Minocqua, Wisconsin. Ray was a giant of a man who took us out on Lake Tomahawk in his 25-foot wooden inboard boat for walleye, bass, and pike, many of which we'd eat during a grand shore lunch in the traditional Northwoods style. Ray and his father Jim were also famous for catching huge muskies, several of which were mounted and hung like famous works of art in the more popular lakeside bars. Some of these fish were close to five feet long and weighed more than 50 pounds. I distinctly recall spending a lot of time just staring at them, many in fancy glass-and-wooden cases with elaborate aquatic scenes. I wondered, *Do fish like this still exist?* And, of more immediate importance, would I ever be so lucky to catch one myself?

On one memorable outing with Ray I actually did have a big muskie attack a small walleye as I was bringing it to the net. I'll never forget peering down into the lake depths at this evil-looking, monstrous creature as it swam slowly around the boat with my fish crosswise in its mouth. I can still see the bloody,

hand-sized tooth marks it left raked across the unfortunate walleye's back.

After many trips with Dad catching my fill of walleye, pike, and bass on live bait and lures, I eventually started to focus like a laser on the only real challenge left … MUSKIE! It was difficult not to. This was the undisputed trophy fish of northern Wisconsin. Everywhere you looked there were mounted muskies, not to mention muskie lures, muskie signs, and muskie bars. Most bait and tackle shops featured a "muskie board" that tallied fish caught that season. A glass-topped display cooler also sat out front where fishers and tourists could check out the latest big catch—usually with a bad case of freezer-burn from being weeks or months old. Everyone, it seemed, wanted to catch a muskie. The fact of the matter was that very few actually did.

Determined to catch a muskie myself, I went straight to the local library and read everything I could find about this exotic new fish and how to catch one. Since this was well before the Internet and fishing videos, I had to work hard to find any solid information on this elusive species. I was a motivated and enthusiastic kid on a serious mission—I absorbed everything I read like a sponge and proceeded to try to figure out the best time, place, and tackle to catch my first muskie.

My exhaustive research told me that June was an excellent month to catch a muskie in the Midwest with active post-spawn fish and a better-than-average catch rate on the most productive lakes. As for where to fish, I was simply looking for my first muskie—not the next world record. I chose a small lake near Boulder Junction with a large population of fish. (What better place than the Muskie Capital of the World?)

The tackle I purchased was standard issue for the sport: a six-foot Heddon fiberglass, stiff-as-a-pool-cue baitcasting rod matched with a high-speed reel; 40-pound braided Cortland Dacron line; heavy-wire leaders with ball-bearing swivels; and a variety of lures, including huge wooden "jerk" baits, top-water lures that looked like bath-tub toys, and massive multi-bladed spinners in every color of the rainbow.

I was fortunate to be fishing on my first day with another great Wisconsin guide by the name of Earl Mayo. Earl was a man of few words but his calm demeanor, leathery skin, and steely gaze told me he spent plenty of time on the water and knew just what to do to help me catch my first muskie.

"So you really want to catch a muskie, young man?" he asked when I met him early that morning at the dock. I responded with an enthusiastic, "Yes, sir!" and peppered him with a litany of questions revealing both my youthful excitement and ignorance.

Before we pulled out of the boat slip that misty June morning I watched expectantly as Earl looked over my newly acquired tackle, checked my knots, and set my drag. "Try this one," he said handing me one of the more popular oversized spinners I had recently bought. I'd never thrown a lure this big and was still somewhat amazed any freshwater fish would eat such a bizarre combination of bucktail and metal. Earl ran the boat a short distance and cut the engine, positioning us over a wide, newly emerging weed flat where he told me to start casting. Before I could even make the first cast he cautioned me with seven words I will never forget: "Keep a close eye on your lure."

At first I had a few of the proverbial "bird's nests" common with a free-spooling baitcasting reel but I soon got the hang of casting such a big lure with heavy Dacron line. Within an hour or so, I had my first official "follow." It was a small fish and I clearly saw the splash of its tail when it turned at the boat. Within minutes, I hooked and landed an undersized muskie that boosted my confidence and determination. This small fish also gave me a valuable lesson on

striking and fighting a muskie on baitcasting tackle—something I'd never done before. *I am going to catch a big muskie*, I now thought to myself with each cast.

Guiding in Alaska was an amazing experience for a kid from the Midwest. Among other important lessons, I learned to fish with absolute confidence wherever I cast a line.

Later that morning, across the lake on a different weed bed, I had a tremendous strike. An improbably large muskie thrashed violently on the surface throwing water in every direction. It took me a moment before I realized it had my spinner in its mouth. "Set the hook!" Earl commanded as I struggled to gain control. I set the hook as hard as I could and tried my best to reel in any slack. Despite my heavy tackle, each time I pulled on this great fish, it pulled back—taking line with ease against a stiff drag. I fought this fish gingerly for what seemed like an hour before Earl expertly netted my trophy. Once it was in the boat, I immediately realized I was shaking from head to toe and had to sit down to catch my breath. "That's a fine fish," Earl said, extending his hand for a congratulatory shake. As I admired my fish, Earl cranked up the engine and headed straight back to the boat ramp.

This mysterious fish in the bottom of the boat was like nothing I'd ever encountered in fresh or saltwater.

It looked a lot like a barracuda or huge northern pike with massive canines, an elongated body, and eyes toward the top of its head. The way it fought, with lunges, twists and twirls, reminded me strangely of alligator wrestling I'd seen on television. It seemed almost prehistoric, like an aquatic dinosaur with teeth and fins. Little did I know this was also the fish of a lifetime, and I was about to enjoy my 15 minutes of fame, at least back at the dock.

That first muskie changed my life forever. The sheer violence of the strike was something I'd read about, heard stories of, and dreamed about all winter

blocks from my home in the suburbs of Chicago. Working there was like a continuous birthday celebration with every kind of fly-fishing tackle imaginable at my immediate disposal. Inspired by this new-found sport, I learned to fly-cast by trial and error in my backyard and with the help of any books I could find on the subject.

Sensing my youthful enthusiasm, my fly-fishing mentors began inviting me on annual outings to fabled trout waters from the Au Sable River in Michigan to the Madison River in Montana. After a few more years I made my first saltwater fly-fishing

Like the aggressive but seldom-seen muskie, the elusive permit ranks among the most sought-after fly-rod species.

but was still totally unprepared for. I had simply never seen or felt something like this before in any kind of fishing I'd done. The muskie's extraordinary size and aggressive behavior combined with the fact they often showed themselves clearly behind the lure before striking was also something I found quite appealing—even addictive. Muskies quickly became my favorite quarry whenever and wherever I fished. I was still only 14 but officially obsessed.

As my fishing education progressed, I also began to learn more about the wonderful world of fly fishing from books, catalogs, and older fishing friends. I got a job working for an Orvis retail operation that had recently opened—quite fortuitously—only a few

trip to Islamorada, Florida, and was amazed at the size, strength, and fighting ability of ocean-dwelling fish such as bonefish, barracuda, and tarpon. The multilayered complexity of fly fishing appealed to my growing desire for a challenge. I soon found myself immersed in entomology, fly tying, rod making, and all the other unique aspects that make this sport so much fun.

Then one day back at home I was reading through an early nineteenth-century book of natural history given to me by my grandfather and came across a section entitled "Muskalonge" (one of many spellings derived from the original Native American Indian word for the muskie). This book described the

Giant steelhead on the fly such as this double-striped monster from British Columbia share many things in common with muskie.

muskalonge as "one of most remarkable inhabitants of the great lakes" noting with much dramatic flair that "the sport afforded by the capture of such leviathans may be easily imagined." What intrigued me most about this description, however, was the following observation, "the fly is never successful; in fact, as may be supposed, I would be quite useless to try it with a fish habitually keeping at so great a depth." With that caveat, the author concluded, "the amount of time and excitement involved in a single capture [of a muskie] is almost equal to an ordinary day's fishing."

Given my earlier encounters with this predator, these words certainly rang true. They hit me like a fishing epiphany: *Muskie on a fly rod!*

I immediately began to figure out the best way to accomplish this supposedly impossible task. First I consulted my older mentors. Like the book I'd read they consistently told me I was wasting my time—and was downright crazy—to even attempt such a sport with a fly rod. Like "shooting tigers with a BB gun" was what some of them said. Other than my grandfather's old book, there was also nothing to be found in the available fishing literature at the time about this new frontier of fly fishing.

Not easily discouraged, I started assembling the proper gear for my quest: heavier, saltwater-gauge 9-

weight and 10-weight rods with matching reels and lines. As for flies, I found that while there were many large streamer patterns and poppers to choose from, nothing was really big enough to get the attention of a fish that regularly eats small birds and mammals for lunch. My search for flies refocused on saltwater and then bluewater patterns where I finally found some that seemed large and enticing enough. I also started tying in earnest, creating oversized hair bugs and streamers that I wondered if I could even cast, let alone retrieve.

But what technique do I use to present these leviathan-sized flies?

My early experiences with lure fishing had fortunately given me some insight when it came to fly fishing for this new species. I knew muskies liked to follow and could be caught with some consistency on large plugs and spinners. Yet I also knew they loved to eat suckers rigged with a hook harness, and occasionally got caught by some kid dangling a worm from a bobber. Because I'd already caught one muskie, I simply figured I'd adapt this rudimentary knowledge when casting for muskies with the fly.

My choice for when and where to fish was simple— June, of course, back on my favorite lake in northern Wisconsin. This water held plenty of fish and I was confident this would be the place to prove Grandpa's book wrong. The very next spring I set out on the lake with my fishing buddy armed with a boatload full of rods, reels, and flies. We made a beeline for my favorite weed bed and started casting.

Our first few hours of fishing produced several exciting follows but no strikes. I was encouraged but still wondered if the naysayers were right about muskie on the fly. Then, as I was casting toward a row of submerged hemlock trees along a steep bank, a small but legal muskie burst from the cover and inhaled my over-sized deer hair popper. I struck back as hard as I could with a limber fly rod. The fight was on! After a quick jump and a few head shakes the fish was mine. We snapped a few photos and released the fish carefully. As I slid this fish in the water I knew this was a profound moment in my fly-fishing career—one from which I'll never recover.

As a small but growing group of muskie fly fishers already knows, the skill and patience required to catch these fish on any tackle inspires an obsession that has only one cure: muskie fishing as frequently as possible. Luck has little to do with this sport unless you believe in earning your luck. Like steelhead and permit, these fish require an almost religious devotion to succeed with many long hours in the aquatic cathedrals they call home. Since my first on a fly, I've been fortunate to have the time and means to fish some of the best muskie waters in North America on a regular basis including the legendary Chippewa and Eagle River flowages in Wisconsin; Leech, Mille Lacs, and Vermilion lakes in Minnesota; Lake Of the Woods and the mighty St. Lawrence River in Canada; Cave Run and Green River lakes in Kentucky; Kinkaid and Shabbona lakes in Illinois; and numerous others around the country. Still, after more than 30 years, I never grow tired of the unforgettable thrill and excitement of an aggressive follow or a violent boatside strike from a fish of any size. Every fish, it seems, is permanently etched in my memory and the source for inspiration during the inevitable slow days.

The legendary muskie has been aptly labeled the "fish of 10,000 casts" for very good reason: These fish are always tough to catch, even on the best water under ideal conditions. While this angling cliché may or may not ring true depending on when and where you fish, the fact of the matter is confirmed catch rates for muskies are very low as compared with other game fish. Throughout the muskie's range, success rates vary widely—from 50 to a couple of hundred fish in a season for the better guides on the best water to only a handful of fish in an entire season on some lower-population or pressured fisheries.

Individual catch-rates for the muskie angler also remain predictably low compared to other species with most putting in an average of somewhere between 30 and 60 man-hours—3,000-plus casts— for a single legal fish, according to recent fishery surveys. As the old-timer who congratulated me on my first fish warned, many also go home skunked. Despite these poor odds, all muskie anglers share a common belief that tomorrow—or the next cast— will bring them the fish of their dreams. No wonder this fish inspires a unique passion among legions of hard-core anglers throughout the country. In fact, it's estimated that roughly half a million anglers fish for muskies annually.

As I've fly fished for various species throughout the world, the closest example to muskie fly fishing I can think of in terms of pure difficulty are steelhead and permit. While these coveted fish definitely hold a special place at the top in the "official" hierarchy of fly-rod game fish, they are in many ways like a muskie in terms of the low percentage of fish caught, challenging conditions, and difficulty of inducing a strike. I've been fortunate to catch my fair share of both species on a fly. Each time I do I'm reminded of the similarities—time on the water, hundreds of casts, and the uncanny way they reject even the best-tied flies and presentations. Just like muskie fishing.

Globe-trotting anglers fortunate enough to fish for peacock bass in the Amazon, golden dorado in Argentina, tiger fish in Africa, and giant taimen in Mongolia will no doubt find muskie fishing a close second with mind-blowing surface strikes and the real potential for a monster fish in freshwater. Although these coveted gamefish rank among the most exciting on a fly, their exotic international locations means fishing opportunities are limited at best.

Unlike steelhead, permit, or other challenging gamefish species, muskies are indigenous to the much closer lakes and rivers of eastern North America. Thanks to a catch-and-release ethic among most anglers and progressive fishery management practices on most waters, muskies of all sizes are now found in 35 states and in fishable numbers well beyond their original range. For the dedicated angler looking for an alternative fish fix, this means that by reading and studying this book, and taking the time on the water to really understand your quarry, you may soon find yourself enjoying truly "exotic" fishing opportunities right in your own backyard.

In my many years of muskie fishing with a fly rod, I've grown from feeling like some crazy outsider with a ridiculously long rod, huge flies and "heavy line" to

The object of my desire: Muskie on the fly represent a new frontier in freshwater fly fishing. Once you experience a heart-pounding strike—or just a follow—from this amazing predator there's no turning back!

one that always approaches the water with a solid sense of confidence and anticipation. Like the early days of saltwater fly fishing, what was once an impossible challenge is now a reality due to angler creativity, perseverance, and improved technology. As I'll discuss in the following chapters, the techniques, flies and presentations I've adapted and developed allow the fly rodder to approach muskie fishing in a variety of new and exciting ways. While the fly rod will never afford the casting efficiency of a 6:1 high-speed baitcasting reel, or duplicate the exact movement of a giant, water-pushing top water lure, spinner or jerk bait, in the right hands it allows for a more precise and nuanced presentation—one most conventional anglers can only dream of imitating. In fact, during certain times of the year and especially in highly-pressured waters, the fly rod is a highly effective and enjoyable way to catch muskies day in and day out.

Most muskie anglers I know are always looking for the next big thing when it comes to baits, locations, or strategies. While it's doubtful they will all convert to fly fishing, in many ways the fly is the ultimate "think outside the box" approach to a fish that is already very hard to catch. Who knows? Maybe they will find a way to make these techniques a regular part of their fishing arsenal.

As you'll soon discover, muskies are in many ways

an exceptional fly-rod quarry. Whether you land a fish or not, the serious angler who devotes the time and patience it takes will eventually be rewarded with some truly memorable experiences, great fish stories, and "bragging rights." Most of all, you'll enjoy a great sense of pride and accomplishment with any fish caught and released regardless of size.

Much has been written about fly fishing for various individual gamefish species: steelhead, permit, tarpon, pike, even carp. Until now, however, no book has been devoted exclusively to catching muskies on a fly. In this comprehensive volume I'll cover everything you'll need to know about muskie fishing with a fly, including this fish's unique life history and behavior; how to get started with the proper gear and flies; what strategies and seasonal tactics to use when approaching a given body of water; how to fight, land and release your fish; what a select few muskie fly-rod guides can teach you; and even some of the best places to fly fish for muskies in the United States and Canada.

I hope reading *Muskie on the Fly* will give you a heightened passion for this new frontier in fly fishing, and a better understanding of the thrilling, often close-to-home opportunities that await you in pursuing this amazing game fish.

CHAPTER 2

THE MAGNIFICENT MUSKIE

"Muskies are a lot like northern pike except…
you can actually catch northern pike!"
—ANONYMOUS CANADIAN FISHING GUIDE

P UT A GROUP OF SERIOUS FLY FISHERS TOGETHER IN A ROOM— better yet, a lake, river, or seaside bar—and after a few drinks the conversation invariably gets around to the merits of their favorite game fish. Whether it's Atlantic salmon versus steelhead, tarpon versus permit, or even large-mouth bass versus smallmouth bass, everyone it seems has a strong opinion about his or her favorite fish, and why it's the most challenging to catch or the best fighter. When it comes to muskies, however, because so few fly fishers have seen one—much less actually hooked one—there's a distinct lack of understanding about what this fish really is, what it eats, and how it behaves.

Before you embark on your first muskie encounter with a fly it is important, at least at the beginning, to try to understand as much as you can about the life history and unique habits of this giant predator. This specialized knowledge will come in quite handy as you try to fool the legendary fish of 10,000 casts with only a fly rod, a hook, and a bunch of feathers. And it will definitely enhance your overall fishing experience.

The popular name "muskie" is short for muskellunge. The nickname is one of many this coveted gamefish has earned since it was discovered. Depending on where you fish in North America, you may find the muskie referred to with different names and spellings including musky, mascalonge, muskallunge, tiger, waterwolf, freshwater shark, or plain old "lunge." For the record, I've also heard muskies referred to with some colorful and graphic names that would make even a prison guard blush. Whatever the case, the name muskellunge is thought to have originated with the Native American Indian word maskinonge—quite literally meaning ugly fish.

The scientific name for the muskellunge is *Esox masquinongy* (Mitchell, 1824) reflecting its close relationship to the more common northern pike (*Esox lucius*) and pickerels (*Esox niger* and *Esox americanus*). Interestingly, all pike species are members of the Esocidae family of fishes and, from an evolutionary standpoint, are closely related to much smaller but very different species.

As the largest member of the pike family, the muskie shares many similarities with its smaller cousins in general body shape, spawning behaviors, food preferences, and habitat. However, as my wise Canadian guide knew all too well, there are many important distinctions making the muskie a considerably more elusive and challenging quarry.

While it is not unusual to mistake a smaller muskie for a northern pike—at least at first glance—with a little knowledge and understanding this kind of error can easily be avoided. This is especially important when fishing water where both species occur and special regulations are in place.

Like all pike species, muskies have an elongated body—much longer than it is deep—with single soft-rayed dorsal and anal fin located near the tail. In addition, all muskies have a set of pelvic fins located about halfway between the pectoral fins and tail. The muskie's tail is also forked with lobes that are more distinctly pointed than that of a pike, which are rounded.

Wisconsin Department of Natural Resources fishery biologist Frank Pratt, Jr., notes that the muskie's elongated body shape—like that of other fish and reptile species such as barracuda, taimen, pike-minnows, snakes, and crocodiles—literally makes it a long, swimming, digestive tract.

The legendary head and mouth of the muskie is large and broad like a giant duck's bill. Its jaws and mouth are lined with hundreds of razor-sharp teeth from top to bottom. The muskie's eyes are widely separated toward the top of its head, making it a perfect ambush hunter, especially from below. This unique eye location is also the source of speculation regarding the muskie's ability to see forage—or a lure or fly—at extremely close range.

The coloration and markings on a muskie vary widely depending on various environmental and genetic factors. These differences in appearance have led to confusion among anglers thinking they had

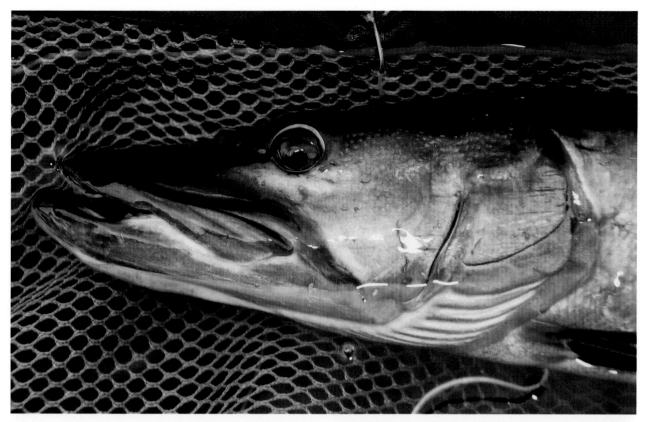

They may not be as pretty as some popular fly-rod species, but muskies hold their own special attraction for those who pursue them.

captured a unique new species of muskellunge. Today these color and pattern variations are considered by most of the scientific community to be environmentally driven phases of the same basic fish, much like those observed in trout or bass from different waters.

The muskie's long sides are most commonly patterned with either dark vertical bars or spots against a lighter greenish brown or silver background. The overall shape of the muskie's lateral markings give rise to the common distinction of the "barred" or "spotted" phase. Both barred and spotted muskies are found throughout the fish's natural range from the upper Midwest to the St. Lawrence River system. While most muskies show some evidence of spots or bars, in more turbid waters they adopt what is called the "clear" phase with light, almost silvery blue, bronze or green sides absent few, if any, distinct markings.

In the spring of 2005, for the first time in history, biologists with the Wisconsin Department of Natural Resources netted, tagged, and released a natural albino muskie just shy of 33 inches and eight pounds, adding yet another unique "phase" to the list of possible muskie variations.

Northern pike, on the other hand, typically feature light-colored bean-shaped spots or patterning against a darker background, much like a brook trout or other char. Smaller pike species such as pickerel also

Muskie Identification

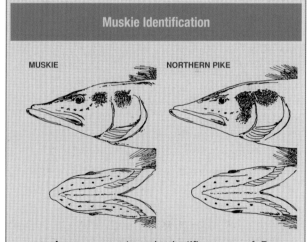

MUSKIE   NORTHERN PIKE

A more accurate and scientific means of *Esox* identification is the exact location of head scales and number of lower jaw sensory pores. The muskie's cheek and gill cover is typically scaled only on the top half versus the pike which has a fully scaled cheek with the top half scaled on the gill cover, and the pickerel which has both cheek and gill cover fully scaled. The muskie has six or more lower jaw pores on each side while the northern pike and pickerel have five or fewer pores on each side. When there is any doubt, the location of scales on the cheek and gill covers and the number of sensory pores is the most definitive method of muskie identification.

No problem seeing this fish follow: Wisconsin Department of Natural Resources Fisheries Biologist John Kubisiak holds a rare albino muskie netted on an Oneida County lake in 2005.

evidence this coloration but with a unique chain-like pattern giving rise to the common name chain pickerel.

From a natural-selection standpoint, the coloration and patterning of all *Esox* species serves as excellent camouflage in shallow water, and allows these fish to remain undetected as they lie in wait to ambush prey.

Yet another distinct member of the *Esox* genus is the tiger muskie. This beautiful muskie variation is a natural or, more commonly, hatchery-produced hybrid of a muskie and a northern pike. As a hybrid fish the tiger muskie is usually sterile and tends to grow faster without the need to waste energy spawning. But it's a deal with the devil: It has a shorter lifespan than the true muskie. It also has the reputation for having a huge appetite and being easier to catch, making it popular for stocking where natural fish are not present. Like the barred form of the pure-strain muskie, the tiger has distinct and dark vertical "tiger" bars along its side against a light background. Unlike the true muskie, the tiger's tail is rounded at the tip much like a northern pike. The head scaling and sensory pore patterns on a tiger muskie reflect the hybrid nature of this fish with scales on most of the cheek and the upper half of the gill cover, and five or more lower-jaw pores on each side. Given their rapid growth rate and voracious appetite, tiger muskies can attain impressive sizes, especially where forage is

abundant. Although large tiger muskies are caught throughout the country every year, the current world record tiger muskie weighed in at whopping 51 pounds, three ounces and was caught in Lac Vieux Desert on the Wisconsin–Michigan border in 1919.

Muskies Past and Present

The evolutionary history of the Esocoid family can be traced back roughly 100 million years. Like many fishes, it is thought that the muskie as was originally an ocean-dwelling saltwater species that invaded freshwater river systems in North America and became permanently trapped by glacial action during the last Ice Age, some 12,000 years ago. Fossilized teeth of prehistoric muskie dating back thousands of years have been found in such unlikely places as Kansas and Oklahoma.

Muskie Distribution

Although muskies in one variation or another are now found from New Jersey to Washington State, its natural range is far more limited. Unlike the pike, which are circumpolar in distribution and can be found throughout the Northern Hemisphere, the muskie is indigenous only to North America. Its native range is primarily confined to the St. Lawrence River basin in the Northeast; the Ohio, Tennessee, Great Lakes and Mississippi River basins in the Midwest; and Ontario in the Northwest. Naturally occurring populations of muskies also exist as far south as West Virginia, Kentucky and North Carolina. As you might expect, within this natural range are many of the best-known muskie waters including the famed St. Lawrence River and Lake Chautauqua in New York; Georgian Bay in Lake Ontario; lakes and rivers throughout Michigan, Wisconsin, and Minnesota; and Lake of the Woods in Ontario.

Today, thanks to numerous state and privately funded hatchery programs, progressive management and regulation of fisheries, muskies are now found in fishable numbers throughout their natural range and beyond. Wisconsin, Michigan, Minnesota, New York, Pennsylvania, and Ohio were some of the first states to recognize the value of the species as a game fish. As a result of good fishery management, these states currently hold some of the best muskie waters in the country. Other states—notably Indiana, Iowa, Illinois, and Missouri—also introduced muskies with much success over the years, and now support sustainable fisheries where none previously existed.

The easier-to-cultivate and fast-growing tiger

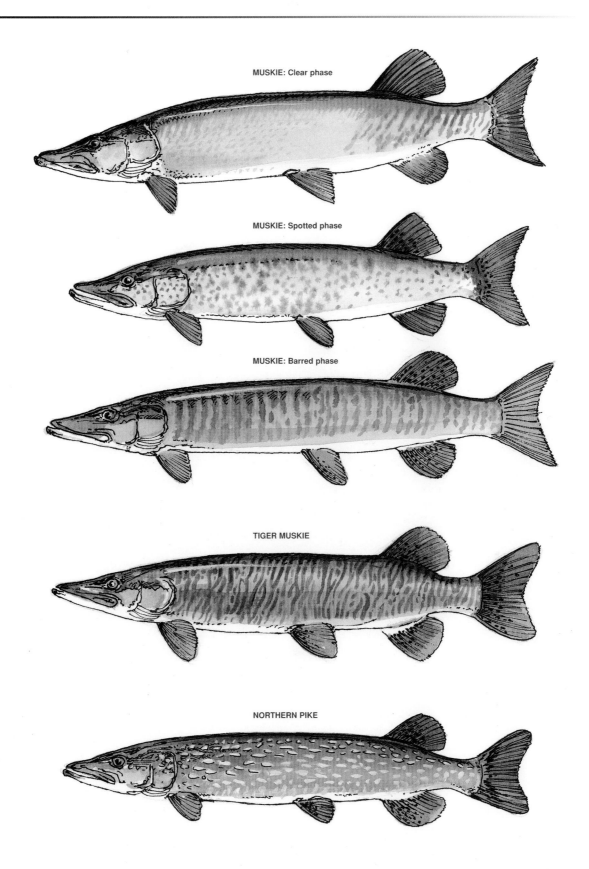

MUSKIE: Clear phase

MUSKIE: Spotted phase

MUSKIE: Barred phase

TIGER MUSKIE

NORTHERN PIKE

Like many species, muskies come in several shades and patterns depending on environmental and genetic factors. Note the unique patterning and rounded tail on the tiger muskie and northern pike. Most tiger muskies are hatchery-produced hybrids.

Although now found in 35 states, the muskies' natural distribution range is quite narrow and unique to North America.

muskies have also been stocked in many states with no history of muskies and less-than-ideal conditions. As a result, many western traditional "trout" states such as Colorado, Montana, Idaho, and even Washington now have good fishing for tiger muskies.

At last count—and of most significance to the fly fisher—some 35 states now have muskie or tiger muskie present in fishable numbers.

The Muskie Life Cycle

The muskie spawn takes place in mid to late spring when water temperatures reach between 48 and 59° Fahrenheit, usually several weeks after northern pike spawn at ice-out. From an evolutionary standpoint, this may help to reduce predation between species where both exist. The actual timing of the spawn varies depending on latitude and how quickly the water warms in the spring. It can happen as early as March or April and as late as June, depending on the location.

Muskies typically spawn in shallow bays, creek mouths, or coves, one to three feet deep, with little current and plenty of muck or other vegetative debris on the bottom that helps to shelter fragile eggs. Like all pike, they are "broadcast spawners," leaving fertilized eggs unattended on the bottom as spawning pairs swim side by side randomly releasing eggs and milt. Research reveals that muskie eggs are not as sticky as

Northern pike fly-fishing authority Barry Reynolds releasing a tiger muskie taken with a fly on Quincy Reservoir in Colorado.

those of northern pike, and as a result they often settle on the bottom instead of clinging to aquatic vegetation. This difficult environment for egg development is thought to be one cause of the lower reproductive rates of muskies as opposed to northern pike. In water where both northern pike and muskie are present, muskies not only spawn later in the spring but also in different, often deeper areas, thus reducing the likelihood of predation. Spawning takes place over several days and nights each spring and, unless significantly altered, is typically in the same areas year after year. Some fish—known as fractional spawners—also spawn more than once in a season, often within two weeks. Depending on its size, a spawning female muskie typically produces from 20,000 to 200,000 eggs—up to a gallon. Incubation of the fertilized eggs takes place within 12 to 15 days under normal conditions.

Although there is no other parental care given to the newly fertilized eggs, the smaller male fish will often continue to hang around the spawning site for some time, while the larger female fish venture out to deeper water weed beds, breaks, or points in search of forage. This post-spawn behavior is well known among muskie anglers. I have taken many fish in a single day—and some of my largest on a fly—at this time of year as they begin to recover from the spawn and aggressively feed again.

Environmental factors such as water clarity, levels, and available forage have a significant impact on the survival of newly-hatched muskie fry. Until a young muskie reaches maturity, predation by other species is always an issue, with other game fish including larger muskies, insects, birds, disease, and humans the primary causes of early mortality.

Although they eat a variety of small invertebrates upon hatching, other small fish are one of the primary food sources for young muskies within a short time. Much like the larger adult fish, even the smallest muskie commonly suffers from the "eyes-bigger-than-its-stomach" syndrome. The small but voracious fingerlings will often attack and eat another fish almost as large as they are, leaving only the tail dangling out their mouth until fully digested.

Muskie Size, Age, and Growth Rates

Muskies are one of the largest and fastest-growing fish in fresh water. While all muskie fishers seek the fabled "50-incher," most muskies caught during a given season weigh between seven and 15 pounds and are shorter than 40 inches in length. Fortunately for us, as can be seen in the graphs below, muskies

have a long lifespan, allowing them to grow very large under the right conditions.

A newly hatched muskie is only one-inch long but grows quickly to a length of 10 to 12 inches by the end of its first full year. During the critical first three years, growth is fastest, and depending on conditions, a healthy muskie can reach 30 to 34 inches within five or six years. Most of this rapid growth takes place in the summer months when temperatures are optimal and food is most abundant. After six years a typical 32-inch muskie weighs roughly eight to 12 pounds and is twice as long as other gamefish of the same age. With fish more than 10 years of age, the growth rate eventually slows to about an inch a year.

Exact aging of muskies is most often done using scale samples to measure growth rings. At one time, 20 years was thought to be the maximum life span for muskies. With larger fish, the cleithrum bone under the gill flap has been found to be a more reliable means of aging. Although the fish must be killed to obtain the bone, fishery researchers have used this

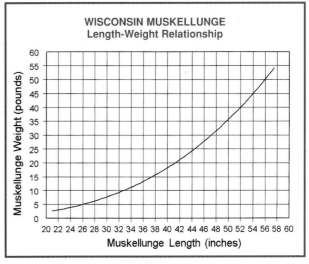

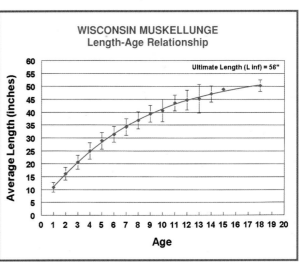

A real-life sea monster: Canadian guide Mike Lazarus and client Ed Barbosa strain under the weight of the all-tackle world-record muskie release—estimated at close to 60 pounds. This fish is likely nearly 30 years old.

method to accurately age very large muskies up to an amazing 30 years.

Once sexual maturity is reached, at roughly three to five years, the female muskie begins to grow faster than the male by three to six inches per year. Thus, by the time he reaches 10 years, a typical male muskie is roughly 36 inches and a female 42 inches. As a result of this difference in growth between gender, most trophy fish longer than 50 inches are females; very few males measure more than 45 inches.

Growth rates and overall size of a muskie vary widely—even within the same population of fish—depending on forage type and availability, environmental conditions, and sex. In some waters surveyed by Canadian fishery biologists, fish of the same length from the same lake varied in weight by as much as seven pounds. Likewise, in certain productive North American waters, such as Lake St. Clair, fish grow very fast and long resulting in generally lower weight for their length. In colder water fish tend to grow more slowly but still manage to develop a girth of enormous proportions thanks to such fatty forage such as ciscos and whitefish. One recent exception to this slow growth pattern is on cold, Mille Lacs Lake in Minnesota where cisco-fed muskies are now growing to more than 50 inches and 30 pounds in fewer than

20 years. At the other end of the spectrum, some lakes with poor growth conditions have actually been known to develop stunted fish. In Wisconsin, the DNR reports some muskie lakes hold fish as old as 20 years but no longer than 30 inches.

How Big Do They Get?

For as long as there have been muskie fishers there have been stories of monster muskies lurking in some lake or river in the United States or Canada. At least one well-publicized report of a Wisconsin muskie weighing more than 100 pounds dates back to the turn of the century. As recently as the spring of 2007, anglers fishing for walleye and smallmouth bass in Green Bay, Wisconsin reported catching and releasing several enormous but out-of-season muskies of potential world-record proportions. Such rumors and reports are part of the legend and lore of muskie fishing and—true or not—keep the die-hard fanatics casting day and night.

While plenty of records have certainly been broken and unbroken over the years, as of this writing, the current Wisconsin and all-tackle world-record muskie still stands at 69 pounds 11 ounces and was caught on October 20, 1949 by Louis Spray in Wisconsin's Chippewa Flowage.

This fish replaced Len Hartman's long-standing St. Lawrence River world-record of 69 pounds, 15 ounces which was disqualified by officials. More recently, in October of 1988, Toronto angler Ken O'Brian caught a giant muskie weighing 65 pounds in Canada's Georgian Bay … trolling for walleye! While increasing numbers of truly giant fish of 40 pounds and even 50 pounds are caught and released every year, the 60-pound mark remains an elusive goal even on the best waters in North America. For those wondering what the potential for a new world record actually might be, scientists who study muskies believe it is possible, under just the right conditions, for a 30-year-plus female muskie to reach a length close to 70 inches and, depending on girth, weigh well over 70 pounds.

Fortunately for the hard-working fly fisher, the possibilities for a quality fish greater than 40 inches and 20 pounds are now better than ever. Thanks to a strong catch-and-release ethic among most serious muskie fishers—more than 90 percent of all anglers according to one survey—and enlightened modern fisheries management, more and larger fish are caught and released each year.

Where They Live

Like a lion on the African Serengeti or a great white shark swimming along the Great Barrier Reef, the muskie is a highly evolved, apex predator that eats whenever and whatever it wants. When it comes to freshwater fishes, this fish is definitely "king of the hill" with very few natural enemies other than man. Getting and staying this big requires suitable habitat and a lot of food. Studies estimate that it takes five to seven pounds of forage fish to produce one pound of muskie. As a result, even the best water can only sustain a limited number of this species without suffering from overcrowding or stunting.

The muskie's large size, food requirements, and spawning and predatory habits result in lower densities compared to other gamefish. Creel surveys on lakes in Wisconsin confirm an average of roughly one adult muskie greater than 30 inches in length for every four to five acres of water. Larger muskie lakes such as the famed Lac Courte Oreilles exhibit even lower densities—but faster-growing fish—with one fish for every 10-plus acres. Overall, it is estimated that the total number of adult muskies in Wisconsin's numerous lakes and rivers is only around 200,000. On other lakes in North America, with longer growing seasons and aggressive stocking programs, this number has been found to be as high as four to six fish per acre, but this is highly unusual.

Louis Spray's controversial 1949 world-record muskie—69-pounds, 11-ounces—remains the subject of much discussion even to this day. Before the original mount was lost to a fire, Spray added a plaque that read, "The good Lord was with me when I caught this fish … for more information contact him."

Prime Muskie Water

Throughout their range, muskies swim in a wide variety of habitats, from lakes and flowages to rivers and streams. Although muskies can be found in small lakes of fewer than a couple of hundred acres and even in small streams, they thrive best in medium to large lakes, rivers, and flowages which offer both a diversity of structure and forage. These various habitats are commonly catagorized as follows:

The lush vegetation and varied structure of natural lakes produce prime muskie habitat.

Oligotrophic Lakes: The geologically youngest and least fertile of muskie habitats, these deep, cold "Canadian shield" lakes represent the northernmost extent of the muskie's natural range. With trout, tullibees, whitefish, and ciscos as common forage, these lakes also produce some of the largest muskies every year. Georgian Bay on Lake Ontario, Whitefish Bay on Lake of the Woods, and Trout Lake in Wisconsin represent some better-known muskie lakes of this type.

Mesotrophic Lakes: The most common muskie lake habitat throughout North America with both natural and stocked fish. These lakes are moderately fertile and hold an abundance of muskie forage from yellow perch, suckers, and walleye, to ciscos and whitefish, depending on latitude and depth. Leech Lake in Minnesota, Lake St. Clair in Michigan, Lac Courte Oreilles in Wisconsin, and Lake of the Woods in Ontario are classic examples of this type of lake.

Eutrophic Lakes: These older, shallow, and fertile lakes often hold large populations of forage and typically stocked muskies. Given the warmer nature of these waters, forage is varied with perch, suckers, crappies, and bullheads making up the majority of preferred prey. Many lakes throughout the muskie's range fall into this category including Lake Chautauqua in New York, the Fox Chain O'Lakes in Illinois, and Spirit Lake in Iowa.

Rivers: Throughout their natural and stocked range, muskies inhabit small to large rivers with slow-to-medium gradients. The lack of diverse habitat in some smaller rivers means holding water is often limited to the deepest or most protected water available. Forage choices in rivers are varied with both rough fish and game fish consumed routinely. The St. Lawrence River along the United States and Canadian border is perhaps the best-known large-muskie river on the continent, and home to several world-record-sized fish.

Flowages and Reservoirs: These man-made lakes hold an abundance of stocked and some natural muskies. Depending on the size, they also offer a

Rivers, flowages, and man-made reservoirs also fully suit the toothy predator.

greater variety of habitat than many rivers, with submerged or standing timber, creek arms, and old river channels representing some of the best habitat. Among other prey species, gizzard shad are the favorite muskie forage in these waters, especially in southern latitudes. The Chippewa Flowage in Wisconsin, Cave Run Lake in Kentucky, and Lake Shelbyville in Illinois are good examples of the more popular muskie flowages and reservoirs.

An ideal muskie lake or river offers a wide range of water depths and variety of cover and is fertile enough to support an abundance of preferred forage. Among the better waters, eutrophic and mesotrophic muskie lakes and flowages are often quite shallow, typically with stained water and an abundance of aquatic plant life. These forage-filled waters tend to support larger numbers of smaller muskies but still produce some very large fish. Many oligotrophic lakes and some reservoirs are very large and deep with clear water and little aquatic vegetation. They typically support sparser populations of muskies but produce

larger individual fish because of the abundance of certain forage species such as ciscos and shad.

Preferred Muskie Habitat

"Fish the weeds" is probably the most common advice given a new muskie fisher. While weeds are certainly a good place to start fishing, muskies have definite preferences for certain weed types—and conditions—over others. As always, the best muskie structure provides the all-important balance of forage, cover, and protection.

Aquatic weeds are among the preferred natural habitats for muskies in many water types. They grow in small clumps early in the year and expand into massive weed beds as the season progresses. In most muskie waters, certain preferred weeds are like fish magnets, drawing and holding fish until conditions change. Some of the muskie's favorite weeds can be seen in the illustration on page 34.

Submerged wood, rock, and sand structure is another common natural habitat for muskies, and is

The predator's lair: Always alert and hungry, a muskie suspends close to cover awaiting its next victim.

Aquatic weeds—both submergent and emergent—are among the preferred natural habitats for muskies in a variety of water types. Some of the favorites shown above include (1) lily pads, (2) bulrushes/reeds, (3) milfoil, (4) cabbage, and (5) coontail.

Muskies love wood, especially when it provides substantial cover and an opportunity to ambush forage.

found in most waters throughout the muskie's range. This structure provides both fish and forage with excellent cover throughout the growing season. When water temperatures are cooler in the spring and fall this structure also retains heat, providing an added benefit.

Like brown trout, muskies in rivers and streams tend to hold in slower moving, protected areas out of the main current flow with a particular fondness for swirling back eddies, large boulders, undercut banks, log jams, and deeper pools below rapids, islands, or dams.

The majority of a muskie's time is spent feeding in and around cover in water shallower than 20 feet. On most waters, this is where the preferred forage and habitat is—and where the vast majority of muskies are caught. This fact alone makes the muskie an attractive fly rod quarry. While muskies in deeper lakes and rivers are sometimes found at depths greater than 50 feet—or suspended over even deeper water structure—this behavior is primarily associated with the migratory patterns of forage during certain times of the year. In some less-fertile, large bodies of water with little available shallow water cover or

feeding opportunities, some muskie populations may remain in deep water for most of their lifespans.

As a general rule, muskies prefer to stick close to cover except when moving around to spawn or to find preferred forage and water temperatures. This is especially true in the summer months when temperatures and environments have stabilized. While more than one muskie may inhabit a weed bed or rock pile, they are usually more solitary fish than walleye or bass, earning them a reputation for being lone rangers. They are, however, sometimes found in loosely defined schools or "wolf packs" when prompted by weather, seasonal changes, and specific forage movement. Individual muskies also tend to inhabit the same structure or "home range" for some length of time during the prime feeding periods. This presents promising opportunities for the lucky angler who discovers where they live. This unique behavior allows the knowledgeable angler to develop a "milk run" of fish to target through the day, week, or season. As experienced muskie fishers know, quite often once a muskie is caught from one of these prime spots another fish will replace it.

Water temperatures are an important key to

First, the muskie sees and senses the potential prey. Then, the muskie stalks its intended target. Finally, the muskie strikes!

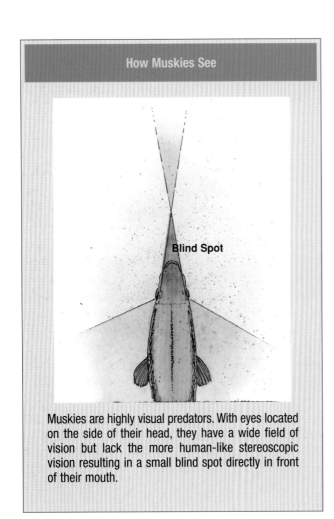

How Muskies See

Blind Spot

Muskies are highly visual predators. With eyes located on the side of their head, they have a wide field of vision but lack the more human-like stereoscopic vision resulting in a small blind spot directly in front of their mouth.

understanding and predicting muskie location. Radio-telemetry tracking of muskies in the United States and Canada confirms that muskies establish at least two home ranges during the course of the year: one in the summer when water temperatures rise above 60°F and another in the winter when temperatures fall below 40°.

These studies also show that a muskie's home range can be as small as 20 acres to well over 1,000, depending on the particular lake or river system. In the transition periods of spring and fall, muskies move when water temperatures rise above 40° and again when they fall below 60°. Depending on the water type and environmental conditions, the distance traveled during these times can be as little as several hundred yards to 20 miles or more.

Because they spend the majority of time in shallow water, muskies are clearly a warm-water-loving species. Depending on the latitude, the ideal feeding-temperature range for most muskies is in the mid-60s. Although they can tolerate water temperatures as high as 10° warmer than northern pike, once temperatures exceed the mid- to upper 80s, muskies tend to become less active and seek cooler temperatures under cover or in deep water. When water temperatures reach these extreme levels, stress-related injury to the fish is more likely. Angling is discouraged to protect the fish.

Following ice-out, muskies commonly stage in basins and along breaks adjacent to spawning areas. After spawning in the spring, they remain shallow and first begin feeding regularly when water temperatures approach 50°. This early period of intense feeding activity is known as the "spring bite" and can be particularly productive for large numbers of smaller battle-scarred male fish.

When water temperatures become more uniform in the summer months, muskies live at a variety of depths, wherever forage, habitat, and water temperatures are most desirable. Muskies at this time of year are typically more aggressive but can be harder to find due to the wider variety of suitable habitat.

In the fall months, as water temperatures begin to drop again, muskies continue to feed aggressively in lower water temps—down to 40° or lower—as they actively search for forage before winter sets in. Muskies at this time of year are often found suspended in deeper water near breaks and rock ledges where migrating forage is concentrated. This phenomenon, known by most muskie fishermen as "the fall bite," is one of the best times of the year for a real trophy fish. In the late fall the muskie's metabolism and movement slows with the falling temperatures but they keep feeding actively until ice-up.

How They Feed

"Nature punishes unreasonable risk-takers. The risk/opportunity ratio seems to be calculated very carefully for fish."
—Thomas Sholseth
How Fish Work (2003)

Like most fish, muskies feed in part by utilizing a sensory system consisting of both a lateral line and numerous sensory pores on their body and head. The combined use of eyesight and these other predatory senses enables the muskie to find and attack prey. Despite having more sensory pores than the northern pike, the muskie's heavy reliance on sight means they compete poorly with their smaller cousins, especially in turbid water.

In typical shallow-water ambush-feeding, a muskie positions itself in and around weeds, wood, rock, or other cover. It lurks, patiently waiting for prey. When a potential meal appears within range, the muskie springs to attention, its eyes focused like a laser and its fins erect. At the optimum time, it attacks by first coiling into an S shape—much like a snake—and then lunges straight forward at burst speeds of up to 30 miles per hour (44 feet per second!). The speed of this attack is astonishing—even fright-

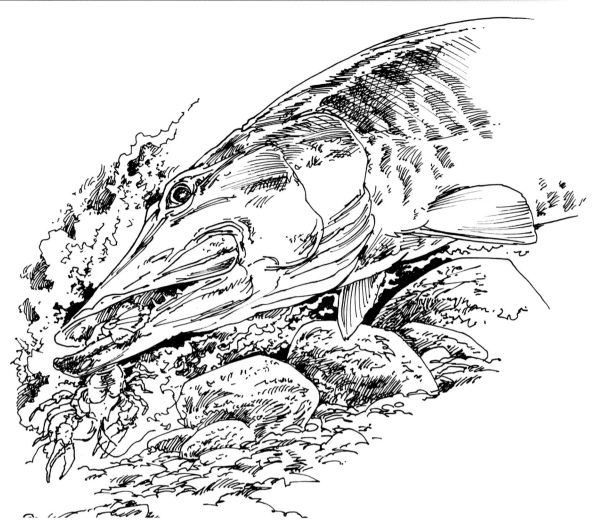

Muskies are opportunistic feeders: Big or small, if it's edible and active they'll take a bite. Here a muskie rolls over to pick a crayfish off the bottom. These and other invertebrates are often eaten by muskies and present overlooked opportunities for the fly fisher.

ening—and one of the great thrills in all fishing. And this is one of the main reasons the muskie fisher must always be ready for a strike. Always.

Unfortunately, as any experienced muskie fisher will tell you, the incredible speed and violence of this strike is also why missing a strike is common with any kind of muskie tackle—particularly when fishing a top-water presentation. Pulling a lure or fly away from a striking muskie is a tough lesson to learn, but it often happens. Another reason for missed strikes has to do with the inherent lack of maneuverability of a muskie once it commits to attack. With a long and narrow body like a torpedo, the muskie can easily move in a straight line at high speeds but lacks the ability to turn on a dime.

When the intended prey is captured, the muskie clamps down with its powerful, pit-bull-like jaws and large, extremely sharp canines, offering little chance of escape (of course, not always the case with a lure or fly). Numerous brush-like smaller teeth on the bottom and roof of the muskie's mouth and tongue also

help to secure prey with a vise-like grip.

After the prey is sufficiently subdued, the muskie rotates the victim in its mouth and swallows it head-first. Some common forage species such as bluegills are more difficult to consume in this manner because they have spiny rays that can become lodged in the muskie's throat. As many muskie anglers know, it is not uncommon to catch a muskie or find a dead muskie with a fish tail sticking out its mouth, a testament to some of the risks associated with this violent feeding approach.

Muskies are also notorious for aggressively stalking or following an intended prey for some time before eventually striking. In some cases they will actually follow a lure or fly repeatedly, nipping at the tail, but never actually eating. In other cases they will strike or boil on a fast-moving lure or fly several times but fail to connect—as if seeking only to injure or stun it into submission. Although it is easy to anthropomorphize this behavior as "anger," "curiosity," or just plain "stubbornness," it seems most likely that this kind of reaction strike is motivated by hunger or a territorial threat.

Among the various feeding triggers, the speed and motion of an intended prey also seem to be a major part of the equation. A fast-moving lure or fly is often the key to success, especially in warmer water temperatures during summer. The fact that speed trolling, where legal, is a productive technique for summer muskies proves that muskies will follow and strike an extremely fast-moving object, even in the prop wash at speeds up to eight miles an hour.

Despite all that's been discovered about muskie biology and behavior, an individual muskie's feeding behavior is often hard to predict. Take the amazing experience of Wisconsin guide Mike Mladenik. One crisp fall day several years ago he hooked and fought the same large and distinctly scarred muskie six times—with the same quick-strike sucker rig—before finally landing the fish. Despite acting as if the poor sucker was its last meal on earth, this healthy 48-inch, 30-pound-plus late-season trophy muskie showed no signs of distress when finally landed. As he does with all big fish, Mike promptly released it to fight another day and took home a fish story worth telling.

What They Eat

While muskies definitely have preferred forage depending on the season and where they live, they are essentially opportunistic feeders. They devour anything they can fit in their mouth, from fish to birds to other muskies.

The majority of the muskie's diet consists of other fish. Some studies put this number as high as 98 percent. Among the various forage fish species, smaller spiny-rayed "panfish" species such as perch, bluegill, and crappies are routinely consumed by muskie when present in large numbers. In fact, various studies have shown that the common yellow perch often makes up as much as 30 to 50 percent of the muskie's main diet in waters where this species is abundant. Other popular game fish such as northern pike, largemouth bass, smallmouth bass, and walleye—even smaller muskies—are also consumed. Despite the concerns of some anglers, game fish generally comprise a much smaller percentage of the overall diet unless they represent the only forage available.

Notably, it's the soft-rayed "rough" fish species including minnows, shiners, shad, bullheads, carp, and suckers that seem to be the preferred forage wherever present—especially among larger adult muskies. Not surprisingly, the elongated, "fusiform" cylindrical and tapered body shape of this preferred forage is a key factor in successful lure and fly design. In deeper, cold-water lakes, other "fatty" fish species such as smelt, ciscos, tullibees, whitefish, and trout

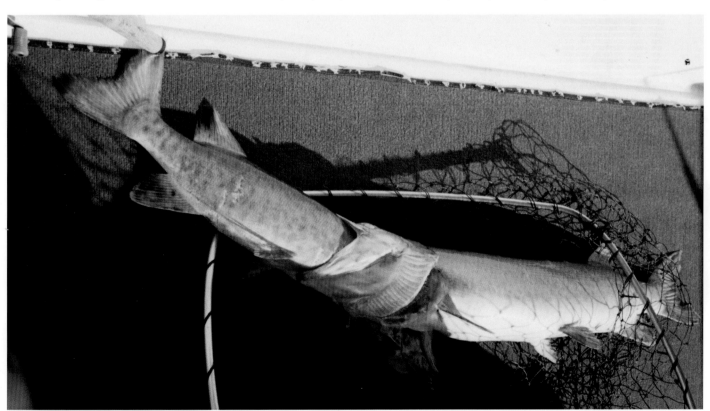

Think your fly is too big? Think again. Although both fish unfortunately died in the process, this amazing photo shows just how big a meal a muskie will attempt to eat. The larger fish is 44 inches and the smaller fish—its intended prey—is 40 inches!

Rough fishes such as this white sucker represent one of the muskie's peferred forage species.

also make up a large part of the muskie's diet. This is particularly true in the fall when many of these baitfish school in large numbers during spawning.

Muskies, particularly younger fish, also eat a number of other smaller invertebrates, reptiles, and amphibians including crayfish, mayfly nymphs, damselfly nymphs, worms, frogs, toads, snakes, and salamanders. Larger adult muskies are also known to eat a variety of birds and small mammals including juvenile and adult ducks and geese, mice, voles, chipmunks, squirrels, and even muskrats. While over the years there have been many reports of muskies attacking even larger animals—including humans—this seems to be more of a case of mistaken identity (dangling fingers off a dock, red fingernail polish)

than intent to do serious harm.

Given their size and energy requirements, muskies rarely seem deterred by the size of prey. In fact, it is axiomatic that the larger the muskie the larger the meal. Wisconsin DNR fishery biologist and fellow fly-rod muskie fisher Frank Pratt, Jr. notes that muskies are genetically engineered to handle prey up to two-thirds their own body size. For example, some studies have shown that the average size of a 30-inch muskie's prey is four inches long while the average for a 50-inch muskie is 20 inches or nearly half its total body length. This is not to say that smaller muskies will not eat a large meal but rather that big lures and flies typically produce bigger fish. Keep in mind that in the fall some muskie experts cast and troll with gigantic diving lures 18 to 20 inches long.

One final and important factor regarding preferred prey is that muskies do not normally scavenge or eat anything that is not obviously alive and moving. As many gamefish anglers in muskie country know, it is not uncommon to have muskie attack a struggling bass or walleye on the line or even after it's been placed on a stringer at boat side. The key trigger in both cases seems to be a fish in distress that a muskie can both see and sense with its lateral line and sensory pores. Hence, keeping your fly moving and looking alive at all times is critical. This piece of knowledge, combined with a basic understanding of muskie behavior, will serve you well as you prepare to fool your first muskie on the fly.

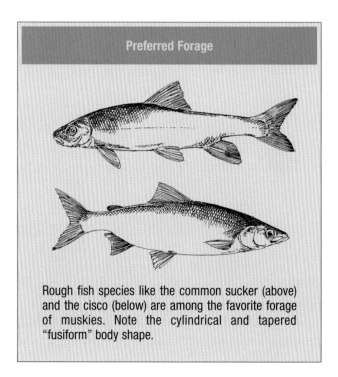

Preferred Forage

Rough fish species like the common sucker (above) and the cisco (below) are among the favorite forage of muskies. Note the cylindrical and tapered "fusiform" body shape.

Yellow perch and other panfishes comprise a large portion of the muskie's diet when available in large numbers.

CHAPTER 3

"The best fishermen I know try not to make the same mistakes over and over again; instead they strive to make new and interesting mistakes and to remember what they learned from them."
—JOHN GIERACH

THE MIND GAME

"**G**ET DOWN!" I YELLED AT MY WIFE AND FATHER as I scrambled to double haul a long cast and a big fly aimed at a muskie in a feeding frenzy. Unfortunately for them, what had been billed earlier in the day as a nice, leisurely boat ride on the lake had just turned into a serious muskie hunt with a crazed fly fisher wielding a large, menacing hook.

As my loved ones cowered on the bottom of the boat, I did my best to put a fly over their heads in the general direction of the fish. I retrieved the fly with great intensity. Nothing followed. I cast again and again to where I thought the fish had moved but for whatever reason could not entice even a follow. Just as I was about to give up all hope, a nice fish of 38 inches appeared out of nowhere and sucked in my fly like a tarpon on a Cockroach. After a couple of acrobatic jumps and a short but lively fight I landed the fish by hand and quickly released it.

I stared across the now-stilled lake surface for any more signs of life. Several minutes passed without a word. Then my father raised his head and somewhat sheepishly asked, "Can we get up now?" I'd forgotten they were even in the boat. My wife—more used to barking the orders in her professional life than being barked at, said without a hint of humor, "What the *hell* got into you?"

MUSKIE was all I could think of…

There's something about seeing a muskie in the water that makes even the best caster a nervous wreck. Like "buck" or "tarpon" fever, even the most experienced anglers forget everything they know when faced with a large muskie about to inhale their fly. Despite knowing exactly what to expect and what to do, I've felt it and seen it happen many times. And each time it's an amazing experience.

One of the most compelling reasons for pursuing muskies on the fly—other than their large size by freshwater standards—is the extreme challenge of getting them to strike. Like fly fishing for selective trout on a spring creek or tailing permit on a flat, the real reason we do this is not because it's the most productive way to fish but because we believe it's a notable accomplishment worthy of our time and efforts. We all know there are more efficient and consistent ways to catch various species, but certainly none as personally satisfying as doing it with a fly rod.

Another reason most of us like to fly fish has much to do with the concept of a "fair chase," that is,

placing certain self-imposed limitations on our approach to make the end result a real test of skill. Hence the growing popularity of catching big fish using the lightest tackle available. In the case of muskie fishing, however, given the inherent difficulty of catching these elusive fish on any kind of tackle, the limitations of a fly rod can start to seem downright absurd. Kind of like climbing Mount Everest without oxygen, it can be done, but there are certainly easier ways to go about it.

As the legendary fly fisher, Al McClane, once said of muskies: "Muskie fishing is hard work … the fisherman who works his baits properly, makes the most casts, and stays alert will, in the long run, enjoy the greatest success, and finally, all muskies are unpredictable." It's this very unpredictable nature that makes fly fishing for muskies so satisfying, but also the source of considerable mental anguish as you struggle to keep focused through the fishing day.

For sheer efficiency and productivity, fly fishing for muskie holds few advantages versus conventional casting techniques. As we fly fishers know, this is decidedly not the point. What is important, however, is that you fully understand and accept the challenge that awaits you.

Before you put down this book and reconsider fly fishing for muskies altogether, consider this important piece of information: Despite the lower odds, fly fishing for muskies can actually be very productive during certain seasons and under specific conditions. In fact, other than fishing live bait for muskies, I believe that when used properly the fly rod can be as effective—if not more so—than certain conventional techniques.

Advantages of Fly Fishing

• Stealthy approach with a fly rod greatly improves your odds of success, particularly in ultra-clear or very shallow water situations with pressured fish.

• Unique, often slower retrieves and presentations possible with only a fly and fly rod are highly effective on pressured or less-aggressive fish.

• Accurate and repeated casting to specific fish or structure is easier to accomplish with a fly rod without the risk of spooking fish.

• Fly fishers can attract—and hopefully hook—more muskies with unique streamer and top-water fly patterns most fish have never seen.

• The figure-8 technique, and other boatside maneuvers, are enhanced and can be more effectively executed with a longer fly rod.

• The limber yet powerful fly rod is an excellent tool for fighting large fish on light line, providing the angler with an exciting and memorable fight no matter what the size of the fish.

• Catching any muskie on the fly is a truly special experience and always a great accomplishment regardless of size.

Despite the unique approach made possible with a fly rod, you can't escape the fact that most of the time, fly fishing for muskies is also a lot of hard work. It demands the most from your equipment and, perhaps most importantly, from your physical and mental stamina. Your mental agility—what I call the "mind game" of muskie fishing—is every bit as important as your physical skills, flies, or equipment. It requires a thorough self-examination if you are to succeed at this sport.

For this reason it is absolutely critical you understand and develop the proper mental skill set for this kind of fishing … even before you pick up a fly rod. These muskie fishing facts of life are an essential part of any successful angler's tackle box—the difference between catching fish and going home skunked.

I'm sure most muskie anglers would agree that starting each day with a positive mental attitude (PMA) is one of the keys to fishing success. While this may sound easy enough to do, there's more to it than simply hitting the water with a smile on your face and a hope and a prayer riding on each cast. For this reason, I've broken down the three most important elements of the proper mental attitude for muskie fishing into three factors:

Conventional versus Fly Fishing for Muskies

Comparing just a few of the pros and cons of conventional casting and trolling techniques for muskies versus fly fishing for them provides an honest and realistic appraisal of the challenges the fly rodder faces in this pursuit:

Conventional Casting and Trolling for Muskies

The Pros

• You can cast and/or troll all day and night (so long as your arm holds up and you don't run out of gas).
• You can cover a large area of water, at any depth, with multiple casts and/or by trolling.
• You can use a wide variety of lure types, weights and sizes.
• You can use much larger lures to attract fish with action, movement and sound.
• You can retrieve lures at high speeds with a high-speed reel or by trolling.
• You can use very stiff rods, heavy non-stretch line, and metal leaders for quick, solid hook sets.
• You can fight fish off the reel using the drag system at all times.

The Cons

• Not many drawbacks other than you are not fly fishing.

Fly Fishing for Muskies

The Pros

• Not many but it's a heck of a lot of fun!

The Cons*

• Tough physically to cast a fly rod and big fly all day and night.
• Limited ability to cover water with a fly rod depending on individual casting skill, boat control, and weather conditions.
• Limited variety and size of flies that can be cast effectively with a fly rod.
• Other than on a top-water popper, or rattle in a streamer difficult to attract fish using sound.
• A longer/softer fly rod necessary for open casting stroke with big flies makes it harder to eliminate slack in the line and set the hook.
• It's difficult to retrieve a fly fast enough for a muskie using only a hand strip and the rod.
• It's difficult to set the hook solidly—at any distance—with a fly rod and hand strip-set.
• It's difficult to keep a tight line and fight a big fish by hand until (and if) you get it on the reel

*There are actually a few more "cons" to fly fishing for muskies than I've listed but I'd rather not discourage you any more than necessary this early in the game.

One for the record books: Determination, confidence, and opportunity—along with a bit of luck—combined to help me catch and release this new line-class world-record muskie on a fly. It measured nearly 50 inches and took a synthetic version of my Muskie Marauder.

1. Determination

2. Confidence

3. Opportunity

While you undoubtedly recognize these as common elements to successful fishing regardless of the species, as you'll see in the discussion that follows, they take on a new dimension when it comes to pursuing muskies with the fly.

Determination

Among the many personal characteristics of a successful muskie fisher, determination ranks at the top. To my way of thinking, a determined angler is someone who exhibits that unique combination of desire, patience, and persistence, resulting in success where others fail.

Of course, we've all heard the old saying that "a good fishermen must have patience" or "you must be persistent to be a successful fisherman." Muskie fishing with a fly really puts these well-worn clichés to the ultimate test. Let's face it: Catching a muskie is a low-percentage sport even with conventional casting gear—on the best water and under ideal conditions. Substitute a nine-foot fly rod into the equation and you've got a real challenge on, or in your hands.

Despite all the tactical and technological advances of the past century—from lures to boats to advanced electronics—even the best muskie guides and anglers in the world know that there are simply no guarantees when it comes to this fishing. As any experienced muskie fisher will tell you, just when you think you've got them figured out the rules of the game seem to change.

Unlike chasing some species of fish where it's normal to have an occasional "slow" day but still catch a few fish, most muskie anglers know that it's entirely possible, even probable, that you won't catch or even see a single fish in a day or week of fishing. Hence the need to remain determined at all times.

A perfect specimen of an unshakably determined angler is my good friend and guide, Mike Lazarus of Montréal, Québec. Mike is highly regarded as one of the most successful professional muskie guides in modern times—perhaps ever. Known by some in the muskie world as the "Dalai Lama," in a given casting and trolling season Mike and his few but happy clients boat somewhere close to 400 fish, many exceeding 50 inches in length. This is an amazing statistic, especially when you consider that some of the best muskie guides in the country take fewer than 200 fish in a good year.

Mike and I have fished together for many years; I have enjoyed much success in his boat. During our days together we've certainly been skunked a few times but we've also had some remarkable days with multiple fish over 50 inches in a day and my largest fish to date on a fly—a 54-inch monster that engulfed my popper like its last meal on earth (see photo on pages 10-11).

During our time on the water we've also fished through extreme conditions including wind, lightning, hail, and snow storms. Late in the season we've even fished among icebergs in search of one last "big heavy." Yet, despite these often challenging conditions, in all our years together I've never once seen him give up and call it quits. Some might call this crazy, but what really keeps a great fisherman like Mike going is a steadfast determination to keep trying despite the odds, fueled by a highly evolved level of patience and persistence.

In my 30 years of pursuing muskies with a fly rod, I've also been fortunate to fish some of the best water in North America on an annual basis, with and without guides. I've been rewarded with many memorable experiences on the fly with anywhere from one to a dozen or more fish landed and released in a single day and many fish over 40 inches in a typical season. I've also been most fortunate to have been in the right place at the right time with my fly rod, landing and releasing several world-record-class fish that taped longer than 50 inches and weighed more than 30 pounds. As you might expect, I've also spent weeks at a time on my feet casting a big fly from early morning until night with only a sunburn, sore arm, and aching back to show for my efforts.

What keeps me going is my determination to be on the water whatever the chances of success. After all, as the guru Lazarus likes to remind me, "You can't catch 'em from the couch!"

A Typical Day on the Water

What can you expect in a typical day of muskie fishing with a fly? Consider this example from a recent outing on Webster Lake in northern Indiana with fly-fishing muskie guide Mark Meritt. Heavily stocked by the state, this lake is known for its abundance of 30- to 40-inch fish with the occasional larger fish up to 50 inches. Because it's close to Chicago and other Midwest cities, it also gets significant pressure from the hard-core muskie crowd, not to mention recreational boaters of all kinds. This amount of pressure adds up to some challenging fishing with any kind of gear.

It was June, and we both knew the chances were good for some shallow-water action with a fly. Mark was fishing conventional casting gear with his normal assortment of spinners, plugs, and plastic jerk baits. I stuck with the fly rod and a big streamer of my own making. As usual, we had high hopes for the day, especially since Mark had already taken several good fish earlier in the week.

Midway through the morning, Mark had already caught and released two fish of 32 and 38 inches, and had had numerous follows on his lures. A great day of muskie fishing by any measure. I, on the other hand, had moved only one fish that followed my streamer lazily before sinking slowly into the depths. We had plenty of casting gear in the boat. Although I was sorely tempted to pick up a rod given Mark's success, I wanted a fish on a fly, and persisted with my casting the rest of the day. During the next six long hours I must have changed flies and tactics a dozen times trying everything I knew to entice and hook a fish.

As darkness fell, Mark was still moving fish and hooked another one he eventually lost at the boat. To say I was discouraged would be a major understatement. There I was with a great guide, fishing prime time on a lake full of muskies, with muskies being caught in the same boat only a few feet from where I stood, and I couldn't catch one to save my life!

Just as I was about to give up all hope for the day, I saw a fish boil and quickly made a long cast with my streamer. The fish hit hard on the first strip and cart-wheeled in the air as soon as I strip-set. After a brief but tense battle I had my first fish of the day in the net, a small but well-conditioned male muskie of 38 inches.

While not exactly action-packed, this day is typical of many I've had over the years. It serves to illustrate the steadfast determination required of any angler hoping to succeed at this game. As tempting as it is to turn to the more-promising lure on such a day, I always stick with the fly rod until the very end.

Despite the inherent disadvantages of fly fishing for muskies noted previously, as I've seen again and again it's the determined angler with a large dose of patience and persistence who ultimately succeeds casting a fly.

Confidence

Chicago Bulls basketball great Michael Jordan once said, "You have to expect things of yourself before you can do them." While this is certainly true of many things in life, it's absolutely the case when muskie fishing with a fly. Whatever kind of fishing you prefer, your confidence on the water is always a key component of your overall success.

When I was first learning to fly fish, I was fortunate to have a number of excellent mentors, including my life-long friend, Victor Shawe from Oregon. Vic is one of the best trout and steelhead fly fishers I know, and without a doubt the most confident. When we first started fishing together I was intimidated by his stories of catching big fish wherever he went. We'd be floating down a river in his drift boat and he'd actually say, "Watch me nail one here." More often than not, within seconds I'd hear, "Fish on!" As our fishing friendship grew I eventually learned that what appeared to be overconfidence to most folks was actually a mental strategy evolved after years of fishing success. Vic, it turns out, really believed he was going to catch a fish on every cast. Whether he did or not, this approach kept him ever focused and always ready for a strike. It's a lesson I'll never forget. It has served me well, especially when put to the ultimate test of mental endurance with muskies.

It's no secret that an angler's confidence level can be affected by something as simple as a new fly, as subjective as the latest fishing report, or as silly as one's horoscope for the day. (For what it's worth, there's a myth that simply carrying a banana on a boat will shatter the confidence of many guides.) Most of all, however, confidence when you're fishing comes from a great deal of experience with a favored species of fish and/or time invested on a certain body of water.

My early experiences as a fly-fishing guide in Alaska taught me a thing or two about confidence and knowing your intended quarry. When I first worked as a guide there in the early 1980s, the truth is I didn't know a darn thing about the rivers and lakes I was preparing to lead others on. As a kid in Chicago, the closest I'd ever come to the Alaskan fishing experience was reading about it in fishing magazines and seeing the action on television. What I did know, however, was a fair amount about fly fishing in rivers for trout and salmon gained from years of prowling Great Lakes tributaries.

Soon after arriving in Alaska, I discovered that despite my lack of practical experience on these foreign waters I was assigned to guide, the trout and salmon swimming there behaved and looked pretty much like the ones back home, give or take a few differences. Within a short time I adapted my experience and skills to each new watershed I encountered. Each day on the water made me more confident; I expected success. After adjusting for the forage base and seasons I was also rewarded with great fishing for my clients, and on days off for me, beyond my wildest boyhood dreams.

While these early confidence-building lessons worked well for me over the years with trout and many other species, muskie fishing with a fly presents a somewhat different dilemma; it's just darn tough to be confident hour after hour, day after day when you don't see or catch anything. Yet, because your opportunities

Beginning each fishing trip with a solid game plan is a good way to increase confidence, even if you have to change it along the way.

with muskie on a fly are limited at best, it's critical that you be confident and focused at all times or you'll miss the one chance you often get in a day to land a single fish. Developing and maintaining your confidence is one of the toughest aspects of muskie fishing with a fly. Like many other things in life, since you just don't get many second (or first) chances with muskie you've got be on your game at all times to succeed.

While nothing can truly take the place of experience and quality time on the water, fortunately there are a few things you can do to build your confidence in this sport even before you go fishing.

In addition to reading and understanding the skills spelled out in this book, perhaps one of the most basic things you can do to develop confidence is to educate yourself about the conventional approach to muskie fishing. This is how I got my start, and it continues paying off to this day. For those purists interested only in fishing with a fly rod, it's still important to understand what the vast majority of folks do when fishing for muskies. I know this may sound like heresy to the hard-core fly-fishing crowd, but believe me, it's the best way to build your confidence and knowledge of these fish.

The conventional approach I'm referring to here includes everything from baitcasting to trolling and, yes, even sucker-fishing techniques. Over the years, far more muskies have been caught using these methods than with flies. It simply makes good sense to take a hard look at the consistently tried-and-true techniques before even casting your first fly.

How you go about this is as easy as looking through a good book or magazine about conventional muskie fishing, a muskie-fishing catalog, or making a visit to one of the many muskie-fishing shops wherever the sport is popular. There you'll encounter an entirely new world of equipment and techniques for catching these difficult fish, including casting rods stiff as pool cues and suitable for saltwater fishing; a myriad of super-sized spinners, top-water plugs and jerk baits bristling with treble hooks; sucker rigs that would make a dominatrix smile; and heavy-gauge wire leaders that could tow a truck.

All this information will help you in building a solid understanding of your intended quarry. Step by step you'll sense your confidence increasing. It's my hard-earned knowledge of these varied techniques, combined with a lifetime of fly-fishing experience, that serves as the basis of many of the strategies, techniques, seasonal tactics, and fly patterns I've developed to catch these fish consistently on flies.

Another confidence-building approach is to book a day or more of fishing with a professional muskie guide. Regardless of the techniques, the real-life experience you'll gain from even a single day with a guide will assist you as soon as you hit the water for the first time with your fly rod. Learning where muskies live, and—if you're lucky—seeing how they react or strike a lure will help build the confidence you'll need. I've benefited from many days on the water with professional muskie guides and I am grateful for all they've shared with me about how to catch these elusive fish.

When choosing a specific body of water or a guide for muskie fishing, I recommend you begin your quest on an "action" lake, flowage, or river with a high concentration of fish. Although this may seem obvious, certain muskie destinations definitely hold more fish than others and are consistently more productive. While the average size of fish in these waters is usually smaller, the probability of seeing and

The thrill and satisfaction of releasing a muskie: Each fish you catch will build confidence and teach you something new.

even hooking at least one fish is much higher than in lower-population "trophy" water. The initial experience of seeing a fish follow your fly and perhaps even hooking or missing one will do wonders for your confidence level as you prepare to take this game to the next level.

For those anglers who can't wait to hit the water with a fly, one final approach I guarantee will help build your confidence before you start fly fishing for muskies is to try fishing first for northern pike. Being in the same *Esox* genus as muskies, but more numerous and aggressive, this species is the perfect "test" fish for an aspiring muskie angler. Best of all, they love to eat flies! Since it's common on the right water for even a beginner to catch and release several pike on a fly, this kind of fishing will provide you with much of the basic education you'll need before

casting a fly for your first muskie.

The fact that pike are so receptive to a fly also makes them the ideal fish for the angler who wants to try this sport but lacks the confidence or understanding of *Esox* characteristics. Since pike exhibit many behaviors similar to muskies, catching just a few will better prepare you for how to respond when a muskie finally follows, boils, or strikes your fly. Moreover, you'll find yourself more comfortable with fighting a fish (or many) of this kind with a fly rod and even how to handle a fish like this safely once you've got it to the boat.

As your muskie fishing progresses I also recommend keeping a detailed diary of your days on the water. Among other things, note weather and water conditions; water temperature and wind direction; barometric pressure and moon phase; fish location

After a long, fruitless day on the water, many a muskie fisher has taken solace in knowing that amazing things can and do happen when fishing for the mighty muskellunge. The much-heralded "Leech Lake Muskie Rampage" is perhaps the greatest example of what is possible when the bite is on.

In July of 1955, during a prolonged summer heat wave, the muskies on Minnesota's Leech Lake went nuts. In a three day period, just about anyone who cast or trolled a line on this lake caught a muskie. The local guides had a field day. They ran trips day and night to make the most of this spectacular opportunity. The totals were staggering: a reported 50 muskies landed in three days and probably more than 100 in the week. As can be seen in one of the few remaining photos (below), many of these fish were clearly of trophy proportions!

A major storm and cold front put an end to this unprecedented fishing but the legend lives on in the minds of every angler who casts a line on Leech Lake or any water where this predator swims. In fact, since that time, Leech and other famous muskie haunts have seen some amazing bites in recent years giving hope to determined muskie anglers everywhere.

and activity level. All are keys to building your understanding of this species. Although muskies can be quite unpredictable, having a record of your successes and failures to refer to will help build knowledge and confidence for the future.

While none of these suggested confidence-builders takes the practical place of time on the water, they will go a long way toward preparing you for catching a muskie on the fly. This critical part of your mental fishing skills will not only make you a better fly fisher but keep you focused when everything at last comes together (see chapter 12 for listings of recommended muskie-fishing resources, guides, and destinations).

Opportunity

It's obvious to anyone who fishes that taking advantage of a fishing opportunity is what good anglers do every day. Opportunities are what give you an edge—something extra to increase the odds. Whether it's an unexpected day off of work, a special fly, a new weather condition, or a particularly good piece of structure, good anglers are always looking for that edge. I'll cover how to do this effectively with a fly rod in greater detail later in this book.

Given the elusive nature of muskies, however, understanding the need to maximize and take advantage of every opportunity you encounter when fishing is a vital part of any successful muskie fisher's mental set of skills. Since muskies are notorious for being

So much for the myth of the fish of 10,000 casts: This cooperative muskie ate my fly after only a dozen casts while filming a segment for Dave Carlson's popular *Northland Adventures* television show. Be warned, though, this is a rarity.

moody fish—and then showing up when you least expect them—you've got to be ready at all times and know just how to deal with these situations whenever and wherever they occur.

Learning to maximize these opportunities when they present themselves is a skill born of experience and often a little bit of luck. When I first started muskie fishing with a fly, I had many long days without seeing or hooking a single fish. Sure, I'd sometimes see a fish follow my fly briefly or swing by the boat just as I pulled my fly from the water. As most experienced muskie anglers will tell you, however, sometimes it's a heck of a long way between a follow and a strike. It wasn't until I started to realize the importance of maximizing this ephemeral opportunity and understood how a following or even a non-aggressive fish could be converted to strike that my success rate noticeably started to improve. As with many kinds of fishing, these small opportunities make all the difference in muskie fishing.

Whatever the season and weather conditions, muskie action often takes place during what most serious fishermen call "windows of opportunity." Sometimes the activity window is open wide, such as in the spring, when post-spawn fish—energized by

warmer water temperatures—are aggressive and hungry and can be caught most of the day if you know where and how to fish. Other times, say, in the cold of late autumn, the window is narrow and closing. Fish are still active and feeding but only for a couple of hours typically during the warmest part of the day or at dusk. Whether you're a throwing a plug, trolling bait, or casting a fly, it's critical to know when these windows are open and what to do to take full advantage of them before they shut.

Fly fishing for muskies, as usual, presents some difficult but not impossible hurdles to overcome when dealing with these small opportunities. Guide Mike Lazarus puts it this way, "Most of the season, all I'm looking for each day is a shot at a fish … when you're fly fishing for muskies it's a hell of a lot more difficult—you're basically now just looking for a shot at a shot!"

In addition to activity windows, the successful fly fisher needs to understand a number of other behaviors. The most important trait unique to muskies is also one of the most exciting things about this sport: the follow. By "follow" I mean when a muskie swims just below or directly behind (often with dorsal fin and back out of the water) and chases a fly or lure for all or a portion of the retrieve. Why muskies do this is the source of much speculation; it reminds me of the false rise of a salmon or steelhead. We'll probably never know the answer to this behavioral mystery but most serious muskie anglers agree this is definitely one of your best opportunities to catch a fish, especially if the follow is aggressive or "hot."

What we do know is that muskies need to eat— a lot. This, combined with their position at the very top of the food chain and inherently aggressive nature, often prompts them to inspect whatever has entered their immediate territory to determine if it's worthy of pursuing further, killing, and possibly eating.

Many anglers, even those who don't fish for muskies, have heard of the muskie follow. In fact, it's such an accepted part of muskie lore that it's common to include it in the fishing report for the day: "Had two fish on and four follows."

If you've read or heard anything about muskie fishing you've no doubt heard about the typical response to a follow … the "figure-8." This last-chance manuver of the rod tip keeps the lure moving at boatside after the retrieve. Like an underwater bullfight, its intended to keep the following fish interested just long enough to induce a strike. When performed properly, the figure-8 is one of the most effective and exciting ways to hook a muskie on any kind of tackle.

The fact that muskies often follow a fly or lure is both a great benefit and a source of frustration to most muskie anglers. It's benefit because you can finally see the fish you hope to catch (knees knocking and heart pounding) and a source of frustration because they may or may not hit your offering (#*&*&*!). Whatever the case, it's been my experience time and time again that a follow might be your one and only real chance on a given day to catch a fish. That's why it is critical to maximize this special opportunity and take full advantage of this behavior whenever it happens. I'll tell you how to do this with a fly in a later chapter, meanwhile never forget you need to be ready at all times for a following fish— and, as my first muskie guide Earl told me, "Keep a close eye on your lure."

Maximizing Opportunities

There are numerous other large and small opportunities and triggers you'll want to look for and maximize when fly fishing for muskies. Although you may not always have the time, skills, or resources to take full advantage of them, you should always keep them foremost in your mind when planning a trip or on the water:

Fish Prime Water: Thanks to progressive management and fishing regulations, muskie fishing in North America is getting better all the time. Find the best muskie water you can—close or far from home— and spend as much time there as possible. Fishing "action" water with higher muskie populations but smaller fish will do much for your confidence level. Fishing "trophy" waters with fewer but larger fish will test your stamina and try your patience but the payoff can be HUGE.

Fish Prime Seasons: Muskies can be caught on a fly any month of the fishing season. On most waters, however, the spring and fall months are usually the best periods for the fly due to ideal water temperatures and clarity, increased aggressiveness of the fish, and preference for shallow water habitat where they are most susceptible to a well-presented fly.

Fish Prime Structure: Fly fishing for muskies is hard work both physically and mentally. The trick is to narrow down your options as quickly as possible. Fortunately for us, muskies tend to stick to certain "home range" areas offering the best habitat and forage throughout the season. Since you can't possibly cover a piece of water like a conventional muskie angler, on your own—or with the help of a guide—locate these hot spots in a given lake or river and spend most of your time there. When you see or catch a fish mark or remember the area and make it part of your regular "milk run" throughout the fishing day.

Fish Prime Patterns: All muskie fishers look for "patterns" or especially good periods of fish activity throughout the year. On some waters it's an obvious preference for a certain lure or retrieve such as the "top-water bite." On other waters it's the time of day such as the "night bite." It can also be a preference for a certain type of fish-holding structure such as the "rock bite," "sand bite," or the "slop bite." Since most of us can't be on the water every day, talk to a local tackle shop or book a guide to find out what the current fishing patterns are for your intended body of water. If you can't figure out a pattern, be sure to learn everything you can from every fish you see or hook.

Fish Prime Conditions: Environmental factors such as water, wind, and weather conditions have a significant impact on fishing success. While any time you can fish is always a good time, dirty-water conditions and unstable water temperatures can turn fish off and significantly reduce your odds with a fly. Look for clean and generally stable water conditions wherever you fish throughout the season. Significant warming trends are also desirable, especially in the spring when fish first begin feeding actively. Weather

Prime conditions: Dedicated muskie fly fisher James Linehan makes one last cast on a Wisconsin lake before heading for cover.

stability remains important through the hot summer months but look for big changes in the pattern—shifts in wind direction, a thunder storm, or a warm or cold front—to really turn fish on. In the fall, muskies really put on the feed-bag, especially when temperatures begin to plummet right up to the first ice. Whatever the conditions, low-light periods due to cloud cover or time of day are always good for muskie fishing and can provide an edge when other conditions deteriorate.

Fish Prime Moon Phases and Photoperiods: Most serious muskie anglers track the lunar phase each month. They strongly believe that the full- and new-moon periods increase muskie activity and improve the odds of actually catching a fish. The daily moon and sun rise and set photoperiod is yet

another important factor to consider when chasing muskies. If possible, when planning a fishing trip, watch the calendar for any significant lunar events and make a point to be on the water when they occur. Should you be lucky enough to find yourself on the water when both a moon phase and photoperiod are occurring at the same time, odds are good you'll see increased action at this time.

Fish Early and Late: The first and last hours of the day are the witching hours for muskies. Regardless of the time of year, many a good fish has been taken on the first and last casts of the day. With fish less wary at this time, fishing early and late also gives you the advantage of less competition from other anglers and less commotion from boat activity.

Fish Smart: With a species as moody and unpredictable

as a muskie, you must be prepared to change flies, tactics, and strategies at all times. Regardless of what conditions normally dictate or what others are doing (or say they are doing), your fishing success can change dramatically if you simply take the time to rethink things and find a new approach. A fly rod and a fly is a very good start, but it's not the only move you can make. Likewise, having a game plan is a good thing, but only if it's working. When fishing is slow, don't keep doing the same old thing—try something new! Muskies do some crazy things when they're on the hunt and you never know what might happen unless you try. Staying alert and being sensitive to any subtle and not so subtle changes in conditions is a real key to muskie-fishing success. It's this kind of proactive approach to fishing that creates opportunity. Some might even say luck.

Visualization: Putting it all Together

Achieving success at the game of muskie fishing requires much more than a combination of the right equipment, boat, and flies. A consistently successful muskie fly fisher must also have an effective set of mental skills. First and foremost, this mental agility includes steadfast determination, unyielding confidence, and the ability to maximize opportunities whenever and however they appear. All the great muskie fishers I have known possess a sixth sense about where, when, and how to fish. By fishing hard and smart, they turn their knowledge into intuition that is usually right.

As with any new skill, once you put in a few long days you'll begin to understand the critical need to maintain a proper mindset at all times. I fully realize

Visualize your success: Imagine a giant muskie lurking behind each piece of cover to improve your odds and keep you focused.

Consistently fooling muskies on the fly isn't a matter of luck or chance. Use the skills outlined in this chapter to increase your odds of success. Combine determination, confidence, and opportunity to beat this predator at its own game.

many anglers would rather "just go fishing" and not worry about these issues. Unfortunately, the very nature of muskie fishing, especially with a fly, soon leaves them discouraged and looking elsewhere for a fish fix.

Fortunately, there is a fun and relatively painless way to achieve the proper mental outlook necessary for this sport. It's called visualization, and over the years I've benefited by employing this technique to keep me focused and in the game. While I know this may sound strange to some anglers, it's no secret that many professional athletes and sportsmen today utilize this very technique to improve their skills and, ultimately, their successes.

To apply visualization to your personal muskie fishing, simply take some time before you fish to imagine yourself on the water you'll be fishing, having a great time casting all day and even catching a few fish. It's a fantasy most of us should be comfortable with and it's easy to do, especially since you'll no doubt be anticipating a great day. Once you're on the

water, focus hard on each and every cast you make. Visualize the structure you're fishing over and where a muskie is likely to be hiding, waiting to ambush your fly. Regardless of whether you see a fish or not, imagine that each cast is being followed by a muskie or that each retrieve will entice a violent boatside strike. If it helps, you can even imagine the next cast will produce a new world record. And you know what? It just might.

That's all it takes to visualize success. There's no right way to do this as long as you keep yourself totally focused and on top of your game.

While it takes some imagination, believing, and pretending you just might catch a fish is an excellent way to improve your fishing. When you do this properly you'll also find yourself ready for a fish at all times. Although simple to do, this visualization technique requires that vital combination of determination and confidence so essential to muskie fishing. When practiced correctly, it also puts you in a perfect position to maximize the opportunity when it finally comes.

CHAPTER 4

"*Every battle is won or lost before it is ever fought.*"
—Chinese philosopher Sun Zi

THE RIGHT STUFF

NOT LONG AGO I EXPERIENCED a personal freshwater fly fishing first: A large muskie broke my rod. Actually, *I* was the one who broke the rod. But the fish deserves most of the credit.

I was doing some late-season "research" for this book with fly-fishing muskie guide, Mark Meritt, on a popular Midwestern lake. We'd fished all day with only a few half-hearted follows and no solid takes. It was a beautiful day for fishing—not for catching. As the sun was setting, my arm and shoulder were getting pretty sore, but I kept casting and stripping a large streamer pattern on a heavy, T-300 line with the hope of at least one fish before dark. My confidence was boosted when Mark noted the deep-water break we were drifting over had given up a 50-inch fish the previous spring. Just then my nine-foot rod doubled over and I strip-struck as hard as I could. It was solid set and I could feel, and then see the golden flash of a large fish as it rolled deep in the clear water.

The instant I set the hook my rod exploded into several pieces. I was momentarily shocked, and left holding only a splintered two-foot butt section and a stripping guide. In a panic, I immediately reached for my line as the fish moved away but had only a few brief seconds of contact before the fish was off. When I retrieved my fly I also recovered the remaining pieces of my shattered rod including the tip-top guide that was actually bent from the force of the hit.

I sat down in the bottom of the boat, took a deep breath, and tried my best to comprehend what had just happened. There was no way to know for sure but we suspected the fish had blasted my fly and kept right on going at precisely the same time I set the hook in the opposite direction. With such intense pressure something had to give. After a brief period of silence I looked up at Mark, Mark looked at me, and we both said "WOW!" shaking our heads in mutual disbelief.

While you probably won't break many rods, choosing the right gear for muskie fishing with a fly is still an essential part of your overall success. This sport is simply too much hard work to waste valuable time and energy worrying about the performance of your equipment. Moreover, getting started the right way and staying on top of your gear requirements will make you more efficient and productive saving you from the many small disasters that can plague even a normal day on the water.

Making a decision about the best tackle for chasing muskies on the fly can be as simple or as complicated as you want to make it. If you're a fly-fishing "gear head" who enjoys collecting as many different rods, reels, and lines as possible for every fish you chase, then you'll really enjoy getting set up for this sport. On the other hand, if you can't afford another new rod, much less a new leader, don't despair—these days there's always an affordable option to fit your needs.

The first place to start looking for muskie equipment is your own fishing closet. With the growing popularity of saltwater fly fishing, many fly fishers have already invested in nearly all the gear they'll ever need for muskies on the fly. The same also holds true for anyone who fly fishes for steelhead or salmon. Both these popular fly-rod species require much the same heavier-weight fly rods and reels that are ideal for this fishing. And you'll be pleased to know that your one-time investment in highly specialized and expensive fly gear now has a brand-new use, often much closer to home.

If you don't already have the gear I've described, the best advice I can give you about choosing the right gear for muskies is: Use the best equipment you can afford and are comfortable casting with all day long. The last thing you need when it really matters is worrying about your ability to make a cast or whether your rod, reel, or line is up to the challenge. Buying the right equipment is the least expensive investment you'll make in this sport compared to

Fly fishing for an elusive fish such as the muskie can be intimidating for some anglers. But it needn't be. With the right gear and plenty of practice, you will soon find it's an enjoyable—and productive—technique for pursing the legendary "fish of 10,000 casts."

time on the water, guides, boats, and—most of all—your mental health.

Choosing a Fly Rod for Muskie Fishing

To better understand the fly rod you'll need, it's helpful to start by examining the standard equipment used by conventional muskie fishers. Take a look inside any serious muskie hunter's boat, tackle room, catalog, or bait shop. Tucked among the many items unique to muskie fishing—wire leaders, jaw-spreaders, hook-outs—you'll find various heavy, saltwater-weight, baitcasting rods of six to eight feet with matching high-speed reels. Some rods specifically designed for throwing certain lures are longer—up to eight and a half feet—but all are pretty stiff compared to other conventional casting rods. With the advent of modern graphite, these rods are also very light, a great benefit when casting long hours with a heavy lure.

The advantages of this unusually heavy freshwater equipment become obvious when repeatedly casting and retrieving large muskie "baits" (what muskie anglers call their lures), setting the hook, and fighting a big fish. Since many conventional muskie lures such as jerk baits and glide baits have no built-in inherent action, a stiff rod is also critical to achieving just the right action necessary to attract a fish.

When you think about it, the same is also true about any fly pattern you might throw … maybe more so. Since virtually all muskie flies lack an effective built-in action, it's entirely up to the fly caster to give the fly enough life-like motion to attract a fish using both the strip retrieve and the rod tip. When fly fishing for muskies, your rod is both an important tool for casting and retrieving the fly as well as for hooking and fighting the fish.

The need to make a lot of casts with a big rod is another special aspect of all muskie fishing, and particularly muskie fishing with a fly. The old myth about muskie being "the fish of 10,000 casts" takes on an entirely new meaning when you consider the number of false casts it might take!

When I first started fly fishing in salt water, I was intimidated by the size and weight of the specialized tackle and flies used for large game fish such as tarpon and sailfish. As a trout fisher from the Midwest, a 10-, 12-, or 14-weight rod was something quite foreign in my hands. The heaviest rods I owned at the time were barely half that line-weight and the thought of casting a big rod all day long was beyond my comprehension. After a few trips in the salt, however, I soon learned that much of saltwater fly fishing actually involves sight-fishing by stalking and/or waiting for a fish to appear—then casting quickly and accurately at your intended target. This was a welcomed relief and served to hone my casting skills for future pursuits.

Fly fishing for muskies is similar to saltwater fly fishing in many respects but with one important difference: When muskie fishing with a fly, most of your time will be spent "blind casting" over suspected fish-holding structure with little actual down time other than to rest your weary arms and hands, usually while moving the boat from spot to spot. Although there are certainly sight-fishing opportunities to be had when muskie fishing—such as with post-spawn fish in the spring or fish busting bait in the shallows—this is the exception rather than the rule through most of the season. Just because muskie and saltwater fly-fishing equipment appears similar in weight, size, and shape, don't be fooled; it still takes a lot of casting to fool a muskie with a fly. Given these myriad considerations, the

Casting a big fly from dawn until dusk is made easier with a lightweight, large-arbor reel such as this Waterworks-Lamson ULA Force 4. It has plenty of guts to handle a big fish and the high retrieve rate will help you pick up line in a hurry.

ideal choice in a muskie fly rod is determined as follows:

1. The muskie fly rod must have a fast yet responsive action to load, cast, and retrieve a large, wind-resistant fly quickly and accurately at short and long distances of anywhere from 20 to 60 feet ... sometimes longer.

2. The muskie fly rod (and reel) must be light enough to cast all day without stress, yet powerful enough to throw and retrieve a big fly, help set the hook, and fight a large, toothy adversary.

Based on these diverse requirements, my ideal, all around rod choice for muskie fishing with a fly is a nine-foot, 9- or 10-weight, fast-action graphite rod. Over many years and on all kinds of muskie water, I've found this rod-weight and action profile offers the very best—and most effective—combination of castability, performance, and versatility for most casters. Moreover, once you've hooked your first muskie, a nine-foot, 9- or 10-weight graphite rod is the perfect tool for fighting a very large freshwater fish while at the same time allowing for ample enjoyment of the fight itself.

Why a 9-or 10-weight rod? While you're certainly welcome to try fishing for muskies with a much lighter rod—say, a 5-weight—it's not a practical choice, unless, of course, you're some kind of fly-fishing masochist. You don't have to be a fishing guide to understand you won't see much action if you can't put the fly in front of the fish.

As for other rod weights, I consider an 8-weight rod great for bass fishing but generally too light for muskie except when casting smaller flies. Likewise, a tarpon-grade 12-weight is, overkill in all but the most extreme big-fly, big-water, or wind conditions. I've caught muskies on rods as light as a 7-weight (usually by accident when bass fishing) but do not recommend this for anyone serious about the sport.

Fly-Rod Action

Rod action—how the rod flexes under the load of the line and fly weight—is equally critical to muskie fishing with a fly. The action of your fly rod is a key determining factor in how well you cast. Although rod manufacturers use a variety of tempting but confusing terminology to describe the action of their rods, most can be categorized simply as slow, moderate, or fast.

As you no doubt have already concluded, slow-action rods have no place in muskie fishing unless you're looking for trouble. In fact, you'll have a tough time finding a slow 9- to 10-weight graphite fly rod unless it's one of the "collectors" items listed on eBay. Moderate-action rods, while still popular with the bass-bugging crowd, typically lack the power required to make the casts and retrieves necessary in muskie fishing.

With the popularity of saltwater fly fishing, today's newer generation of ultra-fast, high-modulus, graphite rods in the 9- and 10-weight category appear to be on the right track. These rods have gone

A fast-action graphite rod such as this nine-foot, 10-weight G.Loomis CrossCurrent GLX is one of many premium choices available to the muskie fly fisher.

So long as you can make the cast muskies aren't impressed by the price tag on your gear: A high-quality, value-priced graphite fly rod and reel such as these offered by St. Croix are the perfect combination for the beginner and experienced angler alike.

through several modifications in recent years. They can best be described as fast, faster, and fastest. In fact, fly-rod actions have become so fast—and stiff— that line manufacturers are now producing line weights one-half line weight heavier than specified just to load these high-powered "cannons." Although many of these new-generation rods certainly cast an impressively long line in the fly-shop parking lot, their on-the-water performance may vary considerably depending on individual casting style, size of the fly, and line type.

My discussions over the years with Steve Rajeff, expert rod designer and world-champion fly caster, confirm this important piece of information. He notes that while an exceptionally fast-action rod such as the new G.Loomis GLX CrossCurrent 10-weight works well in the hands of an experienced caster, a more traditional fast action rod such as the CrossCurrent Series 10-weight is probably an easier rod for most casters to use.

For my muskie fishing, I prefer a more flexible 9- to 10-weight fast-action rod. By "fast-action" I mean a rod that flexes in the upper third of the blank, providing easy loading and good "feel," yet has a fast recovery for constant control and smooth casts. A rod with this action has a progressive taper to load and cast easily, allowing the angler to throw a big fly with accuracy at a variety of distances. As such, these rods are an excellent tool for normal muskie casting distances of 20 to 60 feet with plenty of reserve power for a longer cast when necessary.

A fast-action rod is also the perfect choice for making quick, targeted casts, augmented by a single or double haul. Because your typical day of muskie fishing requires repeated short and long casts—often back to back—you'll have a much easier time throwing a big fly with a rod that loads quickly and requires fewer false casts. Making a lot of unnecessary casts is not only tiring on the arm, back, and hands, but also a good way to get hooked.

Recommended Rods

Selecting the perfect fast-action fly rod for muskie fishing is a little like a certain First Amendment Supreme Court case: You'll know it when you cast it. There's no getting around testing a rod—on the water whenever possible—to see if it meets the muskie fly-rod criteria and suits your individual casting style.

I've fished and tested many of the recommended rod brands over the course of each season and am pleased with their consistent performance. They offer the very best in quality and craftsmanship, and will stand up to almost any abuse you can give them.

While many of these high-end graphite rods are expensive compared to conventional muskie gear, it is possible these days to find a reasonably priced "value" substitute for muskie fishing from the major fly-rod manufacturers or larger fly-fishing retailers such as L.L. Bean, Cabela's, or Bass Pro Shops. Like the trout in Robert Traver's famous "Testament of a Fisherman," so long as you can make the cast, the muskie doesn't care how much you spent on your fly gear!

Fly-Rod Length

The majority of the rods I fish for muskies are the standard nine feet in length. This is because most of the commercially available 9- and 10- weight, nine-foot rods and blanks are designed and tapered to perform best at this length. Since longer rods are typically easier to cast than shorter rods, this rod length serves me well in making both long and short casts. I can put the fly exactly where I want it, regardless of wind conditions.

A nine-foot fly rod is also an excellent tool for performing special boatside maneuvers such as the "figure-8" with a following fish. In fact, some manufacturers of conventional baitcasting muskie rods now offer longer rods up to nine-and-a-half feet for this exact purpose, imitating what is essentially a "normal" fly rod length.

While none of us likes to admit it, a nine-foot fly rod is also helpful to avoid getting hit by your own fly. Because a big, wind-resistant muskie fly with a heavy, sharp hook is prone to dropping on even the best back cast, this is an important consideration to prevent potential injury to yourself or others. Finally, because most muskie fishing is from a boat, there's no real need for a shorter rod to avoid casting obstructions such as trees or high banks.

Over the years, however, I have found a standard nine-foot muskie fly rod does have some slight disadvantages when it comes to controlling your fly in the water or setting the hook. Since any fly rod is by its inherent nature flexible and must bend considerably to load for casting, it constantly requires an extra effort on the part of the caster to control slack when retrieving a fly or setting the hook. Because the strike of a muskie is often quite violent and its mouth is hard as nails, your ability to control line is a critical factor to your overall fishing success.

As a result of this concern, for some time now I have also been including a slightly shorter 10-weight fly rod of eight to eight-and-a-half feet in my multi-rod muskie-fishing arsenal. My objective in fishing a shorter rod is to help reduce the reaction time between the fly and rod tip to either move the fly or set the hook as quickly as possible. Simple logic dictates that the shorter the rod length, the better the leverage and the quicker, more powerful the hook set (assuming you have controlled your slack at the time). A shorter rod is also easier to maneuver, thus providing the angler with an advantage when making quick, short, targeted casts to specific structure or fish. Several fly-rod manufacturers including Sage, Scott, and Bass Pro Shops have recognized this need for specific fishing situations and are now offering fly rods for heavy lines in shorter lengths. They work quite well for muskie fly fishing under certain circumstances.

Other Rod Considerations

To increase my odds while on the water, like most saltwater fly fishers and conventional muskie anglers, I normally carry from two to four rods with me in my boat at all times. One rod is always set up with a streamer on a floating, intermediate, or sinking-tip line. The others are rigged with different streamers or top-water flies, depending on the season.

The reason for this is simple: When a muskie follows your fly—or shows itself in any way—but still won't strike, you must be able to switch your presentation on a moment's notice with the hope of keeping the fish interested and possibly enticing a strike. In addition, since muskie fishing involves casting over many different types of structure and depths through the course of a day, two or more rigged rods allow you to effectively and efficiently cover the water without having to change flies, rods, or lines with every new spot. While it is certainly possible to fish for muskies with only one rod in the boat, two or more fully rigged rods allow you to take advantage of whatever opportunity arises. Given all the abuse your rod will endure in this fishing, carrying an additional rod or two in the boat also affords a backup outfit just in case one breaks.

There are a number of other considerations that can play a big part in your fly-fishing success. One of the most important is the size and style of your stripping guides. For muskie fishing with a fly, I like the strongest and largest stripping guides I can get away with. I prefer at least a 16- to 20-mm stripping guide to reduce friction when shooting and retrieving line. Advances in guide materials have also kept pace with modern fishing needs. I particularly like the newer REC Recoil titanium guides. They are made of super-strong titanium wire and bend instead of

breaking—perfect for the boat fisher.

The size and shape of your rod handle is also important. Although ultimately a personal choice, I prefer a thicker full-Wells grip for most of my muskie rods to provide a solid grip and more leverage with my thumb when casting a large fly and heavy line.

As for the question of a two-piece versus four- or three-piece rods, unless you plan to drive to all your muskie-fishing destinations, I highly recommend a three- or four-piece rod for ease and safety when traveling. While it used to be that a multi-piece rod lacked the same casting action and durability as a two-piece rod, ferrule technology today is such that you can't tell the difference. This fact, combined with the airlines' less-than-stellar track record with checked luggage, makes this an easy decision if you hope to go fishing with your favorite rods when you arrive at your destination. Note: When fishing with any multi-piece rod, check your ferrule connections often to be sure they are tight. Repeated casting with a big rod, a big fly, and a loose ferrule eventually wears the graphite at the point of contact. This increases the likelihood of breakage.

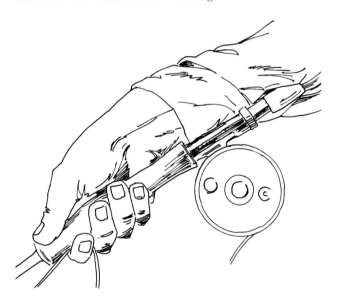

A rod with a full-wells grip and a fighting butt helps increase leverage when casting a big fly and fighting a large fish.

Last but not least, a good fighting butt on your rod is critical when muskie fishing. Most rods in the 10-weight category have one, either permanent or detachable. Some rod manufacturers even offer choices of style in length and shape. When fighting a big fish, a fighting butt provides added support for your lower arm or when propped against your abdomen. It is also especially convenient to hold on to for leverage with your opposite hand when performing the boatside figure-8 technique and striking a fish from a lowered or crouched body position (see the illustration on page 180, figure 1A).

Most important of all when choosing a rod: Fish with the one that meets the criteria I've suggested and *you feel most comfortable with*. Depending on your casting ability and style, you may find the action on a particular manufacturer's 10-weight rod suits you just fine while another one seems too fast or too slow. The best approach is always to take the time before you fish to cast a few different rods side by side and find the one that feels best in your hand. It's also helpful to cast a large "muskie-size" fly on the water and see how the rod performs at various distances. There is really no substitute for casting a rod—ultimately it's up to you to be honest about how well you can throw a big fly 20 to 60 feet, hour after hour, with reasonable ease.

Choosing A Fly Reel

When I worked in a fly-fishing shop as a young man, we told our trout-fishing customers that despite the often hefty price tag, the fly reel is "only" for storing line and backing. This was generally true because we knew that few of our good customers were likely to ever see their 100 yards of backing after we wound it so carefully on the reel spool. This was also probably a good thing since most of the reels we sold back then lacked what would pass as even a decent drag by today's standards.

As saltwater fly fishing became more popular, we eventually had to change our tune regarding the functioning of fly reels. A smooth drag and plenty of backing quickly became the primary concern of all anglers heading to sea. In those early days there were only a handful of really good saltwater reels on the market including the coveted Seamaster and the old Fin Nor Wedding Cake.

Today there are dozens of big-fish fly reels to choose from, all with good to excellent drag systems and plenty of line capacity. In fact, there are so many good reels on the market today, it's hard for the new angler to make a bad choice. The upside for the muskie fly fisher is that you can now find a perfectly acceptable reel for this kind of fishing in the $200 to $400 range. Of course you can also spend as much as $600 for a reel and accomplish just about the same thing, only with more flash. I own and fish a dozen different muskie fishing reels of various price-points including those made by Abel, Bauer, Islander, Orvis, Ross, and Tibor. All these reels have been fished hard and withstood the ultimate test of time on the water.

The major considerations when choosing a proper fly reel for muskie are arbor size, weight, capacity, and drag. Overall durability of the reel is also an important consideration since you'll be fishing most often from a boat. Your reel is likely to be subjected to many rim-bending bumps and bruises while fishing, and as you move from one spot to another.

Large-arbor reels are the perfect choice for muskie fishing. They are exceptionally light in weight, pick up line quicker than a standard small-arbor reel, and have a tough drag system that's more than sufficient. Like your rod, the weight of a reel is also critical—every ounce counts when you're casting a big outfit for extended periods.

Line capacity is less important for the muskie fisher but still should be adequate for your designated line weight and hold at minimum 75 to 100 yards of backing. It's worth noting that I've rarely had a muskie—even big fish over 50 inches—run farther than the length of an 80-foot fly line. On the other hand, backing is cheap insurance for that once-in-a lifetime fish. From a practical standpoint, this also helps to increase the spool diameter on your reel, and, if it's not a large-arbor, pick up line that much quicker.

Although the quality of a drag system is important—and a key selling point for most reels—the truth is most of the time you'll be fighting a muskie on a fly rod by hand, using your index finger on the line and the leverage of the rod as the main source of immediate tension. Nevertheless I always use reels with a quality disc-drag to make sure things go smoothly when—and if—I get my fish on the reel.

The ability to change spools easily is another convenient feature of many of today's better reels. This is especially true if you have only one rod rigged and need to switch from a floating to a sink-tip line. With such a small windows of opportunity when muskie fishing, however, I highly recommend a second or third rod rigged with the lines and flies you need versus trying to take the time to switch spools and keep fishing. The time it takes to re-rig and change spools on even the best reel may cause you to miss the one chance to catch a fish. Further, having a second complete reel provides an all-important backup in case your first one breaks.

Fly Lines for Muskie Fishing

Good news: These days we have a wide variety of high-quality fly lines. Thanks to the growing popularity of the sport of fly fishing, you can now buy a specific fly line for just about every species from stripers to bonefish and, yes, even muskies and pike. You can certainly use a standard fly line in the weight you need for your muskie rod, however, it's a good idea to spend as much as you can afford for the best tools for the job.

To fish effectively for muskies with a fly, you must be prepared for every fishing situation you might encounter. As I've noted already, for me this means always having several fly rods rigged with different lines and flies ready to go at all times. The major categories of fly lines you will use for most muskie fly fishing are:

1. **A weight-forward floating line**
2. **A sink-tip or integrated sinking-head line**
3. **An intermediate sinking fly line**

Floating Lines

Because the majority of muskies are found and caught in water shallower than 15 feet deep, I use my floating or intermediate lines 50 to 75 percent of the time. Whether I'm fishing a top-water popper or a streamer pattern, a floating line allows for an effective and accurate presentation in many productive fishing situations. Yet I still wouldn't be caught on the water without some kind of a sink-tip line for fishing deeper water and other more specialized presentation techniques.

Although a standard weight-forward taper floating line (designated WF-10-F on the packaging and plastic spool) certainly works for most muskie fishing, choose a line specifically designed for casting large, wind-resistant or weighted flies. There are many such specialized lines to choose from today including Cortland's Big Fish/Pike line; 3M Scientific Anglers' Pike/Muskie line; Rio's Pike, Clouser, Outbound, and Accelerator line series; and Airflo's 40-Plus. These floating lines vary slightly in design but all have in common a short and extremely fast forward taper, allowing for increased line speed and distance with a large fly—essentially a floating shooting head. Some even have special finishes to increase line speed and floatation. You'll find floating lines of this design much easier to cast all day, especially when dealing with windy conditions and larger-profile flies.

The fact that extreme weight-forward floating lines do not land softly on the water is not a problem. As apex predators, muskies are not normally shy when it comes to unexpected commotion in the water and may actually be attracted by the sound.

The color of your fly line is not critical but still merits some consideration. Unlike trout fishing in New Zealand where a gray or neutral line is a must, a muskie is not likely to notice your fly line in the air or water. I've been fishing brightly colored orange and yellow fly lines for many years with much success. However, when fishing over pressured fish or in ultra-clear water conditions, a clear-tip floating line may be a wise choice.

The finish and core of your line can have a significant influence on your casting based on weather conditions, water temperatures, and use. Many lines today have a harder-than-normal factory-enhanced slick finish making them easier to cast and shoot on today's faster rods. Some lines are also specifically designed with "low memory" to stay supple in cold weather or maintain their stiffness in hot, tropical-like conditions. Depending on the time of year you fish, this can be a real asset to your fishing: There's nothing more aggravating than a line that won't cast and shoot and tangles repeatedly because it's too stiff due to the cold or too soft in the hot summer sun.

Regarding the issue of line stretch, some manufacturers such as Rio and Monic have recently started offering low-stretch multifilament cores with their lines. A normal fly line has up to 20 percent stretch, so these reduced-stretch lines are worth considering for muskie fishing, especially for longer-range hook-ups.

No matter what the cost or finish, your fly line will get dirty much faster when muskie fishing than you might normally be used to on a clear, clean trout stream. As a result, after only a few hours of casting in warm, shallow, and typically weed-filled water, you'll find your line getting discolored and sticky. This makes your casting even more difficult. While it's hard for any dedicated fly fisher to stop fishing and fix this problem in the middle of the day, over the years I've found it to be absolutely necessary—nothing takes the place of taking the time to clean your line thoroughly with a pad and commercial line cleaner. In order to do this properly you'll want to be sure to carry a good line-cleaning system with you on the boat. Applying a line-slickening agent such as Glide on older lines or Zip-Juice on newer lines after the line is cleaned also helps increase the overall distance and efficiency of your casts.

One final note regarding floating lines: If you're a once-in-a-while trout angler used to using the same old fly line year after year, you might be surprised—and a little disappointed—to know that if you muskie fish a lot you'll likely need to replace many of your fly lines after each hard-fished season. This is in part because the abrasion caused by stripping line constantly against the stripping guide and tip-top will eventually wear off the finish, especially at the transition

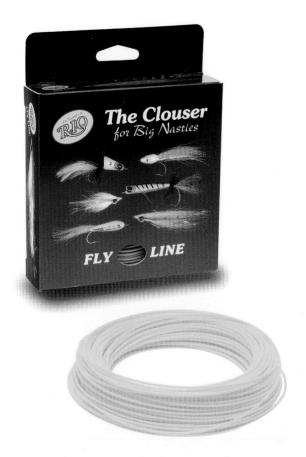

An extreme weight-forward floating fly line such as Rio's Clouser line is an excellent choice for casting large, wind-resistant streamers and top-water muskie flies.

point where the head meets the running line. Fishing out of a boat you'll also encounter many new forms of line abuse including stepping on your line, tangling in the engine or trolling motor, and rubbing along the side of the boat. The combination of this abrasive action and the general wear and tear of fly fishing out of a boat is simply too much abuse for most fly lines, regardless of the cost.

Sinking Lines

A sink-tip or integrated sinking-head line in various grains is your best choice for muskie fishing. Full-sinking fly lines are difficult to cast efficiently all day for most anglers. They have a limited place in muskie fishing, such as extreme deep-water situations where a consistent bottom depth is required. The heaviest lines I use have an integrated sinking-head of 20 to 30 feet attached with a smooth, factory-made connection to a small-diameter floating or intermediate running line making them easier to shoot. Some of the more popular commercially available lines I use are the Teeny T series, 3M's Streamer Express, Orvis's Depth Charge, and also those made by Cortland and Rio. Most of these lines come in a full range of head weights from 100 to 500 grains, but day-in day-out, I'm generally using a 200- or 300-grain sinking head when muskie fishing with a 9- or 10-weight rod.

Mini sink-tips of 10 feet or less are another useful line. They offer less range of depth but are perfect for fishing a streamer pattern over shallow weed beds, sunken wood, or other structure where a floating line doesn't get the fly down quickly enough and a faster sinking line gets snagged or picks up weeds. I also like to use a mini sink-tip when fishing a large diver top-water fly over and along the edge of a weed break. The Teeny Professional Series Pat Ehlers Mini-Sink Tip line is an excellent choice for this purpose. It offers a short eight-foot head attached with a smooth connection to a larger-diameter running line for ease of grip and less problems in the wind.

Intermediate and uniform-sinking fly lines can also be quite effective when fly fishing for muskies in shallow water. Because they sink slower and more uniformly than a typical sinking line, they offer a slightly different presentation by keeping the fly at the same mid-depth range for longer periods of time. Some intermediate lines are now being manufactured in full clear and clear-tip versions. The Cortland Precision Little Tunny Clear Camo Intermediate fly line is a favorite both for castability and stealth. These lines are particularly helpful in ultra-clear-water situations and with pressured fish.

The Jim Teeny T-Series of integrated sinking shooting heads are an excellent choice for getting the fly deep; they always find a place in my boat.

Several major line manufacturers also make a multiple-tip line system allowing the angler to quickly change lines depending on the desired depth and conditions. While these are quite useful if you can afford only one line, your fish will likely be long gone by the time you switch tips and re-rig, I prefer to keep several rods rigged at all times to stay on top of an active fish.

When using any type of sinking line, take time before you fish to experiment in the water and determine how long it takes your fly and the line to sink. Although most fast-sinking lines are typically rated to sink from four to seven inches per second, this sink rate can actually vary significantly depending on the size of the fly and current speed of the water you're fishing.

There are many advantages when using sinking lines for muskie fishing. One is to cover fish and structure effectively at different depths. This can be on a weed line as shallow as three feet or a sunken island in 20 feet or more of water. Depending on your retrieve rate with an integrated sinking-head line, you can fish quite shallow and then deep within the same retrieve. This presentation is quite effective when fishing a weed-line break or rock wall where fish may be hanging on the edge or found scattered throughout structure.

Another more practical reason to use a sinking line is it allows you to make longer casts and shoot line much easier than with a standard floating line and a big fly. With a heavy sinking head and a big muskie fly you'll be amazed how far you can throw

In addition to the popular Pike/Muskie floating fly line, 3M Scientific Anglers offers a wide range of specialty fly lines to fit every muskie-fishing situation.

The old-fashioned way: This 30-pound muskie—possibly the first ever taken on a fly—was caught by champion fly caster William C. Vogt on the St. Croix River in the early 1920s using a three-and-a-half-ounce split bamboo fly rod and a light-test line.

even the most wind-resistant patterns. This comes into play with any windy conditions you might encounter and when you're trying to cover suspended fish in open water and need to get the fly deep with repeated casts.

Finally, the addition of a sink-tip line allows you to strip the fly in a much more erratic and jerky action than a floating line—perfect when utilizing the jerk-and-strip technique or any stop-and-start strip action with the line and rod tip.

One final note regarding line weights for muskie fishing: With floating—and some sinking—lines you might also want to consider over-lining your rod by one or two line weights. This allows the rod to load more quickly at short distances. As noted earlier, most premium fast-action fly rods are powerful enough to handle this extra weight without much problem. Depending on your casting ability it may be just what you need to deliver a large fly with greater ease.

Terminal Connections

Line to Leader

There are several means to accomplish this vital connection, but the most simple and reliable line-to-leader connection I've found is an "end loop" comprised of a short, five- to 10-inch length of stiff .028- to .032-inch diameter hard mono nail- or needle-knotted to the line and a perfection or double surgeon's loop tied on the other end to attach the leader. When building an end loop I like a stiff and abrasion-resistant material such as heavy fluorocarbon or hard nylon to insure proper leader turn-over and longevity.

The choice of a relatively easy to tie "nail-less" nail knot or the more complicated needle knot is entirely personal depending on your knot-tying proficiency and patience level. The nail knot works fine with most fly lines for this connection so long as you use at least six to seven turns of the mono, and the loops are even and tightened securely. When

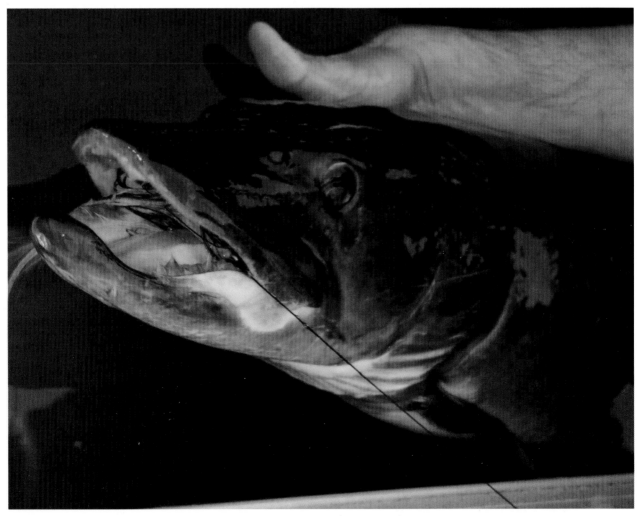

Need I say more? This trophy muskie would have been just another fish story without the use of a wire bite guard.

One of the most significant advances for the muskie fly fisher in recent years is the availability of stainless steel, coated, tie-able wire leader material. Whether you use a pre-made leader or tie them up yourself, the use of a wire bite guard will definitely help you land more fish.

using a sinking or intermediate line—or floater with a special hard finish for tropical fishing—with a solid braided or monofilament core, however, you must use a needle knot or a whipped line loop to create a secure connection.

I use this system with all my fly lines to attach and remove my leader quickly and efficiently with a simple "handshake" loop-to-loop connection. With an easy-to-tie perfection or other loop on the leader tag section, this allows you to change leaders (and flies) throughout the day with a minimum of wasted time (see illustrations on pages 76-78). I've also found it useful with any leader-to-line connection to use a quick-drying rubber agent such as Pliobond to coat the nail knot on your fly line. Because there are many times you'll be retrieving your fly line and leader right up to and through the rod tip—such as when using the figure-8 technique—the rubber coating allows this vital connection to move smoothly through the guides. This helps prevent potential snagging problems when striking and fighting a fish at close range. If this becomes a major concern with your fishing then I recommend you take the time to needle-knot all your leaders to the fly line in advance.

Muskie Leaders

Unlike most trout-fishing situations—where your fly is very light and your long leader is gradually tapered so it will turn over gracefully—muskie leaders are best defined as short and strong. Since the fly you're throwing is usually a six- to 15-inch streamer or popper, it's actually the weight of the fly itself—not the leader—that eventually turns the fly over, usually with a loud SPLAT!

Leaders for muskie fishing can be knotted or knotless and range in length from as short as four feet to as long as nine feet. On average, I use a seven-foot leader comprised of a two-foot tippet of 20-pound test and a 12-inch wire bite guard. Heavy abrasion-resistant materials such as saltwater-grade mono or fluorocarbon are a must. Leader materials manufactured by Climax, Frog Hair, Hal Janssen & Company, Mason, Maxima, Orvis, Rio, Seaguar, and Umpqua are some of the better choices for muskie fishing. All offer excellent tensile and knot strength.

Building your own leader for muskie fishing is a relatively simple process. The key is to avoid using a butt section that is too long and light resulting in a hinge when casting a large fly. For example, I build my standard seven-foot muskie leader using a four-foot section of 40-pound test attached with a perfection loop to a two-foot section of 20-pound test "tippet." With a 12-inch wire bite guard and fly attached to the end of my tippet with a perfection loop, this standard leader turns over nicely and is more than adequate for most muskie fishing situations.

Another approach to muskie leaders is to purchase your favorite commercial brand of tapered knotless or knotted heavy saltwater leader in the breaking strength you desire. After carefully unfurling the leader and making sure it's straight, simply tie a perfection loop on both the tippet end and the knottable wire, and then attach the two together using a loop-to-loop connection.

Note: If you're after a world-record line-class fish, you must consider the length and breaking strength of your "class tippet" and the length of your "shock tippet" (bite guard) attached to the fly. Current International Game Fish Association rules require no more than 18 inches of class tippet from knot to knot, and a maximum of 12 inches from knot to knot for your shock tippet regardless of the material used.

Wire Shock Tippet or Bite Guard

Whatever the breaking-strength of your leader, there's no getting around some form of solid protection to prevent a razor-toothed muskie from cutting your line. Depending on the fly and line I'm fishing, I always use at least 12 inches of 15- to 45-pound-test, small-diameter, nylon-coated knottable stainless steel wire for my muskie shock tippet. Remember: A 12-inch shock tippet in any weight or material is the *maximum* allowed for a line-class record by IGFA.

A wire bite guard of less than 12 inches can be a risky choice especially if the fish decides to inhale the entire fly in one bite.

For what it's worth, consider this strange but true muskie fly-fishing story: While floating a Wisconsin river one summer day with my friend and muskie guide "Musky Joe" Flater, I had a large fish swirl on my streamer next to the bank. "Check this out," I said with confidence, knowing full well this fish was hot and I was about to hook-up ... or so I thought. Joe let out a gruff "nice fish" when he saw the muskie as it turned and made a determined second approach. I kept stripping faster as the fish picked up speed and with a final burst of power devoured my fly head-on. I strip-struck hard, fully expecting to hook-up. Instead, all I got was a "What the hell?" from the back of the boat as I stood dumbfounded with a cut

and frayed fly line dangling from my rod tip. Believe it or not, in the brief time it took to set the hook this aggressive fish had inhaled my entire seven-foot rig all the way to the nail knot ... food for thought when considering leader and wire length.

Fortunately for the muskie fly fisher, there are now several excellent, small-diameter, knottable nylon-coated wires on the market to choose from. Those in particular made by American Fishing Wire/Surflon Micro Supreme, TyGer/TyGer Leader, Rio/Toothy Critter, and Cortland/Toothy Critter are offered in single spools of 15- to 45-pound-test and provide excellent flexibility, knottability, and durability specifically for this purpose. Some wires also come in various colors—or can be easily tinted with a waterproof pen—in case you're worried about spooking the fish.

Pre-made leaders suitable for muskie fishing are now available commercially from Cortland, Climax, Rio, Scientific Anglers, and Orvis. Most are from six to eight feet in length and have a factory-attached wire shock tippet in strengths from 15- to 45-pound test. They all work well and are worth considering if you'd rather not take the time to make your own leaders.

When I first started fly-fishing for muskies the only option we had for wire was stiff, single-strand, stainless-steel piano wire. This wire worked adequately to prevent a bite-off, but its stiffness impaired the fly's action, and it required more work to create a secure leader connection. The advent of knottable wire has truly revolutionized the sport of catching toothy fish such as muskies, pike, barracuda, and bluefish on a fly. These durable wires not only prevent certain bite off, but their flexibility preserves fly action, enhances turnover, and their narrow diameter makes them less wind-resistant.

Some anglers fly fishing for muskies or pike in pressured or ultra-clear water use a shock tippet of 50- to 70-pound fluorocarbon instead of wire. The same is true of conventional muskie anglers when faced with the same difficult conditions. Given the challenge of fooling any muskie on a fly, however, I do not recommend using mono for this purpose, especially where there's any potential for trophy-sized fish. When you consider the vast majority of muskies are caught on conventional tackle using heavy gauge stainless steel or black 40- to 90-pound wire leaders with ball-bearing swivels and snaps, it is highly doubtful a muskie will be turned-off by an unobtrusive small-diameter wire leader attached to your fly. In my three decades of muskie fishing with a fly I have yet to encounter a single fish that exhibited any cautiousness in this regard.

The moment of truth: The last thing you need at this critical point is a faulty knot or defective piece of equipment. Always check—and re-check—your hooks, knots, leaders, lines, rods, and reels to insure everything is in working order while you fish.

Knowing what knots to use and where to use them is a critical part of muskie fly fishing. Among hundreds of specialized fishing knots, the ones I use are easy to master with a little practice and provide the highest overall knot strength. Here are a few of my favorites: Be prepared to tie—and re-tie—them many times in a full day of muskie fishing.

Leader-to-Line Connection

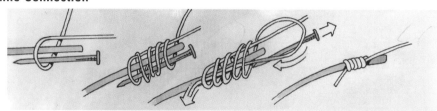

NAIL KNOT: Use the nail knot to attach leader, butt section, or end loop to fly line. A narrow, plastic tube works well as a substitute for the traditional nail and will improve knot quality. For solid-core fly lines use a needle knot or whipped loop to secure leader to fly line. Always trim ends close, and apply quick-drying adhesive to reduce friction through guides.

Line-to-Line Connections

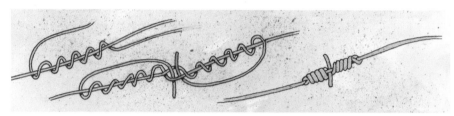

BLOOD KNOT: Use the nearly 100 percent strength blood knot to attach two sections of similar-diameter monofilament when building a leader. Not a good choice for heavy or dissimilar leader material.

SURGEON'S KNOT: Use the easy-to-tie and nearly 100 percent strength surgeon's knot to join two sections of similar leader material. Be sure to use at least three complete turns and pull ends taught uniformly for best performance.

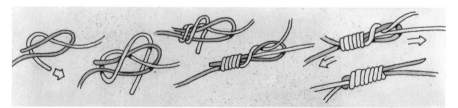

ALBRIGHT KNOT: Use this popular saltwater fly-fishing knot to join leader materials of unequal diameter such as a heavy monofilament or wire shock tippet.

Essential Loops

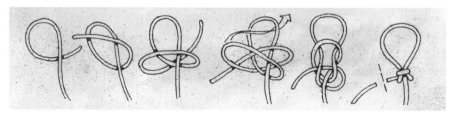

PERFECTION LOOP: Use the nearly 100 percent strength perfection loop for joining two lines with a loop-to-loop connection. It can be used interchangeably with both monofilament and tie-able wire. When tied correctly the tag end should always face 90 degrees perpendicular to the loop.

LOOP-TO-LOOP: When connecting two lines with a loop-to-loop connection be sure the loops fit squarely—like a square knot (left)—and not in a girth hitch (right).

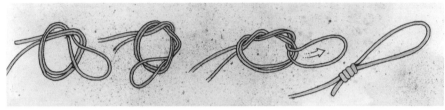

SURGEON'S LOOP: Use the easy-to-tie surgeon's loop to create a loop for joining two lines with a loop-to-loop connection. Always pull both tag ends uniformly taut before trimming.

Essential Knots

UNI KNOT: The strong and versatile uni knot has many applications and is my first choice for attaching my fly to wire bite guard. Once taut, the slip-loop can be adjusted open to allow the fly to swing freely during the retrieve.

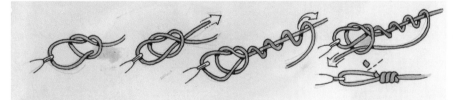

NON-SLIP KNOT: Use the nearly 100 percent strength non-slip loop knot to create a permanent loop when attaching a fly to wire or monofilament bite guard. Use fewer turns with heavier materials to avoid a bulky knot.

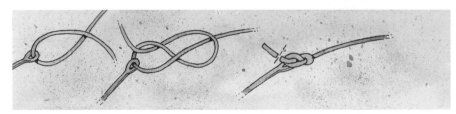

FIGURE-8 KNOT: Use the simple yet strong figure-8 knot to attach fly to wire bite guard when a loop is not required.

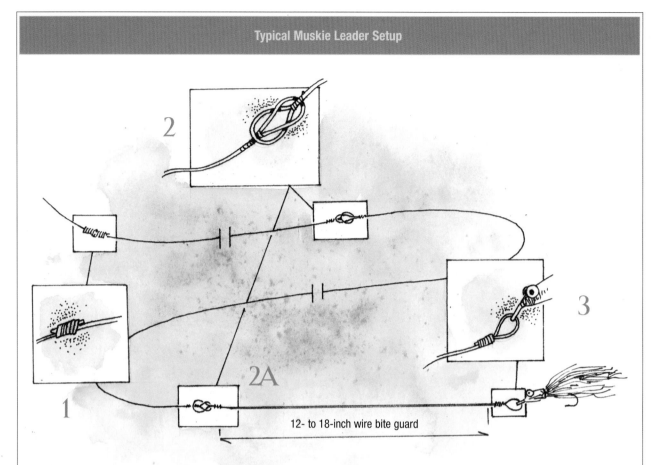

12- to 18-inch wire bite guard

The typical muskie leader setup is simple to build and easy to change depending on fly choice and desired length. Start with a six-to 12-inch end loop of stiff butt leader material attached to the fly line by means of a nail knot (Figure 1). Tie a perfection loop to the end of the leader butt and attach to the end loop using a loop-to-loop connection (Figure 2). Depending on personal preference, use the perfection loop, blood knot, or surgeon's knot to build the leader to desired length. Attach an 12- to 18-inch wire bite guard using a perfection loop and loop-to-loop connection (Figure 2). Finally, attach the fly using the uni knot (Figure 3). Note: Tying a larger loop for the loop to loop connection portion between the wire bite guard and your leader (Figure 2A) allows for easier fly changes by providing a loop sufficiently large to accomodate the fly.

Modern super-lines such as Power-Pro and Fire-Line offer another alternative to wire. Although these lines are certainly tough and strong their suppleness makes them difficult to turn over and they are prone to tangling.

Note: Check all your terminal connections frequently. Be prepared to either re-tie or put on brand-new materials several times a day. This applies regardless of whether you're catching fish or not. With heavy leader material and wire you should be able to see potential problems with routine inspections. When in doubt, run the line slowly through your hands or lips to feel for any less-than-obvious abrasion. There's no excuse for losing the one fish of the day because you were too lazy to check your leader or tippet.

Some knottable wire is also prone to kink when knotted improperly or bent on an obstruction. Be

especially wary of this problem as it can significantly affect the action of your fly in the water. If you find this to be the case, simply cut it off and put on a new section—it's virtually impossible to remove a kink from a wire bite guard.

Leaders for Streamers and Poppers

The length of your leader and the weight of your wire bite guard are determined by your fly and line choice.

When using a streamer with a floating line I typically use a leader of six to eight feet including a 12-inch minimum wire bite guard of 20- to 30-pound-test. This configuration allows the streamer to sink and swim naturally while at the same time minimizing the potential for slack when a fish hits. When fishing a streamer on a sink-tip line, I use a shorter leader of four to six feet with a 12-inch minimum wire bite guard of 20- to 30-pound-test to keep the fly deeper for the majority of my retrieve.

When fishing very deep or to fish holding tight to structure, I often use a leader as short as three or four feet. This helps keep the fly at the exact depth or location you're targeting and, because you usually can't see the fly or the fish, allows you maximum response time for a strike. As a general rule, when fishing any streamer pattern on a sinking line, go as short as possible. The fish don't seem to mind. You're wasting your time if the fish are holding on a deep weed break and your fly is riding high above.

When fishing a top-water popper with a floating line, I typically use a leader of six to eight feet but with a lighter, narrow-diameter wire bite guard of 15- to 20-pound-test maximum. The reason for the short leader and lighter wire is to keep the fly riding high on the surface. This helps achieve a solid and direct pull with each strip of the retrieve. Use too heavy a wire bite guard and you'll normally sink the popper right away, ruining its performance and your odds of success. You'll know right away if it's too heavy since it will take much more work with each strip and pull to get even the slightest effective pop.

You can generally tell if your popper is performing properly by watching and listening for the distinct sound and pop it makes—or doesn't. Conventional muskie fishers use this technique to fine tune their top-water baits throughout the season.

Under certain circumstances it's also possible to fish a popper—or better yet a diver—with a sink-tip line. In this situation I use a leader of six feet or less, but with heavier wire since the fly is going to be fished subsurface for the majority of the retrieve anyway. When using a streamer, popper, or diver, experiment with leader length and wire bite guard weight to achieve just the right balance for each fishing situation.

Essential Muskie Gear

Muskie fishing with a fly requires many other specialized tools and gear not common among or familiar to freshwater fly fishers including:

Fly and Gear Storage

Fly and gear storage presents some new challenges when it comes to muskie fishing. Needless to say, the traditional trout angler's fly vest simply won't work when storing all the big flies and gear you'll need for this sport. With dozens of flies of various sizes and shapes, hook files, pliers, wire cutters, and assorted other gear, muskie fishing requires a practical and efficient way to keep your gear close at hand and yet safely out of the way of your hands, feet, or fly line.

Probably the simplest and cheapest way to store your muskie flies is in a large, see-through plastic box. They come in a variety of shapes and sizes. If the box is large enough it can even accommodate your flies with wire leaders already attached to cut down on rigging time. Depending on where I'm fishing, I carry as many as a half dozen such boxes of flies with me on the water carefully organized by fly type, color, shape, and size.

Large, durable plastic fly boxes such as the Cliff Outdoors Bugger Beast and Ocean Fly Box are another excellent option for storing muskie flies of all sizes. After messing around for many years with a system to store my hundreds of flies and leaders, I've also found that a leader stretcher such as commonly used for tarpon and other saltwater fly fishing works quite well, keeping your flies organized and your leaders straight.

If you're a traditionalist angler who cannot do without some trappings of fly fishing, Fat Cat and Fin-sport make an oversized streamer wallet similar to those used by trout fishers that will store plenty of muskie flies.

Another storage trick for muskie streamers is to place them individually in a clear plastic sleeve or tube with a cap. Many commercially available flies come with these already and can be saved for future use. This simple solution works wonders to keep longer hair synthetic streamers from the inevitable tangles with other flies.

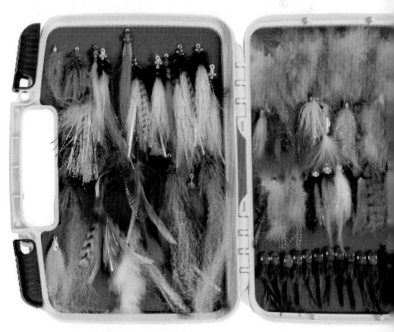

An extra-large, plastic fly box such as this aptly named Bugger Beast by Cliff Outdoors is an excellent choice for storing and protecting large muskie flies.

Ziploc bags are yet another easy and cheap way to store flies, leaders, and assorted gear. Don't tell my wife but I've probably "stolen" thousands of these over the years in all sizes from our kitchen to store my flies and other fishing gear. They work especially well when you're in the boat and want to keep specific items dry and close at hand. It should be noted, however, that these bags do not have any built-in ventilation to inhibit rust. Nor do they provide any protection from sharp hooks so you need to be extra cautious when digging around in a bag of Ziplocs for a new fly.

As for transporting your gear to and from the car or boat, one of the best and cheapest solutions I've found over the years is a large, clear-plastic storage box with a lid, typically used for general household storage. These boxes are inexpensive and are available at most office-or home-supply stores. Best of all, they keep your gear dry, easy to find and in one place when you're fishing. If you're embarrassed to be hauling your gear in a cheap plastic box, Simms, Patagonia, Orvis, and top-other quality fly fishing gear retailers also make some very nice waterproof boat bags that do the same thing for a lot more money.

Stripping Glove

Familiar to most saltwater anglers, the stripping glove is an inexpensive, fingerless glove worn on your casting hand. It has reinforced material around the index and other fingers to provide protection when

Time for a new stripping glove: Casting, stripping, and, fighting muskie on a fly is especially hard on your hands.

stripping. Unless you're exceptionally tough or have been doing this for years, I highly recommend the use of these gloves for all muskie fishing with a fly. On a normal day you'll be hand stripping hundreds of casts a day using only your index finger as both a drag system and as a break to set the hook. After the first serious line cut that hurts like hell and stops you from fishing you'll understand what I mean about this being an essential item in your gear bag. I carry several on the boat with me at all times and go through many in a season. There are several on the market but I prefer the Waterworks "Stripper" Glove and, given my considerable investment to date, I wish I had stock in the company. A single-finger stripping guard is another alternative, but I find them too delicate for most muskie fishing as they tend to move around on your finger and slide off just when you need them most.

Release Glove

Worn on the dominant hand, the heavy-duty release glove is commonly used by conventional muskie fishers and is effective for getting a solid grip on a fish, particularly for a tail hold and when reviving a fish in the water for release. They also help avoid hand cuts and prevent squeezing the fish tighter than necessary for a photo and release. Lindy Tackle and Musky Armor make gloves specifically designed for this purpose.

Wire Clipper

Once you muskie fish a few times you'll find your delicate trout fishing nippers and pliers won't "cut it."

You will need a small but good pair of all-purpose wire cutters to get the job done cleanly and quickly. I always carry two just in case one falls in the water or I can't find it when I need it. Many muskie guides and fishers I know also carry a stronger pair of heavy-duty wire cutters for cutting hooks out of fish (or people). When a muskie is hooked deep with multiple trebles from a lure, this is the surest and swiftest way to get the hooks removed and the fish on its way to recovery. While I haven't often found this tool to be necessary when fly fishing it's not a bad idea if you have the budget and the space in your gear box.

Long-Nose Pliers

A pair of long-nose pliers is essential for pulling knots tight and getting hooks out of fish. A long-handled version is especially nice for removing hooks from a fish that won't cooperate. Most made for fishing also have a built-in line cutter thus potentially reducing the number of tools you'll need to carry.

Jaw Spreaders and Hook Remover

Not your typical piece of fly-fishing paraphernalia, a jaw spreader and hook remover are helpful tools to have when removing hooks from an ornery fish. The jaw spreader works on a spring and, once inserted, keeps a tight-mouthed muskie's jaws open long enough to get a deep hook out. When combined with a long-handled hook remover you can do in seconds what takes a lot of time the old-fashioned way, and still not injure the fish or yourself.

Hook Sharpener

A good-quality hook sharpener is an absolute must for any muskie fisher. Because a muskie's mouth is rock hard and tough to penetrate it's essential you always sharpen your hooks before, while, and after you fish. I use both a short, flat, extra-fine four-inch file and longer diamond-edge type file with a groove to get my hooks consistently razor sharp. Luhr Jensen and Dr. Slick make a variety of files that work well for big flies. Both are available from saltwater fly-fishing retailers, catalogs, and larger tackle stores.

Boga-Grip

This ingenious tool allows the angler to control the fish by lifting it gently with a solid lip-lock while at the same time getting an accurate read on the weight. It can also be used to weigh the fish while still in the net. Using a Boga-Grip properly minimizes handling which is always the preferred method for any successful muskie release. For most muskie

The popular Boga-Grip is a great tool for holding and controlling muskies with minimal injury to angler and fish. Attaching a float to the lanyard is a good idea to avoid a costly mistake.

fishing I use the smaller version for fish up to 30 pounds, but you may also want to use the larger 60-pound model when fishing trophy waters and feeling really optimistic.

Tape Measure

While some anglers may be quite satisfied with a hook up—much less a landed fish—it's always helpful to have a tape measure to know if your fish is legal. An accurate measurment of the fish's length and girth can also help you determine its weight using the simple formula in the accompanying sidebar. If you don't happen to have a tape handy, simply measure your fish against your fly rod, oar, net, or some other length in the boat and mark it clearly for later reference. Some muskie anglers even mark off inches on the side of their boat to allow a quick water-level measurement.

Author's Tip: Calculating The Weight Of Your Fish

Using a tape or other measuring device to calculate length and girth it is possible to obtain a fairly accurate estimation of the weight of your fish.

Here's the formula: length x girth x girth ÷ 800.

So, if your fish measures 42 inches long and has a girth of 20 inches it would weigh approximately 21 pounds.

Is there a doctor in the house? Muskie guide Mark Meritt demonstrates the proper use of a jaw spreader and hook-out tool for removing a streamer fly from a deeply hooked muskie.

Whether made of solid molded plastic or collapsible mesh, a good stripping basket is worth its weight in gold when fly casting from a boat on windy days.

Stripping Basket

Whatever kind of boat you use, a stripping basket is an invaluable tool for controlling any loose or slack line, especially if the wind is blowing your line over the bow or any other places you really don't want it. Stripping baskets are also quite helpful to keep your line clean and tangle-free for shooting longer distances. There are many on the market these days that either stand alone on the deck or can be worn with a belt.

I hate to carry around too much gear and clutter up a boat, so I use often use a lightweight collapsible version. My favorite these days is the Charlie's Total Control stripping basket. This ingenious, lightweight basket, stands about eight inches high and is easy to set up and adjust. Best of all, it fits perfectly along your side for a natural one-or two-handed stripping position. In extremely windy conditions I've also been known to empty my large plastic gear box to hold line when nothing else is available. The only drawback with any larger basket is that it can get in the way of your fishing, especially when you need to move around during the retrieve or with a fish on.

Polarized Glasses

Don't leave home without them! Polarized sunglasses are a must when fishing in any shallow-water sight-fishing situation. When muskie fishing with a fly you'll need to wear them at all times to have any hope of seeing fish or promising structure. Wearing glasses when muskie fishing is also the most important thing you can do to protect your eyes from a large hook or fly line.

I usually carry several pairs with me at all times to cover different light conditions. You'll probably use copper, brown, or amber-hued lenses for most muskie fishing since they provide the best overall contrast. Lighter and darker hues are also helpful to see fish under different light conditions. A side panel of some sort on your glasses will help to cut down on side-glare and protect your eyes. The same is true of a broad billed hat which helps to protect your head from a fly and the sun. It also pays to invest in a proper lens cleaning cloth to wipe your glasses and avoid smudging or scratching.

Camera and Extra Batteries

Catching a muskie on a fly is a momentous event. You'll remember it for the rest of your life. As most of my fishing buddies know, I always try to get off at least a few quick shots of any fish before a release. As for cameras, since I do a lot of writing in the fly-fishing trade I always carry two or three, both 35mm and digital. This gives me several options for print type and helps to insure I always have at least one that works and gets the shots I want. Carrying a simple-to-use 35mm point-and-shoot model, or even a waterproof throw-away camera, is also a good idea since your friend or guide photographer may not be as comfortable using a fancy camera when you hand it over for the shot. Given the various power requirements for cameras today I also carry backup batteries for all my cameras just in case they fail when I need them most.

Be Prepared!

Always carry a backup for every essential item. This is especially important when you're on a long trip or far away from home. When fishing closer to civilization you may be able to find what you need, but you can't always count on it, and, more importantly, it takes extra time and energy away from your fishing.

Essential Muskie Fly-Fishing Gear Check List

- ❏ Rods (at least two)
- ❏ Reels (at least two)
- ❏ Fly Lines (floating, intermediate and sink-tips)
- ❏ Leaders and leader material
- ❏ Wire bite guard material in various weights
- ❏ Line cleaner/pads and slickening agents
- ❏ Stripping glove (at least two)
- ❏ Polarized sunglasses and cleaning cloth or wipes
- ❏ Flies and fly boxes
- ❏ Comb for brushing out dirty, kinked, and mangled synthetic flies
- ❏ Small scissors for fly modification
- ❏ Black waterproof marking pen
- ❏ Trailer hook rigs, add-ons, and extra hooks
- ❏ Split shot or other weight for flies
- ❏ Hook sharpeners (rough and fine)
- ❏ Wire cutter
- ❏ Line clipper
- ❏ Long-nose pliers
- ❏ Jaw spreader and hook remover
- ❏ Boga-Grip, net, or cradle for landing fish
- ❏ Release glove
- ❏ Tape measure
- ❏ Stripping basket
- ❏ Fishing hat
- ❏ Dedicated towel or bandana to keep your hands dry and clean for stripping in line
- ❏ Waterproof Log book to record fish and fishing spots
- ❏ Sun block
- ❏ Insect repellent
- ❏ First aid kit (plenty of Band Aids)
- ❏ Flashlight and head lamp
- ❏ Cameras and extra batteries
- ❏ Rain jacket or suit
- ❏ Ziploc bags
- ❏ Duct tape
- ❏ Reel lube
- ❏ Super Glue
- ❏ Quick-drying rubber adhesive for knots
- ❏ Fishing license
- ❏ Hand-held GPS unit
- ❏ NOAA weather radio
- ❏ A positive attitude
- ❏ Plenty of Advil

BIG FLIES FOR BIG FISH

*"I personally prefer fish that eat other fish
over fish that eat only insects."*

—Dwight Tracy

MY VERY FIRST MUSKIE FLY WAS A LARGE, rather crude version of the now popular Dahlberg Diver. I tied this fly back in the early 1970s on a 2/0 saltwater hook with heaps of purple and yellow deer hair and glued-on doll eyes. It was hard to cast. And it was even harder to fish since it absorbed about a gallon of water the moment it got wet. I kept fishing with it anyway. It was the biggest fly I could come up with and still cast all day given the limited choice of materials at the time. It also looked and sounded kind of like one of my favorite top-water muskie lures—this gave me at least a little hope. Despite its simple design and poor aerodynamics, my ugly concoction worked long enough to entice my first muskie on a fly.

Since that time fly tying has certainly come a long way. Thanks to the imagination and creativity of saltwater and freshwater tiers from around the world, it is now possible to create a fly to match and imitate just about anything you can think of that sinks, swims, or floats in the water. Modern synthetics helped to advance this evolutionary process with a myriad of colors, textures, and finishes to make the fly look and perform in ways never thought possible. Today's flies are also much lighter and more durable than those tied with natural materials, a great benefit to the muskie fly fisher.

As you would expect, warmwater and saltwater flies and tying techniques are the primary inspiration for muskie fly tiers. Although there are numerous patterns available today for various coldwater species, most are simply not substantial enough to attract the attention of a fish that sometimes eats small mammals for lunch.

Among the hundreds of proven saltwater and warmwater patterns developed over the years, the Dahlberg Diver, Lefty's Deceiver, Clouser Deep Minnow, and Blanton Whistler patterns remain some of the best designs when it comes to muskie attractors, especially in the spring. Later in the season, as forage grows larger and fish become more aggressive, large saltwater streamers specifically developed for striped bass, sailfish, and other bluewater species also work well.

While hard to cast all day, gigantic foam and hard-bodied top-water flies normally used for peacock bass, giant trevally, and Mongolian taimen can be just the ticket for achieving the right attention-getting noise and action. With the exception of early season, the major theme with most muskie flies is big, loud, and bold.

Like most trout flies, muskie patterns fall nicely into two distinct categories: impressionistic and realistic. While many talented fly tiers spend hours of time creating the exact imitation of a mayfly or other aquatic life form, this realism is usually not necessary when it comes to muskie flies.

A quick look at a conventional muskie fisher's tackle box will tell you all you need to know about what really works—and what doesn't. Inside you will find an often tangled mess of large spinners, crank baits, jerk baits, and surface baits to name just a few. Most anglers carry dozens of muskie lures. Yet very few of them are as realistic as a well-tied trout fly can be. In fact, most are simply artfully painted metal, wood, rubber, and plastic objects with big

My first muskie fly: It may not look like much, but this crude purple and yellow deer-hair creation worked just long enough to entice my first muskie on the fly.

Battle tested and much abused, this tangled collection of giant muskie lures is standard fare in the muskie hunter's arsenal.

hooks. These lures lack any inherent action other than what is provided by the addition of a lip, spinner blade, or retrieve technique. To the average angler, most look less like the natural forage of a muskie and more like some child's bathtub toy.

Of greatest importance to the fly fisher is the simple fact that all these lures work to attract and trigger a muskie to strike using a combination of action and appearance. In other words, even the most realistic muskie lure or fly will not normally entice a fish to strike unless it also moves through the water in just the right way. This is not to say that muskies are simply mindless predators that will eat anything you throw at them. On the contrary, muskies can be highly

---

Important Muskie-Fly Characteristics

Action
- Sound: fly hitting the surface; noise, vibration, and water disturbance as it swims underwater or pops on the surface.
- Movement: breathability, vertical jigging, and/or horizontal side-to-side movement as the fly is retrieved.
- Sink rate: weighted or unweighted.
- Speed: how fast or slow the fly moves forward on the retrieve.

Appearance
- Size/Profile: large or small, long or short, bulky or sparse.
- Color: match-the-minnow natural colors, "hot" colors, color contrast, color patterning.
- Brightness: light, dark, shiny, flashy, or muted.

---

selective when it comes to preferred forage depending on the water type, season, and conditions. Without the right action, however, you might as well be casting a size 14 Adams.

The full range of possible actions with any fly is obviously more limited than a conventional muskie lure; it's part of accepting the challenge of muskie fishing on the fly. How the fly is fished in a given situation ultimately depends on the conditions and the angler's skill. There are, however, a number of universal muskie attracting and triggering factors you need to consider when tying, choosing, and fishing a fly for this elusive predator.

The importance of the fly's action *and* appearance when muskie fishing is a key lesson fly fishers can take from their lure-throwing brethren. These characteristics enhance the presentation and retrieve of any fly thus increasing the overall attraction.

By choice, muskie fly fishers are limited by the range of patterns and size of flies we can effectively cast and fish all day. As such, virtually all muskie fishing with a fly is done with two types of flies: subsurface streamers and top-water poppers. Within these two distinct categories, however, you'll find a wide variety of similar but distinctly different patterns that don't quite fit the traditional mold including articulated rabbit-strip streamers, Clouser Deep Minnows, gurglers, chuggers, and Dahlberg Diver-like flies. Fortunately, both general fly categories work quite well for muskies throughout the season. With some creativity on the part of the tier, they can also be modified in many ways to increase their action and attractiveness.

Streamers

Like many fly fishers, I carry literally dozens of flies with me when I fish but usually end up using only three or four proven patterns in a day depending on the water, season, and conditions. Among my vast collection, streamers make up the bulk of my favorites. Why? The reason is simple; large or small, they attract and trigger fish in all kinds of water and provide the best overall odds of a hookup. Unlike poppers, streamers can be fished at every level of the water column from top to bottom depending on the line type and rate of retrieve. They're also easier to cast and retrieve all day versus a large, wind-resistant popper, making my time on the water more efficient and enjoyable.

Confidence in a pattern is also why you'll find a streamer on my line most of the day. One of my most productive muskie streamers over the years has been a simple white-and-chartreuse bucktail and saddle

The muskie-fly tier's desk: Hair, hackle, fur, and assorted synthetics allow for endless possibilities and creativity at the vise.

hackle streamer with a bit of flash and glued-on eyes. This basic fly pattern won't win any fly-tying competition, yet it remains effective day-in and day-out in a wide variety of water conditions. Is it because I fish this particular fly with confidence or because the fish think it looks like something good to eat? I'll never know the answer, but whenever things get tough I put it on and know I'll probably catch a fish. Most conventional muskie anglers also have their favorite "lucky" lures and will throw them with confidence—perhaps one of the most important mental factors in fly choice.

Streamer Characteristics

Size and Profile: The size and overall shape of a muskie streamer is a key consideration given the need to attract a fish, hook a fish, and cast all day. The most consistently productive—and fishable—patterns are usually in the five- to eight-inch range. As you might expect, this closely matches the average size of popular muskie lures and, more importantly, their preferred forage. Nonetheless, streamer size can actually vary quite a bit, from as small as three to six inches in length in the spring season to eight to 10 inches or more by summer and fall.

Given the fact that muskies will eat—or try to eat—other fish anywhere from one-fourth to one-half their own size, super-sized flies larger than 12 inches also work. This said, while it is true you probably cannot go too big when it comes to the size of a muskie streamer, the issue quickly becomes one of efficiency and physical strength when dealing with anything larger than 10 inches.

The best streamer patterns I've created use materials and tying techniques that feature a "fusiform," fish-like tapered profile from front to back and top to bottom, providing the overall illusion of bulk without the added weight.

Weight: Muskie streamers can be tied weighted or un-weighted depending on the desired sink-rate and action. Wrapping lead wire on the shank during the tying process is the most commonly used method. However, the weight of a large, heavy-wire hook is usually enough to sink the fly and keep it swimming horizontally and at the desired depth when fishing shallow water on a floating or intermediate line. The addition of an epoxy head and bead or lead eyes is another effective way to increase the weight, noise, and action of the fly. Like a jig, weight adds substantial action to any fly during the retrieve, either vertically or horizontally. Conversely, a keel-weight, such as that used in Blanton's "Lead-Ass" version of the Sarlu-mac, is another design adaptation to consider for increasing the side-to-side action to an otherwise standard streamer.

In deeper water, I normally use a heavy, integrated sinking-head line to achieve the depth I desire rather than adding more weight to an already big fly. In some situations, however, you may need to attach removable split shot or wrap weight to the wire leader to achieve additional vertical "jigging" action and/or get the fly down so it crawls along the bottom. When fishing extremely deep water—20 to 50 feet—a 300- to 400-grain sink-tip line combined with a heavily weighted Clouser Deep Minnow is often the best approach to keep the fly in the desired zone.

Hooks: Hook sizes on most muskie streamers run anywhere from 1/0 to 8/0 depending on the pattern and design requirements. The best ones are tied with shorter shank, 1x to 2x long, wide-gape, stainless-steel, ring-eyed saltwater-grade hooks or heavy duty freshwater hooks commonly used for salmon and steelhead. The main concern with any muskie hook is that it holds a point well and will not bend under the weight of a big fish. The larger-gape and stronger-wire hooks made by Tiemco (TMC 811S and 600SP), Gamakatsu (SS15, SC15-2H, SL11-3H, and SL12S), Eagle Claw (254SS), Owner AKI series, Orvis Pike and Musky hook, Daiichi (2546 and 2461), and Mustad (34007 and C685S) work well for a variety of muskie streamer patterns. Designed specifically for saltwater and bluewater flies, they are more than strong enough to stand up to this tough fishing.

Warning: Be sure to check the hook first before

Large-gape, strong-wire, razor-point hooks are non-negotiable when it comes to hooking muskies on the fly.

you purchase any flies for muskie fishing. Unfortunately, some large commercial pike and bass flies are still being tied on lighter-wire freshwater hooks. As good as they may look in the hand, flies tied on these lighter hooks are not recommended for muskie fishing or any large fish species. There's a definite risk they will straighten under the stress of battle with heavy line and tackle.

Colors, Flash, and Pattern: The muskie's preferred forage base is one of several important factors to consider in color choice for streamers. Although there's no need to "match the minnow" in every situation, with rough and panfish comprising the bulk of a muskie's diet, it makes good sense to tie and fish flies of similar color and pattern. Yet some of the most productive colors and combinations, such as fire-tiger, hot pink, jail bird, and fluorescent orange, are nowhere to be found in the natural world. For what it's worth, the top four color choices used by most conventional muskie anglers are black, white, yellow, and chartreuse. Contrasting color combinations of black and/or white and yellow, chartreuse, orange, red, silver, and gold are also quite effective, suggesting the coloration and patterning of a wide range of forage possibilities.

My color choices for streamers also run the full range of the spectrum from midnight dark to super-nova bright. The most common and productive colors you're likely to use are natural black, green, gray, rust, brown, white, tan, yellow, orange, red, silver, and gold. Combining these natural colors with very bright or "hot" colors such as fluorescent orange, red, yellow, and chartreuse is also quite effective to provide contrast and increased visibility. The old adage "if it ain't chartreuse it ain't no use" still applies when it comes to color choice for muskie flies (and lures). Dyed natural and synthetic materials in these various colors can now be found from many salt and warm water fly tying sources.

Most productive muskie streamers incorporate a distinct vertical and/or horizontal two-tone effect with a light bottom and dark top and/or two distinct colors mixed throughout. Life-like contrast can also be achieved by enhancing the fly with a vertical "barred" pattern on the wing using a waterproof marking pen (I always carry one with me to mark and refresh vertical bars on my streamer flies).

In addition to color and contrast, muskie flies should always incorporate some kind of fish-attracting flash. As Maine fly-fishing muskie guide Dan Legere wisely points out, "I honestly had a tough time getting muskies to hit my flies until I started adding flash."

Dan now catches plenty of Pine Tree State muskies with his flashy streamer patterns. Some of the most common and durable flash materials I use are Flashabou (regular, saltwater, and holographic), Sparkle Flash, Krystal Flash, EP Sparkle, Ice Wing Fiber, Lite Bright, Angel Hair, Mylar, or plain old metallic tinsel. Whether used sparsely or in bulk, these materials all provide much-needed light reflection to any streamer pattern, giving the appearance of life and movement even under low light or dark water conditions.

Although they may not last more than one fish, muskie streamers should also incorporate a distinct set of eyes. Use glued-on or stick-on oversized 6- to 20-mm, 3-D, or prismatic, or doll eyes to give added realism at close range. Fish of all kinds tend to key on the eyes of baitfish over all other forage characteristics. You may also want to consider using eyes of different sizes on the same fly to provide additional side to side motion during the retrieve.

Action: Like a jerk bait, muskie streamers have little inherent action other than that imparted through the angler's retrieve; without the right retrieve technique a muskie streamer is little more than a bunch of material tied on a big hook. The best streamers are those that cast well, maintain a large profile in the water, and exhibit highly variable action. Ideally, your streamer will do one or all of the following during the retrieve: glide, swing, roll side-to-side, jig vertically, and push plenty of water. Streamer materials that breathe, flutter, shimmer, and pulsate during the retrieve or while suspended are always best since they provide a unique and added attraction most lures cannot.

What material you choose makes a significant difference when fooling a muskie on the fly. Various and distinct actions can be achieved using a variety of natural and synthetic materials. All are enhanced with the addition of some flash or light-reflecting component. Natural materials such as bucktail, calftail, schlappen, saddle hackle, rabbit strips, marabou, and peacock are some of the best for muskie flies. Naturally breathable llama hair, Icelandic sheep, and yak hair are also good choices for muskie flies but can be harder to find. As for synthetics, you'll find Fish Hair, Ultra Hair, Polar Fiber, Big Fly Fiber, Bozo Hair, Angel Hair, Rainy's Craft Fur, UV Polar Chenille, Crystal Wrapz, SlinkyBlend, PseudoHair, and the various Puglisi Fibers more durable than natural materials and provide a great silhouette and lifelike action.

Note: When choosing a muskie streamer always test it in the water first before you fish. Although they may look great in the vise or the fly shop bin, many

My what nice eyes you have: Whether tied-in dumbbell eyes or glued-on doll eyes, large, prominent eyes are an essential component of muskie flies adding realism, weight, and a focal point for the fish.

streamers lack the natural breathability and movement necessary to attract and trigger a strike. Look for those flies that exhibit at least some action—even at slow "hang-time" speeds—and swing side-to-side during the retrieve. Flies that do not meet this criteria can sometimes be "tuned" with scissors or addition of weight to achieve the required action.

Sound and Vibration: If there's any downside to streamers, it's the lack of a discernable noise and vibration as the fly moves through the water. This is especially an issue when fishing off-color or stained water where visibility is limited. Adding weight to the fly through the addition of an epoxy head, bead, or lead eyes is one good way to increase the noise level, particularly as the fly hits the water or bumps into an object. The addition of a rattle in the body of a streamer or doll eyes is another effective way to increase the probability your fly will get noticed (and not fall outside the definition of fly fishing.)

Yet another way to increase the sound and vibration of streamers is to tie them using material that retains its bulk, or the illusion of bulk, during the retrieve. This is best accomplished using a combination of spun natural deer hair for support and "hollow" tied synthetic hairs that keep the fly lightweight yet add bulk and push water creating vibration upon retrieve.

Streamer Variations

A more recent and successful adaptation for muskie streamers is the classic tube fly. This traditional "Atlantic salmon-style" fly design works especially well for longer muskie flies (eight to 12 inches) where it's difficult to keep a straight and tangle-free profile

Decisions, decisions, decisions: Fly choice for muskies can be as simple or complicated as you want to make it based on a number of factors. Here the author and famed muskie guide Mike Lazarus check out some attractive top-water possibilities.

with an exposed hook. The use of a tube provides a solid base for material with the hook inserted at the rear as opposed to toward the head. This eliminates the need for a trailer hook. An additional benefit of this style of fly is that once a muskie is hooked, the large fly body often swings free of the hook itself, resulting in less leverage for the fish and less damage to the fly. Accomplished fly tier Jon Uhlenhop of Chicago Fly Fishing Outfitters has created some of the beautiful and productive brass and plastic tube fly patterns for muskies featured in this chapter.

Articulation is another fly modification that adds length and appealing action to any streamer pattern. You can use various combinations of hair, hackle, synthetic materials, and flash of similar or contrasting colors to create an effective trailer fly. For maximum durability and action, securely attach the trailer-hook to the main fly body using stiff stainless-steel wire and a small articulation loop. Placing the trailer hook point in an upward position also helps to increase hooking potential and avoid snags with a longer fly.

Top-Water Poppers and Divers

Top-water muskie flies are great fun to fish and are productive under certain conditions. When fishing in thick cover or dark-water conditions they also provide one of your best options for attracting a fish. While top-water flies can be harder to cast and hook fish with, the simple fact they often trigger both aggressive and passive fish into striking is usually enough motivation to keep me fishing, especially in the heat of the summer.

Most muskie poppers and divers are made of either spun deer hair or dense, closed-cell foam to provide floatation. Natural deer-hair poppers and divers look great in the water, but they eventually retain water and fall apart from the wear and tear of repeated casting or, happily, from a muskie's sharp teeth. While I have caught muskies on smaller bass and pike poppers and divers, the majority of fish have come on much larger patterns intended for the salt.

Top-Water Characteristics

Sound and Vibration: The most important characteristic of a top-water fly for muskies is noise—the louder the better. Unlike a traditional slower-moving bass bug, the muskie popper must "pop" or "chug" loudly and move lots of water. And it must be durable enough to maintain a steady, fast pace across the surface of the water for a long distance without sinking or twisting your line. While I've had the occasional fish blast a top-water fly on the initial "pop" or even a slower "stop-and-go" retrieve, this is by far the exception rather than the rule. Top-water muskie divers must also "pop" loudly when pulled beneath the surface and retain enough buoyancy to pop back to the surface between strips.

Achieving exactly the right "pop" requires a solid, deep concave scoop on the front of the fly to withstand the pressure exerted by the sweep and strip retrieve. Hard bodied, closed-cell foam flies do the best job of withstanding this pressure and producing the required sound. The buoyancy, weight, and solid structure of these poppers also helps to keep them level in the water and not spin with each strip causing your line to tangle.

Examining a popper in a fly shop or catalog will not tell you if it will work for muskies. You'll need to cast and retrieve it on the water first, watching the action and listening carefully to the noise it makes. The exact "popping" sound you are looking for is difficult to describe in a book; suffice it to say it is much more authoritative and deep-throated than any normal bass fly can produce. Most conventional surface lures make this sound with the added benefit of blades or propellers attached to the rear or front of the bait.

Based on their consistent success, some conventional muskie anglers understandably believe that this medium-to-low-frequency sound—rather than a higher-pitched frequency—is a key trigger to attracting muskies and making them eat. Any concerns you might have about a popper being too loud or putting up too great a wake will be quickly put to rest when you see a top-water muskie bait in action. These lures come in several different shapes and sizes but all make a considerable amount of noise compared to anything you can possibly throw with a fly rod. While this action is virtually impossible to replicate, with the right retrieve some poppers and divers come pretty close and make a unique sound that muskies seem to like—if only because they've never heard it before.

Size: The size of most top-water flies and divers used for muskies is usually anywhere from four to eight inches in total length, either single or tandem with a size 2/0 to 6/0 hook. This large size can be difficult to cast but is necessary to attract and trigger a fish on the surface. Although they may look like an injured squirrel or duckling on the water, surface flies do not necessarily imitate a specific type of forage. Rather, they prompt a "reaction strike" from a fish that can't resist the combination of noise and action across the surface. The addition of a bucktail or feather trailer hook with flash accent provides additional length and attraction with a top-water fly and extra hookup insurance with a normally violent surface strike. As with many streamer flies, I also like to insert a rattle into the head to provide added noise and attraction.

Color: Top-water color choice is important but secondary to action and noise. In low-light conditions or on cloudy days I usually fish a solid-black fly to provide the best contrast and silhouette on the surface against a dark sky. On bright days or in shallow or stained water, I often fish a bright or "hot" yellow, orange, green, or chartreuse top-water fly to provide

Only feathers and hair: This freshly "crushed" streamer may not look like much but it just deceived a very large muskie.

some side flash and additional attraction. Conventional muskie fishers also follow this same logic with black the number one most popular color for a surface-bait followed by bright colors such as green, yellow, and orange.

Other Muskie-Fly Considerations

When tying or purchasing muskie-sized flies, there are a number of other critical factors that need to be considered:

1. Castability and Wind Resistance

The most effective muskie flies are those that provide a very large profile yet are aerodynamic and light enough to cast all day. Even the best-looking flies will not work if you can't cast them repeatedly to cover large structure or a specific target.

Wind resistance and water absorption are other major considerations with muskie streamers, especially those made from natural fibers such as deer hair and rabbit strips. Synthetic fibers help to substantially

reduce both the weight and wind resistance of larger and longer patterns, making you more efficient on the water.

As for top-water flies, there is really little you can do to reduce the wind resistance of a large head needed to achieve the right noise. When conditions are especially windy, however, it is possible to fish a narrower diameter, pencil-type head. But this usually results in less fish-attracting noise and surface disturbance on the retrieve.

When choosing or tying any flies for muskie you should always consider their propensity to tangle in the air or during the retrieve. Some long streamer flies (and top-water poppers) look great in the water but tangle with the first abrupt strip or twitch. This is not an efficient way to fish—it will definitely ruin your chances when a fish sees the fly or is following close behind. This also applies to any trailer hooks attached before or after the fact.

To avoid this problem, tie or choose flies with hair and/or hackles tied in and supported at the head with a strong bucktail collar, epoxy, or braided tubing such as E-Z Body to help keep the longer materials straight and less likely to tangle. While more difficult to tie, a tube-fly version of your favorite muskie pattern is another good solution to this problem.

2. Durability: Natural or Synthetic?

When it comes to durability, synthetic materials definitely have the edge. They look terrific in the water, and are stronger and longer-lasting than any natural fiber you can find. On the other hand, many natural materials have a unique action, transparency, or color in the water that simply can't be duplicated with even the best synthetics. Since the goal is ultimately to attract and hook a fish, I fish both natural and synthetic flies—or a combination of materials—with the understanding that my purely natural flies may be history after the first fish.

As with most saltwater patterns, when tying both natural and synthetic muskie flies for durability you should always use a super-strong Kevlar-type thread and repeated coatings of quick-drying super glue-type cement as you tie. Finishing the head with epoxy or Softex also provides a nice profile and helps to keep the bulk of materials in place.

Tip: I always keep a bottle of Zap-A-Gap with me when I'm fishing to do on-the-water repair and extend the life of my flies.

Most high-quality saltwater hooks are extremely durable—they are made to last and hold a bend for species much larger than a muskie. It should be noted, however, that after much abuse some hooks

may bend out from a large fish or particularly bad snag. The most critical issue with hooks is the point, which can eventually be dulled from repeated sharpening or by hitting rocks, wood, or other snags. These flies should always be replaced since the risk of a missed or lost fish is too great.

The good news is you probably won't lose many flies when muskie fishing. Other than the occasional unreachable deep snag or bad knot, with a heavy leader and wire tippet your fly will normally stay on for as long as you can keep fishing. Your fly will, however, put up with a lot of abuse during a day of fishing either from casting, abrasion from snags or, with luck, from repeated strikes from fish.

4. Hooking Properties

Not all flies are made the same when it comes to their hooking properties. Over the years I have seen some enticing-looking muskie patterns that I simply wouldn't fish because of their hook size and design. Perhaps most importantly, any muskie fly you choose or tie should have well-exposed hooks, with a wide gape and plenty of room for penetration. Muskies are not put off by a single-fly hook: Consider the fact that

Opposite page: Natural and dyed bucktail, deer body hair, and rabbit strips are indispensable materials for the muskie fly tier, adding water-pushing bulk and action. Above: Muskie guide Mark Meritt selects a fly from his quiver and prepares to do battle. He's "matching the hatch" with a large, white streamer to imitate the shad forage base on this Indiana lake.

the best muskie lures come armed with several sets of large treble hooks dangling from every direction.

Hook position is not normally a problem with muskie streamer flies but it's best to avoid those with too much material around the hook shank or too close to the bend. These flies may look "fishy" in the water but you'll likely have a problem hooking a fish. Watch the fly in the water to determine if the hook remains exposed when fishing. You may need to simply trim material from around the hook to improve hooking potential.

As for top-water flies, the best patterns are tied with 2x to 3x long-shank, wide-gape hooks such as the Daiichi 2461 and Gamakatsu SP11-3L3H. It's also best to attach the head as high on the shank as possible, leaving plenty of room on the bottom to facilitate penetration. Too many hair and foam top-water flies recommended for bass and pike, even muskies, use either too small a hook or are tied far too bushy to allow a proper hookset. Hooking a muskie on top is certainly hard enough without a hook buried under material too close to the head. Deer-hair poppers may be trimmed to open up the gap but with a hard-body fly there's not much you

Synthetic heads—here Marc Petitjean's Magic Head—create a unique side-to-side action opening up new possibilities for the inventive muskie-fly tier.

can do other than shave the foam with a knife and hope the head stays on.

Muskie Fly Modifications

Trailer Hooks: The use of trailer or "stinger" hooks is the subject of some debate among muskie fly fishers. While there's no doubt they provide an extra edge for fish that consistently strike short or nip the fly, the fact of the matter is that the majority of fish you boat will be solidly hooked just inside the mouth or corner of the jaw on the front hook. This is likely because a feeding muskie takes no prisoners. It has no problem inhaling an easily compressed fly with one bite.

Muskies also commonly attack intended prey—and hit a fly—toward the front and side rather than directly behind where the trailer sits. On the other hand, since there's no way to predict how a muskie will take your fly, a trailer hook can save the day. Using a trailer or tandem configuration on a top-water fly may also increase your odds of a hookup since the surface strike of a muskie is usually quite violent and less than direct.

The use of a trailer hook is ultimately a personal decision; use one if it increases your confidence so long as it does not significantly affect the action of the fly. Heck, the extra confidence it will give you when fishing is reason alone to use it even if you never hook a fish on it. The only real downside is its propensity to snag and pick up weeds which can be an issue in certain water.

When attaching a trailer hook during the tying process I use stiff stainless-steel wire secured through the eye and along the shank of the main hook. The stiff wire keeps the trailer in line with the main fly and significantly reduces tangles. After the fact, it is possible—though not ideal—to rig a trailer hook using tie-able coated wire tied at the bend and secured in place by means of a rubber stopper over the barb. Some saltwater commercial flies also come pre-rigged with a stiff wire trailer-hook loop at the butt. On the water, heavy monofilament may be easier to tie with in an emergency. But it's not recommended due to its propensity to tangle and the likelihood of a bite-off.

Keep the total length of the wire extension for the trailer rig short—two to three inches—from the bend of the main hook, and avoid extending beyond the length of the longest portion of the fly. A gap in the trailer-hook connection that is too long will get snagged repeatedly on the main fly. It also adversely influences the action of the fly.

My what nice teeth you have: Razor-sharp teeth, a powerful jaw, and brute strength make durable flies an absolute necessity.

TIKTAALIK

FIRE TIGER

Overall Length: Eight to 10 inches.

REAR HOOK:
Gamakatsu SL 12S size 4/0 to 6/0.

THREAD: UTC 140 chartreuse.

TAIL: Opal Mirage Saltwater Flashabou topped with fluorescent yellow, chartreuse, green, orange, and red bucktail with orange grizzly rooster cape feathers (two per side).

TRAILER-HOOK CONNECTION:
Thirty-pound TyGer Wire (small articulation loop off back of front hook secured by wrapping tags along shank, through the eye, and back to the bend with plenty of Zap-A-Gap). Note: Rear hook positioned with hook point facing up.

FRONT HOOK:
Daiichi 2461 size 6/0.

HEAD: Rainy's Large Saltwater Popper head, chartreuse with rattle.

TAIL: Fluorescent yellow, chartreuse, green, orange, and red bucktail.

COLLAR: Palmered orange and yellow rooster saddle feathers.

EYES: Large doll eyes or Enrico Puglisi solid plastic eyes.

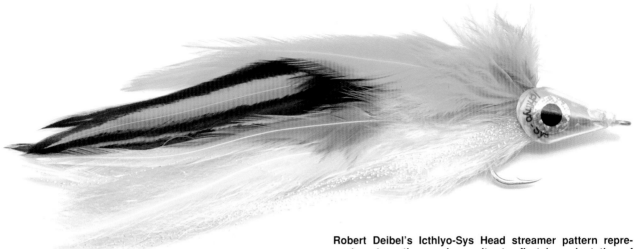

Robert Deibel's Icthlyo-Sys Head streamer pattern represents yet another modern saltwater fly tying adaptation of interest to the creative muskie fly tier.

Trailer hooks for muskie streamers should be of the stainless-steel saltwater or heavy-duty freshwater variety. They should be checked frequently for sharpness, shape, and strength. The hook should optimally be placed in an upward position to counter the direction of the main hook and increase the odds of a hookup. Hook sizes for a trailer should be smaller by a size or two to reduce visibility and drag. The Gamakatsu Octopus hook in smaller (1/0) sizes works especially well for a trailer setup. When tied in upside down, the up-eye design keeps the hook riding straight and in line with the main fly.

Twister Tails: The use of a plastic twister tail on the main hook or trailer hook is a quick and effective way to enhance a streamer's overall attraction and triggering capabilities. This simple modification provides additional action and color while at the same time increasing the overall length and size profile of your fly. These tails work especially well with non-aggressive fish that simply nip at the fly and refuse to eat. And they offer added lifelike action to a fly fished fast or slow.

Twister tails are available in a variety of sizes, shapes, and colors and may be purchased at most fishing-tackle stores. Some even have built-in sparkle for added flash. Because they add significant weight to the fly, the best ones for fly fishing are single or double tails, two to four inches in length. As for colors, white and chartreuse are my favorites but there are many others to choose from.

When attaching a twister tail, center and slide the thickest portion of the body over the point and to the bend of the hook. Exit the body again where the tail begins and slide the remaining body as far as possible along the shank. Before you begin fishing, test the

twister tail a few times in the water to make sure it stays in place and is working properly. You will also need to recheck the tail every few casts to be sure it remains securely attached. If necessary, you may want to apply Zap-A-Gap or other quick-drying waterproof glue to keep the tail securely on the hook.

Spinners and Propellers: The addition of a spinner or propeller to a muskie fly has crossed the mind of many a muskie fly fisher, especially on those tough days when nothing seems to work. Although entirely possible given today's choice of materials and tying techniques, the question invariably arises, *is it still a fly?*

Since the turn of the century "fly" anglers have used such conventional accoutrements with success for many different species from panfish to trout. Although I do not use spinners or propellers when muskie fishing with a fly, some anglers find them to be effective to attract fish and make them strike under a variety of conditions. More recently, some commercial fly manufacturers have also begun offering larger flies with spinners and other lure-like enhancements, including lips.

If you do choose to use them, the smaller size 0 or 1 Colorado or Indiana spinner blades are the best sizes for muskie flies. They are easily attached during the tying process by means of a small split ring and snap swivel attached at the head, or slid over the hook bend. If attached after the fact, use a small, clear plastic or rubber stopper secured on the hook along each side of the swivel to keep the blade in line with the bend and spinning smoothly.

Small metal or plastic propellers used for bass buzz-baits can also be attached to the head of a streamer or top-water fly using a small bead to allow it to spin freely. Although all of these muskie-fly mod-

Natural grizzly and dyed saddle and schlappen hackles provide excellent materials for muskie streamers and top-water patterns.

Modern synthetic fibers open up whole new worlds for the muskie-fly tier by enhancing color and action without adding weight

ifications add a significant amount of wind resistance and weight to the fly, they may work for you, especially in very dark or stained water or with heavily pressured fish when nothing else seems to merit their attention.

Weed Guards: When fishing heavy weeds, wood structure, or tight to the bottom a weed guard is helpful to avoid getting hung up. They are also useful at those times of the year when floating weeds become a serious nuisance.

Effective weed guards for muskie flies can be made using light nylon-coated piano wire, stainless steel, or stiff mono. All work well to avoid some weeds or snags. In heavy weed, however, there's really nothing you can do to prevent a fast-moving, big fly from getting hung up.

Synthetic Heads: The use of synthetic heads on streamers has become popular in recent years with saltwater and freshwater fly tiers. They offer a durable alternative to epoxy or Softex and work well to keep the fly material in place during the retrieve, thus avoiding fouling. Painted, hard-cell foam folded over the head—such as with the crease fly—makes for a truly realistic head, however, this time-consuming technique can be difficult to master for the average tier.

Two of the more exciting developments in this area are the Ready Head invented by fly tier and fisheries biologist Robert Deibel of Ichthyo-Sys (www.ichthyosys.com) and Marc Petitjean's Magic Head (www.petitjean.com).

The Ready Head is a hard, clear, indestructible tapered head that is easily slid on and secured with thread. Each Ready Head kit comes complete with several clear plastic heads for flies sizes 1/0 to 10/0. The kit also includes holographic tape in four muskie-attracting colors (silver, chartreuse, hot pink, and purple) with large stick-on eyes. Although slightly heavier than most glues or braids, these unique heads are easy to use. They give the fly a highly realistic tapered or fusiform shape, mimicking many of the preferred muskie baitfish forage species.

Magic Heads offer a similar, lightweight alternative for muskie streamers heads but with an exciting added twist. These ingenious clear, round, soft heads come in large sizes for muskie streamers from 2/0 to 6/0. They are easily attached to most streamer patterns using thread and can be used with or without weighted eyes. In the swept-back "streamer position" the head acts just like a normal head, allowing the fly to swim straight and/or vertically up and down. By flipping the head forward, however, the head creates resistance during the retrieve, producing a distinct side-to-side, wiggling "walk the dog" action effective for triggering

muskies. These soft plastic heads can also be cut with a nail clipper to produce different actions. They also compress easily and do not interfere with the hook gape, thus preserving the critical hooking capabilities of the fly (see the Yak Attack streamer pattern on page 111).

Author's Recommended Deadly Dozen Fly Patterns: Muskie Flies That Really Work

Fly patterns for muskies can be as simple or complex as the tier's skills allow. Over the years I've seen some pretty ugly examples of "hair on a hook" attract some impressive fish. Beauty is in the eye of the muskie. This is part of what makes this fish such a magnetic species for the fly tier regardless of experience.

If you are new to fly tying, you'll be glad to hear that most muskie flies are really not that difficult or complicated to tie. Sure, you can spend hours on a single pattern but that's more for your individual enjoyment than the fish when it comes to muskies. The important thing is that you can be as creative as you want and still come up with something that will probably work. Many productive muskie patterns are also simple enough for the beginning tier with basic skills. I encourage new fly tiers to give these effective patterns a try. They work well even if not tied to perfection—sometimes even better.

Where applicable I have listed the basic recipes for each pattern to help you get started. As any fly tier knows, it is a great source of satisfaction to catch a fish on a fly of your own making. Given the difficulty of catching any muskie on a fly, this is even more of an accomplishment and worthy of much praise.

MUSKIE MARAUDER

My simple but deadly all-natural streamer of saddle hackle and bucktail has consistently produced muskies on all kinds of water throughout North America. It's easy to tie and fun to experiment using new materials or whatever you've got on hand. This basic, large Deceiver-type fly has an excellent baitfish silhouette that both attracts muskies, and, when fished right, triggers them to strike. It can be tied in a variety of different sizes and colors. Typically white, black, brown, chartreuse, orange, and yellow combinations are best. Inserting a rattle makes this fly even more appealing, especially in off-color water conditions. Using primarily natural materials with this fly means it can get pretty beat up after a few hookups, but the fish still seem to love it even when it's falling apart!

MUSKIE MARAUDER

PERCH

Overall Length: Six to 10 inches.

HOOK: Gamakatsu SC15-2H size 4/0 to 5/0.

THREAD: UTC 140 white.

RATTLE: Medium rattle inside EZ Body braid.

TAIL: (tying order): 1. Six golden olive rooster saddle hackles, 2. two olive rooster cape feathers, 3. two olive grizzly rooster cape feathers.

REAR COLLAR:
Yellow bucktail (bottom), olive bucktail (top).

FRONT COLLAR:
Orange bucktail (bottom), olive bucktail (top).

TOPPING:
Peacock herl.

EYES: Mirage Dome Eyes or doll eyes.

HEAD: Color thread with permanent marker and then seal with clear epoxy.

Chartreuse and white variation—see recipe and photo on pages 120-121.

TIKTAALIK (TIC-TAH-LICK)* POPPER

This basic but very effective top-water fly is responsible for more and bigger fish on the surface than any other in my arsenal. With a large, closed-cell foam head and a bucktail trailer, it has the overall size and noise-making capacity, due to a deep, concave face, to pull big fish up in all kinds of water—day or night. Although not the easiest fly to cast all day, I always keep one rigged for a quick "cast back" when a fish refuses my streamer. All-black and all-chartreuse are my most productive colors. Yellow and even white will work as well. Fish this fly as soon as water temperatures warm above 60°F in the spring, and keep it on until fall.

*The name "Tiktaalik" is derived from recent discovery in far northern Canada of a long-sought "missing-link" fossil of a fish-like creature with leg appendages. Nunavunt tribal elders gave this unique specimen a name that seems quite perfect for this fly: In Nunavut it literally means "large shallow-water fish."

TIKTAALIK POPPER

BLACK AND YELLOW

Overall Length: Eight to 10 inches.

REAR HOOK:
Gamakatsu SL 12S size 4/0 to 6/0.

THREAD: UTC 140 black.

TAIL: Black Saltwater Flashabou topped with black bucktail and yellow grizzly rooster cape feathers (two per side).

TRAILER-HOOK CONNECTION:
Thirty-pound-test TyGer Wire (small articulation loop off back of front hook secured by wrapping tags along shank, through the eye, and back to the bend with plenty of Zap-A-Gap) Note: Rear hook positioned with hook point facing up.

FRONT HOOK:
Daiichi 2461 size 6/0.

HEAD: Rainy's Large Saltwater Popper head, black with rattle.

TAIL: Black bucktail with yellow bucktail on top and yellow grizzly rooster cape feathers (two per side).

COLLAR: Palmered black and yellow rooster saddle feathers.

EYES: Large doll eyes or Enrico Puglisi solid plastic eyes.

Fire Tiger variation—see recipe and photo on pages 98-99.

MUSKIE SNAKE SLIDER

This highly versatile variation on the popular Dahlberg Mega Diver incorporates some of the best aspects of both poppers and streamers. With an enticing combination of deer hair, marabou, and saddle hackle, this slider fly pops on the surface and dives beneath. It creates muskie-attracting allure on all kinds of water. I fish it year-round, especially when I need to move some water and make some extra noise due to water clarity. This fly fishes well with a floating line, but my preferred technique is the Break Dance retrieve with a short, integrated sink-tip to pull the fly over, through, and down the front of weed edges. With non-aggressive fish it's also possible to fish this fly deeper along the bottom with a short leader and heavy sink-tip line, allowing it to pause and rise seductively between each strip. The tail can be made of hackle or rabbit strip to provide added bulk and weight. It should be noted, however, that a 4/0 diver with a water-logged eight-inch rabbit strip tail can be a real bear to cast, even on a 10-weight rod.

MUSKIE SNAKE SLIDER

BROWN

Overall Length: Eight to 10 inches.

HOOK: Gamakatsu SC15-2H size 4/0 to 5/0.

THREAD: UTC 140 brown.

TAIL: (tying order): 1. Eight to 12 brown grizzly rooster saddle hackles, 2. gold holographic Flashabou, 3. rusty brown Krystal Flash, 4. one grizzly brown rooster neck feather over two furnace rooster neck feathers splayed on each side, 5. two brown marabou plumes on each side and one on top.

COLLAR: Golden brown deer-body hair tips flared.

HEAD: Brown deer belly hair, spun, trimmed to diver shape.

Black variation—see recipe and photo on pages 120-121.

MUSKIE BUNNY TWIN TAIL

The unique "twin tail" family of muskie flies found a permanent place in my boat after a heart-breaking refusal—due to an untimely fouled rabbit strip—from a giant lunge on Canada's Lake of the Woods. As anyone who has fished a single or double rabbit-strip fly knows, an unassisted strip can foul around the hook shank, causing the fly to move unnaturally.

The Muskie Bunny Twin Tail, originated by Mark Dysinger and adapted here by master tier Jon Uhlenhop, overcomes this problem with the use of a "lift and separate" looped-wire foul-guard planted squarely between the two rabbit strips. This unique application combined with the tied in tip-first marabou hackle provides a pulsating profile when fished on a fast or slow retrieve. I've found the Bunny Twin Tail a lethal muskie fly on all kinds of water throughout the season. When fished slowly with a distinct pause, it's often just the ticket with those hard-to-convert, post-cold-front, or highly pressured fish.

MUSKIE BUNNY TWIN TAIL

PERCH

Overall Length: Five to eight inches.

HOOK: Gamakatsu SL12S size 4/0 to 6/0.

THREAD: UTC 140 olive.

FOUL GUARD: Fifty-pound-test looped wire.

TAIL: (tying order): 1. Yellow marabou, 2. olive variant magnum rabbit strip, hide up, 3. gold holographic Flashabou, 4. olive variant magnum rabbit strip (hide down), 5. rusty brown Krystal Flash, 6. orange marabou.

COLLAR: (tying order): 1. Tip-tied Yellow marabou, 2. golden olive marabou, 3. dark olive marabou, 4. black marabou, 5. dark olive marabou.

EYES: 3.5-mm orange.

Fire Tiger variation—see recipe and photo on pages 120-121.

MUSKIE DOUBLE BUNNY

Rabbit-strip flies may be hard to cast but muskies love 'em! This effective pattern created by award-winning photographer and fly tier James Linehan incorporates the best of Scott Sanchez's Double-Bunny designs along with a few muskie-enticing natural and synthetic materials. A palmered, cross-cut rabbit strip makes for a full and effective collar. To avoid a twisted tail, reinforce the rabbit strip at the bend using a rubberized bonding agent such as Soft-Tex. As always, the addition of eyes—in this case holographic—provides added attraction.

MUSKIE DOUBLE BUNNY

El Tigre

Overall Length: Five to seven inches.

HOOK: Gamakatsu SC-12S size 3/0 to 6/0.

THREAD: UTC 140 or Kevlar.

TAIL: McLean's or Hareline's orange/chartreuse barred rabbit "Zonker" strip.

BODY: Three marabou quills, one orange flanked by two green.

FLASH: Fluorescent orange Flashabou and Krystal Flash, flanked by two strands of pearl Lateral Scale.

WING: Two to three pairs of orange-dyed grizzly saddles or Deceiver patches.

COLLAR: Cross-cut red rabbit strip palmered forward two to three turns.

HACKLE: Black hackle followed by orange hackle.

HEAD: 5 Minute epoxy with yellow holographic eyes and glitter to taste.

Double Trouble Sucker variation—see recipe and photo on pages 120-121.

MUSKIE CLOUSER MINNOW

As warmwater, saltwater, and coldwater fly fishers the world over have discovered, fly-fishing innovator Bob Clouser's Deep Clouser Minnow series is one of the most effective and adaptable streamer patterns for all species of fish. The same holds true for muskies in many lakes and rivers. I particularly like to fish this super-sized muskie version tied by Jon Uhlenhop early and late in the season. Use the bump-and-grind retrieve with a floating or sink-tip line to get down quickly to the muskie's zone.

Throughout the season, it's also an effective jigging pattern for hitting hard-to-reach smaller pockets in weed or wood when the fish are holding tight. Like so many universal patterns, this fly is easy to tie with either natural or synthetic materials depending on personal preference. It can also be tied with a weed guard and in standard or in Half & Half versions for a different profile.

MUSKIE CLOUSER MINNOW

OLIVE AND WHITE

Overall Length: Five to 10 inches.

HOOK: Gamakatsu SL15-2H size 4/0 to 5/0.

EYES: Large stainless-steel dumbbell(green eye).

THREAD: UTC 140 white.

BOTTOM WING:
(tying order) 1. Olive Ultra Hair, 2. gold holographic Flashabou, 3. opal mirage Flashabou, 4. white bucktail, 5. white Craft Fur.

TOP WING:
(tying order) 1. Olive bucktail, 2. olive Craft Fur.

CHEEKS: Gold Krystal Flash.

HEAD: Thread colored with permanent marker and then sealed in clear epoxy.

WEED GUARD:
Twenty-pound nylon (optional).

Fire Tiger variation—see recipe and photo on pages 120-121.

MUSKIE FLASH-TAIL WHISTLER

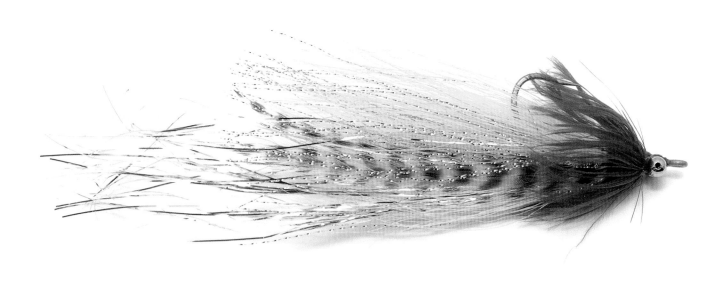

One of many invented by fly-fishing pioneer Dan Blanton, this saltwater classic always finds a place in my muskie-fly box. It works well all season long, shallow or deep, under a variety of water conditions. I especially like to fish it in the spring or on smaller water in rivers where a large profile isn't always necessary to attract a fish. The long flash tail and bead-chain eyes provide added attraction and facilitate jigging action with a slower retrieve. It can also be tied in the "Bad-Ass" version with an offset keel weight for increased side-to-side action.

MUSKIE FLASH-TAIL WHISTLER

RED AND YELLOW

Overall Length: Four to six inches.

HOOK: Tiemco TMC 811S or Mustad 34007 size 1/0 to 4/0.

THREAD: Red Kevlar or 3/0 Uni-Thread.

TAIL: Silver or gold Flashabou or Krystal Flash extending one to two inches beyond the wing.

BODY: Staggered yellow bucktail extending two to three inches beyond the gape of the hook. Red chenille base for collar.

WINGS: Six grizzly saddle hackles, three per side, topped with peacock herl or Flashabou.

COLLAR: Palmered red or orange schlappen (fluorescent works great as well)!

EYES: Bead chain or lead eyes depending upon desired depth.

HEAD: Thread with Zap-A-Gap.

Red and white variation—see recipe and photo on pages 120-121.

YAK ATTACK

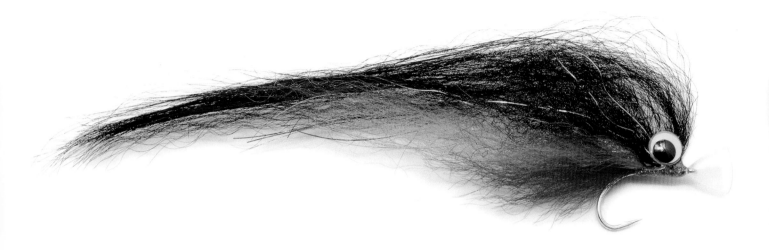

After many long nights of scotch, cigars, and Advil, master fly tier Jon Uhlenhop and I created this beautiful line of muskie patterns using a variety of synthetic and natural materials such as Big Fly fiber and yak hair. These unique flies are perfect for summer and fall fishing on big water when a large forage profile is critical to attract and trigger fish. The "hollow-tied" top wing allows this fly to maintain its massive profile, even during the retrieve. Among many attributes, we've also incorporated rattles and Magic Heads on some patterns to provide additional noise and side to side action. All have big eyes for support and added appeal. These flies fish best on a sink-tip line for ease of casting. They stand up to much abuse both from angler and fish.

YAK ATTACK

BLACK AND ORANGE

Overall Length: Ten to 12 inches.

HOOK: Gamakatsu SC15-2H size 4/0 to 5/0.

THREAD: UTC 140 red.

RATTLE: Large rattle inside EZ Body Braid.

TAIL: (tying order) 1. Red yak hair, 2. orange yak hair, 3. orange Ice Wing Fiber.

WING: (tying order) 1. Black Big Fly Fiber high tied, 2. black yak hair hollow tied.

CHEEKS: Black holographic Flashabou and opal mirage Flashabou.

TOPPING: Black yak hair.

EYES: Doll eyes (15mm).

HEAD: Thread coated in 5 Minute epoxy, Magic Head (No.1 for size 4/0 to 5/0).

MUSKIE RED-TAIL TUBE FLY

FIRE TIGER

Overall Length: Ten to 12 inches.

TUBE: HMH two-inch brass tube.

TRAILER HOOK:
Gamakatsu SL12S size 4/0 to 6/0.

THREAD: UTC 140 white.

RATTLE: Large rattle inside EZ Body Braid.

TAIL: (tying order) 1. Chartreuse Ultra Hair with red EP Silky Fibers, 2. ocean green Flashabou and opal mirage Flashabou.

WING: (tying order) 1. Yellow Craft Fur, 2. chartreuse Craft Fur.

THROAT: (tying order) 1. Bright orange Craft Fur, 2. red Craft Fur.

CHEEKS: Opal mirage Flashabou.

TOPPING: Green Craft Fur.

EYES: Doll eyes (15 mm).

HEAD: Thread colored with permanent marker and then sealed in clear epoxy.

MUSKIE COWGIRL

Named after one of the most effective big-fish muskie spinners of the 2006 season, this all-synthetic streamer pattern incorporates many of the conventional lure's attributes only without the large, pulsating spinner blade. The multiple, stacked layers of Flashabou, Ultra Hair, and Ice Wing give this fly tons of muskie-attracting shimmer, flash, and pulsating action. Although I've fished this fly around the country with much success, I find it works especially well in dark or stained water where fish may have difficulty locating your fly.

When dealing with tough conditions following a cold front, I also find this pattern effective for those hard-to-convert, passive fish that need a motivating trigger. Use this pattern with the pause-and-twitch technique for following fish—and hang on tight.

MUSKIE COWGIRL

FIRE TIGER

Overall Length: Six to 10 inches.

HOOK: Gamakatsu SC15-2H size 4/0 to 5/0.

THREAD: UTC 140 chartreuse.

TAIL: Chartreuse Ultra Hair.

WING: (tying order) 1. Chartreuse Ultra Hair hollow tied (on top), 2. Gold Holographic Flashabou high tied (top), 3. fluorescent yellow mirage Flashabou hollow tied (top), 4. chartreuse Ultra Hair hollow tied (top), 5. fluorescent yellow mirage Flashabou hollow tied (top), 6. chartreuse Ultra Hair hollow tied (top), 7. lime green Flashabou high tied (top), 8. orange mirage Flashabou high tied (bottom), 9. pearl chartreuse Saltwater Flashabou (sides), 10. green holographic Flashabou high tied (top), 11. red Ice Wing Fiber high tied (bottom), 12. green Ice Wing Fiber high tied (top), 13. peacock green Ice Wing Fiber high tied (top). Wing barred with black permanent marker.

EYES: Mirage Dome Eyes or doll eyes.

HEAD: Thread colored with permanent marker and then sealed in clear epoxy.

MUSKIE RED-TAIL TUBE FLY

Tube flies are a time-honored addition to the muskie fly fisher's arsenal. Originally created for Atlantic salmon to achieve a longer profile without fouling, they also make the perfect foundation for large-profile streamers for muskie. With the single hook fit snugly into the rear of the tube, the muskie tube pattern also offers potentially better-hooking qualities and durability once the fly swings free after hook-up. The "hollow-tied" Craft Fur and Big Fly Fiber creations shown here represent many months of trial and error as Jon Uhlenhop and I worked to come up with the right combination of materials and action. I've now fished these productive patterns from southern Illinois to Ontario. I've found them most effective for fishing larger lakes and flowages where giant muskies often prowl deep, open-water structure. Fished with an integrated sink-tip line, these big flies are efficient to cast and maintain an excellent profile that rarely fouls.

MUSKIE RED-TAIL TUBE FLY

BLACK AND ORANGE

Overall Length: Ten to 12 inches.

TUBE: HMH two-inch brass tube.

TRAILER HOOK:
Gamakatsu SL12S size 4/0 to 6/0.

THREAD: UTC 140 white.

RATTLE: Large rattle inside EZ Body Braid.

TAIL: (tying order) 1. Black Ultra Hair with red EP Silky Fibers, 2. black holographic Flashabou and opal mirage Flashabou.

WING: Black Craft Fur. Wing barred with black permanent marker.

THROAT: (tying order) 1. Bright orange Craft Fur, 2. red Craft Fur.

CHEEKS: Opal mirage Flashabou and black holographic Flashabou.

TOPPING:
Black Craft Fur.

EYES: Doll eyes (15mm).

HEAD: Thread colored with permanent marker and then sealed in clear epoxy.

Fire Tiger variation—see recipe and photo on pages 112-113.

CONOMO SPECIAL YELLOW PERCH

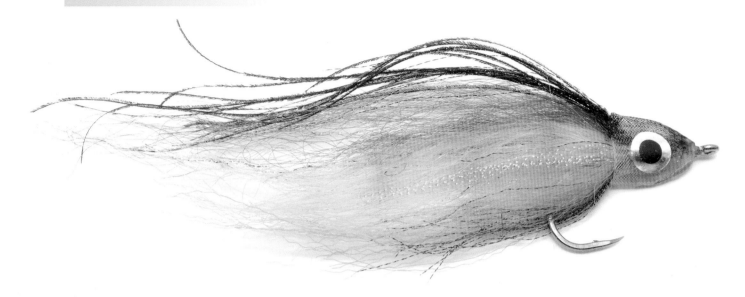

This realistic yet durable pattern was invented by striper expert Rich Murphy for use along his coastal haunts in the Northeast. The natural and synthetic yellow perch variant of the Conomo Special looks seductive in the water and fishes like a dream with appealing side-to-side and glide action. Best of all, the wing stays in place. It won't twist or foul due to the unique use of a durable EZ Body braid. I've fished this pattern with success in all kinds of water. Despite many fish to its credit, I am constantly amazed at the positive response from Mr. Lunge. This one has saved the day when nothing else seems to work.

CONOMO SPECIAL YELLOW PERCH

Overall Length: Six to 12 inches.

HOOK: 8/0 Gamakatsu SL-12.

TAIL: Natural yak hair up to 11 inches long, tapering to a single hair strand, four strands of gold Krystal Flash up to 12 inches, four strands of red Krystal Flash up to 12 inches long.

SPREADER CONE: Extra-large, plain EZ Body.

COLLAR: Yellow yak hair up to seven-and-a-half inches long, sparsely but evenly distributed over the "lower" half of the circumference of the spreader cone, and natural yak hair up to seven-and-a-half inches long, sparsely but evenly distributed over the "top" half.

WING: Ten to 12 peacock herls up to 12 inches long over tapered brown yak hair up to 10 inches long over tapered olive yak hair up to eight-and-a-half inches long over yellow yak hair up to seven inches long.

EYES: Witchcraft 8.0 EY black on silver stick-on.

HEAD: Extra-large, plain EZ Body braid.

FLASH HIGHLIGHTS: Twelve to 15 strands of red Krystal Flash up to five inches long as a beard, 12 to 15 strands of yellow Krystal Flash up to nine inches long on the sides, seven to 10 strands of black Krystal Flash up to 10 inches over the top of the wing.

ANGRY MINNOW

Wisconsin muskie fly fishing guide Brad Bohen came up with this "straight-on, working man's" muskie streamer that is easy to tie, casts well, and looks good in the water. Time tested on the "holy waters" of the northwoods, this fly has worked for me around the country whenever a smaller, more natural presentation is called for. I especially like it for "matching the hatch" when post-spawn fish in lakes and rivers are seeking newly hatched fry for their first meal of the year.

Brad uses big eyes and the "reverse-tie" method for the bucktail to add bulk and create a larger, baitfish-like profile. Natural bucktail material may not stand up to more than a few fish but it's hard to beat the life-like translucence when wet. On more than one occasion I've used liberal amounts of Zap-A-Gap glue to keep it intact for one more fish. Fish this pattern in the smaller 1/0 size in the spring to mimic smaller forage and the larger 3/0 size later in the season.

ANGRY MINNOW

Overall Length: Five to eight inches.

HOOK: Tiemco 811S or Owner AKI size 1/0 to 3/0.

THREAD: Red UTC 140 or Kevlar.

BODY: Red Kevlar wrapped along the shank with repeated coatings of Zap-A-Gap.

UNDERWING: Reverse-tied white bucktail staggered in sparse but even bunches.

OVERWING: Yellow bucktail with black on each side. Gold Flashabou or Krystal Flash laced in between.

GILLS: Red or orange calf tail.

EYES: Three-eighth-inch Mirage eyes set with Softex.

HEAD: Red Kevlar finished with Zap-A-Gap.

Commercially Available Muskie Flies and Tying Materials

If you're not a tier, finding suitable muskie patterns and materials can be a challenge. Until recently, most major and minor commercial fly manufacturers did not see a market in very large, muskie-sized warmwater patterns. What they had were usually tied with lightwire hooks unsuitable for muskies. Although some muskie flies are now available commercially, manufacturers of saltwater flies provide the primary source for most flies and materials that I use. They are obtained from several recommended sources:

Rainy's Flies: Great selection of saltwater and warmwater flies and materials suitable for muskie fishing (see www.rainysflies.com).

Recommended Rainy's Muskie Patterns:
- CF Baitfish Tandem Streamer 3/0 (seven-inch)
- Ocean Candy Streamer 6/0 (twelve-inch)
- Tandem Off-Shore Rattlin' Popper 4/0 (five-inch)
- PSP and Big Mouth Bubble-Head Popper 4/0 (five-inch)
- PSP and Fish-Head Diver 4/0 (five-inch)
- Robrahn's Bluewater Streamers
- Ehlers' Seeker

Note: Wide selection of large and unique saltwater and warmwater streamers in excellent muskie colors including Fire Tiger, chartreuse/white, and pink/white. Many streamer patterns tied with Rainy's own durable Craft Fur. Beautifully painted hard-body poppers with strong tandem hook rigs and rattles.

Enrico Puglisi Ltd: Wide selection of effective saltwater and warmwater baitfish patterns and materials by a master fly tier and designer (see www.epflies.com).

Author's Recommended Enrico Puglisi Muskie Patterns:
- Big Eyes Red Tail Streamer 6/0 (seven-inch)
- Adult Bunker Streamer 5/0 (ten-inch)
- Pike/Offshore Streamer 6/0 (eight-inch)
- Shad/Bluegill/Perch Streamers 1/0 (three- to five inch)
- Rattle Peacock/Pike Streamer 3/0 (six-inch)
- Flex Turbo Popper 6/0 (six-inch)

Note: Numerous realistic and easy-to-cast streamer designs tied with durable synthetic EP-Fibers. Come in a wide variety of colors but Fire Tiger, green/yellow, pink/white, gray, perch, natural and all-green are best for muskies. The larger 10-inch Big Fish and Bunker Flies come complete with a detachable tandem-hook rig. Try the smaller three- to eight-inch

Rainy's Tandem Offshore Popper

Rainy's Fish-Head Diver

Rainy's Robrahn's Bluewater Streamer

Enrico Puglisi Yellow Perch Streamer

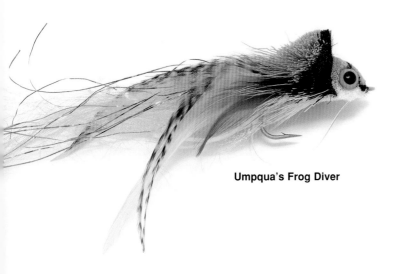

Umpqua's Frog Diver

Baitfish and Pike/offshore flies in perch, natural, and bright colors during the early season for shallow-water fish.

Umpqua Feather Merchants: Huge selection of proven saltwater and warmwater flies and materials (see www.umpqua.com).

Recommended Umpqua Muskie Patterns:

- Barry's Pike Fly
- Clouser Deep Minnow
- Flashtail Whistler
- Gen-X Bunny
- Half & Half
- Lefty's Big Fish Deceiver
- Umpqua Pike Fly
- Umpqua Swimming Baitfish
- Umpqua Swimming Waterdog
- Lemming, Mercer's
- Big Eye Baitfish
- Sea Habit Bucktail
- Super Mushy, Skok's
- Tarpon Snake
- Major Bunker, Kintz'
- Sar-Mul-Mac, Blanton's

Idylwilde Flies: Excellent selection of warmwater patterns by signature tier Hogan Brown and others (see www.idylwilde.com).

H2O Flies: Wide variety of unique warmwater and saltwater patterns for every big fish imaginable, including muskies (see www.flyh2o.com).

Brookside Flies: Offers a nice selection of muskie size streamers, divers, and top-water poppers in a variety of colors (see www.brooksideflies.com).

Pacific Fly Group: Good selection of various warmwater and saltwater patterns suitable for muskies (see www.pacificfly.com).

Spirit River Flies: Another solid source for large freshwater and saltwater patterns suitable for muskies (see www.spiritriverflies.com).

Don Gapen Flies: From the originator of the famed Muddler Minnow comes a superb muskie fly: the Tantalizer. Available in a 3/0 streamer and top-water version (see www.gapen.com).

The Fly Shop: One of the largest fly fishing retailers in the country offering a wide selection of "muskie-sized" saltwater patterns and materials (see www.theflyshop.com).

Feather Craft: Excellent source for muskie fly-fishing tackle, flies, and tying materials (see www.feather-craft.com).

Dan's Custom Flies: Great on-line source for all your muskie fly tying needs including popper bodies and heads (see http://members.ij.net/danscustomflies).

Wapsi: Wide variety of quality fly-tying materials and tools for the muskie fly tier (see www.wapsifly.com).

Hareline: Complete selection of everything for the muskie fly tier including unique synthetic hairs and furs (see www.hareline.com).

MUSKIE MARAUDER

Chartreuse and white
Overall Length: Six to 10 inches.

HOOK: Gamakatsu SC15-2H size 4/0 to 5/0.
THREAD: UTC 140 white.
RATTLE: Medium rattle inside EZ Body braid.
TAIL (tying order): 1. Six chartreuse rooster saddle hackles, 2. four white rooster cape feathers.
REAR COLLAR: White bucktail (bottom), fluorescent yellow bucktail (top).
FRONT COLLAR: White bucktail (bottom), chartreuse bucktail (top).
TOPPING: Peacock herl.
EYES: Mirage Dome Eyes or doll eyes.
HEAD: Color thread with permanent marker and then seal with clear epoxy.

MUSKIE SNAKE SLIDER

Black
Overall Length: Eight to 10 inches.

HOOK: Gamakatsu SC15-2H size 4/0 to 5/0.
THREAD: UTC 140 black.
TAIL (tying order): 1. Eight to 12 black rooster saddle hackles, 2. 10 to 15 strands of black holographic Flashabou, 3. 10 to 15 strands of black Krystal Flash, 4. two black rooster neck feathers over one grizzly rooster neck feather splayed on each side, 5. two black marabou plumes on each side and one on top.
COLLAR: Black deer-belly hair tips flared.
HEAD: Black deer-belly hair, spun, and trimmed to diver shape.

MUSKIE BUNNY TWIN TAIL

Fire tiger
Overall Length: Five to 10 inches.

HOOK: Gamakatsu SL12S size 4/0 to 6/0.
THREAD: UTC 140 chartreuse.
FOUL GUARD: Fifty-pound wire.
TAIL (tying order): 1. Fluorescent yellow marabou, 2. chartreuse magnum rabbit strip, hide up, 3. opal mirage Flashabou, 4. chartreuse magnum rabbit strip, hide down, 5. yellow Krystal Flash, 6. fluorescent yellow marabou.
COLLAR: 1. Chartreuse marabou, 2. orange marabou, 3. fluorescent yellow marabou, 4. chartreuse marabou, 5. red marabou, 6. fluorescent green marabou.
EYES: 3.5 mm orange.

MUSKIE DOUBLE BUNNY

Double trouble sucker
Overall Length: Five to seven inches.

FRONT HOOK: Gamakatsu SC-12S size 3/0 to 6/0.
TRAILER HOOK: Gamakatsu size 1/0 to 3/0.
THREAD: Danville 210.
TAIL: Natural quarter-inch rabbit strip.
BODY: Two tan marabou quills.
FLASH: Gold Krystal Flash.
WING: Two to three pairs of orange-dyed grouse cheeks.
COLLAR: Light gray rabbit strip palmered forward a couple of turns followed by one turn of black rabbit.
HACKLE: Brown roster hackle.
HEAD: 5 Minute epoxy with red holographic eyes.

MUSKIE CLOUSER

Fire tiger
Overall length: Five to ten inches

HOOK: Gamakatsu SL15-2H 4/0 – 5/0
EYES: Large Stainless Steel Eyes (yellow eye)
THREAD: UTC 140 White
WING (bottom) (tying order): 1. Chartreuse Ultra Hair, 2. Ocean Green Holographic Flashabou, 3. Opal Mirage Flashabou, 4. Yellow bucktail, 5. Red Craft Fur
WING (top) (tying order): 1. Chartreuse bucktail, 2. Bright Green Craft Fur
CHEEKS: Chartreuse Krystal Flash
HEAD: Color thread with permanent marker and then seal with clear epoxy.
WEED GUARD: Twenty-pound nylon (optional).

MUSKIE FLASH-TAIL WHISTLER

Red and white
Overall Length: Four to six inches.

HOOK: Tiemco TMC 811S or Mustad 34007 size 1/0 to 4/0.
THREAD: Red Kevlar or 3/0 Uni-Thread.
TAIL: Silver or gold Flashabou or Krystal Flash extending one to two inches beyond the wing.
BODY: Staggered white bucktail extending two to three inches beyond the gape of the hook. Red chenille base for collar.
WINGS: Six grizzly saddle hackles, three per side, topped with peacock herl or Flashabou.
COLLAR: Palmered red or orange schlappen (fluorescent works as well).
HEAD: Thread with Zap-A-Gap.
EYES: Bead chain or lead eyes depending upon desired depth.

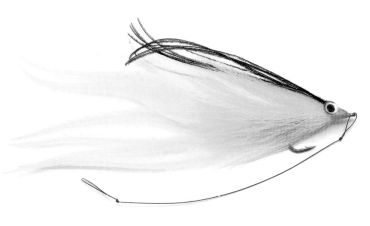

Muskie Marauder

Muskie Double Bunny

Muskie Snake Slider

Muskie Clouser

Muskie Bunny Twin Tail

Muskie Flash-Tail Whistler

ESSENTIAL FLY-ROD SKILLS

WHATEVER FISH YOU PREFER CATCHING—tiny eight-inch brook trout in mountain streams or giant 100-pound-plus tarpon on the flats—your casting and line-control skills are critical to consistent success on the water. Simply being in the right place at the right time definitely has its advantages, but does you little good if you still can't make the fish eat. Despite this fact, few anglers take the time to really work on these skills unless they also have an opportunity to see and catch a fish in the process. After a few missed opportunities, they usually realize it's one thing to be making perfect loops on the backyard lawn or casting pond, and an entirely different proposition trying to cast a fly accurately and swiftly to real, live feeding fish!

As most guides will tell you, when you complicate things further with a boat, a big rod, and a large fly—not to mention wind and waves—things can get dicey for an angler who doesn't have the required skills. To my way of thinking, frustration and anger should not be a part of your normal fishing day—unless it's due to a missed or lost fish. Like making the sometimes difficult transition from freshwater to saltwater fly fishing, there are a number of techniques you'll need to master to make muskie fishing with a fly both a productive and enjoyable experience.

Practice Makes Perfect

Muskie fishing, as should be clear by now, is a low-percentage game with *any* gear. And if you can't get the fly to the fish, it's simply not worth the effort. If you are not already a competent fly caster but still can't wait to catch your first muskie, then I highly recommend you learn to cast proficiently and practice as often as possible. Whatever your level of skill, you'll find it helpful to work on the casting techniques outlined in this chapter *before* you hit the water.

Although this book covers all aspects of muskie presentations, this chapter is not intended as a casting-instruction manual. There are many good fly-casting resources available today, from books to videos, all of which will do a better job of getting you started the right way. There are also many places to practice including your own backyard or a local pond. If this isn't enough, most fly shops and retailers now offer personalized casting instruction by the hour or over several days in a school (see the appendix for list of recommended fly-casting resources). Respected fly-fishing organizations such as the American Casting Association (www.aca.org), Federation of Fly Fishers (www.fedflyfishers.org), and Trout Unlimited (www.troutunlimited.org), are also valuable resources. They offer fly-casting schools and clinics around the country with certified instructors. These are of great value to the beginning and experienced caster alike.

The late Jim Chapralis, one-time muskie guide and noted fly-fishing authority, has written extensively about the various skills you can learn and improve by taking the time to practice casting (www.anglingmatters.com). In his excellent book, *Master Your Fly Casting* (2006), he outlines a number of casting "games" designed to imitate realistic fly-fishing scenarios. His "Bass Bug Event" is particularly applicable to muskie fly fishing; all serious muskie anglers would benefit from reading and practicing this and other casting games before hitting the water.

Muskie Fly-Casting Basics

Before we go any further you should know that fly casting for muskies is not pretty. In fact, despite what you've been taught and practiced all these years, most of the time your wrist will "break," your

Regardless of size, every muskie landed on a fly is a good fish. To catch your first one you'll need to practice and perfect your casting, line control, and other essential skills on and off the water. With time these skills should become second nature allowing you to focus on the fishing, not casting.

loops may be wide and open, and your fly is occasionally going to hit the water with all the delicacy of a bowling ball. For those most comfortable casting a delicate 4-weight fly rod and a size 22 trico spinner to sipping brown trout, these unorthodox techniques may seem rather crude and uncivilized. All this changes quickly when a muskie inhales your fly.

Depending on the water and conditions, most muskie fly fishing requires repeated but reasonable casts of 20 to 60 feet. On a large lake or wide river, longer casts may be necessary to cover the water or reach a particular choice piece of structure. In a practical sense, repeated casts of more than 80 feet are not effective or necessary—it becomes increasingly

difficult to set the hook and control a muskie at these long distances.

When fishing a smaller lake or river you may find your casts limited to 30 feet or shorter. In fact, sometimes a very short cast of 10 feet will be all it takes to hook a fish. Fortunately, since you will almost always be fly fishing from a boat, it is usually possible to get close enough to your intended target to make a reasonable length cast.

Like most fishing, water clarity plays a part in the required distance of your casts. In stained, weedy, or dark water lakes and rivers, as a general rule, you can usually get away with shorter casts so long as your boat approach is careful and quiet. In clear-water

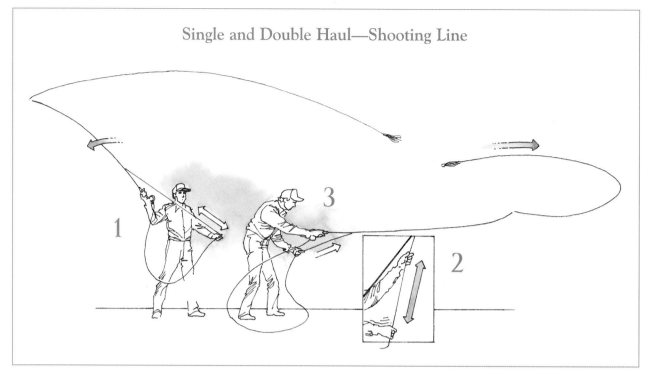

Single and Double Haul—Shooting Line

The haul technique—either single or double—is an essential skill for the muskie fly fisher. With a weight-forward or shooting-head line, the haul increases line speed so you can cast the fly farther and faster than with a normal overhead cast. Start with a low rod tip and strip in all but the head section of the line—usually 30 feet. Lift the rod overhead while at the same time pulling down forcefully on the line—about one foot—with the line hand (Figure 1). As the line straightens for the back cast, allow the line hand to drift backward toward the stripping guide and then pull down again as you make a forward cast (Figure 2). Aim and release the line on the forward cast as the loop unrolls, allowing the fly to shoot toward its intended target (Figure 3).

conditions prevelant in many lakes without significant weed growth or cover, keep your casts as long as possible to avoid alerting the fish of your presence.

Above all, the most important part of fly casting for muskies is the ability of the angler to make repeated, quick, and accurate casts of various distances with a big fly while maintaining constant line control.

The Muskie Casting Stroke

Casting a large, heavy, wind-resistant fly requires a slightly different casting stroke than many anglers are accustom to using. Instead of the traditional, overhead, "tight loop" desirable when trout fishing, it's best to slow down and elongate your stoke to open up the cast in an elliptical arch. Commonly known as the "Belgian cast," this modified stroke helps considerably to smooth out the cast with a large or weighted fly, thus avoiding tailing loops and resulting tangles. To make this cast, use a forceful side-arm, more horizontal stroke for your back cast and then swing the rod tip overhead for the forward cast to deliver the fly along a vertical plane.

Lifting a large fly off of the water and propelling it forward also requires an exaggerated casting stroke, often extending the entire arm away from the body for additional leverage and power. When casting for

muskies always keep your casting stroke smooth—any fast or abrupt movement on the forward or back cast usually results in disaster. Once the fly is off the water, you'll also need to wait longer for the rod to load on the back cast. This is especially true with a large top-water fly that is wind resistant due to its poor aerodynamics. It is important to note, however, that waiting too long for a large fly to straighten on a back cast will result in slack and a tailing loop.

Lastly, it's worth noting that when fly fishing for muskies, you'll be doing yourself a big favor if you take a few minutes throughout the day to take a break and rest your casting arm. Making repeated casts with a large fly and a big rod is hard work. I've found this is the best way to keep up your stamina and insure you are focused and ready for a fish when it finally hits.

Essential Casts

Single and Double Haul—Shooting Line

The most important casting techniques you'll need to master for muskie fishing are the single and double haul. Normally associated with shooting line when saltwater or steelhead fishing, this high-speed, distance-casting technique also plays a vital role in muskie fishing.

Short-line Roll Cast

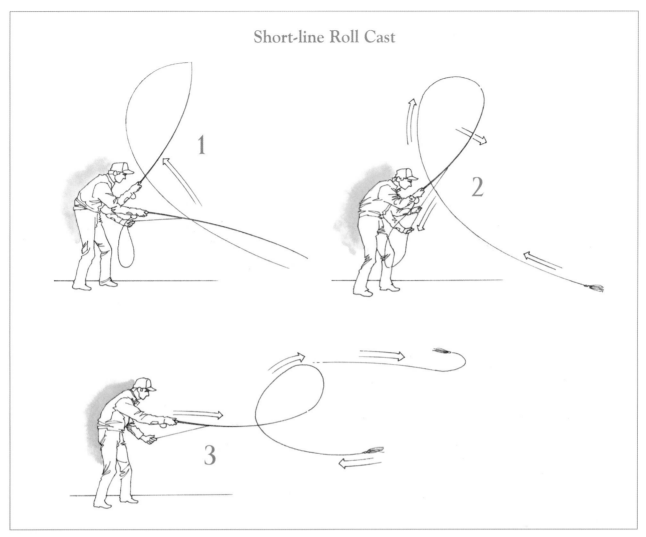

The short-line roll cast is an effective means to pick up line—or make a short cast—with a floating or sinking-head line and a large fly. Start with a low rod tip and strip in all but 10 feet of fly line. Like a normal roll cast, slide the line and fly along the surface until a belly is created behind the rod (Figure 1). Using the surface tension of the line on the water to load the rod, make an accelerated forward cast with a single haul to increase line speed (Figure 2). Once the forward loop unrolls, release the line for a short cast or continue holding it until it straightens, and begin a normal back cast (Figure 3).

I use a single or double haul for all of my casts when muskie fishing to put the fly where I want it quickly and accurately. By reducing the number of false casts, it allows me to maximize my distance with minimal effort. Once you finish your retrieve back to the boat, shooting line with a haul also enables you to quickly pick up the fly and cast again with minimal effort at whatever distance you need to reach the fish or structure. Perhaps just as important, the haul technique helps to avoid unnecessary wear and tear on my casting arm—an important consideration after a long day or week of fishing.

As is common in saltwater flats fishing, during the course of a day's muskie fishing you'll be presented with many visual targets. Sometimes you'll see a fish swimming or even a swirl or a boil. This is where the haul can really help your presentation. False casting

simply takes too much time. Shooting line with a haul is really the only way to take full advantage of these great opportunities.

Any form of haul is made easier with a weight-forward or shooting-head line, whether floating or sinking. Both lines are easier to shoot and significantly reduce the need for false casts. Always keep your hauls short and fast to generate line speed and maintain accuracy.

With an integrated sinking-head line the narrow diameter and added weight of the head allows you to achieve a much faster line speed than is possible with a floating line. The key to casting any shooting-head line is to start the cast with the entire head and a short length of running line outside the rod's tip-top guide. Usually three to six feet of running line is sufficient to execute a proper cast. With a quick roll cast

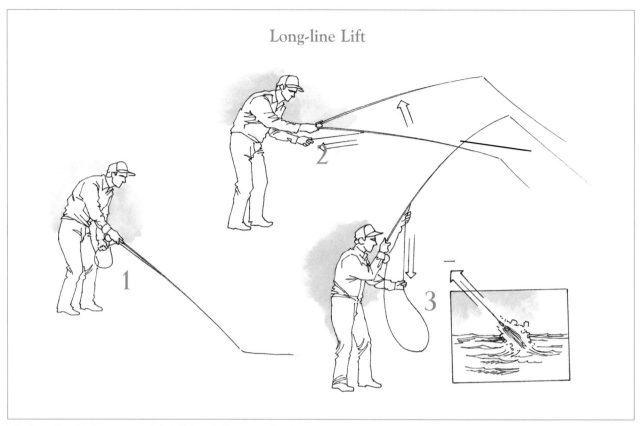

Long-line Lift

The long-line lift is an essential skill for picking up a floating line on the water after a cast without retrieving the fly all the way to the boat. Start with a low rod tip and strip the fly toward the surface (Figure 1). Once the line is tight and the fly is just below the surface, raise he rod slowly overhead using the surface of the water to create tension and load the rod (Figure 2). Once the rod is fully loaded, apply a forceful power stroke combined with a single haul to pull the entire line and fly off the water for a normal back cast (Figure 3).

after each retrieve to bring the fly and line to the surface, it's simply a matter of executing a gradual acceleration—speed up and stop—on your back cast to slide the line off the surface and then shoot forward. With a sink-tip line, aim, then release your forward cast at a higher trajectory to achieve maximum distance. (see illustrations on pages 126 and 127)

Short-line Roll Cast

As you might imagine, it's quite difficult to roll cast a large muskie fly from a long distance, especially with a heavier sinking-head line. With the short-line roll cast technique, however, it is possible to lift the fly and head out of the water before you begin your normal back cast. This technique is also essential to casting a sinking-head line. In this case, the entire head and short length of running line must be near the surface before beginning the cast. (see illustration on page 127)

Note: When using this technique with a sinking-head line you'll need to use more energy to lift the line to the surface, and then begin your back cast immediately after the forward roll cast or the line will sink before you have a chance to load the rod.

Long-line Lift

A long-line pickup or lift with a floating line is a useful technique in a variety of muskie-fishing situations. This is especially true when you see a fish close to where your fly has just landed or when you want to cover a spot again quickly without retrieving the fly all the way to the boat. The real key here is to eliminate any slack in your fly line and reduce water tension on the fly itself by stripping it toward the surface before you begin your cast.

This casting technique takes some practice but is exceptionally useful when drifting through fast water on a river where you may never get another chance to make the cast. (see illustration on this page)

Water Haul

This technique isn't elegant. But it gets the job done by putting your fly where you want it as quickly and efficiently as possible, especially with a sinking-head line. The open and higher trajectory of the loops required for this cast also help the angler avoid getting hit by a heavy sinking-head line and big fly. That's a nasty wallop. The trick here is to use the tension

Water Haul

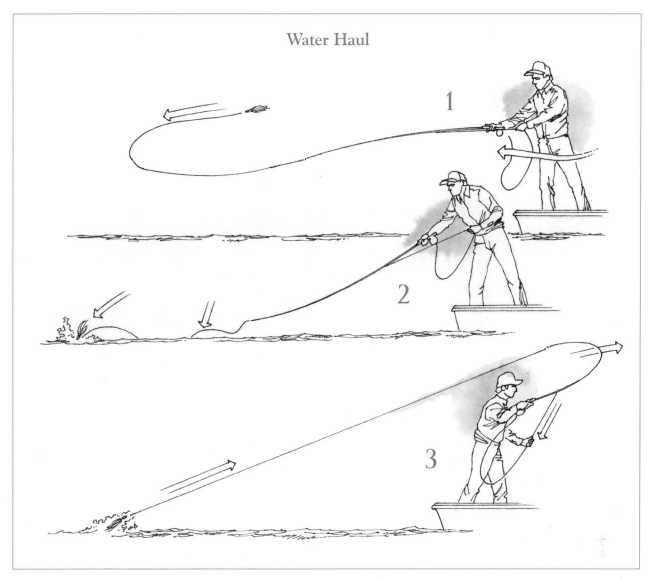

The rather unorthodox water haul or tension cast utilizes the surface tension of the line on the water to load the rod and make a powerful forward or back cast using a floating or sinking-head line. Like the long-line pickup, after you make a short forward cast begin stripping line slowly and lift the rod to bring the line and fly toward the surface. Once the rod is fully loaded, apply a forceful power stroke combined with a single haul to pull the entire line and fly off the surface, and literally lob it behind you (Figure 1). Turn to face your fly and begin fishing or repeat the process by stripping in any slack line and loading the rod again using the surface tension of the line on the water (Figure 2). Apply a forceful power stroke combined with a single haul to pull the entire line off the surface, and lob it forward (Figure 3).

of the water on the line and the fly to help load the rod. This technique can be applied with either the forward cast or back cast, or both depending on your ability.

You can increase the distance of your casts using this technique by stripping and then releasing a short length of line with each water haul, and then shooting line with a short single haul as you cast forward.

Warning: The water haul should not be attempted with a faster casting motion—you'll risk breaking the rod or hitting yourself with the line and the fly. It also works best with a streamer fly; the tension in the water is simply too great with a concave-faced topwater popper. (see illustration on this page)

Change-of-Direction Cast

When fly fishing from a boat you must be adept at casting in many different directions. Regardless of your boating skills or those of your guide, you will eventually find yourself forced to cast backward or behind the boat to beat the wind, target a sighted fish, or cover structure you missed during a drift. The easiest way to do this is to simply turn your body 180 degrees to face the intended target, and then fish your back cast as your forward cast to deliver the fly. This approach works well anytime you need to change direction but especially when you've got a cross-wind blowing into your casting arm.

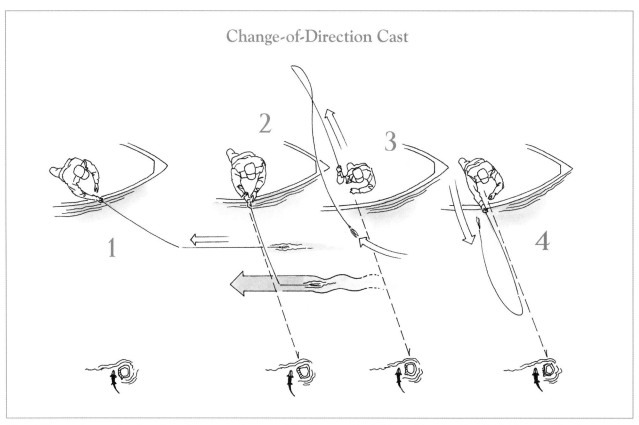

Change-of-Direction Cast

The ability to change the direction of your cast is essential when muskie fishing with a fly. Simply fishing your back cast as a forward cast is one option, especially when dealing with wind or multiple targets. Another option is to reposition your body and rod tip in the direction you want to cast. Regardless of where your fly is to begin, start by stripping in line and turning your body to face the new target (Figure 1). Once you're in position, point the rod tip at the new target (Figure 2) and make a back cast directly opposite where you want the fly to land (Figure 3). Your forward cast should now land on the new target without the need for multiple, time-consuming false casts (Figure 4).

Sometimes it is necessary to change the direction of your cast when a fish appears out of nowhere. Rather than make multiple, time-consuming false casts to reach a new target, the best way to accomplish

---

Author's Tips: Casting Big Muskie Flies

- Keep false casts to a minimum!

- Keep your casts smooth; avoid abrupt movements when the fly is in the air.

- Use a fast but short single or double haul to increase line speed and distance.

- Maintain an open loop by extending the arc and elongating the arm stroke.

- Wait longer on the back cast, to be sure the rod has loaded properly, before starting the forward cast.

- Maintain an elliptical casting stroke using a horizontal, sidearm back cast and a vertical forward cast.

- When the normal cast isn't possible, use the water haul to help load the rod and deliver the fly.

- When you get tired, take a break.

---

this is to reposition your body with your rod tip pointed in the direction you want to cast. With a low rod tip and your line on the water, lift the rod for a back cast that is directly opposite the target you intend to hit. When you make this cast in one continuous motion your rod should load properly and your fly will follow, regardless of where the cast originated from. (see illustration on page 130)

Dealing the Wind

"The wind is your friend."
—Anonymous muskie guide

Wind is always an issue when muskie fishing, especially in open water. Although we all like to fish in nice weather, the fact of the matter is that much of the best muskie fishing of the year takes place in conditions that are less than ideal. Throughout the season, wind is also an important trigger for muskies, so you must be able to fish in it effectively if you hope to take advantage of this opportunity.

Fortunately, when fishing from a boat it's usually possible to change direction so you have the wind

Dealing With Wind

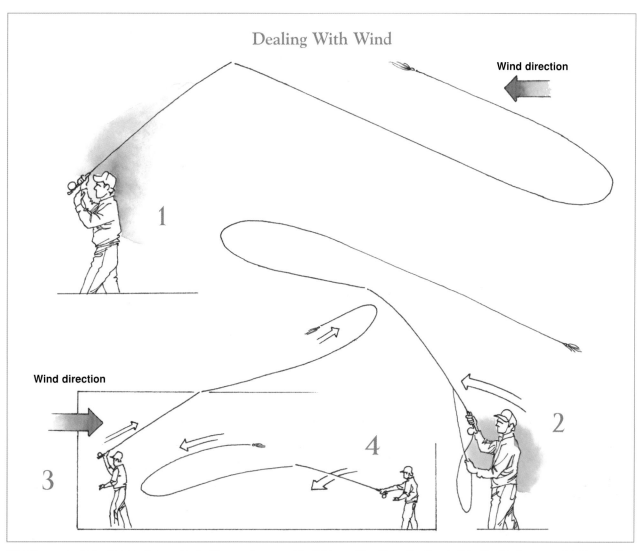

Wind direction

Wind direction

1

2

3

4

Casting on a windy day can be a real challenge when muskie fishing with a large fly. If possible, the best approach is to use the wind to your advantage by positioning the boat so the wind is behind you at all times. Keep your back cast low with a tight loop (Figure 1) and your forward cast higher with an open loop (Figure 2) to maximize the distance of each cast. If you can't avoid a headwind, you'll need to keep your back cast high (Figure 3) and your forward cast low with the tightest loop possible (Figure 4). In both situations, combining each cast with a forceful power stroke and a single or double haul will increase line speed and help to beat the wind.

behind you to help carry the line and fly forward. To make the most of a tailwind, it's usually best to keep your back cast low and tight to get under the wind—using a sidearm cast if necessary—and then make your forward cast higher and more open than normal above the water. This inverted approach allows you to maximize the force of the wind to catch your line and carry it forward.

If you simply can't avoid a headwind, then the opposite holds true with a higher-than-normal back cast and a lower forward cast with a tight loop to punch the line into the wind and toward the water. The key with both a tailwind and headwind is to use a haul and accelerated rod speed to achieve a tight loop to penetrate the wind. Caution: Resist the natural tendency to overpower your cast when dealing with

wind—this will only result in a failed cast and a frustrated angler.

With a crosswind blowing across your casting arm, the situation can become quite dangerous as the wind is constantly pushing the line and fly toward you. With a big fly and a powerful rod, this is not a risk worth taking no matter the odds. In this case it's usually best to use the change-of-direction cast. Simply turn your body 180 degrees and fish your back cast as your forward cast. If the wind is coming from the other direction, then you'll have much less to worry about. You may still need to keep a slightly lower casting plane with a sidearm cast at a 45-degree angle, however, to maintain a proper loop.

When shooting line in a crosswind, you'll probably need to adjust for the wind speed and direct the cast

Ready, aim, fire: A single or double haul combined with a shooting-head line—floating or sinking—will help increase your casting distance and reduce wear and tear on the body when muskie fishing with a fly. Note the large, plastic shooting "basket" by my feet to keep the line tangle free and ready to shoot.

slightly upwind to avoid blowing the fly away from your intended target. In this case it may help to make a few trial casts to determine how far the fly will move before hitting the water.

Line Control

Like casting, good line control skills are an essential component of muskie fly-fishing success. There's simply no room for error when enticing, hooking, and landing big, powerful fish.

Take a moment and think about it: Without the benefit of a high-speed retrieve baitcasting reel, when you finally hook your muskie on a fly, your index finger on the line is the only method for applying resistance until—and if—you can get a fish on the reel. It's the only drag system you've got for casting, hooking, and fighting a fish. Yet another good reason for wearing a casting glove when muskie fishing.

Since it's not uncommon for a muskie to hit a fly the moment it hits the water or right beneath your feet at boatside, you'll always need to be prepared for a strike with the line locked under your index-finger and a firm grip with your stipping hand. Line control is also an essential component of your fly retrieve. A fly's attractiveness to a fish is in large part dependent on how you move it through the water. Therefore you'll need to become adept at stripping while manipulating the line and the rod tip in rapid succession.

All of these skills take time to master so it is important to practice well beforehand—not on your first fish.

Boats and Personal Watercraft

Whether it's a wooden drift boat with oars, a small aluminum fishing boat with an outboard engine, a high-speed muskie boat or a bonefish skiff, a boat offers the greatest advantage when fly fishing for muskies.

Since muskies inhabit a variety of water types and depths throughout the season, a boat's versatility allows you to approach fish in both shallow and deep water, and from any number of directions with very few restrictions. The speed and mobility of a boat also gives you the advantage of being able to pinpoint active fish quickly over a large area and, in some cases, return as many times as necessary.

Another distinct advantage to fishing from a boat is that you can stand safely and comfortably above the water when fishing. This heightened position significantly improves your ability to see structure, make effective fly presentations, watch for following fish, set the hook, and fight the fish.

If you don't have access to a conventional fishing boat, it is certainly possible to use a personal water-craft—canoe, kick-boat, pontoon boat, kayak or even a float tube—to reach the fish. Some anglers I know do this successfully with conventional and fly-fishing gear, but usually on smaller lakes and rivers where range and mobility is not as crucial. When you consider the inherant disadvantages of sitting down while fly fishing for muskies, however, these alternative modes of water transportation are not exactly ideal. Imagine trying to "figure-8" a following muskie with a nine-foot fly rod as it swims around your legs and you'll get an idea of what I'm talking about.

Consistent line control is essential when muskie fishing with a fly. Whether casting, retrieving, or hooking a fish you must maintain control of your line using the stripping hand and/or index finger at all times.

Some kick-boats and pontoon boats now offer a casting platform and/or "lean-bar" option for the angler who wants to stand; these portable water craft are a much better option for the muskie fly fisher on rivers and small lakes.

Wading can be productive for those anglers who prefer a more traditional approach and know exactly where fish are located. Some muskie fly fishers I know do this with consistent success on their local waters.

A stable, inflatable boat such as this Outcast Sporting Gear two-person pontoon with a lean-bar is an excellent choice for muskie fly fishing on rivers and small lakes. On larger lakes and rivers a more traditional fishing boat with an engine allows you to cover more water and increases the odds of finding active fish.

However, given that these are seasonal opportunities at best, a boat remains your best option to cover more water and increase your opportunities.

Angler Safety

Safety is always an important consideration when fly casting for muskies. With a big, sharp hook traveling at high speeds there's always a danger of hooking something you don't intend. Although none of us like to admit it, there's no getting around the fact that your back cast is going to drop occasionally with a big fly and a heavy, sink-tip fly line. This is especially true in windy conditions when it can be difficult to control your cast regardless of your skill.

It's always safer to position yourself in the boat so your back cast is made over the water instead of over the middle of the boat. If you must cast directly over the boat to reach a fish and you're not alone, always communicate your intentions and look first to make sure your fishing partner is sitting down or at least out of the way before you do.

Although most conventional muskie fishers fish with two—sometimes three—anglers casting from a boat at the same time, this is not recommended when fly fishing. Regardless of your casting skill, the risk of hitting another angler or the guide is simply too great in such close confines. This is certainly the case when fishing from an open-hull skiff or bass boat where there's little room to hide. If the boat is long enough, however, it may be possible to allow two experienced anglers to fly cast at the same time provided the person in the stern keeps a close look out for the person in the bow. Fly fishing out of the back of a boat near the engine can be frustrating due to limited space and numerous other obstructions, but it may be worth it if the fish are active and it's not "your" turn on deck.

One advantage to having two casters fishing simultaneously is that it allows you to fish different flies and presentations over the same water. With one angler fishing deep with a streamer and another on top with a popper, it is possible to cover all water levels, and quickly determine what the fish want on a particular day. This approach requires constant communication and team work. Warning: It may result in some tense moments, especially when "your" fish takes your fishing pal's fly!

Standing upright on the elevated front deck of a boat and waving around a nine-foot slender tube of graphite is not a good idea when there's any significant threat of a storm or lightning. Although it is true that muskie fishing is often lights up just before a storm hits, always keep a close eye on the weather. Judge for yourself when it's time to put down the rod and head for cover. Remember, lightning can strike long before and after a storm passes. Seeing a storm cloud pass or lightning in the distance is no guarantee you're safe to continue fishing. This is yet another good reason to keep a National Oceanic and Atmospheric Administration (NOAA) marine weather radio on board at all times to provide adequate warming of an impending storm. Many cell-phones also offer this valuable, life-saving option.

Boat Control

Boat control is an often overlooked yet critical factor when muskie fishing, regardless of the technique. Whether sitting still, drifting with the wind or current, or moving under the power of a trolling motor or oars; the speed, direction, or angle of the boat has a significant impact on your ultimate success.

Generally speaking, fly fishing for muskies requires that the boat move at a consistent distance parallel to structure and at a much slower speed than when conventionally fishing to accommodate the time it takes for each retrieve. This approach allows the angler to make each cast perpendicular to the boat and retrieve in a straight line without developing additional slack. Depending on the rate of retrieve and the speed at which the boat is moving, casting ahead of the boat can result in too much slack. Likewise, casting toward the stern or directly behind the boat may pull the fly too fast.

Maintaining an ideal boat speed places the angler in the best position to see a following fish and take advantage of it with a figure-8 or other boatside maneuver. A boat moving too fast in this situation may result in the fly swinging towards the stern or under the boat making a hook-set difficult if not impossible. Experienced anglers and guides understand this dilemma and use the trolling motor or oars to slow down the boat after each cast before moving again.

Regular communication with your fishing partner is the key to effective boat control. Given the variables of wind and current on all types of water, it is imperative that you remain aware of each other and make adjustments as necessary. If your guide or fishing partner is used to fishing with conventional muskie gear, you should always be sure to point out the fact that the fly-rod retrieve is generally slower and requires more time between each cast to make a proper presentation.

Author's Tips: Casting from a Boat

- Maximize each retrieve by keeping your casts perpendicular to the boat as often as possible.

- Keep the boat moving slowly: always cast and retrieve the fly in a straight line whenever possible to avoid slack during the retrieve (unless, of course, a fish is following)

- In open water over larger structure, use longer, evenly spaced fan casts to cover the water methodically from several directions.

- When fishing smaller structure, position the boat as close as possible, and use short casts to cover the water thoroughly.

- When drifting a river, keep your retrieves moving cross-current and downstream, not upstream against the current.

- Approach sighted fish in shallow water quietly with the oars or trolling motor before casting; make your retrieves perpendicular to the fish to give your fly the best profile.

- Keep your casts longer and farther apart in clear or open water and shorter and closer together in stained or dark water and thick cover.

- Maintain constant communication with your fishing partner to achieve the best boat speed and position.

Team work: Effective boat control requires constant vigilance, communication, and attention. Here guide Mike Lazarus watches intently as I retrieve my fly over a weed bed. He's also using the trolling motor foot pedal to position the boat and maximize each cast.

Blind Fishing vs. Sight Fishing

When blind fishing open-water structure, such as a deep-water rock hump or isolated weed bed on a large lake or river, use the oars or the trolling motor to control your speed as you drift. Keep your casts long—40 to 60 feet—to cover as much area as possible. Fan casting these areas with multiple, evenly-spaced casts is usually the ticket until you have a follow or a hit. Depending on the size of the structure you are fishing, the distance between each cast can vary from two to ten feet. You may also need more than one drift to cover the water effectively and allow the fish time to see the fly. Whenever I start seeing fish, I carefully note the specific details of the area they came from and try to focus my efforts there on the next pass.

When fishing a specific structural target such as a river log jam, large boulder, or small reed patch, use the trolling motor or oars to position the boat before you start casting. Make your first casts perpendicular to the edge of the structure and then parallel once you get closer. If the water is clear, as a general rule, keep the boat as far away as possible. And use longer casts to avoid spooking fish. However, if the cover is particularly thick, hit it from afar and then as close and as many times as possible to cover the target. This is an ideal situation for presenting the fly and responding to strikes or following fish. You usually see the fish first, giving you ample time to get tight to the fly and react quickly with a strip-strike—if it strikes. Smaller structure is easier to cover thoroughly with a fly rod. And it gives the fish more opportunity to see, hear, and feel your fly.

When floating a medium to small river in a drift or aluminum boat, it's normal to be fishing tight as the boat moves directly over or very close to shoreline or mid-river structure. If possible, try to hit each selected downstream target at least once before you reach it to avoid disturbing the fish in shallow holding water. As the boat approaches the target, hit it again but from a slightly different angle—just to be sure you cover the water thoroughly. This approach can create some excellent hookup opportunities: River fish often strike as soon as the fly enters the water, especially on ambush points such as below a long jam or the head of a pool below rapids.

Sight-fishing for muskie requires a slightly different approach with the boat. When you see a fish move, boil, or simply sunning on the surface, don't gun the trolling motor or slap the oars in an attempt to reach the fish quickly. While muskies are not normally spooky, it's smart to adopt a careful approach to a fish that is often in shallow water and close to the surface. As you would when watching a rising trout, take your time and slowly approach the fish. Avoid making a big wake. When you reach reasonable casting range, throw beyond the head of the fish by a foot or two. Retrieve the fly past and in front of the direction you think it's facing or can see it facing.

As with Atlantic salmon or steelhead, you want your fly to pass sideways *by* the fish, allowing the largest and most attractive profile. If this isn't possible, and the fish is still showing, move the boat quietly and try a different angle and/or a different fly.

Depending on the conditions, some fish may not show any interest, but at least you'll know you didn't ruin your chances before you made the first cast.

Whatever the fishing situation, you or your guide should automatically approach each fishing spot as quietly and stealthily as possible to preserve your chances for encountering a fish. The same goes for any other common boat noises such as a squeaky oar lock, tough-to-position trolling motor, rough-running engine, or dropping heavy items on the bottom of the boat. These are all simple steps you can take to improve your odds for a fish that's already extraordinarily tough to catch.

The Casting Deck

The casting deck in a boat can be as simple as the small front seat of a row boat or the expansive front deck of a bass boat or bonefish skiff. Whatever kind of boat you use, always position yourself as far above the water as possible to cast, retrieve, and see the fish clearly. Saltwater flats boats are certainly ideal for this kind of fishing. But there are only a handful in use on muskie waters. You'll most likely find yourself on a

A classic McKenzie-style drift boat such as this watercraft by Hyde is another excellent choice for drifting rivers for muskies. Easily maneuverable and stealthy, this stable boat offers a perfect casting platform from which to stand and cast a fly.

Here are a number of other line-management techniques that will improve your presentations and overall fishing efficiency:

• Clean and stretch your line: One of the best ways to avoid a knotted or kinked line is to stretch it thoroughly and keep it clean. Before you start fishing each day take a moment to stretch the first 20 to 50 feet to eliminate any memory from the reel. A dirty line is also more prone to sticking, catching, and looping on itself than a clean one. While most of us do not want to take the time to clean line while fishing, this is an absolute must when muskie fishing. Taking a few moments through the day for a quick rub with a commercial line cleaner and than a slickening agent such as Glide goes a long way to helping your casting and avoiding this problem when it really matters.

• Don't fish with too much line: Although we all like to make long casts, the fact of the matter is most muskies are caught within 20 to 60 feet. By cutting down on the length of line you strip off the reel, you prevent unnecessary loose line on the deck and potential tangles when you cast. If you need to make a longer cast, you can always strip line quickly from the reel and then reel it back up when back to fishing normal distances.

• Use the right fly line for the conditions: As noted in Chapter 4, most modern fly lines have cores and coatings specifically designed for use in different weather conditions. In cooler air and water temperatures in the spring and fall, use a line with a softer braided nylon core that remains supple and won't coil. In warmer summer temperatures use a "tropical" line with a mono core that remains stiffer in the heat and is less likely to stick when you cast.

• Use a stripping basket: Whether you spend $10 or $50, a good stripping basket is worth its weight in gold on windy days. Although there are many options to choose from, one of the easiest solutions is a cheap, large plastic storage container placed on the boat deck by your feet. If you prefer using a conventional stripping basket, I highly recommend one that is adjustable, lightweight and collapsible such as that offered by the Charlie's Total Control Stripping Basket shown in the photo (www.flyfishbasket.com).

• Use the cockpit: On especially windy days, standing to the rear edge of the bow deck and using the boat cockpit

as your stripping basket works well to hold line out of the full force of the wind. If necessary, you can also place a wet towel on the cockpit floor right behind the front deck to help to keep line in place. When things get really bad, as a last resort you can stand in the cockpit and cast from a lower position then step back up to the deck for your retrieve. This is not ideal for most presentations but may be your only option when the wind kicks up. On these really windy days you may also find it necessary to retrieve a floating line or running line with your rod tip under water to prevent the line from blowing off the surface.

bass boat, drift boat, Jon boat or other all-propose fishing boat with either bench or elevated seats. To achieve an even higher casting deck, guide Mark Meritt has built a special wooden, carpeted platform on the front deck of his boat to elevate the fly angler as far as possible above the water.

When fly casting for muskies from a boat, you should use the largest and widest flat surface area you can find in the bow or the stern, depending on the

boat. This is usually not a problem with a drift, skiff, bass or Jon boat with a large front deck built specifically for fishing. With smaller V-hull, aluminum rowboats your options may be more limited. In this case you may want to consider standing on a forward seat to gain elevation and a better field of view. If you try this, be careful not to put yourself in a precarious position or you'll soon find yourself in the water or on the bottom of the boat when it hits a wave or a rock (believe me it hurts!).

Clear the Deck!

A clean casting deck is essential to making one good cast or a thousand. There's nothing more aggravating than missing a fishing opportunity because your line is twisted around a boat cleat, your shoes, a piece of loose leader material, or a forgotten pair of pliers. This unfortunate situation is bound to happen with even the best casters, especially if it's windy and your line is blowing around the deck. Fortunately there are several tricks to make your casting from a boat more efficient and pleasurable.

One of the first things you should do in a typical bass boat is remove and stow any detachable boat seats or butt rests found on the front deck. This simple move will give you a lot more room to work with and make your day much more enjoyable. Now take a look at your overall casting area and identify any obstructions. Look for cleats, anchors, ropes, trolling motors, control pedals, depth finders, and wires. Sharp or rough edges on the boat hull and cockpit also present potential hazards to your line as you fish. All of these present potential impediments to your casting proficiency. They must be stowed, covered, or moved as far away as possible before you start fishing.

Bare feet and fancy free: Although I've burned the tops of my feet a few times, if conditions allow, going barefoot in the boat helps to keep track of your fly line on the deck when casting and retrieving.

Through the day, *stay vigilant*. Routinely check your casting area to make sure you haven't cluttered it up again with flies, tools, or other equipment.

If it's all right with your guide (or if the boat is yours), one of the easiest and cheapest ways to cover many permanent boat obstructions is to simply place a strip of duct tape across any line-catching obstructions or edges near the front deck of the boat. I always carry a roll with me in the boat for this and a number of other repair jobs. This technique works especially well on boat cleats and boat storage handles which seem to grab fly line like a magnet whenever you're trying to cast.

The same result can be accomplished by covering these obstructions with an old towel or shirt, soaking them first in water so they won't blow away. In an emergency, I've even used the shirt off my own back. As they dry through the day simply soak them again and place them back where needed. A larger towel or blanket soaked in water can also be used on the casting deck or the boat floor to effectively keep the line in place on especially windy days.

Another trick to making more efficient casts from a boat is to remove your shoes when fishing. Doing so will help prevent you from stepping on your line when casting. It's especially important when there's a strong wind, and you can't possibly keep track of your line and your target at the same time. It should be noted, however, that when muskie fishing with bare feet you need to be especially careful to keep any loose flies or other sharp objects off the casting deck and out of harm's way. If it's too cold for bare feet, try wearing socks which still allow you to feel your fly line and stay a bit warmer.

Staying Fit for Muskies on the Fly

No discussion of casting big flies all day long with a 10-weight rod would be complete without touching on the importance of staying and keeping fit to prevent injury. Like golf or other repetitive outdoor activities, it pays to spend time strengthening and stretching your muscles before and after you go after muskies with a fly rod. Some of the easiest exercises involve using free weights or machines to build hand, wrist, arm, back, and leg strength. A small hand exerciser or stress ball is also a convenient tool for building strength in the hand, fingers, and forearm. Before and after I fish, I also always take the time to stretch my wrist, arms, shoulders, back, and legs using a doorway, car door, boat trailer, or other solid object for support and balance.

Just a few minutes of this preventative self treatment will go a long way to keep you fit and focused on fishing instead of pain. For anyone seeking more detailed advice on how to prevent and treat fishing-related injuries, I highly recommend the excellent book *Fit to Fish* by Stephen L. Hisey, PT and Keith R. Berend, MD (2005). Co-authored by a fly-fishing physical therapist and surgeon, this book offers a wealth of information and instruction on how to identify, prevent, and treat the most common aliments known to fly fishers.

PROVEN
PRESENTATION
TECHNIQUES

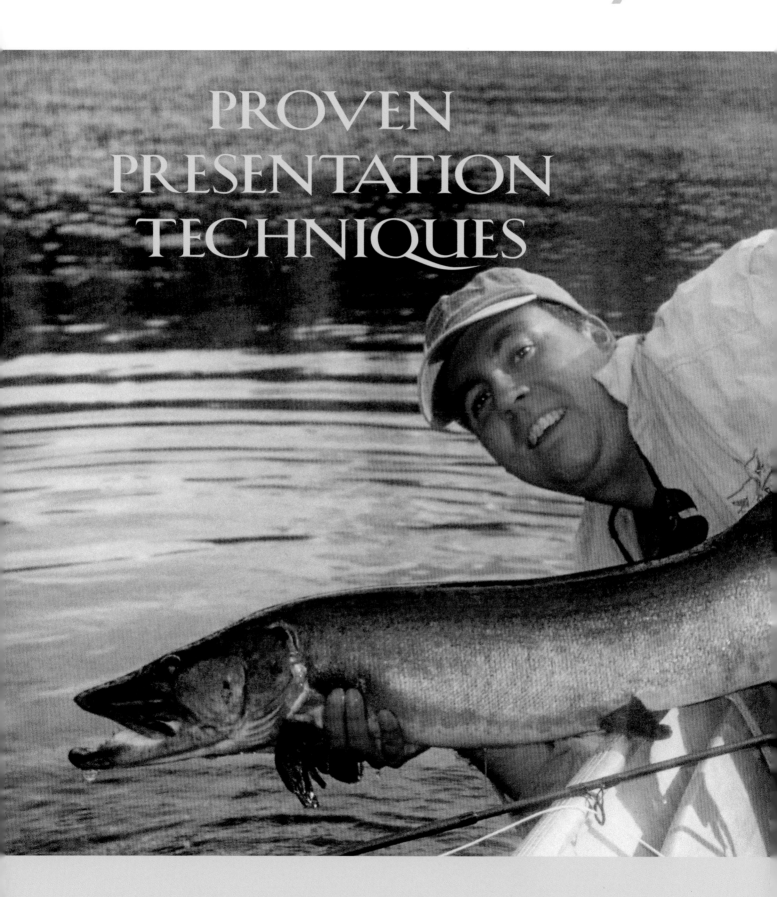

THE NOTORIOUSLY UNPREDICTABLE NATURE of the muskie has spawned hundreds of lures in every size, shape, and color imaginable. This cornucopia of choices is a testament to the imagination—and sometimes gullibility—of muskie anglers as they search for the one magic bait to finally make "old mossback" hit. Some lures certainly look and move a lot like the muskie's favorite forage while others look like nothing from this solar system. Despite all the energy devoted to the design, testing, and marketing of these different lures, at the end of the day some experienced muskie fishers will freely admit that fooling a muskie actually has little to do with the lure itself. Sitting in a boat filled to the gunnels with rods, reels, and tackle boxes overflowing with lures, they go on to tell you that success in this sport is really much more a matter of the right presentation at the right place and time than anything else.

In many ways they're exactly right. Like fly fishing for Atlantic salmon or steelhead, it's often more a matter of making the first swing, splat, or *plop* in front of a fresh fish that counts more than the fly on the end of your leader. While there's no doubt color or size is important to catching a muskie, it is often simply a case of the right cast and retrieve in front of the right fish that ultimately triggers the fish to strike. Since most muskie lures—and all flies—require the angler to retrieve them in a specific manner to produce the right action, the proper fly-rod *presentation* technique is clearly a key factor for success wherever you fish.

This rather disconcerting truth was made evident to me many years ago on a large Canadian shield lake. I was fishing with a buddy in late October with the hopes of one last big muskie on a fly before ice-up. With water temperatures in the low 40s, we knew the fish would probably be suspended off deep breaks near the shallows in search of larger prey such as migrating ciscoes and whitefish. After spending most of the day casting fruitlessly in open water with a giant 15-inch cisco-colored streamer and a 400-grain integrated sinking-head line, I needed a break. To the distinct surprise of my buddy, for a change of pace, I decided to try fishing a large top-water popper on my floating line.

After a couple of lazy casts to get my rhythm back, I directed the popper toward a distinctive rock saddle and began my retrieve. Within seconds I was thrilled—and surprised—when I saw the unmistakable push of a large muskie below the surface. I instinctively increased the speed of my retrieve with the hope of enticing a strike. The fish immediately lunged forward and inhaled my fly like a great white shark on a helpless seal. With a length of 51 inches and a girth to match, this giant of a fish was exactly the trophy I'd hoped for. While certainly not expecting anything to happen on the surface in these cold, late-fall conditions, this fine fish stands as one of the many examples of the unpredictable nature of muskies. And the importance of being in the right place at the right time!

With the notable exception of the size of the fly, the presentation techniques used to catch muskies on a fly are similar in many ways to other species you may have fished for. If you've ever blasted the bank with a streamer for big browns, popped a bass bug for largemouth in the lily pads, stripped a Clouser deep along a rip for stripers, or teased a bonefish on the flats, you already have some idea of what muskie presentations are all about. Depending on the water and the season, muskie presentations represent a combination of these and many other commonly used fresh- and saltwater presentation techniques. As your muskie fishing advances you'll also see that there are many unique things about this fish that necessitate using the fly rod in some pretty creative and unusual ways. This is what makes this sport so fun. And it's an extreme challenge for the fly fisher looking for something entirely new and exciting.

How a fly fisher effectively presents and retrieves the fly to entice a muskie is the subject of this chapter. We'll cover the proper casting and stripping techniques for presenting and retrieving both streamers and top water flies. We'll also cover a variety of specialized techniques for triggering strikes in and around the best muskie-holding structure. These unique presentations can be used with success any time you hit the water but are intended for fishing specific kinds of structure through the season.

The Predator Pose

Regardless of what kind of water you're fishing, your basic muskie presentation must be focused, efficient, and aggressive at all times. Any momentary failure to heed this advice usually results in great disappointment as the one good opportunity of the day dissolves right before your eyes. To help maintain my composure when faced with this challenge, over the years I've adopted what I call the "predator pose." This athletic body attitude is something I've done for as long as I—or anyone I fish with—can remember. There are no guarantees in this sport, but I promise this approach will go a long way to help insure you're at least ready for a fish at all times.

The basic elements of the predator pose are detailed in the accompanying sidebar. With time and practice they should become second nature. As you might expect, during my retrieve I rarely look at anything else but my fly and the area immediately around it—not even a bird or pretty sunbather. I scan the water between casts occasionally to see what's coming, of course, but never during the retrieve. Like driving a car, you can't afford to daydream—even for a moment—when your fly is in the muskie's zone.

I realize this all sounds rather extreme, but in order to be a successful muskie angler you have to give yourself every edge you possibly can. During the normal long days on the water, I've found the predator pose approach keeps me alert, and in the best position to see, prepare, and strike a fish should it hit or follow my fly. This is a decidedly aggressive approach to fly fishing that requires your undivided attention from the moment the fly hits the water until it reaches the boat. Unless you've just caught a fish, there's no sitting back, watching the scenery, and enjoying a cold one while fly fishing for muskie. As my old friend Victor likes to say, "You've got to be armed and dangerous at all times."

Streamer and Top-Water Casting and Line-Management Techniques

There are several casting and line-management techniques that will improve your efficiency and effectiveness with any muskie presentation. After each forward cast, don't simply release the line and

The Predator Pose

- Face your intended target squarely with your weight evenly balanced, your feet slightly staggered, and your knees slightly bent.
- Grip the rod handle with your thumb firmly on top and your index finger wrapped underneath for leverage and line control.
- Make a cast and lower your rod tip toward the water as the fly lands.
- As the fly lands, lean forward from the waist and immediately get control of your line by placing it under your index finger. Strip any remaining slack tight to the fly.
- Focus on the area around the fly for any movement or other signs of fish activity, particularly after the first strip or pop.
- Begin your retrieve maintaining this position while at the same time remaining focused on your fly and the area around it.
- Throughout the entire retrieve, remain alert and poised, turning your body if necessary to face the direction of the fly. Be ready for a strike.
- As you finish your retrieve, watch closely behind and around your fly for any signs of a follow before picking up for the next cast.
- Keep the fly moving and do not pull it out of the water until you are confident there is no fish following!
- Repeat the same presentation for the next 10,000 or so casts...

hope it lands where you intend. This may make for long and impressive casts but it's a waste of time if your line gets knotted and your fly lands in a tangled mess. Instead, it's always best to maintain constant and continuous control by feathering the line with a loose grip through your stripping hand fingers. Another option is to create an "O-ring" using your thumb and forefinger to reduce tangles, though this technique offers less direct control.

The predator pose in action: Muskie fly fishing requires mental and physical stamina to make an effective presentation. Note the low rod tip, the staggered feet for balance, and the full-arm strip with the line.

I also always use a "check haul" on my casts with a pinch or slight haul on the line just before the fly lands. In most cases, this technique forces the fly to "turn over," significantly reducing the chances it will tangle on the line or itself. And it makes each retrieve more efficient from the first pull. When fishing a specific target or shoreline, applying a check haul also helps to control the distance and accuracy of each cast as well as avoid snags by making last minute adjustments before you overshoot. As you might have guessed, stopping the fly short with a check haul forces it down hard on the water, usually with a loud SPLAT. This is a good thing. The loud noise and commotion caused by this controlled crash landing is an effective way to attract and trigger a nearby muskie even before you begin your retrieve, especially in dark water.

When casting and stripping any fly, a small amount of slack is always created as soon as the fly lands, moves forward, swings sideways, or drops. When this happens, it is critical that you continue to maintain control and pull in this slack quickly in preparation for your next strip. As a result, when fishing a muskie fly, your stripping hand is always in motion, whether making the strip itself or picking up the slack from the previous strip. This is a lot of work with a fly rod. But it's absolutely essential to make sure you are connected—or at least close to being connected—at all times with your fly. If you apply these techniques correctly, you'll always be ready to strip-strike when a fish hits.

Be forewarned: Although it would be great to see every muskie that eats your fly, the simple fact is that because of different water and light conditions, the only thing you may see is a large boil, sudden push of water, or "drive by" side flash when the fish strikes. This is one of the most difficult things about fly fishing for muskies. The strike is often so violent and quick that you can't possibly respond in time, especially with a long line and, more often than not, some slack between retrieves.

The Basic Retrieves: Streamers and Top Water

The retrieve is the heart of your presentation. It is the real "art" of muskie fishing with a fly—where you make your fly come alive and hope to fool a muskie along the way. Like many fishing techniques, experience and time on the water are always the best teachers. There are several concepts you should keep in mind, however, to get you started the right way.

Consider this fact: Many popular muskie lures such as jerk baits and glide baits are simply painted pieces of wood or plastic with several sets of treble hooks and no "built-in" action. As such, it is entirely up to the angler to give life to these giant lures with a stiff rod and a strong arm and back. Having fished with many talented muskie anglers over the years, I can honestly say working a lure this way is a unique skill worthy of the highest regard. This is also one of the more successful conventional techniques for catching muskies on any water.

Like jerk baits, a typical muskie fly also has no inherent action other than what the angler can successfully create with the line strip and the rod tip. *Your retrieve, then, is the art and practice of moving and manipulating the fly in such a way to attract a fish.*

Happy angler and angry fish: The thought of big-headed trophy fish is what keeps me focused and casting all day and night.

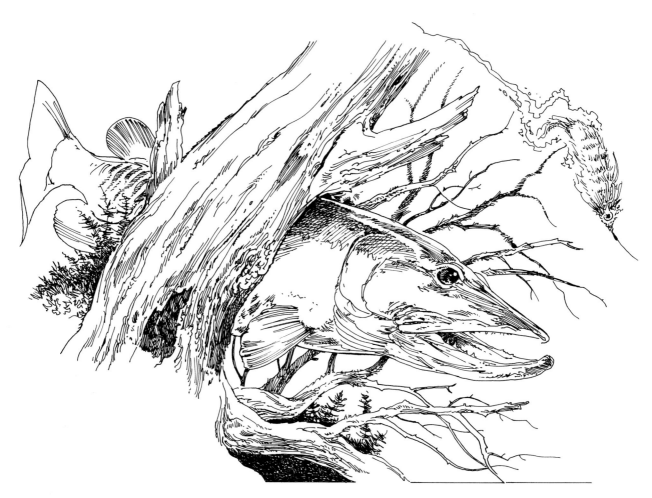

Be the streamer: When making a streamer presentation for muskies always keep the fly animated and looking vulnerable. During the retrieve keep an eye out for visible structure, and be sure to cover any probable ambush points like this enticing log cover.

We all know the old saying that 90 percent of the anglers catch 10 percent of the fish. Among the many things top anglers are doing better, I humbly suggest that the retrieve is a big part of their success. As we've all seen, many times just a simple change in the speed or direction of the retrieve is all it takes to trigger a fish. Other times you can try everything you know and still not interest a fish. That's fishing—and especially muskie fishing—regardless of the approach.

Muskie Streamers

Streamers are my "go-to" fly for most muskie fishing regardless of the water, season, and conditions. Compared to a large top-water popper, they are easy and more efficient to cast and retrieve at any distance. This keeps your fly in the water where it belongs. Equally important, they provide an excellent forage-fish profile in the water. When fished correctly, they exude a tantalizing side-to-side and/or stop-and-start motion that triggers muskies to strike.

Because muskies tend to actually "eat" streamers rather than "blow up" on them, they also provide what is probably the best hookup success rate for the fly fisher. The only real downside to fishing streamers for muskie is their lack of significant noise and vibration during the retrieve—a significant issue in dirty or dark water. This negative can, however, be overcome to some extent with the use of rattles and special water-pushing materials and tying techniques.

The Muskie Streamer Retrieve

Be the Streamer

Before you start casting a streamer for muskies, take a few minutes to think about muskie behavior and visualize what the fly should look like in the water.

Would a muskie eat a slow-moving, lifeless baitfish without any visible sign of distress? Probably not.

Would a muskie eat a fast-moving baitfish that is behaving erratically and struggling as it moved away? Definitely!

These are exactly the kind of images to keep in mind each and every time you cast a streamer for muskies. Remember: *Be the streamer.*

Muskie Streamer Retrieve

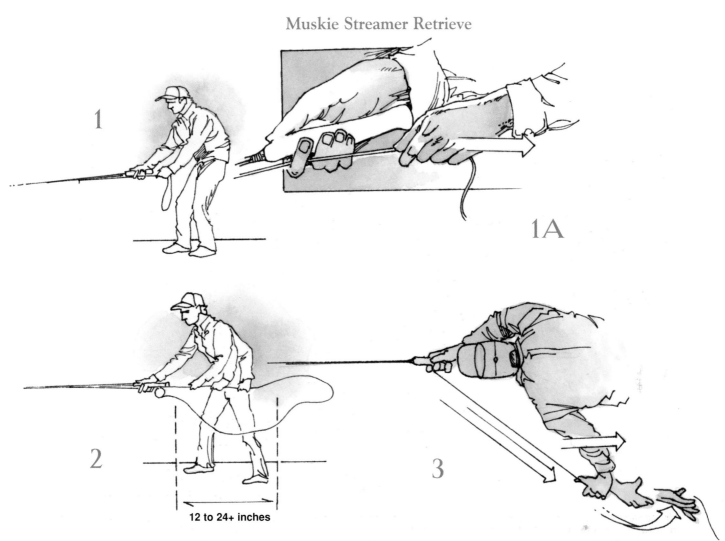

The basic elements of the muskie streamer retrieve: Start by making a cast and assuming the predator pose with a lowered rod tip (Figure 1). As the fly lands, immediately get control of the line by placing it under your index finger and stripping tight to the fly (Figure 1A). Watch for signs of fish activity and, with a firm grip on the line behind your index finger, begin retrieving the fly with fast or slow strips of 12 to 24 inches or more depending upon the desired action (Figure 2). At the end of each strip accelerate the fly by turning your line hand away from the body (Figure 3). After each strip, immediately recover any slack line and reposition the rod for the next retrieve sequence.

It's also helpful to observe a few of the most effective subsurface muskie baits in the water to see how they move. When fished as intended, jerk baits, twitch baits, and glide baits move in a side-to-side and/or up-and-down fashion with a spastic, stop-and-start action. Depending on how fast they're fished, they also incorporate plenty of tantalizing "hang time" during the pause between jerks. Muskie-sized crank baits have a solid plastic or metal lip that causes the lure to dive and wobble at various speeds depending on the size, shape, and speed. Spinners are also worth watching. They trigger fish with a combination of speed, flash, and vibration from the blade and a body made of natural and/or synthetic materials that undulate seductively during the retrieve.

There are many variations on streamer retrieves to use in imitating these various actions—sometimes even on the same retrieve. You can also create your own retrieves offering the muskie something entirely new to chase. How you accomplish these actions is dependent on your individual skill with a fly rod. Whatever your ability, you'll need to master the basic muskie streamer retrieve as outlined in the illustration above.

Variations on the Muskie Streamer Retrieve Using the Strip

"Consistency is the last bastion of the unimaginative."
—Oscar Wilde

Given the inevitable slow times between fish, figuring out exactly what streamer technique to use on a given day can be rather frustrating. Until you finally hook up or start seeing fish, the only things you've got to go with are your confidence and unyielding faith in the water, your presentation, and your fly. Once you do connect, however, your odds improve tremendously. Each fish you encounter reveals telling clues about fish location, prey preferences, and aggressiveness. These valuable clues should form the basis of your fishing strategy for the day.

The best streamer game plan is usually to mix up your retrieve's length and speed with a combination of long and short, fast and slow strips. The length of most muskie strips is normally 12 to 24 inches, but utilizing the entire arm to pull more line—up to four and a half feet in my case—is also effective. It's also more work due the additional slack you'll need to recover. If this basic variation isn't producing, get creative by changing the speed and tempo with a combination of faster and slower strips during the same retrieve. You can also impart additional action to the streamer during the retrieve by shaking or wiggling your rod tip up and down and/or side to side at the same time you're stripping.

When you see a fish approach your fly, always speed up your retrieve with faster strips and a change of direction with the rod tip to entice a strike. This fleeing or escape behavior simulates the response of natural prey and forces the muskie to make a split-second, instinctual decision. Unless the fish are particularly moody, I don't recommend slowing down or stopping the fly mid-retrieve—an unnatural response that usually results in the fish immediately loosing interest.

Here are a few other streamer retrieve variations to consider:

- **Short, fast strips combined with long, slow strips:** short–short–*long*–*long*–short–short OR short–*long*–short–*long*–short–*long*

- **Fast, long strips with a distinct pause allowing fly to glide sideways and hang or drop:**

  strip–pause–swing–drop–*strip*–pause–swing–drop

- **Slower strips increasing steadily to fast strip:** slow strip–slightly faster strip–faster strip–*fastest strip*

- **Continued very fast strips the entire retrieve all the way to the boat.**

- **Continued slow, steady strips the entire retrieve all the way to the boat.**

- **Two-handed, saltwater "cuda" strip with rod propped under arm.**

Any combination of the above.

Variation on the Muskie Streamer Retrieve Using the Strip and the Rod

The Muskie Jerk-and-Strip Streamer Retrieve

Speed is without a doubt one of the key triggers that motivates a muskie to strike. To achieve more speed—and action—with the streamer retrieve, I use a unique combination of both the strip and rod motion known as the "jerk-and-strip." This effective trout-fishing streamer technique was first popularized by Kelly Galloup in his fine book *Modern Streamers for Trophy Trout* (1999). And it works for muskies.

When done correctly, the jerk-and-strip technique causes the fly to accelerate faster and move farther—and in a slightly different direction—than can be accomplished with a single "in-line" strip. This burst of speed, in turn, produces a seductive side-to-side swinging action that attracts fish of all kinds, especially muskies. It also causes the fly to stop and start abruptly. This creates more hang-time appeal as the streamer material flairs and pluses during the brief pause between strips. The combined actions produced by the jerk-and-strip work especially well to imitate the natural fleeing behavior of prey. This often triggers an impulsive reaction strike from muskies—even those fish that might not be ready to eat. Just be sure to maintain constant control of your slack and get tight to the fly between each jerk-and-strip or you'll miss the first fish that hits. (see illustration on page 149)

Muskie Streamer and Top-Water Presentations for Sighted Fish

The streamer presentations outlined at the beginning of this chapter are intended primarily for blind-casting to structure without visible fish. Casting to sighted fish requires different presentation techniques to be effective with a fly. Like bonefishing or tarpon fishing, when you approach a sighted fish in any of these situations, be prepared to cast quickly and accurately to any fish you see. This means standing at the ready with fly in hand, and always making sure your line is tangle free.

Boiling or Rolling Fish

Seeing a muskie boil or roll on the surface is a good sign that muskies are present and probably feeding, usually by attacking individual or schooled baitfish from below and pushing them toward the surface or against structure. When this happens you might even be able to see individual or schools of baitfish jumping on the surface trying to get away. This activity can

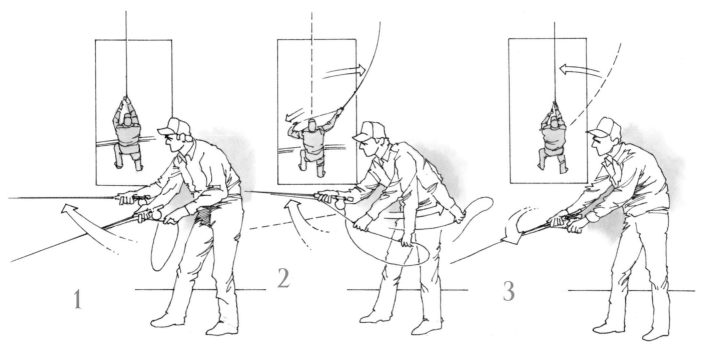

The basic elements of the muskie jerk-and-strip streamer retrieve: Start by making a cast and assuming the predator pose with a lowered rod tip. As the fly lands, immediately get control of your line by placing it under your index finger and stripping tight to the fly (Figure 1). Watch for signs of fish activity and, with a firm grip on the line behind your index finger, begin retrieving the fly by forcefully sweeping the rod down or sideways at the same time you apply a fast, 12- to 24-inch or longer strip (Figure 2). After each jerk-and-strip, immediately recover any slack line and reposition the rod for the next retrieve (Figure 3).

The jerk-and-strip technique triggers muskies to hit by moving the streamer in an erratic—almost spastic—stop-and-start motion much like the natural, fleeing behavior of prey.

happen all year long but is most common in the spring and fall when certain forage—such as shad—are concentrated and often suspended in open water. You'll find this behavior associated with different structure including deep, open-water basins, creek mouths, rock bars, and weed beds where preferred prey species often congregate.

If you can't actually see the fish after it boils, try to make an educated guess as to where the fish is moving, and fire off a couple of casts as *quickly as possible*. Even if you're wrong about the source of the commotion, it's always worth a cast. The key here is timing and depth since the fish is most likely moving around actively in search of prey. If you don't get a response on the first cast, make a couple of more tightly spaced fan casts. Retrieve the fly at various depths and various speeds. Cover the entire water column from top to bottom—with luck you'll find the fish along the way.

Don't be surprised if a fish comes to the fly late, often on a deep follow. In these situations I always use a figure-8 or other tactic at the boat to keep the fly animated at close range.

In shallow, clear water it's sometimes possible to see the fish itself—or at least a shadow—moving underwater right after it boils. While it's not necessary to hit the fish right on the head, you still want the fly close enough to get noticed. Try leading the fish by a foot or two and then strip the fly as close as possible before the fish moves again in search of other prey. An active fish usually finds your fly within the first few strips, but always fish the entire cast just to be sure.

Laid-Up or Sunning Fish

During the spring and summer months it's not uncommon to see perfectly healthy muskies laid-up like baby tarpon "sunning" themselves on sand or

Like a backwater tarpon, muskies often "lay up" in shallow water. Approach these fish with caution and make your first cast your best.

muck bottoms, or very close to the surface. Why they do this is a mystery. There are several plausible theories relating to digestion, water temperatures, and other environmental conditions. This behavior is best observed in early morning or late evening when the water is normally calm and undisturbed. Because you can often see the fish before it sees you, this makes for a truly unique opportunity on the fly.

When you spot a fish under these conditions, make your approach as quiet as you can. Cast your fly three to five feet past the front of the fish and retrieve it at the fish's depth, allowing for a full side profile whenever possible. In this situation, it's usually best to begin with a streamer to provide the maximum versatility. An active fish should immediately take notice and either strike or at least follow. If the fish isn't interested,

fish "cruisers." It's an experience much like trout fishing in a beaver pond. I've observed this behavior throughout the season, but it's most common in the early spring before and after the spawn. Although these early-season fish are often less aggressive because of cooler water temperatures—and the rigors of spawning—they can be fooled with the right fly and the right cast.

When approaching a fish in this situation, make a cast and lead the fish by a few feet, just as you would a bonefish or cruising trout. Allow the fly to sink and then retrieve it at the fish's eye level, watching for any reaction. If the fish shows any sign of interest—turning and moving toward the fly, opening and closing its mouth—continue stripping at the same or faster pace until the fish eats. These fish are not overly aggressive so twitching and pulsating the fly with the rod tip when the fish approaches is often an effective way to trigger a sudden strike.

The objective of these streamer-retrieve techniques is to provide you with options to draw the muskies attention and trigger a strike. It's always a challenge when a fish shows but won't eat. On most days, being creative and varying your retrieve is the best approach—you never know what they may want on a particular day. The real key here is to always watch for a fish, judge its behavior, and respond accordingly.

The Muskie Top-Water Retrieve

The Muskie Sweep-and-Strip Top-Water Retrieve

Catching a muskie on a top-water fly is one of the most exciting and visually intoxicating events in all of fly fishing. Although I've fished around the world for many different and exotic species, for me nothing compares to the sight of a large muskie aggressively pushing a V-wake while following my popper across the surface, kicking up water with splashes of its tail, or blasting it from below and jumping sky-high with my fly sticking out of its mouth.

As nerve-wracking as this fishing can be, it's also a productive way to fly fish for muskies under the right conditions and with the right techniques. One of main the reasons it's effective is the muskie's shallow-water and surface-feeding orientation through much of the peak warm water season. Depending on water temperatures and regulations where you fish, the top water popper can also be used with confidence as early as March and as late as November.

The popper is also the only type of fly that produces a significant level of noise, commotion, and fish-

it probably hasn't seen the fly or doesn't want to eat. Before giving up, try casting again from a different direction or with another pattern, perhaps something loud on top, to get its attention.

Cruising Fish

On some muskie lakes and rivers it's common to spot fish in shallow, clear water swimming slowly along the bottom. If they're not spooked, I call these

attracting vibration almost on par with some conventional muskie top-water baits. This added attraction has resulted in many of my biggest fish each year.

A top-water fly is an excellent choice for searching the water, especially in stained or low-light conditions where a streamer might not be as visible or effective. Before you try top-water fishing for muskies, however, you should know that this is also one of the more difficult techniques to master. It requires a steady hand, a keen ear, and a practiced eye.

To understand better how to fish a top-water fly for muskies, it's worth taking a look at the wide range of muskie surface lures to see how they move through the water and what they sound like. Although there are dozens on the market, the most effective lures incorporate various combinations of side-to-side or "walk-the-dog" wobble. Some even have fore-and-aft propeller blades, or arms that kick and sputter water leaving a defined bubble trail as the bait moves along the surface. Some surface baits are meant to crawl slowly in calmer water. Others work best at faster speeds. Both conventional surface lures and top water poppers trigger muskies to strike with an irresistible combination of noise, vibration, action, and speed.

Because I enjoy fishing poppers, I always keep a rod rigged with a top-water fly to use when conditions are right—or as a backup fly in case of a follow. A top-water fly can be just the ticket for a fish that refuses a streamer. Keeping an extra rod rigged and dedicated for this purpose makes switching to a popper quick and efficient. I also enjoy throwing a top-water fly simply for a change of pace since it requires a different casting stroke and retrieve technique. It's just plain fun to cast a top-water fly and watch as it pops and gurgles all the way back to the boat. You can almost imagine it crying "Help me! *Help me!*" as it struggles across the surface.

If you've fished a popper for bass you are well on your way to understanding what it takes to fish on top for muskies. Many of the same surface retrieves that work for bass also work for muskies, only on a much larger scale. There are, however, several notable differences in the technique, timing, and energy required to cast and pop the fly.

Many anglers have difficulty casting and turning over a large, air-resistant popper. By slowing down the cast and extending the stroke to open the loop, most should be able to achieve the minimal distances required. Adding a short but firm haul on your back and forward casts also helps increase line speed and distance with a large popper. They are not for distance casting. When fishing any large, wind-resistant fly, take the time to position the boat within reasonable range of your target before you cast.

How you retrieve a top-water fly for muskies is the most critical part of this equation. A typical bass popper or diver requires a relatively fast but short strip of the line to make it move, gurgle, and pop as intended. A muskie popper, on the other hand, displaces far more water as it moves across the surface. This necessitates the combined—and very aggressive—use of the rod tip and the strip to achieve a loud and steady pop throughout the entire retrieve. (see illustration on page 153)

Other Top-Water Retrieve Considerations

When using the sweep-and-strip top-water technique, it's important to make every pop count—but especially the first one. If you try to pop the fly too soon after it lands, more often than not it simply skips quietly over the surface or comes flying back at the boat, risking injury and wasting a perfectly good cast. In most situations, it's best to make the initial pop as large and loud as possible by keeping the rod tip low on the water, eliminating any slack, and making sure the fly is sitting upright before your begin your retrieve.

It is also important that you begin each retrieve using a slow and steady rhythm much like a conventional top-water muskie lure. For whatever reason, muskies prefer a moderately paced, steady, and uninterrupted *pop, pop, pop* rhythm that leaves a

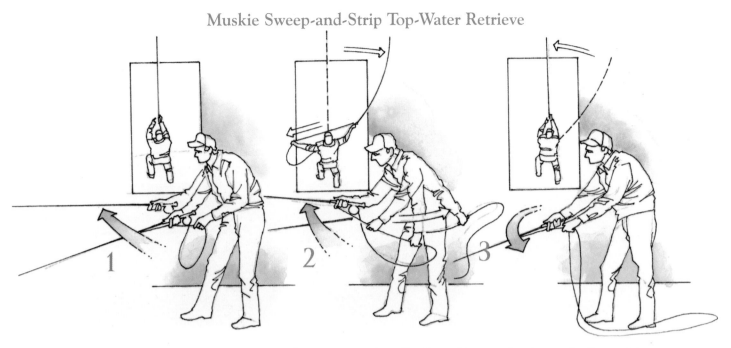

The basic elements of the muskie sweep-and-strip top-water retrieve: Start by making a cast and assuming the predator pose with a lowered rod tip. As the fly lands, immediately get control of your line by placing it under your index finger and stripping tight to the fly (Figure 1). Watch for signs of fish activity and, with a firm grip on the line behind your index finger, begin retrieving the fly by forcefully sweeping the rod sideways at the same time you apply a fast, 12- to 24-inch or longer strip (Figure 2). After each sweep-and-strip, immediately recover any slack line and reposition the rod the next retrieve (Figure 3).

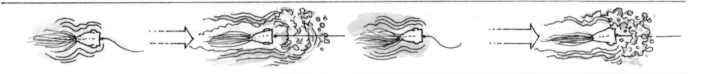

The sweep-and-strip retrieve triggers muskies to hit by creating a very loud and visible boil on the surface of the water.

distinct bubble trail as opposed to working it back very slowly with a distinctive pause. Resting the fly for long periods and letting the rings completely disappear between pops as is common with a bass bug is not normally the most effective approach.

If you're not getting any action with the fast-paced, steady retrieve rhythm, try the slower one-pop-at-a-time technique. It can't hurt and you just might catch a fish. I've taken fish this way but typically they're located on a small piece structure I know holds one good fish. One or two pops is all it takes. Whatever happens, if a fish is following, always pick up speed gradually and/or change direction with the rod tip to trigger a strike.

The most critical thing about top-water fishing for muskies is achieving the proper speed and noise throughout the entire retrieve. This may sound relatively simple but it is actually dependant on many things including the type and shape of fly, water conditions, and even your leader. Under most conditions I choose a large deer-hair or hard closed-cell foam-

body popper with a deep, concave face. Of the two fly types, the hard foam-body popper definitely pushes the most water and makes the loudest possible sounds with a fly rod. In my experience, muskie poppers that consistently create the lowest frequency, loudest "blurp" noises are usually much better at attracting muskies than a higher frequency, softer pop. Watch and listen to your fly during each retrieve to make sure you're achieving the right commotion with every cast.

In calm water, making the fly move, pop, and gurgle properly is usually not an issue. When the wind is causing wave movement on the surface—often prime conditions for top water—the popper will still work just fine but you've got to wait a moment between waves or the fly will skip with each sweep and strip. In rougher conditions, it's also a good idea to use the largest and loudest top-water fly you can cast to draw the fish's attention.

Whenever you use a top-water fly, I suggest using a lighter, thinner, wire shock tippet of 15- to 20-pound-test to avoid weighing down the head of the

Problem: Fly skips on the surface when I try to pop.
Solution: After you cast, let the fly settle in the water, lower your rod tip so it's touching the water, and strip in any slack line before beginning your sweep-and-strip retrieve. Always make sure the fly is upright and facing forward toward the rod tip before the first pop. In extremely windy or wavy conditions, slow down the pace of the retrieve and apply the sweep-and-strip between each ripple or wave.

Problem: Fly twists on the surface when I pop, twisting my fly line and leader.
Solution: Check your wire, knots, and the fly for any damage or weeds. Kinks in the wire, large knots, or even a nick in a hard-body popper can make the fly turn and roll as you retrieve. After repeated casting—or a fish—the body of the fly may become detached from the hook causing it to roll during the retrieve. Flies with trailer hooks also tend to roll if attached with a stiff wire connection that has been bent and is no longer in line with the fly.

Problem: Fly doesn't make a large and loud enough pop.
Solution: This common problem is usually caused by not waiting long enough for the fly to settle in the water between pops or not having the rod tip low enough and your tight line before popping. If you've got any slack, pop too soon, or are at the wrong angle, the fly cannot capture enough water in the head to make any noise or push water. Wait for the fly to settle, lower your rod tip so it's touching the water, strip in your slack, and then begin your sweep-and-strip retrieve.
    Tip: This problem may also be caused by a dirty line sinking the fly or a damaged head. Clean your line regularly and check the fly for signs of wear and tear, replacing if necessary.

Problem: Line slaps loudly on the surface when I sweep-and-strip, making an unnatural noise.
Solution: "Line slap" is a common problem with top-water flies caused by too much slack. You can easily eliminate most of this unwanted noise by keeping the rod tip low to the water and always stripping line tight before each sweep and strip. Holding the rod tip underwater also helps to avoid noise and slack, but tends to pull the fly too deep reducing the noise level of each pop.

Problem: Fly is difficult to pick up off the water.
Solution: A large top-water fly with a concave face can be difficult to pick up off the water, especially at longer distances. Before beginning your back cast, eliminate any slack line, and raise the rod slowly, lifting most of the line and leader off the surface first. Once the rod is at the 11 o'clock position, cock the wrist back and apply a short but powerful single haul to finally lift the fly off the water for the back cast.

fly and deadening the action. You should also use a heavy, stiff-butt, monofilament leader of six to eight feet with at least 20-pound-test tippet, to facilitate turnover and prevent the fly from falling to one side as it lands. Abrasion-resistant fluorocarbon is not recommended for top-water muskie flies: It sinks faster than nylon monofilament, dulling action during the retrieve.

Top-water poppers can be fished with a wide variety of rhythms depending on the conditions and aggressiveness of the fish. Like streamer fishing, being creative with your retrieve just might be what it takes to trigger a fish.

Variations on the Muskie Top-Water Retrieve

Popping Techniques:

• Cast and let the fly settle … wait a moment…then give the fly one *BIG POP.* Wait for another moment, look for fish or signs of fish, and then begin a moderately-paced sweep-and-strip retrieve all the way back to the boat.

A muskie popper in action: The explosive boil of a muskie popper is the key to attracting fish and making them strike.

• Cast and let the fly settle … then begin with a slow, then increasingly faster sweep-and-strip retrieve until you reach the boat. Tip: you can go only so fast with most top-water flies before loosing an effective pop. When you reach this point, maintain it for the duration of the retrieve.

• Cast and let the fly settle … then begin popping with a steady but extra hard and long sweep and strip, making the fly move side to side and put up a larger-than-normal wake—and a much louder and obnoxious noise.

Teasing 'em up: Keep the popper moving aggressively along the surface with a steady, faster paced rhythm and minimal pauses between each sweep-and-strip retrieve. Note the large wake created as the fly pushes water.

Chugging Techniques:

• Cast and let the fly settle … begin a slower-paced, steady retrieve with only a slight sweep and strip, making the fly chug quietly instead of popping loudly: *chug, chug, chug, chug*. Tip: This approach works best in extremely calm conditions where the noise of a top-water fly is more noticeable.

• Cast and let the fly settle … then begin "walking the dog" by using the rod tip and body position to change the retrieve angle and swing the fly from side to side as it chugs along steady and slow.

• Any combination of all these techniques.

While the top-water fly is less versatile than a streamer, it's still an important part of your muskie-fishing arsenal. Although the hookup percentage is not as good, the top-water fly is an excellent choice for searching the water and locating active fish. I've used this approach on many occasions to find—and sometimes miss fish—only to come back at a different time and catch them on a streamer. This is especially true in the warm-water months from late spring through early fall when muskies are often shallow and aggressive, making them more susceptible to a surface presentation. It's also a perfect fly to throw at night and in dark or stained water where visibility is an issue. When an aggressive fish won't eat your streamer but keeps chasing the fly to the boat, casting a top-water fly right away or later in the day to the same fish may be just the ticket to prompt a strike.

A spot on a spot: Whether it's a weed bed, rock pile, or stump field, muskies often hold very tight to cover. Specialized retrieves targeting these spots are the best way to pull them out and make them eat.

The sheer excitement of seeing a muskie hit or chase a fly on top can make it difficult to set the hook properly. The way these fish blast a popper and the natural urge to strike when you see a fish hit is simply too great for even the most experienced anglers to resist. How to do this effectively is covered in detail in Chapter 9, but always remember to keep your line tight and the rod tip pointed at the fly. Wait a moment until you see the fish turn and/or feel the fish pull line before strip-striking and then lifting the rod to set the hook.

Top-water fishing can also be frustrating when the fly doesn't act exactly as you want on each cast. See the sidebar on page 154 for a few helpful tips to make your top-water presentations more effective.

Weeds, Rocks, and Wood: Specialized Streamer and Top-Water Presentations for Lakes and Rivers

Depending on the specific muskie structure you fish throughout the season, you'll be presented with many different opportunities requiring a wide variety of specialized retrieves. In a broad sense, when the water is cold in the early spring and late fall—temperatures below 60° Fahrenheit—your presentations should be low and slow. Although muskies have been known to hit a top-water fly just about any time of year, during these times it's usually best to present the fly as close as possible to their comfort zone to entice a strike. In the late spring, summer, and early fall months, when water temperatures climb to 70° or 80°, your fly should ride higher in the water column—or on the surface—with a much faster and aggressive strip on the retrieve. Once fish zero in on a fly in these water conditions, they often move a long way to hit or follow. In the late-fall months with dropping water temperatures and slowing metabolism, a lower and slower presentation is generally more productive.

When muskies are located on, in, or near specific structure such as weeds, rocks, and wood, I use a number of specialized retrieves to cover the water as thoroughly as possible. Because muskies often hold very tight to structure—a spot on a spot—the distinct advantage of these techniques is that they increase the overall visibility of the fly, always a challenge when fly fishing for muskie. Once seen, these presentations trigger reaction strikes with a combination of movement, sight, and sound. See the following illustrations for graphic examples of how to exicute these retrieves.

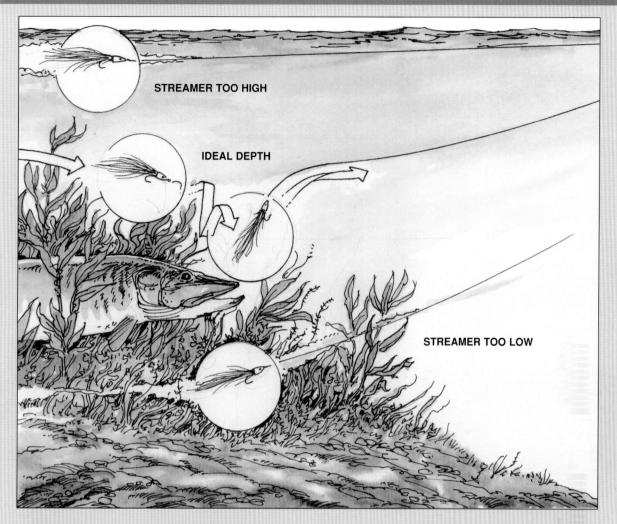

STREAMER TOO HIGH

IDEAL DEPTH

STREAMER TOO LOW

SOME OF THE BEST FLY-ROD OPPORTUNITIES of the year occur in early spring on lakes, flowages, and reservoirs when muskies are just beginning to feed again following the spawn. At this time of year, smaller battle-scarred male muskies are often found in shallow water close to spawning areas, often suspended or close to the bottom. As the water warms, muskies of all sizes begin to feed more aggressively, chasing smaller, freshly-hatched baitfish now abundant around emergent weeds. Fish seek out the newest emerald-green weed growth—the greener the better—and remain there until the weeds change color. Later in the fall, muskies are again found back in the shallows in search of forage hiding in and around weeds. Look for any remaining green weeds that provide both oxygen and cover.

When fishing muskies in submerged vegetation, I like to use the tick-and-twitch technique with a floating or sink-tip line and a small streamer pattern fished just over the tops of any shallow, green weed cover. The best approach is to make a cast and allow the fly to sink until it's just above any visible green weeds. Using moderate to fast-paced strips of 12 to 24 inches, retrieve it as close as possible to weed growth. Ideally, your fly will occasionally "tick" the tops of the weeds during the retrieve, even pulling or bending a

few along the way. Weed growth is rarely uniform in height, so you'll undoubtedly get hung up a few times. But the temporary inconvenience of having to clean off your fly every few casts is well worth the intended result.

Frequent pauses and twitches of the fly using the jerk-and-strip technique are also quite effective in getting the fish's attention. The combination of ticking and twitching action is an excellent trigger for fish lying deep within or along the edge of weeds that may not notice a fly swimming higher in the water column.

Tip: If you wait too long and let your fly sink all the way to the bottom, you're bound to get hung up. The best way to avoid this is to use a check haul to hit your intended target and begin retrieving very slowly allowing the fly to sink in the water column. When you reach the desired depth just above the weeds, start stripping faster throughout the balance of your retrieve, steering the fly with your rod tip toward any green weeds you think look promising. Remember: It's okay if you tick some weeds along the way—that's the point! Simply speed up your strip whenever you think you're about to get seriously snagged.

STRIKE ZONE JUST AS FLY
RIPS THROUGH WEEDS

AS SURPRISING AS IT MAY SOUND, intentionally retrieving and "ripping" a streamer through weeds is an excellent way to trigger a strike from a muskie. This technique works best in the summer months, when weed growth is at maximum density and height and muskies are most aggressive due to higher water temperatures. It also works well in stained or dark water where fish may not be seeing or sensing your fly as much as you'd like. Whatever the conditions, the sudden commotion created when a fly rips or hits weeds can move a fish to strike when a free-swimming streamer fly is not yielding results.

Start ripping the streamer by scanning the water for any visible weed edges, clumps, breaks, or pockets. Cast the fly to the intended target using a check haul to control the distance. As you begin your retrieve, steer the fly using your rod tip so it heads directly for the weed structure you want to fish. Just as the fly is about to hit the weeds you've selected, make an exaggerated long, fast strip combined with a forceful downward sweep of the rod to actually rip the fly through the submerged vegetation—very much like a jerk-and-strip retrieve.

This technique can be difficult to execute. With a fly rod it's hard to generate the speed and power necessary to

actually break free *and* end up with a clean fly. On the other hand, if a fish is following or lying just inside or below the weed line, the action created by a fly breaking violently through the weeds is often too much for a muskie to resist. Look for strikes as soon as the fly gets to the other side, even if it has picked up some weeds. This technique also works especially well if the weeds are silt laden and appear to "blow up" when hit by the fly.

Tip: Although quite effective in submerged muskie weeds such as coontail and cabbage, ripping streamers is not recommended when fishing emergent weeds such as lily pads or reeds. As you'll quickly find out if you ever snag a lily pad or single reed stalk, these tough plants thrive in hard bottoms and have root systems like small trees. It's virtually impossible to rip a fly through them without getting hung up. Using a weed guard may help, but you must slow your retrieve when approaching any potential snag—never a good thing when muskie fishing.

ALLOW FLY TO DROP BETWEEN WEED CLUMPS.

LUSH, SUBMERGENT AND EMERGENT WEED GROWTH normally reaches maximum height and density in the summer. As ambush hunters, muskies in lakes, flowages, and reservoirs love to use this shallow-water structure for cover and foraging opportunities. The same holds true for submerged and standing wood, especially when close to deeper water. Whether along the shoreline or on top of a saddle, weeds and wood provide a ideal targets for the fly fisher. To effectively fish this thick cover, you'll need to get the fly down in the muskie's zone even if it means risking a few snags along the way.

An effective approach for fishing dense cover is to jig the fly using a floating line and a weighted streamer or Clouser Minnow. While many streamer patterns are suitable for this technique, I particularly like those with lots of flash and shimmer such as the Flash-Tail Whistler or the Muskie Cowgirl. Start by casting as close as possible to your intended target using a check haul to control the distance. In this situation, it always pays to keep your casts short to maintain control and avoid snags. Begin stripping immediately to keep the fly riding above the weeds or wood.

Assuming you don't have a follow, when you reach an obvious ambush point—a clean break in the weed line or a gap between wood downfalls—pause the fly briefly allowing it to fall freely. As it drops, use the rod tip and stripping hand to jig and twitch the fly adding further attraction. As soon as the fly reaches the bottom, or as close as you dare go, get tight and apply a quick strip to dart and pull the fly out, up, and then over the structure you're fishing. Ticking weeds along the way is alright so long as the fly remains relatively clean. Continue stripping and jigging the fly with each opportunity you see until you reach the boat.

Depending on the depth and clarity, a fish that hits a jigging fly may do so undetected due to the slow speed and inevitable slack created on the drop. Always maintain control as the fly drops using a slow strip to take up any slack. Watch closely for signs of a fish—a flash or a boil. In dark water sometimes abrupt line movement is your only indication of a strike.

Tip: This technique is perfect for a weighted Clouser pattern that is essentially a jig fly. This fly pattern tends to ride hook up, reducing the amount of snags in tight cover. You can also adapt any streamer pattern to work for this situation with a small split-shot on the head to provide front-end weight and jigging action.

KEEP STREAMER IN THE FILM THROUGH ENTIRE RETRIEVE.

THIS EFFECTIVE TECHNIQUE is one of the many adapted from the conventional muskie hunter's game book. It requires the fly angler to retrieve the streamer at a high rate of speed, creating a distinct and noisy wake as it displaces water across the surface.

This technique works best in warmwater conditions of late spring and summer with more aggressive, surface-oriented fish. Calm water is generally preferable; it's tough to move the fly very fast against any wave action on the surface. That said, when you encounter a wind-blown point, saddle, or shallow rock bar—especially one with high weeds within inches of the surface—it's well worth trying this technique for a few casts. I also use the bulging technique whenever fish are forced by reduced water clarity to rely more on motion and noise than sight such as during the mid-summer algae bloom.

To bulge a streamer for muskies, select a bushy, buoyant fly tied with less-absorbent materials such as bucktail or synthetics. Make a normal cast, and stop the fly short in mid-air using a check haul. This forces the fly to hit the water with a noisy splash, one hopes drawing the attention of any fish nearby. Begin your fast retrieve as soon the fly hits the water to prevent it from sinking. Use your rod tip to lift the fly on the surface, and then lower it as you strip aggressively so the fly swims just below the surface in a straight line. Ideally, your streamer should be "in the film" the entire retrieve, pushing water and leaving a wide, distinct wake. If this isn't prompting any action, using the rod tip to move the fly in an erratic or zigzag pattern during the retrieve can also be effective.

As the fly gets closer to the boat you'll find you don't need to strip as fast to keep the fly riding on the surface— *but it must never slow down.* If a fish follows to the boat, try using the lift and sweep technique to accelerate the fly and change direction at close range.

Tip: Using a two-handed saltwater retrieve can be effective to maximize your retrieve speed with this technique, but it's extremely difficult—nearly impossible, really—to achieve a solid muskie hook-set using this approach. Rather than miss a fish, I prefer to use a fast single-hand strip and then the lift-and-sweep at close ranges. As with any high-speed retrieve, the hit itself can be violent. Be prepared at all times to set the hook using the strip and the rod tip if necessary.

PAUSE AND THEN TWITCH!

WHEN MUSKIES GET MOODY and won't respond to the normal retrieve techniques, I always give the pause-and-twitch technique a try to trigger a strike. Although most conventional muskie anglers would never, *ever* stop a lure mid-retrieve, over the years this has proven to be a surprisingly effective finesse technique with a fly rod and non-aggressive fish. Pull it out of your quiver any time of the year. It works during every season and all kinds of water but especially well with pressured fish and/or when fish are not aggressive due to cold fronts or other difficult conditions. You'll know it's time when you see fish repeatedly follow but only nip at the tail or open and close their mouth without actually striking the fly. Most anglers would eventually leave these frustrating fish and find another "player." Fly fishers, however, still stand a chance if only a small one.

To do this effectively, simply cast and retrieve your fly normally in open water or over visible structure. When the fly approaches the boat and is just visible—instead of speeding up and going straight into a figure-8—give it a fast, short strip. Let it pause. The hackles, hair, or other material will flair noticeably as it drops and flutters. Add a few follow up twitches with the rod tip while the fly drops or suspends before resuming your retrieve. The idea here is

to make the fly look as vulnerable as possible even as it moves *very* slowly.

When you stop the fly, continue stripping in any slack with short micro-strips. And be ready for an unseen fish that may be following and only needed this subtle trigger to strike. In stained or dirty water you may only see the fly disappear—or you won't see or even feel the fish until you strip. In this case, strike anyway when you see anything unusual with the fly or the water. When the fly is very close to the boat you'll probably see the fish first so be prepared with a low rod tip to set the hook properly with a strip-set or tip-set. When a fish eventually hits, it may turn and run immediately or simply stop in the water while it figures out what happened. This is an easy way to loose a fish! Be careful to read the strike behavior before striking with this retrieve.

Tip: This technique can be used quite effectively with a non-aggressive, slow-moving but following fish or, as a regular part of your muskie presentation lineup. Keep in mind that it is not necessary to see a fish when using this technique. More than a few times I've experienced an unseen fish—following from far behind or below—charge out of nowhere and eat when all I did was simply stop the fly and use the deadly pause-and-twitch.

The best way to fly fish most lily pads and reed beds is to position the boat within casting distance and cast parallel or perpendicular, retrieving the fly as close as possible along the edge. Keep your casts tightly spaced to make sure you cover the water thoroughly. As you make your casts from this position, always take full advantage of any snag-free open pockets and narrow lanes within the weed line. Targeting small, isolated lily-pad or reed patches away from the main bed is also a good approach: Muskies often use these secondary points to ambush prey.

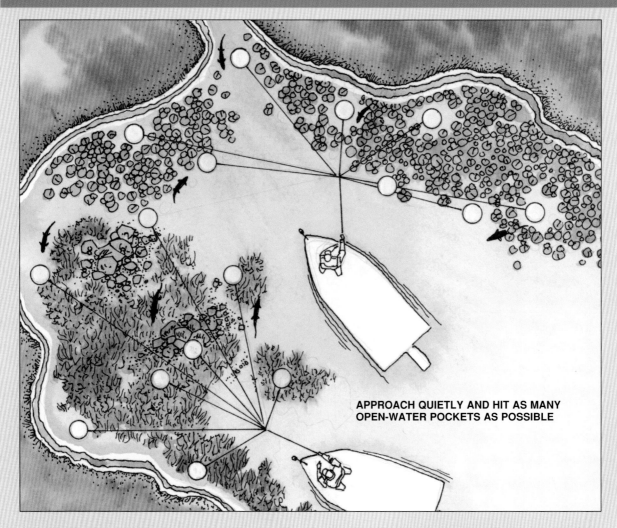

APPROACH QUIETLY AND HIT AS MANY OPEN-WATER POCKETS AS POSSIBLE

THIS FUN AND PRODUCTIVE streamer and top-water technique reminds me most of bass bugging or pocket-water fishing on a trout stream with a streamer or dry fly. It can be used throughout the season but is particularly effective in the summer months on lakes, flowages, river backwaters, and reservoirs when weed growth is typically lush and full. While you probably won't see them until they hit or spook, muskies love to hold deep inside or tight to heavy "slop" cover such as cabbage, lily pads, reeds, or milfoil. Depending on the water, weather conditions, and location, each of these various weed types provide good cover, shade, and forage opportunities throughout the season.

When you approach an area of dense surface cover, keep an eye out for any open-water pockets, lanes, and gaps from a foot to several feet across. These may be located right in the middle of a dense area of cover or along the shoreline in between the first weed growth and the bank. Once you spot a likely target, get as close as possible to the area you want to hit without risking a spooked fish (you'll know it when you start to see large or small wakes disturbing the vegetation.) Take your time to get in position and make a targeted cast to the very edge of the area you want to fish.

As with most shallow-water streamer presentations, begin the streamer-slop retrieve before the fly even hits the water using a check haul to keep it straight and clean. This approach cuts down on snags before your fly has a chance to be effective. It also makes a noticeable splash alerting any fish in the immediate area. As soon as the fly enters the open pocket you want to fish, give it one sharp, pulsating strip. Use the rod tip to impart additional twitch and flutter action to the fly as it drops. Streamer patterns that incorporate a lot of naturally breathable materials, combined with synthetic flash and sparkle, work quite well for this technique. If a fish doesn't take right away, resume your retrieve for as long as possible or use a long line lift to pull the streamer out of the hole before it gets snagged.

THE SLOP-FISHING TECHNIQUE can also be used successfully with a top-water popper. In this case, the fly rod is a perfect tool for targeting casting to ring-tight pockets where muskies often hold. In most cases, you must hit the pocket square on or you'll get snagged and ruin the all-important first pop. If a fish doesn't move right away, make a few more pops before picking up to cast again using a long line lift.

Depending on the density of the surrounding weeds, you may not see the fish as it rushes forward to nail the fly. Other times, the entire weed bed will erupt with a muskie on the end of your line! Typically, the fish will not have to move very far so always be prepared with a low rod and a tight line to set the hook *after you feel the fish*.

It's also possible to fish a light, deer-hair popper or diver with a mono weed guard right through the middle of thickest, matted slop. With this technique, use a softer forward power stroke and cast the fly *gently* over the slop keeping a look out for any logs or other surface obstructions that might prevent a clean retrieve. Allow the fly to settle in the water—or on a lily pad—and begin a very slow steady, retrieve. Instead of popping the fly right away, steer and slide it with long, smooth strips and a high rod tip

directly over and around any vegetation. If you do this slowly enough, you'll find the light fly and the weed guard work quite well to avoid snagging. When the fly reaches a promising opening or gap in the weeds, recover any slack and give the fly a sharp, hard pop with the strip and rod tip. If you're lucky, a fish will hit it right away. If not, you may actually see a fish move from several feet away, so be prepared to hold tight and pop once more as the fish approaches. Assuming you don't get snagged, you can fish a fly quite a long way using this technique. Strikes often come at the open water edge where the weed line ends.

Tip: Slop fishing with a streamer or top-water fly is best done with a full floating line and a short, stiff leader of four to five feet. With the entire line suspended on the surface you'll have a much easier time stripping and lifting for the next cast. As you might expect, a sinking line of any kind in this situation tends to tangle immediately in the slop causing all kinds of unwanted headaches for the muskie fly fisher.

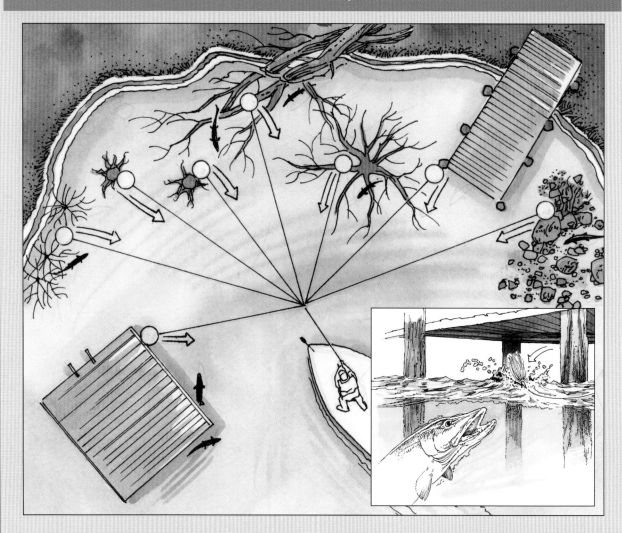

THIS SUMMERTIME TECHNIQUE is specifically designed for fishing exposed and submerged rock and wood structure such as large boulders, logs, downfalls, stumps, or piers. This prime structure is always worth targeting and common in muskie waters throughout the country including lakes, rivers, flowages, and reservoirs. Clear-water conditions are ideal for this technique. Obviously it's best if you can actually see the subsurface structure you want to fish to avoid getting snagged. If the water is stained or dirty due to algae bloom, this is still an effective method—just be prepared to get snagged more often.

Once you spot a likely looking piece of rock or wood, take your time and cast the fly—streamer or top-water—toward the intended target using a check haul to control the distance. Bring the fly down loud and hard. Casting the fly sidearm with a skip cast is one good way to place the fly close to or directly under exposed structure and produce a fish-attracting splash. If you should hit the structure itself, don't worry; the noise of the collision alone can be helpful to trigger a fish lurking close by.

Another approach is to cast a few feet past the structure. As the fly approaches the target, speed up your retrieve. Stop it abruptly, using the rod tip to direct the fly along the way. The force of the strip-and-stop action bumps the fly into the structure, making its presence more noticeable to a fish lying in wait.

Although it is hard to avoid the occasional snag—and damaged fly—a muskie sitting in ambush beside a boulder, under a deadfall, below a pier support, or next to a stump will definitely know your fly is there by sensing vibration alone. As soon as structure contact is achieved, speed up your retrieve back to the boat while looking out for a following fish or a strike.

Tip: Single-hook fly fishers have an advantage when using this technique. In fact, conventional muskie fishers normally switch from a treble to a single hook when fishing heavy weeds or wood with this and other heavy-cover techniques. A stiff mono weed guard on the fly may help to avoid potential snags along the way but is no guarantee you won't get snagged.

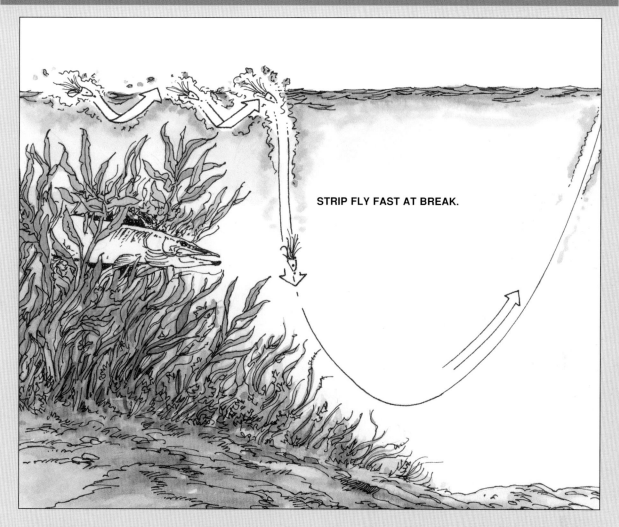

STRIP FLY FAST AT BREAK.

DISTINCT WEED EDGES CLOSE TO DEEP WATER provide perfect ambush points for muskies, especially in the summer months when fish are more aggressive and weed growth is at maximum height. The break dance technique targets these hot spots using a floating/diving popper pattern and a sink-tip line.

When using this technique, I like to use a large, noisy diver pattern such as a Muskie Snake Diver or Rainy's Fish-Head Diver with a leader of six to eight feet. A shorter integrated sinking-head line such as the Teeny Pat Ehlers Mini-Tip Plus is also helpful since it allows the diver to float yet still has plenty of weight to plunge it over the edge. Leader length is important here to keep the fly popping effectively on the surface and then pull it as deep as possible along the weed edge. Use a leader that is about a foot longer than the depth you're fishing to provide the best action.

When you see an obvious weed edge or break line with weeds within a few feet of the surface, position the boat along the outside edge and make a cast over the main body of weeds well beyond the break. Allow the sinking-head to sink to the desired depth, and then begin popping the diver over the weeds back to the boat toward deeper water. With a long enough leader, the diver should pop and dive close to the surface without snagging weeds. As soon as the fly reaches the weed edge, lower the rod tip and give it a forceful sweep and strip using the sinking-head line and the angled shape of the diver head to pull the fly deep and straight down along the face of the break. Keep the fly moving and pulsating underwater at the desired depth using faster strips and the rod tip as it moves.

Muskies often hit the fly as soon as it dives over the weed edge but may follow for a while before hitting closer to the boat. Always keep a look out for these fish, and if possible convert them with a figure-8.

The real beauty of the break-dance technique is that it allows you to effectively fish the entire water column in the same cast, from shallow weeds to weed edges and bottom structure. When fish are lurking deep in the weeds, a loud and abrupt rip over the edge is often just the ticket to pull them out and trigger a reaction strike.

Tip: This technique also works well when fishing rock, sand, or gravel points close to deeper water. While some weed growth or wood structure is always preferred, muskies using these areas for ambush throughout the year are more likely to hit your fly when it moves abruptly down (or up) an edge. As you complete your retrieve, increase the speed to tick deeper weed tops and/or other structure that you may have missed with the normal retrieve.

MUSKIES ARE NOTORIOUS FOR FOLLOWING a lure or fly a long distance without striking, even in deep water where you can't possibly see them until it's too late. Although they may take any time during the retrieve, the last few feet are critical to triggering a deeply following fish to strike. This technique is adapted from a conventional crank-bait technique where the angler literally "rips" the lure up vertically toward the side of the boat at the end of each cast. It also works well on very windy days when it's often difficult to maintain contact with your fly during the retrieve.

To do this with a fly, make a long cast using a sinking-head shooting line, and allow the fly to sink to the desired depth. As the fly and line are sinking, lower your rod tip into the water so at least half the rod is now submerged (Figure 1). You'll probably need to bend at the waist and lean over the side of the boat to do this properly. With your rod pointed down at a 45-degree angle, start stripping line aggressively with long and/or short strips, throwing slack into the boat behind you (Figures 2 and 3). As you near the end of your retrieve and you can see the sinking head is about to reach the rod tip (usually with a color change), make one last, long strip. Lift the rod upward with a sweeping motion using your wrist for leverage against the fighting butt (Figure 4). This maneuver results in a very fast upward "fleeing" movement of the fly and is often just the action needed to trigger a deep following fish to hit.

Tip: When a fish hits at close range using this technique, you'll need to use a tip-set, or let the fish turn before setting the hook with a very short back-set or strip-strike.

SHALLOW TO DEEP RETRIEVE

DEEP TO SHALLOW RETRIEVE

THIS COLDWATER STREAMER RETRIEVE is an effective approach in the spring or fall when muskies are suspended close to deeper structure or right on the bottom. Depending on the depth of the water, when bottom bouncing a streamer for muskies, it's best to use a short leader of four to six feet and an integrated sinking head of 200 to 300 grains or heavier to get the fly to the maximum depth for most of the retrieve. In shallow water, use a lighter sink-tip or floating line and longer leader of six to nine feet to insure your fly is getting down. You're bound to lose a few flies when fishing close to the bottom, so this technique obviously works best over cleaner substrate such as mud, sand, rock, or gravel devoid of significant snags.

To employ this technique, make a cast and let the fly, leader, and sinking head sink all the way to the bottom. As it does keep a tight line and be ready for strikes during the drop. Maintaining contact with your fly using micro-strips during the drop will help to detect fish and prevent potential snags. When the fly reaches the desired depth just off the bottom, keep your rod tip low to the water and begin a slow, steady retrieve using short strips of three to 10 inches combined with frequent and distinct pauses. Adding an occasional twitch with the rod tip or a longer, faster pull off the bottom never hurts to draw attention to your fly. Placing your rod tip

completely under the water helps to keep a tighter line and avoid slack between strips. Once the fly reaches the boat, watch for follows and be prepared to figure-8. If the water is deep enough, I recommend using the deep-rip technique to trigger any unseen fish before the fly reaches boatside.

Bottom bouncing with a weighted Muskie Clouser or other muskie streamer with a weed guard is also an effective deep-water approach when combined with an integrated sinking-head line. Ideally, the weighted fly will drag and bounce along the bottom kicking up debris but remain relatively snag free due to the weed guard or hook riding up.

In shallow-water situations, bottom bouncing with a lighter sink-tip line and diver pattern such as a Muskie Snake can also be effective in triggering strikes. By increasing the speed of your retrieve, you can pull the diver deep in shallow water, causing it to scrape and dig along the bottom. Between strips, the natural buoyancy of a deer-hair diver causes it to rise enticingly off the bottom and avoid potential snags.

The strike of a muskie using the slower bottom bouncing retrieve may be as subtle as a bluegill's tap-tap-tap, a heavy snag-like dead weight, or a violent jerk of the rod tip. All are exciting ways to hook a fish and will warm you up quickly on a cold day.

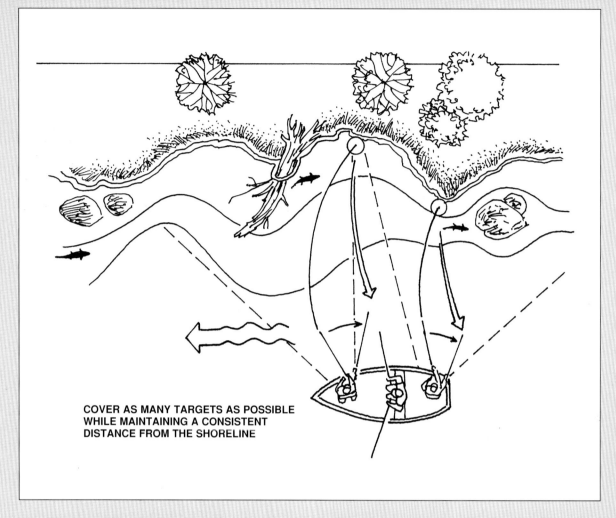

COVER AS MANY TARGETS AS POSSIBLE
WHILE MAINTAINING A CONSISTENT
DISTANCE FROM THE SHORELINE

THE NAME OF THIS TECHNIQUE alludes to the popular fall sport of trout fishing and bird shooting on the same day. When muskie fishing with a fly, the "blast" part is not from a gun but from the fish when it blows up the water and inhales your fly! The cast-and-blast technique works best when drift fishing fast-water or rapids sections on a small- to medium-sized river. Muskies in rivers love to hold in shallow, protected water tight to the bank and/or small pockets near midstream structure, so you need to cover as much of this structure as possible as you move with multiple, targeted, quick casts.

Unlike open-water lake fish that have plenty of time to examine your fly, with fast water river fish it's not always necessary to retrieve the fly all the way to the boat to trigger a strike—unless, of course, it misses or follows. Instead, cast your streamer or top-water fly tight to the bank or other shallow structure using a check-haul to control the distance and alert the fish. As soon as the fly lands, begin stripping, twitching, or popping aggressively. You typically don't have much water to cover in this situation so be sure to make the first move your best effort. Watch for signs of a fish either from below or nearby before you pick up. If you think you spotted a fish, depending on the speed of the current

and abundance of snags, you can buy some time by using the current and a downstream mend to keep the fly moving parallel to shore before picking up again.

If nothing shows after the first few strips, pick up immediately using a long-line pickup technique with a quick, single haul. On the next cast, scan the water for the next target downstream and continue casting and blasting until the current slows enough to make a longer retrieve necessary. This is fast-paced fishing. And it's quite exciting, especially when your casting rhythm is suddenly interrupted by a muskie ambushing the fly as soon as it hits the water.

Tip: As when trout fishing with a streamer, it's best to maintain a consistent distance from the shoreline while floating downstream so you can continue hitting targets without continually readjusting the length of your casts for each spot. If a fish swirls on your fly but you don't connect for some reason, then by all means continue stripping or popping the fly to the boat and figure-8 if necessary.

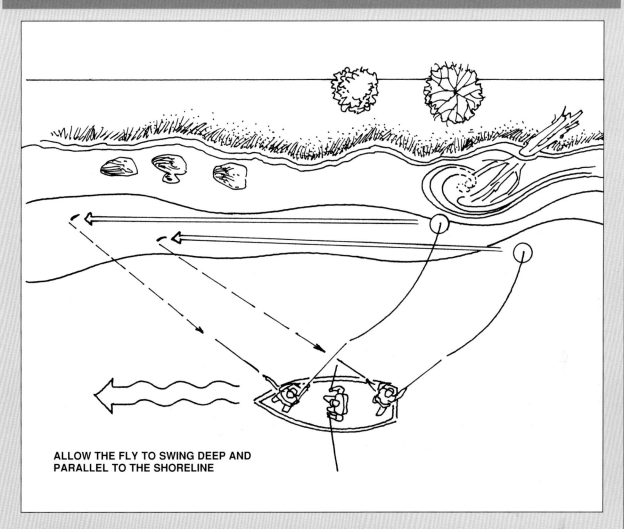

ALLOW THE FLY TO SWING DEEP AND PARALLEL TO THE SHORELINE

MUSKIES HOLDING ALONG DEEPER SECONDARY SEAMS require a lower and slower presentation to draw their attention. Shallow fish may also follow the fly off a break, and then nail it as it reaches the main current. I like to use a sinking integrated-head line such as a Teeny T-300 for these situations to keep the fly in the muskie's zone for as long as possible.

When swinging a fly for these deeper fish keep the boat positioned just outside the deep break and maintain a consistent distance. Cast the fly directly across stream toward the shoreline using a check haul to control the distance. Depending on the depth near shore, you might have to begin stripping immediately to avoid getting hung up before you reach the desired seam. Whenever the fly touches bottom, simply lift the rod tip and pick up your retrieve speed to keep it swinging smoothly. As the fly swings into the seam, allow the line to move with the current while applying short strips and twitching and pumping with the rod tip.

Ideally, the fly should move downstream parallel to the shore or structure break, providing a side profile to the fish. If the current allows—and your oarsman agrees—you can also use the oars to pull back away from the bank extending the drift. This also allows the fly to cover the typically deeper middle section of the river where fish often hold. Let the current swing the fly below the boat before finishing off your retrieve with a deep rip or a figure-8.

Tip: As you make your way downstream keep an eye out for fish-holding midstream structure such as logs, large boulders, weed beds, and deep holes. While shorelines are always a tempting target, depending on water levels, muskies may hold in the middle of the river as well as along the shore.

CONVERTING FOLLOWS

"Muskies ... all other fish are just bait."
—Anonymous

SEEING A MUSKIE FOLLOW YOUR FLY TO THE BOAT—and not strike—is one of the most exciting (and frustrating) things about this sport. There is simply nothing in the world of fly fishing like the long, dark shape of a muskie slowly rising from the depths or one that pushes a V-wake behind your fly, its dorsal fin and tail slicing the water, ready to pounce. The same can be said for a hard-charging "hot" fish that comes out of nowhere and takes your fly just inches from the rod tip on a well executed boatside figure-8 maneuver.

This common yet unique behavior is both a blessing and curse for all muskie fishers. A blessing because you can finally see the fish you're after, and a curse because it usually happens when you least expect it. Needless to say, a following fish is not a caught fish. It may or may not take your fly depending on how well you handle the situation. Whatever the case, a following muskie is without a doubt one of your best chances to actually hook a fish if you know exactly how to take advantage of this great opportunity. In fact, whether you're casting a lure or a fly it's fair to say as many as half of your fish may be caught on a follow within the last 10 feet of your retrieve. On some highly pressured lakes with more "educated" fish, the percentage of fish caught on follows can be much higher.

Exactly why a muskie follows has been the subject of speculation for as long there have been muskie fishers. For many anglers it simply doesn't make sense that a fish this big would hesitate to eat anything that comes its way. Yet it happens all the time. As fly fishers we're easily reminded of the "false rise" scenario common with trout, steelhead, and salmon. As with all these species, we'll probably never know exactly what triggers a following response but our inquisitive minds can't resist trying to figure out why.

Based on my own experience and after speaking with many great muskie guides, anglers, and biologists, I think it's safe to say this unique behavior has something to do with a strong territorial or feeding reaction combined with a general lack of fear and innate curiosity as the biggest predator on the block. Bottom line: these fish don't get big without being smart!

The word "follow" is commonly used by all muskie fishers to describe several different fish behaviors. Sometimes you'll see only a short, standing wave of water as the fish stalks the fly from below.

Other times it's much more obvious with the muskie's entire back and tail undulating on the surface with its nose glued to your fly. And sometimes you won't see anything until at the last minute a muskie suddenly appears out of nowhere, follows, and then hits like a heat-seeking missile.

One thing is for sure: A follow from a muskie can happen at anytime during your retrieve, from the moment the fly hits the water until the time you pick up for the next cast. The simple fact that muskies like to follow means it's critical you pay attention and watch carefully for signs of a fish on each and very retrieve. The last thing you want to be heard saying as a muskie fisher is, "Oh, there goes one."

One of the many unique and exciting aspects of muskie fishing is that even with a fly it is not all that unusual to have up to a dozen or more follows on a given day. Sometimes the same fish will follow on consecutive casts or at different times of the day. On really good water in the prime "following" seasons of late spring and summer, I've actually had as many as 30 or more different fish follow my fly on the same lake. Many guides I know have had similar days with both lures and flies—and still not hooked a single fish. Other times you may see only a fish or two follow but still hook several anyway. As you can imagine, it's always great to see a muskie following your fly but it can get pretty frustrating playing this aquatic game of cat and mouse when they simply won't eat. To make up for this, muskie fishers always include this information in their report of the day's fishing results: "Hooked two and saw six fish."

For as long as anglers have fished for muskie they've been trying to figure out the best way to convert a follow into a solid strike. This fascinating behavior has led to many different theories and techniques over the years as to the most effective approach. Like

The art of the figure-8: Fooling a muskie on the fly with this time-honored technique takes practice and patience. It's an exciting game of cat and mouse even if the fish won't eat.

casting a crab fly for permit, the fly is important but it's mostly a matter of the right technique and the right fish. When understood and executed properly, the highly specialized methods described in this chapter will increase your odds of success if the fish gives you a chance.

The Figure-8

The most common angler response to a following muskie is the "figure-8." This classic and time-honored conventional technique keeps the fly or lure moving at close range by extending the life of each retrieve with a smooth, wide sweep of the rod underwater as if drawing an "8" pattern with the rod tip.

The main goal of the figure-8 is to keep the fish focused on the fly or lure—instead of the boat—long enough to trigger a strike. Often the strike will come quickly as the fly or lure speeds up or changes direction as it reaches the boat or within the first wide turns of the figure-8. Other times the fish may disappear for a moment and then crush the fly or lure just when you've given up all hope. With a really aggressive fish it's often possible to keep the fish motivated for some time and literally walk it back and forth next to the boat like a dog on an imaginary leash. More often than not, a muskie will follow briefly and then spook

or simply lose interest and drop out of sight.

Since you can't always see a following fish clearly due to water and light conditions, most muskie fishers employ the figure-8 on every cast whether they actually see a fish or not. There are many other variations on this theme but the general idea remains the same: Keep the muskie's interest long enough to trigger a boatside strike. When this doesn't work some anglers will cast back immediately with the same or a different fly or lure, usually with a faster or more erratic retrieve. Others mark the spot and leave the fish to try again when conditions are different. All these techniques will work depending on the fish and the day.

Muskie fly fishers can do a number of things with a following fish to duplicate these techniques with both streamers and top water flies. These include the lift-and-sweep, the figure-8, and moving the fly in an L, J, U or O pattern. Since the fly has no real inherent action, however, you are limited by the amount of motion you can create with a short line and your rod tip. One distinct advantage you do have is that the fly rod is an excellent tool for moving the fly at different depths at close range. Certain flies can also be finessed and manipulated at slow speeds not possible with a conventional lure.

It has been said that your chances of successfully

hooking a following fish on a lure are 50/50 at best. This is both the result of an angler not being mentally prepared for a fish after casting all day without any action, and the fact it's difficult to hook any fish, much less a muskie, on a short line right off your rod tip. Conventional muskie anglers have the advantage of a very stiff rod and high-speed reel that helps to make up for any momentary loss of concentration. Yet even skilled anglers still miss and lose plenty of fish at close range. Hooking a following fish on a fly rod is even more challenging because the rod is by its very nature much softer at the tip than the butt and your line is controlled by your hands alone. This means you need to be prepared with a tight line and a proper set while at the same time keeping the fish interested by moving your fly with the rod tip.

Despite the difficulty of hooking a fish at close range, there are a number of things you can do to help improve your success rate with a fly rod when converting a follow into a strike:

1. Seeing the fish as early as possible
2. Reading the follow: hot or not?
3. Fly rod lift-and-sweep, figure-8, and L, J, U, and O retrieves
4. Changeups
5. Practice

Ultimately, each of these factors and techniques will determine what you can and should do to successfully convert a follow into a strike. Let's take a look at various following fish scenarios and what you should do with your fly in each instance:

Seeing the Fish

It should go without saying that the earlier you see a fish following your fly, the better the chances you'll have of converting a fish to strike. Yet many anglers have a difficult time understanding this important concept and fail to see fish before it's too late.

As with most sight-fishing in salt water, the earlier you can see a fish, the better prepared you are to

The follow: Seeing a muskie follow your fly is one of the greatest thrills in fly fishing. Riding high with its head, back, and tail fin out of the water, this aggressive fish is definitely hot!

make a good cast, execute a retrieve, and eventually set the hook. As anyone who has fly fished for bonefish knows, it can take some time to learn what the gray ghost looks like on even the shallowest of flats. Once you do learn the tell-tale signs—nervous water, flash of a tail, or a mud—the odds of catching a fish improve markedly. Muskies, while very big fish by freshwater standards, can also be tough to see depending on the water conditions and structure where you fish. Once you figure out what they look like in the water, however, you'll be much better prepared to do whatever it takes to convert a fish to strike.

Whether you're fishing on top or below, as soon as your fly lands in the water, get control of your line and begin scanning the water for signs of a fish. Sunlight, water clarity, and depth play a major role in your ability to see a fish in this situation. Because muskies are often found in stained water, you need to look for minor and major water movement as well as the fish itself. This can be a ripple, wake, splash, or boil from a fish near where your fly just landed or as far as several feet away.

For the record, I've had muskies attack my fly from quite a long distance in shallow water, leaving an obvious roostertail wake across the surface as they charged. Another equally exciting scenario is when an aggressive fish lunges at the fly as soon as it lands, leaving a heart-stopping boil the size of a bathtub. An interested muskie may also "flash" near the fly as soon as it lands—what I like to call a "drive-by"—leaving only a brief indication that a fish is present and about to hit. Keep an eye out for these obvious and ephemeral signs. And be prepared for a hit.

It is not uncommon for a muskie to completely miss the fly during the retrieve—or for the excited angler to miss the fish. When this happens it's essential that you continue with your normal retrieve. Watch closely for the fish. And stay alert for a strike at any time. If no fish follows right away, always keep the fly moving at boatside with a figure-8 just in case. When you're sure no fish has followed, this "miss" is well worth casting to again. You may just get a second chance.

If you don't see any signs of fish immediately after your fly lands in the water, continue with your normal retrieve always watching above and below the water for any signs of fish activity. Notice here I didn't say "watch your fly" but rather watch for fish. This means looking directly behind, below, and around your fly—not always at the fly itself.

In some cases you may clearly see the full body form of a muskie riding high and following your fly. Whenever this happens be sure to keep the fly moving

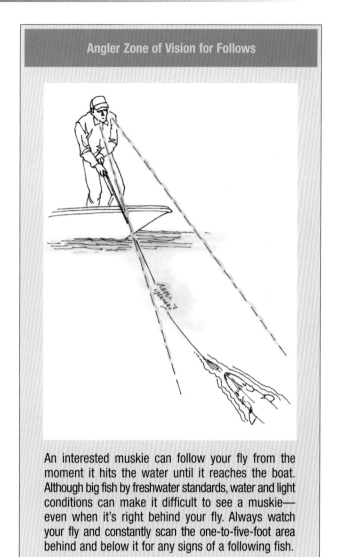

An interested muskie can follow your fly from the moment it hits the water until it reaches the boat. Although big fish by freshwater standards, water and light conditions can make it difficult to see a muskie—even when it's right behind your fly. Always watch your fly and constantly scan the one-to-five-foot area behind and below it for any signs of a following fish.

at a steady or faster pace, and try to convert it to strike with a slight change of direction along the way or at boatside with a figure-8.

Other times you won't see anything but a small standing wave of water or an additional V-wake as the fish pushes water directly behind your fly or from just below. This can be quite subtle with even a big fish depending on how high it is in the water column. It is best described as any additional and unusual nervousness in the water not associated with the fly or any existing wave action. After a long day on the water it's easy to start imagining a push from a muskie, but once you see it you'll know just what to look for. As with nymph fishing, it's always best to err on the side of caution and be ready to strike at the first sign of anything unusual in the vicinity of your fly.

One of the best opportunities for seeing fish is when your fly reaches the very end of the retrieve. At this critical point, even though you may not have seen any visible signs of a fish through the entire

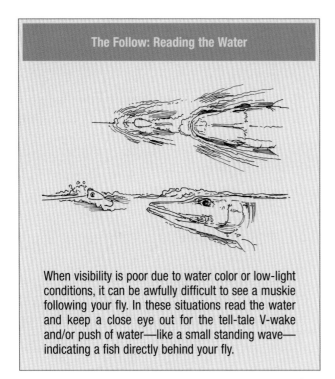

The Follow: Reading the Water

When visibility is poor due to water color or low-light conditions, it can be awfully difficult to see a muskie following your fly. In these situations read the water and keep a close eye out for the tell-tale V-wake and/or push of water—like a small standing wave—indicating a fish directly behind your fly.

retrieve, it's a good bet to perform a figure-8 or similar maneuver, just in case a fish was following slowly or deeply. As you do this, keep a close eye on the area behind and around your fly as well as scanning the wider five-to-10-foot area away from the boat. Muskies are notorious for staying deep or hanging back and then finally showing themselves or striking just as you pull the fly up for the next cast—even after a couple of figure-8s.

While it is entirely possible to hook a fish this way, it's usually not for long. With your rod in the worst position overhead and no leverage to set the hook, the fish will usually shake off well before you even have a chance to get control of your line. Other times, after you pick up for the next cast, a muskie may suddenly appear where your fly was and sit motionless as if waiting for you to feed it. This is a good sign to start using the figure-8.

Even when I'm "damn sure" nothing has followed, I always anticipate a late follow and, more importantly, take full advantage of it by keeping the fly moving for as long a possible close to the boat.

Reading the Follow: Hot or Not?

A muskie follow can be categorized in one of two ways based on its observed aggressiveness: hot or "player" fish and neutral or "curious" fish. Both types of muskie follows can be successfully converted into a strike with a fly but of course a hot and aggressive fish is by far the easiest to convert.

A hot muskie is one that actively stalks your fly all the way to the boat, never giving up. These fish are players. You should do everything you can to get them to strike on their first appearance. Speed and proximity to the fly are the main factors that distinguish these fish. You'll know when a fish is aggressive when it's swimming fast and riding high in the water with its mouth right on the fly. Often its entire back is out of the water as it chases the fly, flipping water with its tail as it pushes forward in perfect rhythm with the fly retrieve.

Other hot-fish behaviors include aggressive opening and closing of the mouth or nipping at the tail of the fly. They might even strike and miss the fly several times as you make your retrieve. While it may be hard to see this depending on the clarity of the water, a really aggressive fish will also appear brightly colored and "lit up" in the water with eyes focused and gills flared ready to eat your fly as if it was its last meal on Earth.

Some late-following fish can also be considered hot but are harder to anticipate and hook. These tough fish typically arrive at boatside "out of the blue" and either hit or miss the fly entirely, disappearing as fast as they came. They might also slash, boil, or strike and miss the fly as you start to pick up for the next cast … just moments after you were certain there were no fish following. I've actually had fish miss the fly and hit the side of the boat or the oar with an audible thud. Some guides I know have even had them jump in the boat. These muskies are definitely HOT!

Slow-moving, neutral, or non-aggressive fish are even tougher to convert. But it's always worth a try. These fish are quite common on highly pressured waters where the presence of other anglers or boat activity has changed their behavior to the point that they always take a long and hard look before they eat. On other waters, these fish simply appear smarter than the rest and exhibit a cautiousness unrelated to the conditions. These "curious" fish typically swim slowly behind the fly or hang well back or below it as if not really that hungry and only mildly interested in your offering. Sometimes they hang and suspend around the boat for a while and even follow again and again only to move away when the fly or the boat gets too close.

Occasionally a non-aggressive fish will take a half-hearted nip at your fly when drawn close to its mouth, but this is far from a solid muskie strike. While it's hard not to try to catch such a passive fish—especially if it's the only fish you've seen all day—the best approach is really to mark the specific area on your map or with a landmark or buoy and come back later when conditions and hope the fish's attitude has changed.

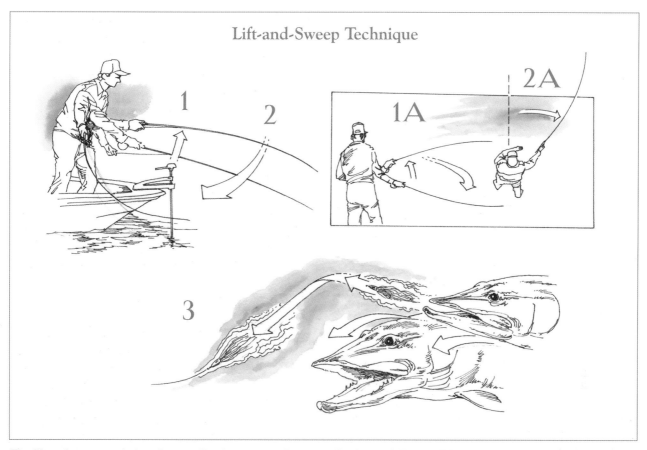

Lift-and-Sweep Technique

The lift-and-sweep technique is one effective way to trigger a strike from a following fish using a streamer. When you see an interested fish behind your fly, immediately strip in any slack and grip the line firmly under you index finger. Keep the fly moving by lifting the rod (Figures 1 and 1A) and then extending your arm and turning your body to sweep the rod sideways (Figure 2 and 2A). The rapid upward movement of the fly, combined with an abrupt change of direction, is often just enough to convert a fish from a follower to an eater (Figure 3).

A hot and aggressive fish is a golden opportunity for a muskie on a fly. The key, as always, is to keep the fly moving and the fish interested. This can be accomplished best using a figure-8 technique or other similar maneuvers as follows:

Fly Rod Lift-and-Sweep, Figure-8, and L, J, U, or O

Streamer Follows

Streamers are an excellent choice of fly for converting a following fish. They cast well in a variety of conditions and can be stripped fast to keep the fish interested. They can also be fished at different levels of the water column allowing you to put your fly exactly where the fish is. Once at the boat, streamers can be manipulated smoothly with a fly rod in various ways to induce a strike. They are in many ways like the fly version of an in-line bucktail spinner, only without the blade. It's no wonder bucktails and other spinners are among the preferred lures for enticing and hooking a following muskie with a figure-8.

Let's assume it's late spring, and you're fan-casting a streamer over an emerging weed bed on a flowage.

There's a nice southwest wind, and the temperatures have been rising since the morning. You've been diligently figure-8ing on each and every cast but have still not seen a single fish. Suddenly you spot the V-wake of a muskie riding high and tight behind your fly. Wherever you are in your retrieve, when you finally encounter an aggressive fish like this following your fly you should always continue stripping your retrieve at the exact same pace or faster.

By all means don't lose focus and slow down, hesitate, or stop your retrieve!

This is the worst thing you can do with a following fish. Nonetheless, it's difficult to avoid, especially when it's a large fish. A muskie that senses any unnatural movement or hesitation in your fly will normally lose interest and spook or sink away.

As you continue stripping the streamer at the same pace or faster, watch the fish closely. Is it moving faster when you strip faster? Many times a fish will kick up water with its tail as it moves through the surface film to eat a fly. This is a sure sign a fish is about to hit. If so, pick up the pace until you reach the boat or hook the fish. Sometimes a slight increase in speed

Figure-8 Technique: Lead Up

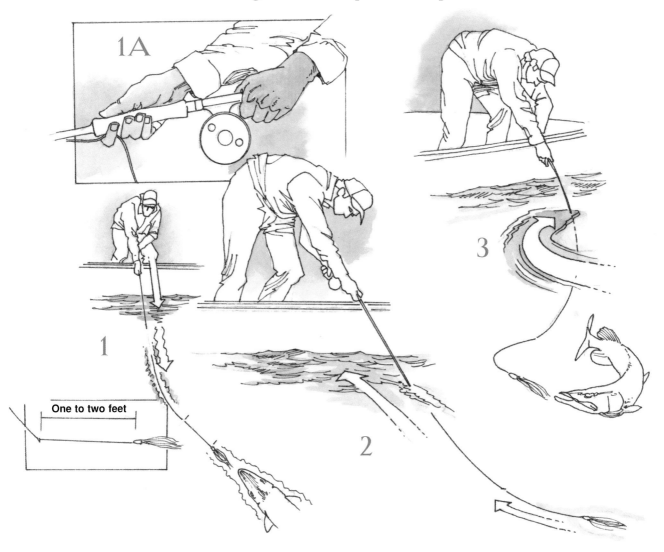

The figure-8 technique is a highly effective—and visually exciting—way to convert a following fish to strike a streamer. Start by stripping in all but one to two feet of leader (Figure 1) and locking the line under your index finger (Figure 1A). Without stopping the fly, place your other hand firmly on the fighting butt (Figure 1A) or handle for leverage, and immediately begin lowering the rod into the water to keep the fly moving deeper and toward the side of the boat (Figure 2). When the rod is nearly vertical underwater, abruptly change direction—to the right (L) or left (J)—by swinging it up toward the surface with an accelerated, wide, arching motion (Figure 3).

combined with a change in direction is all that it takes to induce a strike.

The Lift-and-Sweep

One simple and effective technique for increasing the speed and changing the direction of the fly when it's close to the boat is the lift and sweep (see lift-and-sweep illustration on page 179). This technique is perfect when the fly is running a few feet below the surface with a fish following closely behind. I first learned the secret of this technique while fishing the Florida flats for barracuda. Although I spent the majority of my time chasing permit, I always carried a 'cuda rod just in case a toothy predator got in my way.

Like the muskie, a 'cuda will regularly follow a fly close to the boat but lose interest the moment it slows down. By lifting and then sweeping the rod rapidly to one side once the fish is close, this technique immediately increases the speed and direction of the fly at close range without stripping, often resulting in a violent boatside hit.

The Classic Fly-Rod Figure-8

When the streamer is close to the surface with an aggressive fish following closely behind, the classic figure-8 is usually the most effective way to keep the fish interested and convert a follow. You don't really have much choice here. The fly and the fish are now very

Figure-8 Technique: Follow Through

4

5

One to two feet

6

As the rod tip and fly approach the surface away from the boat (Figure 4), without ever stopping the fly, change direction again by sweeping the rod in an accelerated, wide, turn back down toward the bottom and side of the boat, completing the first half of the figure-8 (Figure 5). If the fish continues to follow, complete the second half of the figure-8 pattern on the opposite side. Repeat for as many times as necessary to elicit a strike (Figure 6).

close to the boat. You'll soon be out of fly line to strip and room maneuver. Unless you do something instantly to keep the fly moving, most fish will lose interest or see the boat and spook. So take a long, deep breath. With one smooth and continuous motion:

1. Strip in any slack, pulling in all but a few inches of the leader and wire tippet extending from the rod tip (one to two feet total). This allows you to control the fly much better than with a longer length of line. Smoothly and quietly extend your arms and lower the rod tip into the water, stripping any excess line and immediately locking the line against the rod handle with your index finger.

2. At the same time, with your body now extended over the water and both hands on the handle (or the other hand gripping the fighting butt of the rod if you have one) keep the fly moving by lowering the entire rod deeper underwater, toward the bottom. Depending on the depth of the fish at this point it may be necessary to plunge the entire rod up to the handle to perform this maneuver. This initial downward swing moves the following fish deeper in the water column keeping it focused on the fly and helping to reduce any potential distractions from you or the boat.

3. As the rod and fly approach the maximum depth, change direction again by swinging up rapidly to one side or the other with a smooth, wide, upward arching motion. Depending on where you have the most room to maneuver, you'll either be swinging the

rod to the right with an "L" or to the left with a "J" away from the boat. Throughout this entire maneuver it's critical to watch the fish's response and keep the fly moving and looking alive using both the speed of the swing and the motion of the rod tip.

4. When you reach the end of the first rapid upward swing away from the boat, without stopping the fly, change direction again by making a wide but definite turn back down towards the bottom completing the first half of the figure-8 pattern. Note: The following fish will often chase the fly as you accelerate upward and away for this first swing and then eat it the moment it changes direction for the next downward swing. Be prepared!

5. If the fish continues to follow back down, once the fly approaches maximum depth, reverse course with another wide but definite turn, swinging the fly upward rapidly in the opposite direction and away from the boat. When you reach the opposite corner of each "8," swing the rod to turn the fly back again. Repeat the same pattern as many times as necessary to elicit a strike. (See two-part illustration of the figure-8 technique on pages 180 and 181).

Finer Points of the Figure-8

• As you figure-8 with the fly rod, imagine painting a large, sideways underwater "8" with your rod tip. This simple visualization technique should help you to understand and maintain the pattern required to move the fly.

• Once you get the hang of this, try increasing the speed and direction of the ovals so the backside swing is away from the boat and up toward the surface and the forward swing is deep and back toward the side of the boat.

• The depth of your rod tip and fly in the water is dictated entirely by the level of the fish in the water column. Some fish may follow wherever your fly goes while others remain on or just below the surface or go deep for the entire figure-8. In some cases you may even find you need to plunge the rod right up to the reel to maintain the fish's line of sight.

• The figure-8 technique can be used in very shallow or deep water. If used in shallow water, simply make the ovals more sideways and direct your fly to avoid snagging the bottom. In a deep follow scenario, the fish may stay below the fly for the entire figure-8 and only be visible when it strikes.

• Be especially careful not to cut too tight a corner with any swing or you'll risk pulling the fly out of the fish's line of sight. Muskies are agile predators but their long body prevents them from turning on a

dime. All your turns should be wide (three to five feet) and smooth. Allow the fish to follow yet think the fly is just about to get away!

• Even with a nine-foot rod, the proper figure-8 technique usually requires you to bend over, or even get on your knees, and extend your arms to work the rod tip at the exact depth necessary to reach the fish. As you get into position, keep you body movements and noise level to a minimum. Abrupt body movements and loud noises may risk spooking the fish at close range.

• Try to anticipate the best boat position for a figure-8 with each cast. Placing your casts and retrieving the fly perpendicular or parallel to the front of the boat is usually best for maximum maneuverability. Casting this direction also allows a much wider range of motion both above and below the water than casting toward the stern where you always risk tangling in the engine or other obstructions.

If you've done this right and it's your day, the fish will follow the fly close through the first downward swing and then crush it on the first upward swing or change of direction. If not, continue the next swing of the figure-8 at a faster pace and try to induce a strike on the next turn, and so on. You can repeat this pattern for as long as the fish remains interested and your arms can take it. However, your odds of getting a fish to strike, while still good with a figure-8, diminish the longer the fish follows but does not strike.

When a fish is really hot on the fly but still won't eat, another effective technique during the figure-8 is to slow or pulse the fly briefly just before the turn and then pull it back right across the fish's face. With some fish it seems this abrupt about face with the direction of the fly combined with an easy meal literally touching its lips is simply too much for a muskie to take. It will open wide and inhale.

Whenever performing any figure-8 pattern, it's critical to have a clear boat deck to work with and to be able to move quickly wherever you or the fish wants to go. Ideally you'll be able to keep the fish toward the front of the boat during this maneuver but as the boat drifts you may need to reposition yourself. The fish may also move away and then come back for another look. More than once I've had a fish follow off the front of the boat, disappear, and then suddenly reappear off the stern where I finally hooked it on a figure-8.

As noted above, when the fish is very close—especially on the surface—try to keep as low a profile as possible by taking a step back away from the edge, crouching or bending over, even getting down on

One key to converting an opportunistic muskie on the figure-8 is to create the illusion of an easy meal: Always keep the fly moving to maintain interest, and accelerate through each turn to trigger a reaction strike. It's also just as important to make each turn wide and smooth to give the fish plenty of room to maneuver—and voraciously eat!

your knees with the rod. You'll probably need to do this anyway to work the fly properly, but you should still be careful not to spook the fish unnecessarily with any sudden body movement or loud noises. In clear- or low-water conditions, wearing natural or camouflaged colors may also help to avoid detection when the fish is very close.

This aquatic game of cat and mouse with muskies can go on for some time with the fish either right on the fly following every turn as if it is actually hooked or hanging back and taking swipes at the fly as it pleases. If you lose track of the fish, by all means don't stop your figure-8! Instead, keep actively "figure-8ing" and looking in a broader area around your fly for some signs of a fish. You may see only a momentary flash or glimpse of its head, tail, or belly. Other times your fly will just stop and disappear when the fish decides to eat.

If it seems like the fish is slowing down and losing interest, try changing the speed or direction of your fly abruptly or making the loops of the figure-8 even wider and more erratic. Sometimes the fish will move deeper during the figure-8 yet still show some interest. Assuming you've got the depth to work with, when this happens take the fly to the fish's level by crouching over—even hanging over the gunnels—and submerging

the full nine feet of the rod and reel with both hands firmly planted on the cork grip. This deep-water version of the figure-8 is admittedly pretty extreme, but sometimes it's the only way to keep a fish interested when it moves deep and out of range.

While it's always tough to give up on a fish, at some point you must decide if it isn't going to eat and try another approach—or move on to the next opportunity. If, on the other hand, you've got the stamina and the fish remains interested with fewer but very real signs of being aggressive, then by all means keep figure-8ing. The importance of this cannot be overstated. On more than one occasion I've almost given up on a "repeat follower" and then, when I'd given it my all—and my buddy was about to pull the trolling motor—the fish decided it couldn't take it any longer and blasted the fly.

Top-Water Follows

The figure-8 techniques used with streamers can be applied just as effectively when fishing a top-water fly. When you encounter an aggressive fish pushing water behind the popper on the surface or following from below, keep the fly popping at a steady pace or faster as it nears the boat. Read the fish's behavior to decide if you should pick up the pace to elicit a strike.

Often a slight change of speed or direction will trigger the fish to eat before the fly reaches the boat.

As with a streamer fly, do not hesitate or stop the fly at any time during your retrieve.

If the fish still hasn't taken the fly by the time it reaches the boat, you'll once again face the fly fisher's dilemma of not having enough room or fly line left to strip to give the popper any action. In this situation, the best technique is to use the top-water figure-8 as

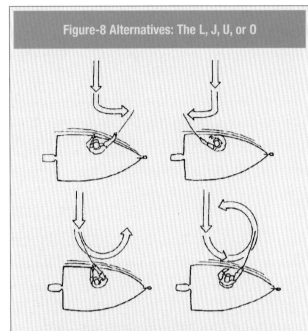

Figure-8 Alternatives: The L, J, U, or 0

An abbreviated and less-complicated version of the figure-8 can also be done with a simple L, J, U, or 0 pattern at the end of each retrieve. To do this, as the fly reaches the boat, simply lock the line under your index finger and swing the rod tip swiftly underwater to the right for an L, the left for a J, or a half (U) or full circle (0) after each cast. If possible, it's usually best to lean over the gunnels and use two hands on the handle when doing this maneuver to increase control and leverage with this technique.

Although it's been my experience that the full figure-8 is still the best way to convert a fish to strike, sometimes you just don't have the time, energy, or space in the boat to do this as you'd like. Consequently, I usually reserve these abbreviated techniques for those "out-of-the-blue" hot fish that leave you totally unprepared and a little embarrassed. When fishing in dark water or low-light conditions where it's often impossible to see a follow—even at close range—these abbreviated techniques work especially well to insure you don't miss a hook-up opportunity at the boat. In any of the above situations, if an aggressive fish shows but doesn't eat immediately it's entirely possible to extend the L, J, U, or 0 into a full figure-8 by completing the turns back toward the boat as described above.

illustrated on the following page. Once the fly is within one to two feet of the rod tip, in one smooth motion lock the line under your index finger against the handle, and start using the rod tip exclusively for your pops. Bring it gradually toward and then parallel to the gunnels. This is easier said than done. It requires some practice to get it right. Continue popping the fly with a gradual L turn to right or J turn to the left, depending on where you have the most room to maneuver. If the fish is still interested and holding tight under the fly, you can then perform a full figure-8 pattern on the surface until it hits or spooks. If it's an especially hot fish you may even be able to walk it around the front or along the side of the boat several times using this technique with wide swings of the rod. As with any figure-8 technique, the main goal is to keep the fish focused on your fly by making it look alive, and then make it eat when it thinks its next mouthful is getting away.

Another top-water technique that works very well with aggressive muskies is to actually submerge the fly in front of the fish. While this may seem contrary to most fly-fishing techniques, this sudden and unexpected change of direction with the fly seems to act as an additional trigger. It often moves a noncommittal fish to strike. If the fish does not take as soon as the fly submerges, you can also try moving the fly underwater in a figure-8, L, J, U, or 0 pattern as you would a streamer. A foam or hard-bodied popper has little inherent action when submerged, so continue twitching or pumping the popper with the rod tip to keep the fish interested. You can do this with any kind of muskie popper—even a large, concave-faced hard popper—so long as you keep it moving fast enough once it's underwater. A large diver-type fly also works especially well in this situation since it is meant to swim above and dive below the surface.

The effectiveness of this approach was made very clear to me several years ago on a small Midwest lake. It was the first top-water bite of the year. The conventional guys were nailing fish every day on their usual assortment of bathtub toys. I was working a piece of newly-emerged emerald-green weed near a deep break when I saw a fish boil just outside casting range. I didn't want to risk spooking the fish by moving the boat. Instead, I made a "Hail Mary" cast in the direction of the fish. After a few aggressive pops a V-wake appeared behind the fly. I kept up my steady retrieve. The fish was glued to the fly as it approached the boat. With no room left to strip, I submerged the popper right at the boat, and the fish hit as soon as it broke the surface.

Figure-8 Technique: Top Water

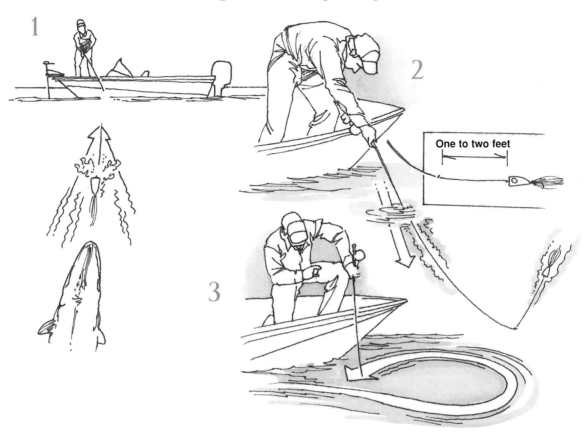

One to two feet

The fly-rod figure-8 technique can also be effective with a top-water fly with a few added twists. Like the streamer approach, start by stripping in all but one to two feet of leader and locking the line under your index finger. Continue popping the fly on the surface toward the boat using the rod tip—instead of the strip—and place the other hand firmly on the fighting butt or the handle for leverage (Figure 1). As the fly approaches the boat, make an abrupt turn to either side along the gunnels depending on where you have the most room to maneuver. Move the popper in a wide, smooth, figure-8 pattern along the surface with accelerated turns to trigger a strike. If the fish is still interested but not overly aggressive, try submerging the popper (Figure 2) and then moving it in a figure-8 pattern like a streamer underwater (Figure 3).

Instinctively, I did a backset as the fish moved away. As often happens, the fish jumped as soon as it felt the hook and pulled free on a short line. Within seconds, I saw the same fish again, on the other side of the boat swimming slowly away. I was so pissed off at losing this fish, I made an immediate cast almost as if to hit it on the head. To my surprise and that of my buddy, the fish moved on the fly and ate it again! I set the hook solidly this time and soon landed a fine 43-inch spring fish … hooked twice and landed once.

Changeups and Finesse Tactics

Whenever you encounter a following muskie it's really a judgment call on your part to decide when to keep casting or figure-8ing, and when to give the fish a break and try again later. Like resting an Atlantic salmon or a steelhead after it "missed" your wet or dry fly, a brief pause in the action may be just the thing to convert a fish from being a follower to an eater. On the other hand, on a slow day it's awfully hard to

leave the only fish you've seen, especially a big one. If you're like me, in the back of your mind you'll always be wondering if the next guy casting over this spot—most likely with a lure—might just get lucky and catch "your" trophy.

Once you've determined a particular muskie is simply not interested in your figure-8 or other creative boatside maneuvering, there are several other good "changeup" options you can still use to try and catch the fish. As usual, there are as many theories and approaches to this situation as there are muskie fishers.

Fly Rod Changeups and Options:

1. **Cast back right away with the same or similar fly.**
2. **Cast back right away with a totally different fly.**
3. **Change the speed and direction of your retrieve.**
4. **Mark the spot and come back later with the same or a different fly.**

Casting back quickly with the same fly is a natural response for most anglers. On more than one occasion I've seen excited anglers cast the water into a froth in a desperate attempt to conjure up a following fish. Unfortunately, this is not always a good approach, especially if the fish has already followed once or twice and had a good, long look at what you're offering. Casting back with a similar but different fly, however, may be just the thing to make an aggressive fish turn again and eat. By a slightly different fly I mean switching from a smaller fly to a larger fly (or visa versa) of the same general pattern or profile or from a sparsely tied fly to one that is bulkier (or visa versa). If this doesn't work, then a complete color or pattern change from bright to dark, flashy to muted, or vice versa can be just the thing to turn a fish on.

For fish that are clearly non-aggressive as indicated by a slower, deeper follow, it may be necessary to make a more dramatic change. In this case making a switch from a streamer to top-water fly and/or a completely different retrieve may be just the thing to increase the interest level and produce a strike. This is perhaps the most important reason for always keeping another rod rigged with a fly and prepared to cast.

If you're fishing with a buddy and are feeling generous, you can also have your friend cast to the fish. This is always quicker than picking up another rod, stripping line, and making a cast. I've used this teamwork technique with success many times. For those of you who can't stand the thought of missing (read: *sharing*) a fish, another option is to always keep another rod out with line stripped and ready to go.

Changing your retrieve speed or direction of the cast is also a good option with a fish that has stopped following. This can be done quickly with the same fly, but a different pattern and presentation is usually the best approach. With an aggressively following fish I usually opt for a very fast and aggressive retrieve with either a streamer or top-water fly. On the other hand, a slower retrieve may be just the ticket so it pays to be creative in this situation. This is especially true in early spring and late fall when water temperatures are lower and the fish are not as likely to chase a fly for very long.

You can also alter the position of your boat and casting direction to give the fish a new and different profile of the fly. I've used this technique on both lakes and rivers, but it can be difficult in a strong wind or current. If possible, try retrieving the fly from the left or right side—or the exact opposite direction from where you think the fish is now holding. If you're in open water and the fish seems to be holding on a certain piece of structure—a rock bar, for instance—you can also try to circle the area with narrowly spaced fan casts. Note: Because this approach requires some extra time and using the oars or a trolling motor to reposition the boat, you always risk the possibility of spooking the fish when trying this maneuver.

When a passive fish is clearly not interested in eating, your best game plan is usually to mark the spot it came from on your map, depth finder, or with a buoy marker or shoreline landmark, and come back again when conditions have changed. The time you take to do this can vary from a half hour to a couple of hours to much later in the day. Since muskies often hold for a long time in the same area or spot, consider trying again the following day or even week if you have the time. The key in this situation is to look for some significant change in environmental conditions that might trigger a fish to strike: lower light, a change in the barometer, increase or decrease in wind speed, or the passage of a frontal system.

Following-Fish Finesse Tactics

Finessing a streamer fly for muskies using the pause-and-twitch retrieve can be an effective tactic for converting non-aggressive follows into strikes (see illustration on page 161). Despite the universal prohibition of slowing down your retrieve when muskie fishing, I've had this work many times when the fish are in a funk. The slower speed of your retrieve and the natural movement of a muskie streamer—even at rest—can be just the ticket on a tough day, especially with pressured fish or a cold front.

In the typical scenario, a non-aggressive fish swims slowly a few feet behind or below the fly all the way to the boat. Other times a fish may swim leisurely into view well after you've made the next cast and then suspend close to the boat as if looking for a handout. These fish provide the angler plenty of time to decide what to do but the odds of converting them are much, much lower. Since the fish in both scenarios are curious enough to inspect my offering, however, I always assume there's still a chance they can and will be caught with the right finesse approach (positive mental attitude).

Practice, Practice, Practice

Whatever technique you employ with a following fish, it's always best to test your fly first, observing exactly how it reacts at fast and slow speeds on a very short line at the side of the boat. You'll have plenty of opportunity to do this while you're fishing, but I recommend doing this prior to fishing with any streamer or top-water fly you choose to cast. Some flies look attractive at any speed while others tend to die in the water without any assistance from the rod tip. Top-water flies are especially difficult to keep moving with a short line. So determine in advance what rod motion is necessary to keep the fly popping and looking alive above and below the surface.

Never, ever, give up: Whether you can still see the fish or not, it's always worth doing the figure-8 for as long as you can hold out. If the fish goes deep, take the fly to the fish by lowering your body and plunging the rod right up to the reel if necessary.

CHAPTER 9

GETTING HOOKED UP

"The finest gift you can give to any fisherman is to put a good fish back, and who knows if the fish that you caught isn't someone else's gift to you."

—LEE WULFF

S EVERAL YEARS AGO I WAS FISHING ONE OF MY FAVORITE northern Wisconsin rivers on one of those perfect Indian summer days. It was late October, but daytime air temperatures were still in the 70s with a light "fishy" southwest wind. I was just happy to be out on the water this late in the year without getting frostbite. Legendary muskie guide "Musky Joe" Flater met me that morning with a broad smile I knew meant only one thing: It *was* going to be a good day.

As predicted, within a few casts of the put-in I had my first follow. Joe laughed when he saw the fish as it swam under the boat and said in his typical Wisconsin twang, "Come on, Robert, let's get the next one." After a few more follows, I eventually got the hooks into a small but active fish that jumped several times just like a salmon. My confidence level was high. The faster the follows and strikes came, the faster I fished. A few bends downstream I missed a nice fish that blasted my streamer midway back to the boat. Sensing my frustration, Joe wisely suggested I take a break and figure out what the heck was going on.

"Slow down, Robert, we're not in the big city anymore," Joe said. He noted that while the sun was shining and the air was warm, the water temperature was still quite cool. This would keep the fish on the lethargic side. On the next strike I forced myself to wait for the fish to turn—and was immediately rewarded with a solid hook up. Despite a tough start, at the end of this amazing day I had moved more than a dozen fish to the fly and landed a grand total of eight "fatty" fall muskies up to 44 inches. I also learned something new about muskie fly-rod strike techniques to add to my long list of "lessons learned."

While not every day on the water is this productive, once you find the fish, you need to know exactly what to do when a muskie finally inhales your fly. How you go about hooking, fighting, boating, and releasing a muskie on the fly is, therefore, the next logical step in your education.

Muskie Hits and Misses

Hooking a muskie is a challenge regardless of what kind of tackle you prefer to use. Whether you're bait casting, trolling, or fly fishing, these fish have an uncanny ability to avoid getting and staying hooked. The combination of an extremely hard mouth, vise-like grip, and long, powerful body are a big part of what make this fish among the toughest in fresh water. The tendency to strike close to the boat also presents a number of problems unique to this sport. More than once I've had a muskie on that I was sure was solidly hooked, had it fight for some time, and then—just when I thought the battle was won—simply open its mouth and swim away. Most conventional anglers have had the same experience only with lures armed with several sharp sets of large treble hooks. Like a dog with a stick, it's as if these fish want to play a game just to see how long they can hold on.

Despite being mentally prepared for the challenge, and even seeing a fish clearly before it hits, it's always a bit of a surprise when the strike finally happens. Given the muskie's tendency to attack prey on short notice—at bursts of speeds up to 30 miles per hour—there's usually precious little time to react before the fish is gone. As a result, it's common for even an experienced angler to "blow" a fish by striking too soon, too late, or not at all, depending on the hit.

As ambush hunters, the strike of a muskie is by its very nature fast, aggressive, and violent. These efficient predators require substantial amounts of food to maintain their large size. They can't afford to use anything but lethal force to achieve this goal. Over the years muskie fishermen have predictably come up with a number of choice verbs to characterize

A classic fall "fatty": There's nothing finer than fly-fishing for muskie on a perfect Indian summer day. This memorable fish was one of many that taught me a thing or two about fly rod hook sets.

the indelible strike: crush, inhale, destroy, annihilate, pulverize, obliterate, and, my favorite, "T-Bone." One minute you're casting away and the next there's a fish thrashing violently on the end of your line. It's a heart-stopping thrill that leaves you weak in the knees and ready for more.

Hooking a muskie on a fly is probably unlike anything you've ever encountered as a fly fisher. In fact, the closest examples that come to mind are the spectacularly violent strikes of a barracuda, golden dorado, or peacock bass. All these fish hit with great speed and force. They thrash, jump, throw, or completely miss the fly in the process. Other times the strike is surprisingly subtle such as when a 100-pound tarpon quietly "hoovers" a Cockroach or a large brown trout sips a size 22 Pale Morning Dun off the surface imperceptibly.

It's this wide variation in strikes that keeps the successful muskie angler on his or her toes and prepared for anything. As for the hook-setting technique,

there's no room for typical overhead "trout sets" here. Think tarpon or bonefish. The critical demand is to continue stripping line until you feel the fish, strip-striking to set the hook solidly in a hard mouth, and then using the rod to add leverage and cushion the shock.

Above all you should know that hooking a muskie on a fly rod is an amazing experience. It's an event you should be justifiably proud of—even if you don't actually land the fish. The goal, however, is to get the fish to the boat, and there are a number of specific techniques you'll need to know to accomplish this task.

Muskie Hook-Setting Essentials

1. Sharpen your hooks
2. Stay focused and be prepared
3. Correct body, foot, and hand positions
4. Strip-strike technique
5. Line management

Sharpen Your Hooks

Other than a proper hook-setting technique, there is nothing more important to your ultimate success than a well-sharpened hook. Most anglers simply do not take the time to sharpen their hooks properly or consistently (or even at all). This seems to be most common with freshwater fly fishers who don't normally worry about sharp hooks when fishing small flies for trout or other species. Saltwater fly fishers, on the other hand, know all too well about the importance of a sharp hook; the most successful ones do not take any chances when it comes to this aspect of their sport.

When sharpening a fly hook for muskies, use a large two-sided hook file to achieve a three-sided triangular point. You can forget about your smaller trout-hook hones when muskie fishing. Our sport requires saltwater-grade sharpeners for large hooks. There are many hook files on the market today specifically designed for this task. Most have a large handle which makes it easier and safer when sharpening a larger hook. Some incorporate a long hook-sized

Author's Tips: Hook Sharpening

TRIANGULATED HOOK POINT

1

LARGE BARB

2

DULL HOOK POINT

REDUCED BARB

To sharpen a muskie hook properly, start with the rougher side of the file to achieve the basic tapered angle you desire. Use the fine side of the file to finish off the point until it's razor sharp. (Figure 1)

Many large saltwater hooks are produced with a barb that is larger than really necessary to hold a fish. Use a file to reduce it to roughly half its original size. This not only helps to drive the hook home but also prevents a far larger hole in the muskie's mouth during the fight. Filing the barb helps both your hookset and the ease of release while ensuring the fish remains hooked. (Figure 2)

slot to achieve a consistent angle while sharpening.

You can easily check the sharpness of your point by dragging it over your thumbnail at a 45-degree angle to see if it catches. If it does, then you probably have a good point that will penetrate cleanly with a proper hookset technique. If not, keep filing until you're sure it's razor sharp. In some cases you'll find the hook point is simply too worn down or bent to be effective. This is quite common with stainless steel and other saltwater hooks. Although it may be the last one of your favorite pattern, my recommendation is to put it aside, and put on a new one with a sharp hook. This is yet another good reason for bringing along plenty of your favorite flies with sharp hooks.

Like most muskie anglers, I always sharpen my fly hooks *before* fishing. This is especially important with a brand-new fly which is rarely sharp enough out of the box. I also constantly check my fly throughout the day for any signs of abuse. As you can imagine, stripping a fly all day through muskie water and fishing from a boat can do a lot of damage to a hook. It may not be necessary to check your hook on each and every cast, but each time you hit a rock, stump, or a snag you are potentially bending or dulling your point. Always take a moment to check your hook and make sure it's sharp. You'll be glad you did when a fish finally hits.

Stay Focused and Be Prepared

Staying focused and prepared for a strike is one of biggest challenges in muskie fishing. Yet even the most intense anglers start to lose focus and let their minds wander, especially after a long day on the water with little or no action. Allow me to say that the only thing worse than boredom is missing a fish because you stopped paying attention. Muskies seem to have an uncanny ability to sense this and strike in a variety of unusual ways—always when you least expect it.

For the record, I've had them take my fly the moment it landed or just as I was pulling it out of the water for the next cast. Just as commonly, I've had them follow, strike, and miss my fly several times before finally nailing it right at boatside on a figure-8. Some fish actually chase the fly with such speed and determination they hit the side of the boat with a loud "thud." Some even jump in the boat. While not a recommended approach, I once caught a nice muskie on my water-haul back cast the moment it hit the water. While such strikes are not the norm, these varied and unpredictable behaviors mean you'll need to stay focused on your fly and the area around it at all times for any signs of a fish.

Ready for anything: The unpredictable nature of muskies requires the fly fisher to remain focused and prepared for a strike at any time during the retrieve. Note the predator pose with staggered—sock-clad—feet for feel and balance and stripping hand ready to strip-strike.

For those anglers wondering just how far a muskie will move for a fly, consider the unusual story of Wisconsin muskie guide Don Larson, a.k.a. The Pond Monster. Fishing one of his favorite, clear-water flowages on a crisp fall day, he made a cast and immediately saw a bright, fluorescent-orange shape 40 feet away moving with great speed toward his fly. Undetered he kept retrieving. The fish—a muskie, after all—hit hard, putting up a fierce fight. As Don landed this fish he soon discovered the source of the color he'd seen: a large, Dardevle spoon stuck in the fish's back. He carefully removed the spoon and released this unfortunate and now less-visible muskie to fight another day.

One of the main benefits of staying focused is the extra time it gives you to prepare for a strike. Even if it's only a few seconds, the sooner you see your fish, the better odds you'll have of achieving a good hookset. This includes assuming the proper body position for a strip-set and clearing any loose line. Seeing what's happening as early as possible also gives you a chance to alert your fishing buddy to be prepared, help clear line around your feet, and put the boat and motor in proper position.

Hookset Mechanics

Successfully hooking a muskie with a fly rod is more about skill and technique than brute physical strength. Although muskies can grow to enormous size, even the most fragile angler can hook a big fish if he or she employs the proper mechanics when setting the hook. Because the muskie's fight is rarely long and drawn out, a solid hook set is really the most critical part of landing a fish.

The actual hook-setting technique you use for muskies on a fly depends on a number of critical variables including the aggressiveness of the fish, the type of fly you're using, and the distance the fish is away from you when it finally hits. However, there are some basic mechanical skills for a proper hookset to consider at all times when fly fishing for muskies:

1. Body and foot position: As discussed in Chapter 7, whenever you fly fish for muskies you should assume the predator pose with your body bent forward from the waist, with head and shoulders squarely facing the direction of each cast. It also helps to stagger your feet with one foot is slightly forward to maintain balance and stability.

As the boat moves, always "follow the fly" by rotating your body position through each retrieve to maintain the proper angle. This is true whether floating down a river, fishing a lake shoreline with the wind, or a trolling motor moving you forward. In addition to giving you the best possible view of your fly and the area around it, this arm, body, and foot position provides the angler with the best overall stability and mobility to set the hook when the fish hits.

2. Rod hand and arm position: When retrieving the fly, your rod tip should be at the water's surface and pointed directly in front of you. Leaving the rod tip high or to the side only creates more slack and reduces leverage should a fish hit. Your rod hand should be firm yet relaxed with the thumb on top for maximum power. The rod arm should extend forward from your body while your stripping hand reaches ahead to pull line from behind your index finger for each strip. While it's often necessary to sweep the rod tip down or to the side as you strip to achieve more action with the fly, the rod should always return to a tip-down, extended-forward position after each strip to be ready for a strike. The objective here, as always, is to keep the fly looking alive during your retrieve

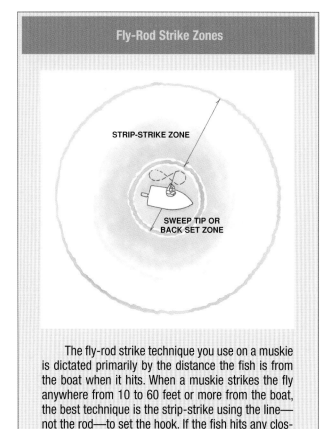

Fly-Rod Strike Zones

STRIP-STRIKE ZONE

SWEEP TIP OR
BACK SET ZONE

The fly-rod strike technique you use on a muskie is dictated primarily by the distance the fish is from the boat when it hits. When a muskie strikes the fly anywhere from 10 to 60 feet or more from the boat, the best technique is the strip-strike using the line—not the rod—to set the hook. If the fish hits any closer to the boat—say, within 10 feet—the strip-strike is less effective since you've run out of room to strip line. And the rod is already nine feet long. In this case you must use the rod to set the hook with the sweep, tip, or back-set techniques outlined in this chapter.

while at the same time maintaining constant tension by continuously recovering any extra slack.

The Best Hookset

Setting the hook with a fly rod is quite different from conventional muskie-fishing techniques. When a conventional angler sets the hook, he has the advantage of a high-speed reel to take up slack, no-stretch line, a powerful drag system to maintain tension, and a very stiff rod to drive the hooks home. The rod does most of the work. This approach seemingly leaves little room for error but still results in lost fish depending on the angler's skill and the nature of the strike.

In many ways, the fly rod is the exact opposite of a conventional muskie rod. It is soft, slow, and flexible. It's designed to cast a line and fly effectively. As a result, the fly rod—even a fast graphite stick—is not the ideal tool for setting the hook on a hard-mouthed muskie. When you consider the fact the rod tip is always low to the water for most of the retrieve, it's also obvious that it simply takes too much time to

move the long and limber fly rod in any direction for a quick and powerful hookset. Moreover, without the aid of a conventional reel to retrieve line quickly, it's entirely up to the angler to maintain the right amount of tension by hand alone until, and if, the fish can be brought tight to the reel.

By far the most effective hookset for muskie with a fly rod is the strip-strike method using the line—*not the rod*—to set the hook. This is the same technique used when fly fishing in salt water for bonefish, tarpon, and billfish where a solid, tissue-penetrating hookset is essential for a proper hookup.

Let's assume you've just cast your streamer in a likely looking area and begun your retrieve. About half way back to the boat a nice muskie comes out of nowhere, follows, and then inhales your fly from behind: What should you do?

The natural inclination for most anglers is to raise the rod tip high, and then strip in line as quickly as possible, trying to keep tight to the fish using the leverage of your rod. Unfortunately, given the inevitable slack in the water during any retrieve, and the relatively soft tip of even a heavy 10-weight rod, this natural response is not an effective way to set the hook on a big fish with a very hard mouth. Sure, you may have the fish on for a little while and may even land it if you're lucky, but odds are you have not really set the hook solidly, and the fish will eventually get off.

Instead, the best way to set the hook on a muskie is to use the strip-strike technique as follows (also see the illustration on the following page):

The Strip-Strike

1. Keep your arms extended with the rod tip low and pointed directly toward the fish. As with any retrieve, your line should already be secured under your index finger for control. Your stripping hand should be as far forward as possible, ready to strip line or set the hook.

2. As soon as you see or feel the fish strike the fly, keep the rod pointed at the fish and pull straight back on the fly line with a long, hard, and fast strip *pulling directly on the hook*. Do not lift the rod! Keep pulling until you feel the line tighten and the weight of the fish. If possible, take a step or two backward in the boat when stripping to further eliminate slack and help set the hook. Ideally the strip-set is accomplished with a single strip of the line, but may require additional strips depending on how much slack you had when the fish hit.

3. As soon as you feel a solid connection with the fish, sweep the rod directly to one side or the other to

Strip-Strike Technique

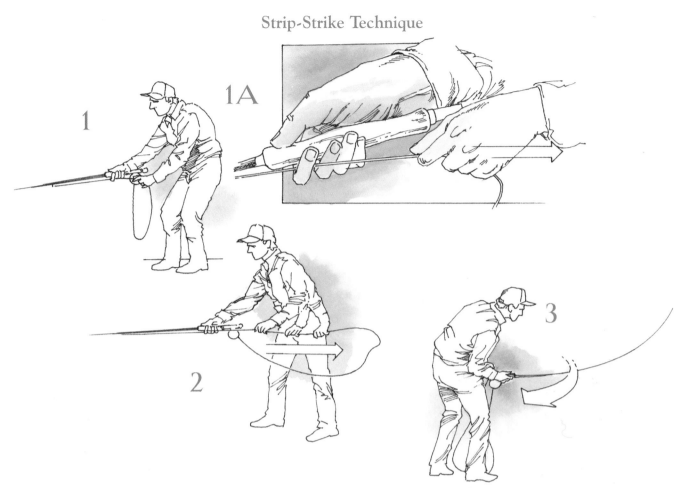

The strip-strike technique is by far the best way to achieve a solid hookset on a muskie. When a fish hits, keep the rod pointed directly at the fish (Figure 1) with your stripping hand ready to strip (Figure 1A). As soon as you feel—or see—the strike, pull back straight and hard on the line without lifting the rod (Figure 2). Once the fish is hooked, immediately employ the full power of the rod by sweeping it to the side for additional tension and leverage (Figure 3).

take up any remaining slack, rotating your body if necessary. This immediately helps to absorb the shock of the initial strike. It also applies additional leverage on the fish. The direction of your rod sweep depends on the direction the fish moves after it strikes, your body and boat position at the time of the strike, and the location of any obstructions in the boat. Hopefully, the fish will turn after striking and you'll be able to sweep the rod freely in the opposite direction the fish is facing.

In order to master this important technique, there are several other key points to understand:

• Although the muskie strip-strike technique is described in step-by-step detail, in real life it all happens very fast in one, smooth, controlled, continuous movement from the strip to the set.

• The moment a fish strikes, your rod and stripping hand should be extended forward and ready to strip line as with any normal muskie retrieve. In reality, this may not always be possible due to the fish hitting between strips or at the end of a retrieve. In

this case, resist raising the rod overhead. Instead, reach forward quickly to strip line from as close to your index finger as possible to maximize the overall length of your strip-strike.

• Once you set the hook, the index finger of your rod-hand becomes your entire drag system allowing you to control line and maintain constant tension—until and if—the fish can be fought from the reel. This is one reason I always wear a stripping glove to protect my finger(s) from the intense friction created by line tension during the strip-strike and the fight that follows.

• If you can't possibly recover enough line when the fish hits or the fish continues swimming directly toward you, then—and only then— strip in as much line as physically possible and aggressively sweep the rod upward or sideways (downward will only hit the side of the boat and prevent a full sweep) to set the hook. Use the rod now as your main tool of resistance. Rotating your body and taking a couple of steps backward in this situation helps to further eliminate slack (just

The death roll: Muskies are notorious for rolling on the surface once they get near the boat. There's not much you can do except keep tension with the rod held high and hope they don't get off or injure themselves in the process. This particular snub-nosed Canadian fish eluded me for several seasons until I finally got her to eat one of my black Tiktaalik poppers.

be sure you know where you're going before you try this!). This is probably the least effective way to strike a muskie with a fly rod but may be necessary when you don't have a choice.

The strip-strike technique as described usually works best when the fish takes the fly from directly behind. Muskies, however, don't always take the fly the way you want. They strike from any direction they choose—including from either side or below, sometimes even from above like a cat on a mouse. When a fish takes the fly from the side, it's usually best to wait a moment, and let the fish continue turning before you strip-strike. This approach allows you to use the weight and motion of the fish to your advantage to pull the line tight before strip-striking, typically leaving the fly firmly implanted in the corner

of its mouth as it swims away from you. When a fish strikes from directly below the fly, the same technique applies, but you'll need to keep the rod tip low to the water, or even push it into the water and wait a moment before strip-striking to control the fish and prevent it from throwing the fly as it thrashes on the surface or jumps.

A major tactical benefit of the strip-strike is that if you miss the fish (or it misses the fly), you still have time to induce another strike within the very same retrieve. Instead of lifting the line to make another cast, continue retrieving the fly (knees shaking), and be ready for another strike. With your fly still in the zone where a fish has already seen it, the odds are good it will try to eat again or at least follow. This is especially true with a fish that boils or takes a swipe at the fly during the retrieve but doesn't connect. More than once I've had a fish miss the fly early in the retrieve and then return for another try only to be hooked in the process. It's an exciting way to fish and one of the many great things about muskie fishing with a fly.

Muskies are notorious for striking a streamer in the brief seconds between strips and pauses of your normal retrieve. Like the classic jerkbait strike between wide, side-to-side swings, this response is triggered by a brief pause in motion signaling an opportunity to pounce. Since it's difficult to predict exactly when this will happen—even when you can see the fish—it's important to keep a tight line by continuing to recover any micro-slack with short three- to five-inch strips even while the fly drifts forward or to the side. As always, stay focused and keep the line locked under your index finger between each strip.

Once the fish is on, as tempting as it is to set the hook several more times using the full force of the rod, this is not recommend in most situations. As long as you achieve a solid strip-strike, the pressure of a tight line on a long fly rod should keep the hook firmly implanted in the fish's mouth and allow you to fight the fish. As many muskie anglers know from experience, even the slightest temporary slack line created by dropping your rod to reset the hook can only lead to a critical loss of tension and ultimately a lost fish. If you didn't achieve a good hookset, you may still be able to fight the fish long enough to land it by simply keeping gentle pressure on your line and avoiding strong tension during the fight.

The basic strip-strike technique works best 90 percent of the time when a muskie takes a streamer anywhere during the retrieve within the normal casting range of 10 to 60 feet from the boat. This distance is usually far enough from the boat to effectively strip the line tight yet close enough to still maintain some control. With fish that hit beyond this distance, achieving a solid strip-strike is more difficult due to the overall amount of line in the water. The inevitable slack in the water and fly line stretch also become more of an issue, so be extra vigilant to eliminate as much slack as possible before strip-striking with a longer line.

Short-Line Strike Techniques

Striking a muskie on a short line of less than 10 feet from the rod tip requires a different technique

I missed this fish several times on the popper until I learned to wait a moment to feel the weight of the fish before setting the hook.

Sweep-Set Technique

When a muskie hits close to the boat, you'll need to use the rod to help set the hook rather than a strip-strike with the line. One option with a short line strike is the sweep set. When a fish hits in this situation, strip quickly to get tight to the fish, and then immediately sweep the rod low and sideways to maintain leverage and control. Another advantage to a low rod is it helps prevent the fish from jumping, thrashing, and possibly throwing the hook.

than the strip-strike. Since there usually isn't nearly enough line necessary for a solid strip-strike, the fly rod itself now becomes your primary tool for setting the hook. This, as I've pointed out, is not ideal. A fly rod's inherently soft tip is not suited to this kind of work, especially as compared to a conventional muskie rod. As you might have guessed, simply lifting the rod tip over your head for a "trout set" is also a sure way to lose a short-line fish. In addition, when a muskie hits near the surface on a short line at boatside, it will typically jump and/or begin thrashing and twisting wildly on the surface. Result? Many lost fish.

Boatside strikes within 10 feet of the boat are very common when fly fishing for muskies and, like all muskie fishing, present their own special set of challenges. Nonetheless, there are certain short-line striking techniques that improve your odds of hooking a fish under these conditions.

The Sweep-Set

1. As the fly and fish approach the boat, continue stripping line to eliminate slack and keep the rod tip low to the water. Lock the line firmly against the rod handle after each strip to prevent slippage when you finally set the hook.

2. When you see or *feel* the fish finally hit, in one continuous motion make a final hard and fast strip to get tight to the fish, securely lock the line under your index finger, and rotate your body while sweeping the rod aggressively sideways at a low angle. Once the fish is hooked, maintain pressure with a low rod angle

until the fish moves away from the boat. In most cases with a short line, a muskie will strike and then stop and thrash or turn and run as soon as it feels the hook. When this happens, use the weight and motion of the fish to maintain pressure while resisting the natural tendency to yank as hard as possible on a short line. Keeping the rod tip low also helps keep the fish lower in the water where it is less likely to jump or thrash and throw the hook. Don't panic and raise the rod directly over your head. Not only does this rod position lack sufficient leverage to set the hook properly, but it lifts and holds the fish on the surface where it has a distinct advantage with a poorly set fly. Moreover, with the fish and fly on or near the surface, if you miss the fish or it pulls out you stand a good chance of hitting yourself, the boat, or your buddy.

3. Depending on the speed and aggressiveness of the particular fish, with a short line strike it may be necessary to allow the fish to turn away briefly after it hits close to the boat. In this case, it's usually best to let the fish pull the line tight *before* sweeping the rod sideways for a sweep-set. Some fish strike and stop dead in the water while others strike and keep moving like a freight train. The angler must read the strike and anticipate which striking technique is best in a given situation.

4. After the fish is hooked, maintain constant pressure with the rod bent at a 45-degree angle, and a tight line. In some cases, after the initial hookup it may be best to let the fish move away from the boat instead of trying to hold it close on a short line where it is more likely to thrash on the surface and pull free.

When a fish hits at boatside at the end of a normal retrieve and/or during the figure-8, the leverage of the rod is the only option left to set the hook. In this situation, be sure to maintain a solid grip on the line under your index finger and either lift the rod directly—and firmly—overhead for the tip-set (Figure 1) or, once the fish eats on a figure-8, sweep the rod in the opposite direction the fish is moving for a back-set (Figure 2).

The Tip-Set

When a muskie hits at close range such as during the figure-8 or appears suddenly on your fly, you may be forced to lift the rod straight up using a tip-set to drive the hook home. This also is common with an exceptionally passive fish that simply "nips" or "mouths" the fly but does not fully commit. When you feel any resistance in this situation—or see the fish eat—immediately sweep the rod upward, literally using the rod tip and the weight of the fish to help set the hook. If you have room in the boat, you can even try to pull the fish forward in the water as you do this to apply more pressure at close range. Tip-set and lip-hooked fish like this are notoriously hard to hold on to but may be fought and landed if you "baby" them with steady but light tension during the fight.

The Figure-8 Back-Set

If the fish does not hit during the final stages of a retrieve, you will no doubt attempt to convert it with a figure-8. As you perform this unique short line maneuver, there are several strike techniques you

need to know to achieve a solid hookset without the benefit of a full strip-strike:

1. As you swing the fly underwater with the figure-8 or other maneuver, keep both arms extended with the line locked tightly under your rod hand index finger. The other hand should be firmly planted on the handle or fighting butt for control and leverage.

2. Continue swinging the fly through its paces and watch the fish closely for any signs of a strike. Although the strike is often lightning fast, you may be able to observe the fish as it kicks its tail to move forward, opens its mouth, and lunges towards the fly. Depending on the depth and clarity, however, you may only feel a nip, tug, or sudden stop from the full weight of the fish on your line when it finally eats. When in doubt on a figure-8, strike as hard as you can when you feel any resistance.

3. When you *see* and/or *feel* the fish lunge forward and strike the fly, since you can't possibly strip any more line for an effective strip-set, grip the line tightly and immediately sweep the rod *upward* or *backward* depending on the position of the fish and where you've got the most mobility. Of the two rod move-

ments, the backset works particularly well in this situation since a muskie will often turn and hit as the fly is moving rapidly up and away on the outside turn of the figure-8 pattern. Although not an easy technique to master, the reverse back-set strike technique uses the forward motion and weight of the fish to help the hook penetrate deeply and maintain pressure on a very short line. When performed properly, it not only provides a solid hookset—usually in the soft corner of the muskies mouth—but also keeps the fish lower in the water during the initial stage of the fight.

Depending on the fish and the situation, sweeping the rod upward (or forward) during a figure-8 may be necessary and unavoidable to achieve a set. This short line strike option will work so long as you achieve a solid hookset on the initial upward sweep—usually in the muskie's beak—and can re-position the rod quickly to maintain side pressure to avoid thrashing on the surface with a short line.

4. Once the fish is hooked on a short line, apply constant pressure by pulling and directing the fish with the rod tip low and to the side, stripping in line

as necessary. Again, depending on your body position at the time, this may require some awkward movements within the boat in order maintain tension.

With all this moving around you will also need to be aware of any loose fly line on deck and make sure you're not getting tangled in the process. If the fish wants to run, let it go while feathering the loose line away from the rod and reel until the line is clear. Fighting any fish on a short line is problematic. Letting the fish move away from the boat is always a good idea so long as you've got a solid hookset. Before trying any of these techniques, be sure to take a quick look around the boat and in the water. Beware of any obstructions that might interfere with your body, foot, and rod motion. Trolling motors, engines, and oars are all important tools for muskie fishing but can present a significant problem when you're striking a fish with any length of line.

Dealing with Top-Water Strikes

There is no doubt that fishing top-water flies is a highly effective way to search for, attract, and catch

It's all about the take: This long and lean muskie came out from under a nasty log jam and nailed my fly only inches from the rod tip. Without any line left to strip, I used the sweep-set to drive the hook home, resulting in yet another great memory and release.

Muskie guide Mark Meritt displays a fine Vermilion Lake, Minnesota fish taken on a Rainy's Offshore Popper. Setting the hook with a top-water fly requires considerable skill and self-control to avoid pulling the fly away from the fish. Mark always says "God save the Queen" to help him remember to wait a moment and feel the fish before setting the hook.

muskies. Hooking a fish, however, is another matter unless you know exactly what to do. The same strip-strike techniques apply when fishing on top, but with a major exception: It is absolutely critical that you keep the rod tip low and wait a moment after the strike to *feel the weight of the fish pull the line before attempting to set the hook.*

Although the surface strike of a muskie is typically an explosive event, and cause for most anglers to strike reactively, mentally prepare yourself for this technique or I guarantee you'll blow every fish. As is often the case when dry-fly fishing for trout, Atlantic salmon, or steelhead, it's the pause in the strike that allows the fish to turn and help set the hook itself before you pull it away. Most conventional-gear muskie anglers are well aware of this problem with top-water strikes, yet they still miss fish regularly by pulling the lure away too soon when they see a violent hit on top.

This important lesson was made frustratingly clear to me in my early days of muskie fishing with a fly. I was fishing with guide Mike Lazarus on a small Canadian lake that held a good population of fish up to 50 inches. I'd taken many fish there on streamers over the years but never one on top. The water that July was warming rapidly. We knew a top-water bite from post-spawn fish was a distinct possibility. I decided this was a good time to test an early version of what I now call the Tiktaalik popper. This new pattern had a chartreuse body and a matching bucktail trailer. Witnessing its appealing sound and action in the water, we were both confident it would work despite never having hooked a fish with it before.

After an uneventful morning with no action other than a few chunky smallmouth bass, I was losing hope and ready to go back to my favorite streamer. Mike encouraged me to stick to the surface, reminding me—as he always does—that it was "just a matter of time." I cast my popper tight to a weed edge close to deep water and began to retrieve with a steady and loud *chug, chug, chug.* About half the way back to the boat the water exploded. A nice muskie was suddenly suspended in the air with my fly in its mouth. I struck back right away and was rewarded with only my fly—

Strike! In this amazing series of photos captured by publisher Tom Pero you witness the full excitement of a top-water take. In the first two frames the popper boils noisily along the surface of a quiet cove. In the third frame, the fish hits from below with a typically violent splash. In the final frame the fish jumps clear out of the water with my fly in its mouth.

no fish. I was disappointed but kept fishing with the knowledge we finally had a technique that worked. A few minutes later the exact same thing happened!

Now I was really getting discouraged. When it happened for the third time, I was ready to hang it up

---

Author's Tips: Top-Water Strikes

Here's a helpful tip to improve your odds with a top-water taker: Before you set the hook, try saying the words "God save the Queen," "I've got you," or just about anything you can think of to remind you to pause a moment before striking. The real trick, of course, is to resist lifting the rod when you say it. When done right, this technique provides that critical extra few seconds of time you need for the fish to turn before your strip-strike. I learned the value of this for the first time when trout fishing with guide Noel Jetson on Lake of the Pines in Tasmania, Australia (hence the "God Save the Queen" part) many years ago. It always comes in handy when I find myself missing fish by striking too quickly whether trout or muskies.

---

and try another sport or go find a bottle of scotch.

After some heated lunch-time analysis of both fly and fisher, we determined the probable source of my problem: My top-water strike was simply too quick. Although most dry-fly fishing requires a quick set with the rod tip as soon as the fish takes the fly, my natural striking reflex was one I would now have to resist to catch a muskie on top.

We decided to apply this theory to our afternoon's fishing. A nearby bay with newly emerging lily pads seemed perfect for a test run. I cast the popper to the edge of the pads, made a few strips, and a fish exploded on my fly. Contrary to every fiber in my body, I kept my rod tip low and waited until I could actually *feel the pull of the fish on the line* before striking. When I did finally strike, to my amazement, the fish was on, and I had my first muskie on the surface.

Line Management When Fighting a Fish

Once you hook a fish, eliminating slack and maintaining tension with your index finger is much more important than worrying about getting the fish on the reel immediately. Sure, if the fish hits on a long

line the moment the fly hits the water, you may have no problem quickly reeling up the slack with your large arbor and fighting it off the reel. More than likely, however, the fish will hit midway during your retrieve or at right at boat side. You'll be left with a lot of line in the water or the boat to worry about. This situation is particularly tricky if the fish runs right away taking line as it goes. As with tarpon, permit or bonefish, make sure your line is free of any knots, kinks, or loops that could get snarled in the guides. Also avoid stepping on your line or having your slack jump off the deck and wrapping around your rod, reel, or fighting butt. Here are a couple of line-management techniques I've found useful over the years:

• When you hook a fish, immediately look down and make sure your line is clear and free of any obstructions. If it is and the fish wants to run, keep your rod bent sideways or overhead at a 45-degree angle to maintain tension. Use your stripping hand to "feather" the line low and away from your body. The farther you keep the line away from your rod, the better the odds it won't tangle. As the fish pulls line, you can also control line and reduce tangles by forming a small "O" with your thumb and forefinger away from your body. Both saltwater line-management techniques help prevent the line from jumping off the

deck and tangling as the fish runs.

• If the fish doesn't run immediately, keep the rod raised at a 45-degree angle and continue stripping to maintain tension. Allow the fish to pull against the bend of the long rod. Resist the temptation at this point to yank on the fish to control it. You can also use this brief opportunity to untangle or clear any loose line on the deck. Muskies often thrash and head-shake in one place immediately after being hooked—your best option is to keep a tight line and be ready for a run when it comes.

• When you set the hook with the strip-strike, try to keep the rod butt tight against your forearm for additional leverage and to avoid tangling any loose line around it when the fish runs.

• Get some help! If you're fishing with a buddy or a guide and your line is not clear, use whatever language it takes to call for assistance. Clear the line as quickly as possible before the fish gets off. This beats trying to untangle a bunch of line by yourself. It allows you to stay focused on your fish. The same rules apply for eliminating any potential boat obstructions such as a trolling motor, anchor, or loose tackle. If you're fishing alone, then my best advice is to always keep a clear deck, check constantly for tangles, and hope for the best when a fish finally hits.

Fish on: The long and limber fly rod is an excellent tool for fighting large fish like the muskie. Use the full leverage of the rod—much like a shock absorber—to control your fish until it tires. Always keep an eye on the fish and any potential snags that might cause serious problems during the fight. Note this fish is bull-dogging straight toward the protective cover of a midstream log.

Playing a Muskie

Playing a muskie on a fly rod is one of the greatest thrills in fly fishing: the combination of a long, limber fly rod, and holding your line directly to fight the fish by hand until—*if*—you can get it on the reel. You literally feel every movement of the fish as it attempts to get off. The fly rod is also an excellent tool for fighting a muskie because it allows you to exert a substantial amount of leverage while not overly stressing the line or the fish. Compared to fighting a muskie on conventional tackle, it is a very tactile and intimate experience, one that you will never forget.

Although muskies are not physically capable of long powerful runs like tarpon or bonefish, they more than make up for it with spectacular jumps, violent head shakes, short powerful lunges, and alligator-like "death-roll" twists and turns. They also like to run under the boat when they get close resulting in some interesting contortions of both angler and rod. Once you've set the hook properly it's time to start dealing with a whole new set of issues.

Controlling Your Fish

The first few seconds after you hook a muskie on a fly are the most critical to boating your fish. The excitement of hooking a muskie combined with the unpredictable nature of the fight make for some tense moments until the fish is brought under control. Whatever happens at this stage, the primary goal is to keep a tight line and eliminate slack using the rod, the strip, and the reel in the most efficient way possible.

Although each fight plays out in its own way, once hooked, a muskie usually reacts with one or all of the following behaviors: jumping, shaking its head, thrashing, rolling, twisting on the surface or below, and strong, short runs. Here's some advice for dealing with each of these common situations:

Jumps

Muskies often jump once or even several times as soon as they're hooked on a fly. Although I've seen it happen many times using conventional gear, it seems to be much more the norm when fly fishing. While it is certainly a thrill to see a muskie several feet in the air with your fly hanging out of its mouth, it is also a speedy way to lose a fish if not handled properly.

When a muskie jumps, the first thing you need to do is resist the natural tendency to pull back and risk dislodging the fly. Rather, the best approach is to "bow" to the fish. This well-known technique, adapted from tarpon fly fishing, requires the angler to momentarily lean or "bow" forward, extending the rod hand toward the fish to reduce tension on the line and the fly. As much as your natural inclination is to pull back immediately when the fish jumps, with a longer fly rod it is especially critical that you give the fish momentary slack at this time. This technique takes practice. It may not go quite as planned the first few times. But in most cases it's vital to get through the initial jumping stage of the fight.

Head Shakes, Thrashing, Rolls and Twists

Once hooked, a muskie normally reacts with violent head shakes, trashing on the surface or below, and

Bow to the fish: Like fighting a tarpon or Atlantic salmon, it helps to "bow" to a muskie when it jumps to avoid excessive pressure on the line. The trick is to anticipate the jump. Muskies—especially fly-caught muskies—often jump as soon as they feel the hook and then again when close to the boat. Look for this spectacular moment, and remember to bow to the mighty muskellunge.

fast "alligator" rolls, spinning and twisting in one spot. This response usually happens when a fish hits right at boatside. But it can happen any time a muskie hits depending on the fish and the strike. It is a critical time during the fight when many fish are lost on any kind of gear. The best way to deal with this situation is to sweep the rod tip down and to the side while maintaining a tight line. Although you may be tempted at this time to lift up and back on your rod, this only serves to keep the fish on the surface, increasing the risk of loss. When done properly with a fly rod, this maneuver forces and directs the fish's head back down into the water instead of allowing it to remain in one place. This technique is difficult to perform in the excitement of battle and without the benefit of experience. Practice it mentally. It should become almost automatic whenever you encounter fish at close range.

Sometimes a fish rolls, spins, and twists so rapidly that it entangles itself helplessly in the line. While it is possible to land a fish in this condition, it is not the most sporting way to fight a fish. It may injure the fish or result in the hook being dislodged. If the opportunity presents itself, pull gently on the line using the rod tip to guide the line and allow the fish to unroll while it rests on the surface.

Runs and Lunges

After the initial jumps and surface thrashing, a muskie normally makes several short, powerful runs. While I've had some larger fish make long runs of 30 to 50 feet—and even pull a smaller boat in the process—most of the time they take only five, 10, or 20 feet of line before stopping to rest. With the exception of big fish or extremely swift current, under normal circumstances it's unlikely you'll see your backing when fighting a muskie with a fly rod. Sometimes these runs are combined with rolls, twists, and turns; other times they're simply straight runs with the fish holding deep or close to the surface.

When a muskie runs, use the fly rod to your full advantage by allowing the fish to work against it like a big shock absorber. This does not mean holding the rod straight over your head or bending the rod in half. Rather, you should hold the rod at a 45-degree angle with the butt section near your waist. Allow the entire rod to absorb the pressure. Let the fish run when it wants but keep control and tension on the line either by letting it slide under your index finger or off the reel against moderate drag.

When the fish stops, strip quickly or reel in any slack line and pull back *steadily* on the fly rod to one side or the other to turn the fish. Do not tug or jerk

Catch and release: Guide Mike Lazarus and I take a moment to admire a hard-won Canadian muskie on the fly. The release cradle is one of several good options for landing your fish and ensuring it survives to fight another day.

violently! Changing the angle of pull imparts sideways pressure on the fish—a good way to keep it under control. Use your body to apply additional leverage and turn the fish when necessary. The goal at this point is to keep constant pressure; never let the fish rest.

During the fight, always face your fish squarely to maximize leverage and control. In some cases, you may even find it necessary to walk around the deck or even to the back of the boat, especially if the fish is getting close and is near the engine or other obstruction. For some unknown reason, many anglers like to stand in the same place as they fight a fish—this is definitely not the best way to land a muskie on a fly.

Another advantage to facing your fish is the ability to see any underwater obstructions a hooked fish almost invariably seeks out. Muskies are at home in shallow water. They head right for any heavy weeds, wood, or other natural cover they can find in an attempt to hide or shake the hook. Any time a fish gets close to these potential snag areas you risk losing it. If the fish gets deeply tangled in weeds or wood but remains hooked, don't give up. I've saved many a "lost" fish by approaching quietly and untangling my line with the rod tip or an oar.

The Final Stages

The total time it takes to fight a muskie on a fly rod depends on a number of factors: the water you're fishing, the size of the fish, and your skill. Muskies are known more for their elusiveness and the way they hit than for their fighting stamina. With most fish the fight lasts anywhere from five to 15 minutes. I have had some large fish over 50 inches in open water or heavy current take as long as 20 minutes to land but

this is more the exception than the rule. Occasionally you'll find a small fish that fights exceptionally hard for it size. This is always fun. On the other hand, I've also had large, impressive fish barely fight at all. You never know what to expect. It's really more about the thrill of fooling a muskie with a fly than anything else.

It's important *not* to fight your fish to total exhaustion. Doing so will only cause extreme stress to the fish, making its full recovery less likely. This is especially important in warmer water temperatures during the heat of summer. Playing a fish for an extended period of time also increases lactic acid buildup in the fish's muscle mass, significantly reducing the odds of recovery. The fish may swim away looking healthy but turn belly up when out of sight. With a fly rod it is possible to subdue your fish in short order, avoiding additional or unnecessary injury.

Once a muskie has finished fighting, it typically rests or floats on or just under the surface. You'll know the battle is over when it no longer resists your pull and you can steer it easily with the rod. Don't be fooled at this stage of the fight. Although the fish might be worn out, it is still very much capable of a last-minute short burst, jump, or roll. Many fish also run under the boat at this stage in search of a final hideout.

Use the leverage of the rod and a gentle touch with your index finger on the line to control the fish at close range. Once again, *do not lift the rod directly overhead*. Keep it at an angle while applying steady pressure and control. If the fish does make a last dash under the boat, simply follow it underwater, submerging the entire rod if necessary. If it wants to move to the other side of the boat, then swing the long rod under the boat making sure to avoid the engine or trolling motor in the process.

If you've had a chance to get the fish on the reel by this point, make sure the drag is light. Use your hand to "palm" the bottom of the reel to maintain tension instead of holding tight on the reel handle.

Whether fighting the fish by hand or off the reel make sure your line is clear so that the fish can still run if it wants to. It is common for a hooked muskie to bolt at the sight of the boat or a net—be prepared for this likely event right up to the final moment.

Catch and Release

Boating and Releasing Your Fish the Right Way

Whether fishing conventionally or with a fly, most muskie anglers today practice a strict ethic of catch and release. Muskies Inc., the anglers' group that has promoted this practice since 1970, estimates that as many as 98 percent of all muskie anglers now release their fish to fight another day. Release data from this organization's "Lunge Log" indicates that the number of fish over 50 inches has increased from only 186 from 1970 through 1986 to more than 2,500 in current years. This modern practice has clearly resulted in improved fishing on many regulated waters. It has also fostered a greater community understanding that the muskie is a splendid gamefish species worth protecting. When you consider the fact that a trophy fish exceeding 40 or 50 inches has lived 10 to 20 years—and that it is highly unlikely a fish of such size will soon be replaced by Nature if reduced to possession—catch and release becomes even more vital.

It's worth noting that as recently as 20 years ago most legal muskies were killed on the spot and headed straight to the taxidermist or the local cooler for display. In fact, until the 1950s, shooting a muskie in the head with a handgun was still the accepted method of dispatching most fish, large and small.

With the advent of plastic fish replicas by skilled taxidermists, it is no longer necessary to haul your fish back to the dock to put it on the wall. A high-quality mount can be created using photos and careful measurements. Lax Reproductions (www.laxreproductions.com) and Fittante Replicas (www.fittantereplicas.com) are two talented taxidermists specializing in muskie replicas.

How you land and release your fish is critical to its survival. There is simply no point in catch and release or higher size limits if the fish you catch is going to die anyway. As most fly fishers know, however, it's one thing to take pride in releasing a trophy and another thing to do it properly and with care.

Probably the two most important factors to a muskie's survival are using a lure or fly versus live bait, and keeping your fish in the water as long as possible. As a fly fisher using a single-hook fly, you will rarely encounter a fish that has taken your fly deeply. This is no guarantee a fish won't die of other causes, but it is markedly better treatment than impaling the fish deeply with multiple hooks that require extensive removal. More than likely your hook will be in the corner or side of the muskie's mouth, allowing for relatively easy reach and removal.

There are a number of other important considerations and techniques when landing and releasing a muskie depending on the size of the fish, hook placement, and your available equipment.

Be Prepared

Always carry long-nosed pliers or a hook remover for gripping and removing a hook. A jaw spreader is also helpful when removing hooks to keep the fish's mouth open long enough to reach the hook. Many

How not to hand land a muskie: In a moment of over confidence, I chose to land this hard-fighting muskie by hand. Bad call. Although I didn't feel a thing, it took only seconds for my hand to start bleeding as if I'd just been in a bar fight. Note the retracted trolling motor and the deeply bowed rod in the first frame as the fish seeks shade cover underneath the boat.

anglers carry a wire cutter or small bolt cutter for cutting hooks which cannot be removed without possibly injuring the fish. Another useful item for landing a muskie is a "release glove" made of tear-resistant material to protect your hands and control the fish.

Keep Your Fish in the Water

Once the fish has tired, if at all possible, it is best to keep your fish in the water instead of lifting it into the boat by hand or with a net. For obvious reasons, fish tend to remain calmer in these situations than those hoisted out of the water. Handling the fish as little as possible also helps protect the fish—and you—from serious injury. While not all fish will cooperate, it is possible with many fish to measure and remove hooks while the fish sits horizontally in the water next to the boat. It also helps to have a floating ruler or tape-measure markings on the outside of the boat at the water line for a quick measurement. After measuring the fish it is often possible to remove the hook by simply gripping it firmly at the bend with pliers and letting the weight of the fish pull or twist against it.

Hand Landing a Smaller Muskie

It may be necessary to use your hands to grip a small muskie to remove a hook. In this situation it's best to leave the fish in the water and lift the fish's head by gripping just above and behind the gills where the back begins to narrow. Assuming the fish cooperates, you can then get the angle you need to remove a hook with either pliers or hook remover. This technique is commonly used by pike anglers, and is quite effective with smaller fish of up to 40 inches. It's important when using this grip to avoid touching the fish's eyes in any way to avoid injury.

Hand Landing a Large Muskie

With fish longer than 40 inches, it may be necessary to use a different hand grip to control the fish. Try sliding your hand under the inside of the gill cover to the point where the flesh meets the underside of the jaw. When done correctly, it is possible with this grip to avoid touching the gills. Try to maintain control long enough to pry open the mouth and remove a hook. When using this grip with a large fish it can be

difficult to maintain a hold when the fish begins twisting as they often do. To prevent injury, simply slip the fish back in the water instead of dropping it on the bottom of the boat.

Whenever using a hand grip it is important to wet your hands first to prevent further injury to the fish. You also may want to consider using a release glove, wet cloth, or towel—this will give you a better grip and protect your hands and the fish.

Boga-Grip: A Boga-Grip is an exceptionally useful tool for both handling fish of all sizes and determining their weight. With its vise-like jaws and 360-degree swinging rubber handle, it assures you will not injure yourself or the fish. When using the Boga-Grip an angler must be careful not to lift the fish vertically for any longer than necessary to avoid internal injury. After the weight is taken, it is best to support the fish under the belly with the grip held to one side.

Nets versus Cradles: There is much debate among muskie fishers regarding the use of nets or cradles. Some swear by nets while others will only use a cradle or nothing at all. While both offer a good option for landing a fish, they need to be used correctly to insure the best release possible.

• Nets: Probably the most important thing about a net is using one big enough to hold your fish. A small net does more harm than good. It may result in the loss of a fish that can't fit, leaving only your fly behind in the mesh. Most muskie fishers use a long-handled net with a 40-inch or larger basket for easy capture. Many nets today also utilize rubber-coated netting that helps avoid injury to the fish. Frabill muskie nets (www.frabill.com) are widely considered the best when it comes to large nets for this sport.

Proper netting technique takes practice. When netting a muskie it's essential not to swipe or stab at the fish. Wait until you have a fish moving slowly or resting quietly on the surface. A fish that sees the net may also make a final run so it's critical to be prepared for this ahead of time. It's best to net a muskie head first, using a firm sweep of the net and then lifting up quickly once it's inside the entire basket. After the fish is in the net, leave it in the water until the hooks are removed.

• Cradles: Among the serious muskie crowd, cradles are increasingly popular. Typically made of

Swimming with the fishes: As a dedicated practitioner of catch and release, Mike Lazarus will go to any length—and embarrassment—to ensure a fish has fully recovered. Always watch your fish after it's released to make sure it can swim on its own power.

Good release: The personal satisfaction of catching and releasing a muskie on the fly is a feeling beyond words. After you release your fish, take a moment to enjoy this noteworthy accomplishment—and think about what lessons it may have taught you before you begin fishing again.

strong mesh netting or cloth stretched between two buoyant wood or plastic poles, they offer a perfect, custom-made "stretcher" for muskies of all sizes. Given the elongated shape of a muskie it also makes sense to use this approach, rather than a net, which can contort and injure the fish. To use the cradle you simply slide the fish into one end and then lift or pull the poles together locking the fish in place. The cradled fish can then be left in the water the entire time allowing for easy access to remove hooks and prepare for release. The only real drawback to a cradle is it requires two anglers to be used properly.

Holding the fish and taking photos: With the popularity of catch and release, the camera has become a popular accessory to record your success. We all like to have photos of our fish. Holding the fish the wrong way or for too long, however, can result in injury to or even the death of your prize. When taking photos of a muskie, keep the fish in the water while your prepare your camera. This is much better than trying to hold and manage the fish while your camera man tries to figure out where it is and what button to push.

When the camera is ready to shoot, lift the fish gently from the water using a Boga-Grip or hand hold on the lower jaw with your other hand on the belly. You can also do this by holding the tail wrist with one hand and placing the other hand under the belly. The key in both instances is to keep the fish supported horizontally instead of vertically. After you take a few photos, place the fish immediately back in the water and prepare it for a quick release.

Reviving and releasing a fish properly: Once you remove the hook, hold the fish horizontally in the water with a firm grip on the tail and/or under the belly. When the fish is ready for release it will resist your grip and attempt to swim away. With fish that show obvious signs of stress, be sure to hold them in the water until they are fully revived. If necessary, you can assist the fish by gently pushing it back and forth in the water, directing more water through its gills. After the fish has been released, watch it swim away for the enjoyment of a good release and to make sure it does not show any further signs of stress. If the fish is not fully recovered, it may swim off and then resurface again. Observe the area carefully to be assured that your release was successful. If not, take whatever steps are necessary to revive the fish again.

A SEASON
ON THE WATER

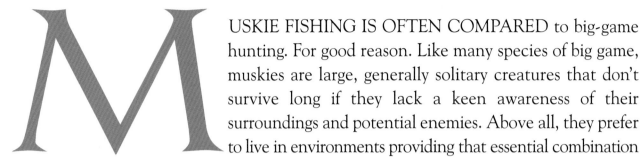

MUSKIE FISHING IS OFTEN COMPARED to big-game hunting. For good reason. Like many species of big game, muskies are large, generally solitary creatures that don't survive long if they lack a keen awareness of their surroundings and potential enemies. Above all, they prefer to live in environments providing that essential combination of food, comfort, and security—moving only when prompted by reproductive urges, water temperatures, forage location, or danger. Though ever changing, these predictable migratory and feeding patterns throughout the year are what provide the skilled hunter with an opportunity for a shot (or a bite) when things go right.

Contrary to popular wisdom, hunting for muskies with a fly is productive throughout the entire fishing season, not only in the spring and fall. My own experience has shown that from the first warm breezes of spring right through the first snow flakes of winter, it is entirely possible to catch muskies consistently on a fly. Although there are certain seasons and patterns when muskies are more active and most susceptible, whenever this fish decides to eat I believe it's vulnerable with the right presentation and fly.

As with all fishing, your success ultimately depends on understanding where muskies feed, what they prefer to eat, and how to fish the fly in a wide range of conditions. Among these critical factors, the relationship between predator and prey may be the most significant. As respected Illinois and Minnesota muskie guide and fisheries biologist Chad Cain notes, "Find the forage and you will find the fish."

Your fishing game plan also must take into account the specific type of water you fish and the best fish holding structure within that water as the season progresses. Finally, you need to consider that effective fly choices, retrieves, triggers, and presentations change as conditions and water temperatures fluctuate.

While each specific body of water has its own particular fish-holding "hotspots" and patterns, this important chapter focuses on the best overall lake and river tactics and strategies for finding and catching muskies on the fly in the spring, summer, and fall seasons. You should approach any fishing situation with the understanding that most areas in a given body of water hold very few fish. The real key is to stay focused, find those areas that have the highest percentage, and work them to the best of your ability with a fly.

Timing is Everything

Although we humans like to categorize the seasons into months, Mother Nature has other ideas about what actually happens throughout the year. This has become increasingly evident with global heating and other extreme changes in normal weather patterns making predictable fishing seemingly more difficult. The main point is that fish behavior and levels of activity are dictated not by the month you fish but by certain natural imperatives, such as biological urges, environmental changes, and water temperatures.

The reproductive urge is clearly the overriding factor dictating the aggressiveness and location of fish in the early season. Each spring muskies make a predictable migration to shallow-water spawning areas and hold there until conditions—warmer water temperatures and hunger—dictate a need to move. Once summer is in full swing, muskies are generally more active and aggressive because of the uniformity of warmer temperatures throughout a given body of water. Other environmental factors, such as available cover and forage ultimately determine prime summer holding areas and peak feeding times. Summer fishing pressure can have a negative effect on fish location due to increased angler and boat activity. In the fall months, falling water temperatures, remaining viable cover, and forage location are critical to determining where and when fish will feed right up until ice-up.

Spring—Prime Time

Water Temperatures: +/- 45° to 65°Fahrenheit

Spring is one of my favorite times of year for muskie fishing with a fly. With fish increasingly active and

Why I love the spring: Fly fishing for early season muskie can be excellent when the weather and fish cooperate. This nicely marked Indiana lake fish was one of many that ate my streamer fished tight to newly emerging weed cover in shallow water.

feeding more regularly due to rising water temperatures, they are uniquely susceptible to any kind of artificial, especially a well-placed fly. Muskies concentrate in greater numbers in shallow water, significantly increasing your chances with the fly presentation. Your opportunities in the spring are further increased by the fact water clarity is usually very good on lakes because of the lack of significant weed growth.

The prospect of early season muskies is always a welcome opportunity after a long winter of no fishing. As muskie fly-fishing guide Mark Meritt likes to say, "In the spring of the year there are always some fish, somewhere, doing something!" Not surprisingly, conventional muskie fishers do quite well with this first "spring bite" fishing live bait and a variety of smaller spinners, bass plugs, and twitch baits.

Fly fishing for muskies in the spring can be your very best opportunity of the year for single or multiple fish. In fact, it's not uncommon on the right water to see and catch several fish in a day on a fly. Many of these fish—especially smaller males—bear scars and bruises from the rigors of spawning. With rising water temperatures and generally more active fish, also expect to start seeing frequent following fish and fish that are either swimming, sunning, or boiling on the surface. Keep an eye out for these spring fish behaviors and you will increase your odds with a fly.

In the early spring, muskies of all sizes are usually found in very shallow water close to spawning areas. Depending on latitude, water temperatures, and weather patterns, you are likely to find these fish in various stages of the spawn including pre-spawn, spawning, or post-spawn. Although muskie fishing is closed in many northern states at this time, I discourage anglers from fishing to visibly spawning fish—where the season is open—to preserve the fishery.

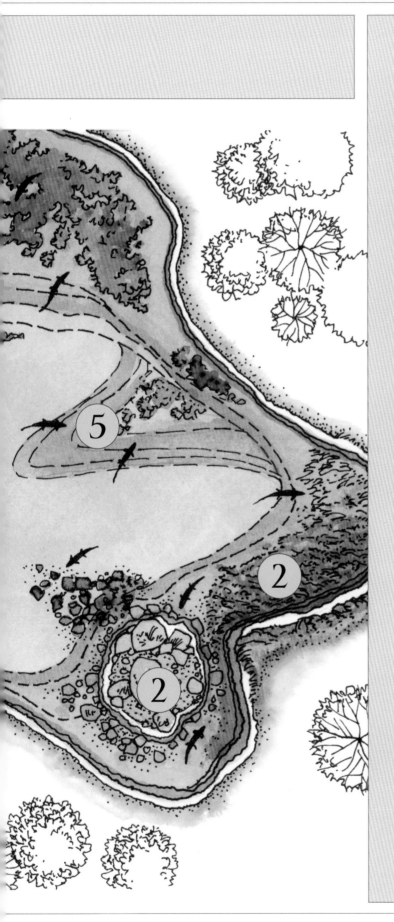

Where to Find Muskies in the Spring:

(1) Shallow, weedy bays, marshes, flats, and coves: Large or small, these areas provide plenty of forage and shallow cover for muskies following the spawn. Always a good bet with a fly rod, especially when newly emerging green weed growth is present.

(2) Gravel, rock, mud, and sand-bottom bays and bars: This darker bottom structure warms quickly with the spring sun and retains heat well. Muskies spawn here and remain in these areas after spawning for some time to recuperate and feed. Once water temperatures begin to warm, deep and shallow rock bars directly outside spawning areas also hold fish early in the season.

(3) Shoreline weeds and wood: Newly emerging weeds, reed beds, fallen timber, and stump fields provide plenty of cover for forage and muskies, especially in lakes, flowages, and reservoirs. When close to deeper water, spring fish will stick to these areas for security and food throughout the spring.

(4) Creek mouths, inlets, and channels: Typical of bigger rivers, flowages and reservoirs, these areas are where muskies commonly spawn and then resume foraging. They hold good numbers of fish depending on water levels and clarity. Once the water warms above 60°F some fish begin moving out to deeper water breaks directly adjacent to these areas in search of forage.

(5) Deeper weed edges, breaks, flats, and points close to spawning grounds: As the water temperature increases to above 60°, larger female muskies are the first to move out of shallow spawning grounds, suspending near these spots to recuperate and feed. Look for newly emerging green weeds and warming trends to provide opportunities for a bigger fish at this time.

Post-spawn fish tend to stay quite shallow through the spring, feeding on newly hatched forage until the first transition period when water temperatures rise above 60°F. While smaller male fish usually dominate the catch at this time, larger female fish are particularly vulnerable in late spring as they venture out to recover from the rigors of spawning and begin to feed again.

I first discovered this big-fish springtime opportunity when fishing in northern Wisconsin with guide Mike Mladenik. We were fishing a large flowage. I had high hopes for the day. Mike quietly maneuvered the boat to the edge of a newly emerging weed bed when I thought I spotted a good fish swirl on the surface. I couldn't see the fish but made a long cast with my favorite white bucktail streamer and began a steady retrieve. A fish hit hard after just a few strips and stayed deep—an indication it was probably big. After

Influence of Sun and Wind

Structure location relative to the angle of the sun and wind direction play an important part in spring fishing. Being highly sensitive to water temperatures, areas offering the most direct sunlight usually hold the most fish, so long as they also provide adequate holding structure and forage. Given the angle of the sun in the spring, areas with shallow structure and direct sun exposure on the north side of a lake or flowage warm faster, prompting the earliest weed growth. As a result, these areas draw more potential forage and, therefore, more muskies.

If the wind is out of the north for a sustained period of time, warmer water is pushed to the south, eventually moving the fish with it. The opposite holds true when the wind is from the south, providing an ideal setup with both sun-lit northside structure and a good wind direction.

a long tense fight, I landed and gently released a beautiful 47-inch female muskie: a nice way to start the season!

In the northern states and Canada, most spring muskie fishing takes place during May and June. Depending on where you live, these months usually coincide with the opening season for muskies and offer your first legitimate shot of the year at a fish. In states with no closed season, such as Illinois, Indiana, and Kentucky, you will often find good fishing as early as February, March, or April. These southern-latitude lakes and reservoirs warm sooner than those in the north, resulting in active fish much earlier in the year. How warm the water temperatures are when the season opens in your state depends on the year and the type of water you plan to fish.

During the spring months you can normally expect water temperatures anywhere from a low of 40° to a high of 70°F. The gradual—sometimes rapid—rise in temperatures during these months is a key factor in fish activity and aggressiveness to a fly. Though I've caught muskies on a fly in water as cold as the low 40s, typically the better spring fishing occurs once the temperatures reach the mid-50s to mid-60s. When considering a spring trip, check the forecast often and keep a look out for a rapid rise in air temperatures, usually driven by a southwest wind following a major change in the jet stream pattern.

Where to Fish Muskies in the Spring

As a general rule, the most productive springtime muskie fishing is found closest to spawning areas in water four to 15 feet deep. Following spawning, some fish remain quite shallow as they recover while others move to the closest deep weed-line break or edge. As the water temperatures rise above 60°F, fish movement increases as muskies begin to make the transition from spring to summer patterns. This typically takes place by June but with warmer springs fish will sometimes be in summer locations by as early as late May.

Shallow, more fertile eutrophic and mesotrophic lakes, flowages, and reservoirs offer some of the best early-season action with a fly. These water types typically contain a wide variety of ideal heat-retaining cover such as weeds, wood, and rock. They also offer the most abundant early forage choices providing plenty of food for smaller but aggressive fish.

Deeper, clearer, and colder oligotrophic lakes also offer good fishing in the late-spring season with fewer but larger fish. Because these less-fertile lakes warm slowly, muskies normally seek out the warmest water they can find in and around heat-retaining sand,

River fishing is productive in the spring once water levels stabilize and the first weed growth appears. This typical Great Lakes spotted muskie came from a the edge of an emerald green, cabbage weed bed on the mighty St. Lawrence River in Québec.

gravel, rock, mud, or vegetation-covered bays and flats. Muskies also remain shallow for longer periods of time since the main lake body takes longer to warm up.

The very nature of oligotrophic lakes means there are typically fewer prime fish holding spots to target during the spring. If you or your guide knows where these spots are you may find good but limited opportunities with the fly rod. Given the numbers and activity levels of fish in more fertile waters, however, it's usually best to focus on these trophy fisheries later in the year.

Most river fishing at this time of year can be risky because of typically high water levels and water dirty from runoff. Even if it is possible to fish, because of the volume of water the fish are usually spread out and hard to target with a fly. Depending on water levels, some larger river systems with clear backwaters and sloughs offer good fly-rod opportunities for post-spawn muskies. (see illustration on page 216-217)

Spring Presentations, Retrieves, and Flies

My spring choice of presentations, retrieves, and flies is dictated by several factors: forage size, the aggressiveness of the fish on a given day, weather conditions, and water temperature. As a general rule,

in the spring you'll have the best success using smaller streamer patterns three to eight inches in length. This fly choice makes perfect sense when you consider the average size of most spring forage such as newly hatched panfish, gamefish, and rough fish. It is also reinforced by the fact most muskies are not yet focused on a larger forage profile so common later in the season.

This is not to say a really big fly will not work in the spring, but with colder water the majority of fish are more likely to strike a more natural, smaller profile. Conventional muskie fishers have followed this line of thinking for years. They catch the majority of their early season fish using live chubs and minnows and smaller lures such as in-line spinners, jigs, twitch baits, and bass plugs.

In the relatively cold water temperatures common in the early spring, you'll have the most consistent success fishing your smaller streamer fly with a slower, deeper strip retrieve combined with frequent pauses and the occasional twitch or pump using your rod tip. The added attraction of the twitch is critical at this time of year—it makes the fly look alive when moving at slower speeds. In fact, one of the most productive springtime baits for conventional muskie anglers is the "twitch bait."

The speed of your retrieve is the real key to catching fish in the spring. In the earliest part of the spring, with chilled water temperatures, fish typically will not move very fast or far for your fly. Fish slow and low keeping the fly in the fishes' zone as long as possible. As the temperature rises your retrieve speed can also be increased. Smaller males respond well at this time to a faster moving fly, but larger females may require a slightly slower retrieve given a longer recovery time from the spawn. It always pays to experiment with retrieve speed to find something that works.

When water temperatures rise above 60°F in the late spring you should start having increased success in shallow water using both streamers and top-water flies. As with the streamer, fish the top-water fly at a moderate to fast pace, keeping an eye open for follows. If you don't move any fish, it may also help to retrieve the top-water fly erratically with an occasional stop, burst of speed, or sudden change of direction. On warmer days, fishing both a top-water fly and a streamer over the same water can be an effective technique to trigger a fish.

The most effective fly presentations in the spring are

Spring Muskie Fly-Fishing Summary

Best Water Types: Shallow, fertile, eutrophic, and mesotrophic lakes and most flowages. Oligotrophic lakes have limited spawning areas but hold fish shallow for longer periods. Lakes and reservoirs in southern climates offer good fishing very early in the season due to warmer water temperatures. Rivers are often high and dirty due to runoff; look for fish in backwaters and sloughs.

Hotspots: Any shallow water structure that warms quickly and where fish hold before, during, and after spawning. Look for signs of cover, especially wood, rocks, and newly emerging green weeds.

Best Flies: Smaller three-to eight-inch streamers and Clouser Deep Minnows work well early in the season. Fish on top when the water temperature rises above 60°F. Natural colors are best in clear water and brighter colors in stained or shallow water.

Best Retrieves and Triggers: Early season fish slow, deep, and steady. Use tick-and-twitch and bump-and-grind techniques to induce strikes from fish tight to cover. Use the pause-and-twitch to trigger a strike from following fish. Pick up the speed of the retrieve as water temperatures increase.

Best Presentations: Blind fishing and sight fishing. Cover the water methodically with multiple casts in the same area. Sight fish to any fish you see. Top water can be very effective when the water warms.

---

blind casting over shallow water structure and sight fishing.

When blind casting it's best to fan cast each area slowly and methodically, keeping your casts tightly spaced. In areas with newly emerging weeds, use the ticking and twitching technique to attract fish holding tight to cover. In areas with wood, use the bump-and-grind technique, placing the fly as close as possible to the structure—or making contact—to trigger a fish. Spring muskies often hold very shallow, so it also pays to place a few casts right against the shoreline in water only a few inches deep.

Sight fishing with streamers to shallow-water muskies can also be very productive in the spring. Mostly you'll encounter smaller males suspended or cruising in or just outside a shallow spawning bay. When you see a fish, approach it with caution. Cast well ahead so your fly intercepts the fish as it moves. Always watch the fish closely for a reaction; any increase in speed or opening and closing of its mouth usually means a fish is about to strike. If the fish is only mildly interested, but still following, use the pause-and-twitch technique to prompt a strike. Reading an individual fish's behavior is the key to success with this method.

A wide variety of fly colors work in the spring depending on the preferred forage, weather conditions, and the specific water and structure. In clear-water conditions commonly found on natural lakes it's usually best to stick with more natural colors that "match the hatch" in terms of forage. This means fishing flies with a predominance of yellow, white, black, brown, gold, copper, and gray. In stained-water conditions such as commonly found on a flowage, it's usually better to fish flies with more contrast and brighter colors such as yellow, orange, and chartreuse. In both clear- and dark-water situations, it also helps to have some flash on the fly to provide added attraction.

Fly fishing for muskies in the spring is reliable, assuming the weather holds and you don't have a major cold front. Unlike summer and fall months when your windows of opportunity can be smaller, once the water warms you will find fish susceptible to the fly throughout the day. Spring fishing action typically increases with daytime heating so early mornings are not as important as fishing in the heat of day and into the evenings.

Summer—Anything is Possible

Water Temperatures: +/- 65° to 80°F

Depending on the latitude, the peak summer months of July and August offer some of the best muskie fishing of the year. With ideal water temperatures

Lake St. Clair fly-fishing guide Brian Meszaros cradles a magnificent early season spotted muskie caught by his client on a 2/0 perch pattern Clouser Minnow. Regardless of size, muskies like this trophy will often eat a relatively small fly if presented properly.

tures and plenty of larger forage, muskies become increasingly aggressive on all types of water and structure both shallow and deep. This period of active feeding also means that fish caught in the summer are on average heavier than those caught in the spring, a trend that will continue through the fall.

With more anglers on the water in the summer, it's no surprise these traditional vacation months are when the majority of fish are caught each year.

Fishing during the so-called "dog days" of summer can also be very tough, especially on pressured water, water with reduced water clarity due to weed growth or bloom, or when you encounter prolonged periods of heat with little or no change in conditions. On the other hand, dramatic weather changes such as fronts and storms can be just the thing to trigger a summer bite.

Speed trolling for muskies is a good example of just how aggressive these fish can be in the summer. Where legal, this effective technique involves trolling a lure just off the back of the boat on a very short line—sometimes right in the white-water of the prop wash—at speeds of up to eight miles an hour. The first time I witnessed this I was highly doubtful a fish would hit something moving this fast and close to the boat. Sitting right next to the boat engine I watched intently as the large spinner twirled and flashed in the prop

wash literally inches from the churning propeller. Then it happened: A 50-inch muskie appeared out of nowhere and inhaled the lure. I was in shock, and the reel was screaming for attention—definitely food for thought when considering how fast to retrieve your fly.

Depending on the year and where you fish, summer water temperatures on most muskie waters can be anywhere from the mid-60s to a high of well into the 70s. During unusually warm years, or in the muskie's most southern range, it is also common to find temperatures into the 80s. These warmer water temperatures make for active and more aggressive fish but also tend to spread fish over larger areas, making them harder to find. The extreme heat of summer can also raise water temperatures beyond the muskie's comfort zone. When this happens, muskies often suspend off summer feeding grounds in cooler, deeper water.

The time of day you choose to fish for muskies becomes much more important as summer progresses. In early summer, fish are more active during low-light periods of morning and evening. This is especially true in shallow-water eutrophic lakes and flowages where feeding periods tend to be shorter because of abundant forage. As the summer progresses the window of opportunity narrows further because of recreational

Summer muskie hotspot: Emerging cabbage beds with the tops barely visible are ideal spots to cast a streamer or top-water fly. Work these areas thoroughly from the shallow and deep sides keeping a keen eye for any additional structure variations that might hold a fish.

Super-sized poppers such as my Tiktaalik are an excellent choice for warm-weather muskie fishing. Although it works year-round, the movement and sound of a large popper really seems to grab a muskie's attention during the dog days of summer. This fish followed out from under a thick patch of lily pads and sucked my popper in like a trout taking a dry fly.

pressure as well as increasing water temperatures. During mid-summer it is often best to fish shallow early and late, leaving the mid-day period to search thicker, shade-producing cover, or deeper water for suspended fish.

The mid-summer "night bite" is one of the best opportunities for summer muskies. Nighttime fishing for muskies is no secret. It is a highly effective approach in the heat of the summer, especially on clear lakes. Pressured by increased summer boat traffic, some muskie populations change their feeding patterns, and feed more aggressively once the sun is down. Fly fishing at night with a loud popper or water pushing streamer over productive daytime structure is an effective way to trigger a spine-tingling strike in the darkness.

Where to Fish Muskies in the Summer

With more stable water temperatures and abundant food, muskies can be found almost anywhere in the summer. Although many fish species such as walleye seek out cooler temperatures in deep water, muskies remain active in both shallow and deep water, providing plenty of opportunities for the fly fisher.

In eutrophic lakes and shallow flowages, muskies tend to stay shallow all summer long due to reduced oxygen levels and lower clarity in deeper water. Although there is plenty of forage in these water types, weed growth and algae blooms can make summer fishing with a fly difficult—the fish can't see your fly. In deeper mesotrophic lakes, muskies are found in both shallow and deep water where they often suspend in early summer near structure and close to forage.

In the late summer, reduced oxygen levels on some mesotrophic lakes will eventually push fish back to shallow water to feed. Oligotrophic lakes remain relatively cool all summer long, and muskie activity in these lake types increases as temperatures rise, particularly in late spring and summer. Rivers are always a good summertime option with reduced flows, weed growth, and improved clarity. (see summer lake hot spots illustration on pages 226-227 and river hot spots illustration on pages 228-229)

Summer Presentations, Retrieves, and Flies

Your choice of fly patterns during summer is determined mainly by the water depth you plan to fish, water conditions, and the observed aggressiveness of the fish. With large forage more abundant in the summer months, I routinely use flies larger than the flies I throw in the spring. On average my summer streamer patterns are six to 10 inches in length. Some

are as large as 15 inches—huge!

Although these flies are more difficult to cast all day, it's worth keeping in mind that most conventional muskie anglers are now consistently casting and trolling big spinners, crank baits, jerk baits, and top-water lures to 10 inches in length, some even longer. When water clarity becomes a major issue because of weed growth or algae bloom on some waters in late summer, you may be limited to fishing a loud top-water popper or large water-pushing streamer in shallow or deep water just to attract a fish.

Summer fly colors are typically gaudy and bold. While I still fish plenty of natural, white, and black patterns with success, I also start fishing a lot of chartreuse and hot oranges and yellows for increased visibility. These bright colors appeal to the aggressive nature of summer fish. And they sometimes trigger a reaction strike from a neutral fish. Another reason for using brighter colors is that weed growth and algae bloom on shallower muskie waters significantly reduces visibility.

It is not uncommon at this time of year to switch back and forth between a surface fly and a streamer, covering the same water several times through the day as you attempt to trigger a fish. Warmer water temperatures and aggressive fish also means more follows. Carrying several fully rigged rods with different flies is essential at this time, allowing you to quickly present a variety of flies to the same fish.

The summer months are the perfect time to build a "mail route" of fish to target. Provided conditions remain stable, summer muskies routinely hold in the same home-range areas for several weeks. When you see a fish follow several times from the same area, you know you've found a spot worth hitting again and again, especially with a different fly later in the day or when the weather changes.

Fly speed is critical to your summer fishing success: You can't possibly fish your fly too fast. To take full advantage of this trigger, keep your fly moving as fast and erratically as possible during the entire retrieve. This applies to both streamers and top-water flies. The key is to keep the fly looking alive yet vulnerable. With the rare exception of non-aggressive fish, do not stop your fly at any time during the retrieve, especially if you've got a hot fish following close to the boat.

Fly fishing for muskies on top is another exciting summer opportunity. Once you've witnessed a large muskie parting the water with its mouth open to inhale your chugging surface fly, you may not want to fish anything else. Summer fish often show well

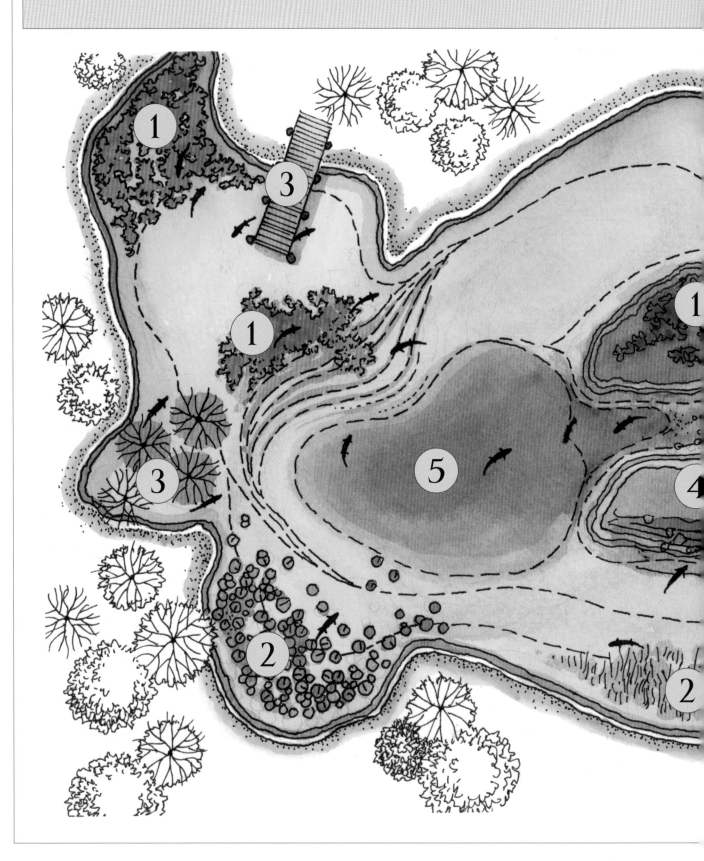

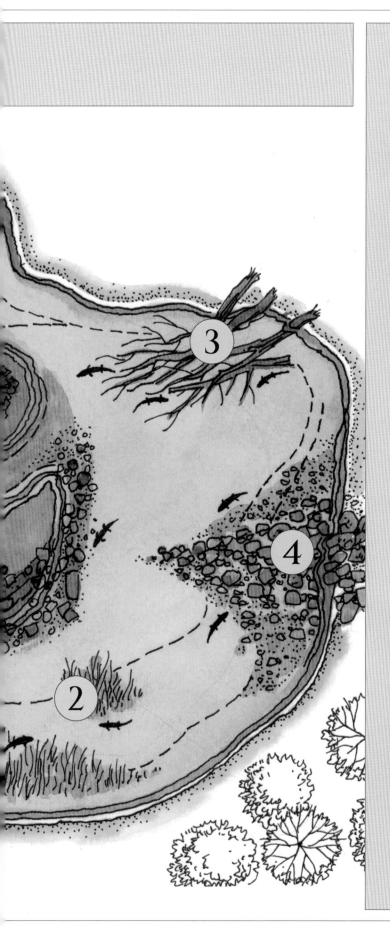

Where to Find Muskies in The Summer

(1) Weed and cabbage beds, flats, points, secondary points and saddles: These classic muskie hotspots offer both forage and cover throughout the summer months. In deeper lakes and flowages look for weeds that extend closest to deep water or provide a saddle between two shorelines. Muskies often hang right on top of saddles and off the edges to ambush prey. Isolated shallow weed structure is also an excellent summer muskie location, especially when located well away from the shore and surrounded by deep water.

(2) Lily-pad beds, reed beds, and bulrush banks: Although technically weeds, this type of structure grows rapidly during the summer months and provides plenty of cover with easy access to forage. Typically the greener, more recent growth holds the most fish in the early summer. Fishing a fly right in the thick of this shallow-water "slop" can also be productive as fish hold in these areas in search of cooler water and overhead cover. As the summer progresses and weeds begin to die off, muskies move into other shallow areas with reeds and bulrushes, or seek out green weeds in deeper water.

(3) Wood structure: This common fish-holding structure includes natural downfalls, logjams, and submerged timber, as well as man-made docks, piers, fish cribs, and boathouses. Muskies seek out this type of structure for cover and forage, especially in rivers and reservoirs where aquatic plant life is often limited. As with any shallow structure, the closer to deeper water the more likely it is these areas will hold fish.

(4) Rock, gravel, and sand bars, reefs, and points: This heat-retaining structure holds fish in most muskie habitats but is best in colder lakes and rivers. In mesotrophic and oligotrophic lakes look for muskies to hold close to shallow rock and sand structure early in the summer and deep rock-and-gravel humps and bars extending to even deeper water later in the year. These areas act as fish magnets, particularly after cold fronts or when weed growth begins to die off. On rivers, rock structure serves primarily as a current break, providing a perfect ambush point from which to feed.

(5) Deep water: The summer months are also a good time to start fishing deep-water structure such as rock and weed humps, points, and channels. Although most muskie fly fishers prefer to fish shallow structure they can see and target, there is no doubt larger fish in the summer will suspend in these areas searching for food and comfort. These deep-water areas are best fished with a sinking line and a streamer during the midday period when shallow-water fishing may be less productive.

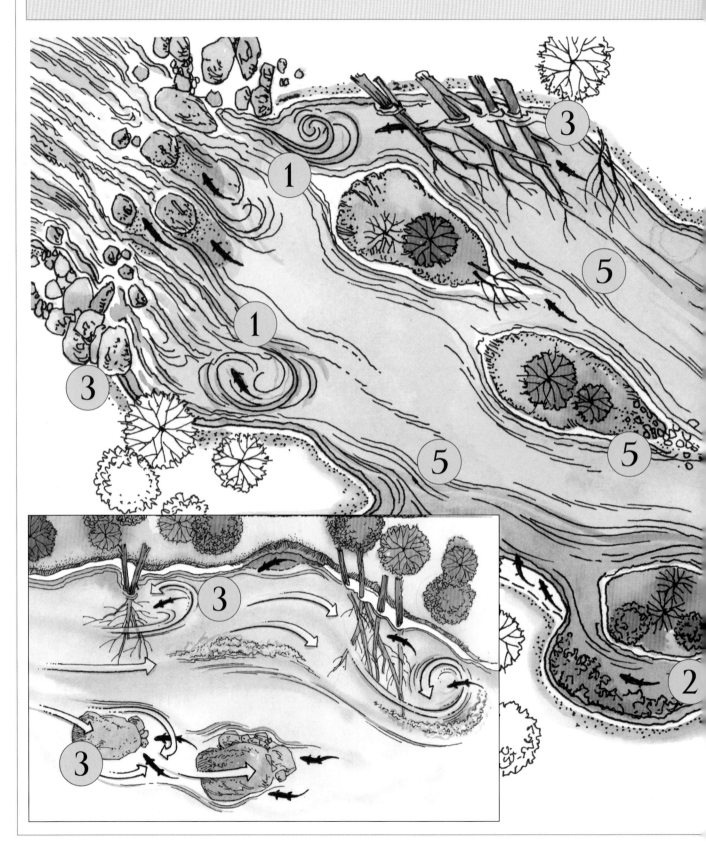

Where to Find Muskies in Rivers

(1) Fast water: Commonly found at the head of rapids, pools, and dams, these areas provide a natural ambush opportunity for muskies. Although not generally a fast water species, in the summer and fall months muskies will concentrate in these areas in search of oxygen, cooler water temperatures, deeper water, and forage. Look for fish holding high or deep just behind larger rocks and to the slower side of any fast-water current seams and breaks.

(2) Undercut banks, side channels, and backwaters: These muskie hotspots offer the perfect combination of food and protection, especially when close to faster, deeper water. Cover these areas thoroughly with a fly by fishing both shallow and deep. The presence of any additional structure such as wood, weeds, or rock will always enhance the prospects of a fish.

(3) Large boulders, log jams and beaver houses: A natural muskie hang out, these areas provide plenty of cover to ambush prey. When approaching a typical log jam, target your casts to cover the entire structure from front to back and from the upstream to downstream sides (see inset illustration of holding spots around large boulders and log jams). As with any river fishing, the older the log jam, the better the fishing. Beaver houses are another classic muskie hangout in rivers. Look for fish holding tight to the deepest areas directly in front of the house (provided a beaver hasn't slapped its tail and spooked everything in sight).

(4) Bridges and other man made obstructions: Many rivers offer good muskie fishing close to road and railway bridges. These large structures often provide a substantial break in the current and, as a result, plenty of opportunities to ambush forage. Look for fish both above and below these areas depending on the depth and current speed. Older bridge abutments and pilings are also well worth a cast in slow or fast water.

(5) Midstream structure and slower water: The deepest, slowest part of a pool or stretch of river is a prime muskie hotspot. These areas offer both depth and protection with plenty of forage. Look for those areas with definite breaks, variable depth, and any additional structure such as rocks, weeds, or wood. Tailouts behind islands are also well worth fishing, especially if they hold debris and offer proximity to deep water.

behind your fly before striking. They may chase a fly several times before hitting. They will also hit a top-water fly during all times of the day—even at night.

Heavier weed growth in the summer offers excellent lake and river opportunities for the muskie on the fly. Although snagging weeds can be a frustrating experience with any kind of fishing, you can turn this situation to your benefit by using the twitching and ripping techniques to trigger fish.

Submerged wood is another fish magnet in the summer with fish often holding along deeper edges. To get the attention of these fish, use the bumping technique, making contact with the wood whenever you can.

All of these effective techniques work well when fishing shallow water structure in the summer.

In lakes, flowages, and rivers with poor water clarity due to natural stain or summer algae blooms, fly fishing can be a real challenge. The fish must rely almost exclusively on their lateral line and sensory pores to detect and find forage. If this is a normal condition and not the result of recent siltation or runoff, muskies usually continue feeding in shallow water but require a specialized approach to be caught with any consistency. The best shallow-water structure for fly fishing under these conditions includes thick weed growth—lily pads and reeds—rock and boulders, and made-made structure such as boat docks, piers, and diving platforms.

A fish may not detect your fly on the first cast. The trick is to hit the same piece of structure several times and from different directions before moving on. The best presentation is to fish a steady retrieve with a water-pushing streamer or loud top-water fly. Help the fish zero in and eat it! Rattles inserted into or attached to the fly can also help the fish to locate your offering.

Follows and boatside strikes are also common under these conditions. Watch your fly closely as it nears the boat. Perform a figure-8 or other variation before lifting the fly for the next cast. You may not see any sign of a fish in these conditions until your fly is in its mouth.

Weather and lunar conditions are an important consideration in the summer. Significant atmospheric changes tend to trigger muskies into striking, especially when fishing has slowed due to high water temperatures. An approaching front, new or full moon, or wind change are all reliable summer muskie triggers. One ideal summer-fishing situation is a long period of hot, humid weather followed by a storm and/or a front on a new or full moon. If the front is warm, fishing should remain good throughout this period of change. If the front is cold, fishing can still be quite good until the front approaches but slows considerably once it passes and temperatures drop.

In these difficult situations muskies usually move vertically off normal structure and into deeper water or bury themselves in heavy cover where they hold until conditions stabilize. If you're fly fishing after a significant summer cold front, slow down your retrieve and fish a smaller, more subtle fly pattern. During the warmest period of the day concentrate on specific areas you know hold fish.

Fall—Big-Fish Time

Water Temperatures: +/- 60° to 40°F

Next to the spring season, the fall months of September, October, and November are probably the

---

Summer Muskie Fly-Fishing Summary

Best Water Types: All muskie water types including lakes, flowages, reservoirs, and rivers. Some shallow water lakes and flowages may become difficult to fish due to heavy algae bloom.

Hotspots: Shallow and deep water with enough structure to provide cover and easy access to forage. Weeds, wood, and rock all hold fish during the summer months depending on the water type. Fish shallow early and late. Fish deeper water for suspended fish during the day. Nighttime fly fishing for muskies is also effective on clear-water lakes with little natural cover and intense recreational pressure. River fishing begins to improve with lower water levels and clarity.

Best Flies: Big and bold. Fish larger streamers and top-water patterns with a fast retrieve. Look for more aggressive follows and boat-side hits. Attempt to convert any follows with increased speed or a quick change of flies. Remember where fish are holding and fish your mail route at different times with different flies. Top-water flies are especially effective day and night in warmer water temperatures and with more aggressive fish.

Best Retrieves and Triggers: Fast and varied. Use both the strip and the rod tip to create erratic fly movement to trigger and convert aggressive summer fish. Fish the fly all the way to the boat. Pay close attention for any signs of fish approaching.

Best Presentations: Blind fishing with streamers and top-water flies in shallow and deep water as well as target fishing to sighted fish. Work prime areas thoroughly at different times of the day and with different flies to trigger fish. Fish deep structure areas with a streamer and a sinking line when shallow waters are unproductive.

"Incidental" species such as this trophy smallmouth bass are common when muskie fishing with a fly. In fact, depending on where and when you fish, it's not unusual to catch a variety of other popular game fish—northern pike, largemouth bass, even walleye.

most productive times of the year to catch a muskie with a fly. Unlike the early spring months when the water is cold and the fish are just beginning to feed again, fall fish are already aggressive and increasingly hungry in anticipation of the approaching winter. Early egg production in female muskies also means fish will feed aggressively in anticipation of harder times to come. As fall-loving muskie guide Don Larsen, a.k.a., The Pond Monster, likes to say, "muskies in the fall are like feeding pigs!"

The warm Indian summer days of late September and October following the first frost offer some of the best muskie fishing of the year both in terms of numbers and size of fish. Some of my personal best days have come at this time: more than a dozen fish landed and many others missed, seen, or lost.

On certain lakes and flowages, once the weed growth begins to die off after turnover, muskies are concentrated seeking forage close to structure such as steep dropoffs and breaks. While the best activity in the fall is often limited to the warmest part of the day, when the fish do eventually turn on it can be

downright scary how many are eager to eat your fly. These fall fish are not only extremely aggressive but in prime condition, showing off increased girth and weight.

The change of seasons combined with colder water temperatures and shorter days makes for fine fly fishing in all kinds of muskie water including lakes, flowages, and rivers. Although muskies continue feeding actively well into December, as water temperatures cool and their metabolism naturally slows they become less and less susceptible to all but the most hardy fly fisher willing to put in long hours in difficult conditions. This is certainly not to say you should not try fly fishing in the late fall or early winter months, but your range of presentations becomes severely limited by Mother Nature as the season progresses.

This season is probably your best and last chance of the year for a trophy fish over 40 inches—a 50-inch-plus monster is not out of the question.

As most serious muskie anglers know, this is the time of year when most world-record fish have been caught (or claimed to have been caught). Gigantic

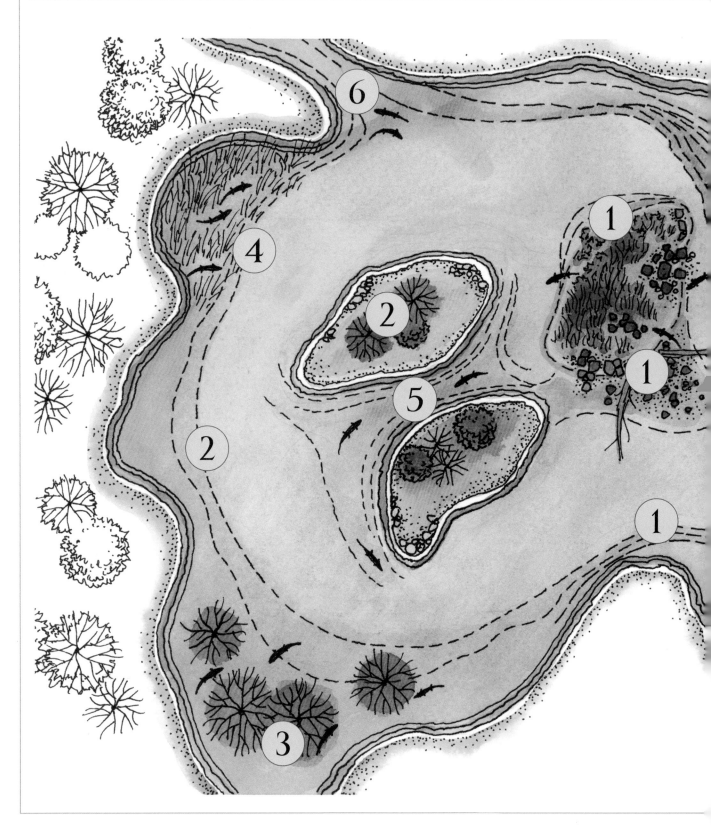

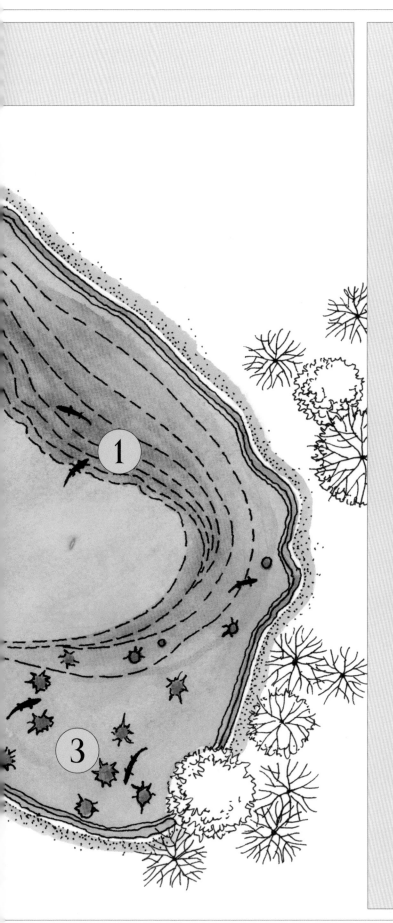

Where to Find Muskies in the Fall:

(1) Deep Weed and Rock Edges, Basins, Humps, Points and Breaks: A classic fall hotspot on most muskie lakes. As the water begins to cool, forage of all kinds such as perch, walleye, and suckers school off these areas, attracting muskies on the feed. Look for the steepest breaks and drop-offs with any remaining green weeds, wood, and rock for the best action.

(2) Shallow Reefs and Points: Rock, gravel, or sand reefs and points close to deep water hold muskies throughout the summer. They are real fish magnets as the water cools in late fall, especially on mesotrophic and oligotrophic lakes. Fish suspend close to structure, cruising back and forth onto shallow flats in search of spawning ciscoes and whitefish.

(3) Sunken and Standing Timber: A typical fall flowage and reservoir hotspot, muskies seek out this structure for cover and forage once the bulk of weeds die off. Full trees and stumps hold fish, but fishing sunken timber in the fall with a streamer is difficult due to unseen snags. If the water temperature remains warm enough, try a fishing top-water fly slowly.

(4) Remaining Green Weeds, Reeds, and Bulrushes: Any remaining green weeds combined with structure are worth fishing in the fall. They provide both forage and cover. While most broadleaf weeds may be dead by late fall, reeds and bulrushes can remain green and hold fish until late in the season. Fall muskies often follow forage into very shallow backwaters with reeds so long as deeper water is nearby.

(5) Open Water Shoals, Reefs, and Saddles: A classic late fall big-fish structure, muskies will congregate close to these shallow, protected areas in search of forage such as ciscoes. Windy and rough fall conditions push forage into these areas but can make for very tough fly casting.

(6) Stream and Creek mouths: These areas attract many species of spawning fish in the fall and thus hungry muskies. Look for fish to hold close to the mouth and on deeper outside edges. Any additional structure such as rocks, wood, or green weeds make this a prime fall hangout.

Wisconsin fly fisher Derek Kuehl proudly holds his line-class world-record muskie taken on a streamer in October. While a trophy fish by any measure, Derek respectfully released this impressive muskie to fight another day.

fish of 40 to 50 pounds are still caught with some consistency each year on prime waters throughout the species' range right up to the close of the season. While most of these giants are often caught trolling with plugs or using a live-sucker rig, I have caught very large fish exceeding 50 inches in length on a fly as late as December where the season is still open.

The fact that live-bait sucker fishing is probably the most popular traditional method of fall muskie fishing tells us a lot about how and what these late-season fish really want to eat. Once the water temperature drops below 40°, sucker fishing is considered by some anglers to be the only viable way to catch muskies in the late fall, though casting large jerk baits or slow trolling in open water with enormous plugs is also effective.

Two Seasons in One

The fall muskie season has two distinct phases. The first is the early fall, pre-turnover period of September and early October. Water temperatures at this time drop into the ideal range of the high 50° to 60°F, keeping the fish both active and aggressive. This initial drop in water temperatures is a key transitional trigger. The result is good fly-fishing opportunities just about everywhere you fish, especially in shallow water. It's very similar to the spring bite.

Depending on where you fish, this is also the time of the fall turnover on some lakes. During this turnover, the surface water becomes cooler and denser than it is in deep water. The cooler, denser water eventually sinks. There's a temporary reorganization of the water column until the lake once again stratifies with uniform temperatures throughout. As the water begins to cool during this brief period, muskie fishing can be great, especially in very shallow water. On lakes where this is actively taking place you will notice a rapid deterioration of weed growth— and tough fishing. Depending on the water and weather, the fall turnover can last from one week to several weeks.

The second phase of fall fishing occurs after the first frost of late October and early November. Depending on its severity, water temperatures begin a precipitous drop from 50° to 40° and lower. The movement and metabolism of the fish begin to slow noticeably. The fish become more passive, and fly fishing is less productive. Fishing with the fly during late fall can still be good, however, with the right presentations and under the right conditions. But it's much less consistent than early fall fishing.

Where to Fish Muskies in the Fall

The best opportunities for fall fishing happen at different times on different waters. In all cases, however, reduced forage choices, fewer oxygen-producing green weeds, and less-than-ideal temperature ranges combine to concentrate fish and provide targeted fly fishing opportunities until the water freezes.

Shallow, eutrophic-type lakes offer some of the earliest fall fishing. They cool off, turn over, and clear more quickly. In deeper mesotrophic and oligotrophic lakes, the fall bite is later, when muskies follow migratory forage such as ciscoes and whitefish into shallow water as they spawn. This presents a unique opportunity to target big fish in shallow water—a paramount interest to the fly fisher.

Because oligotrophic lakes stay generally cool throughout the season, the fall muskie bite happens later but still finds much improved fishing with fish holding tight to any heat-retaining structure such as rocks, sand, and gravel until late in the season. Flowages, reservoirs, and rivers all fish particularly

This well-conditioned fish is a prime example of why the fall is one of my favorite seasons to be on the water. As the water cools and days shorten, muskies go on a feeding binge, adding substantial girth and weight in anticipation of leaner days to come.

well this season due to reduced water levels, scarce forage, and concentrated holding water. Dampened fishing pressure in the fall also makes for more enjoyable and often productive days on the water.

Fall is perhaps the best time of the year to tackle muskies on flowing water. With typical low-water conditions, muskies congregate anywhere they can find enough cover and foraging opportunities. Some of the best fish-holding structure includes any remaining deep pools, eddies, backwaters, and pockets behind boulders. If it looks like it might hold a fish, it probably does. With less weed growth, fish also tend to hold close to any wood structure or remaining reeds, even in very shallow water. (see fall lake hotspots illustration on pages 232-233 and river hot spots illustration on pages 227-229)

Fall Presentations, Retrieves, and Flies

Recognizing that most muskies in the fall are caught on live suckers, large deep-diving crank baits,

plastics, and trolling plugs, it's hard to choose a fly that is too big this time of year. On the other hand, in the early fall before lake turnover, many fish are still taken on top-water baits and even spinners in very shallow water. Based on this variety of bait choices, the best overall fall fly patterns are large streamers of six to 15 inches in length and loud, water-pushing surface poppers.

As the season progresses and water temperatures drop below 50°, fish move deeper in lakes. Your chance of taking a fish on top decreases sharply. On rivers and flowages, however, you can still effectively fish flies on top well into fall. In the late fall just before ice-up, large streamers fished deep and slow become the only practical fly choice on most waters.

One major exception to this general rule is when muskies are feeding on tightly schooled or spawning forage fishes: ciscos, shad, and shiners. You'll see fish and forage boiling on the surface. When this happens, it is sometimes possible to fish a top-water fly over the massacre and trigger a strike. Although streamers are the predominant fly choice in late fall, keep one rod rigged with a floating line and a top-water fly in case you see a fish crashing bait on top. Over the years I have taken several fish using this late-season technique, some as late as December. The odds of being in the right place at the right time, however, are highly dependant on the vagaries of weather and water.

Color choice in the fall remains much the same as summer. Weather and water clarity are the main determining factors. Many lakes, flowages, and rivers feature improved clarity due to less weed growth and lower water. Natural colors such as yellow perch, black, and white are all good choices. In lakes and flowages with large numbers of suckers, spawning ciscoes, and whitefish, it's best to match the hatch

with oversized light-and-dark-colored streamer patterns that imitate this color scheme. When fishing stained water or deep-water structure, try fishing brighter colors such as fluorescent chartreuse and orange to trigger an aggressive fish.

Fan casting a streamer using a slow retrieve over shallow and deep structure is one of the most effective fall techniques. Shallow weed line or rock edges close to deep water are prime fall muskie hotspots. That's where the food is. Cover these areas thoroughly with multiple casts of a streamer on a sink-tip line fished at varying depths. Working the streamer both parallel and perpendicular to this structure allows for the fullest coverage and gives the fish plenty of opportunity to see your fly.

Try casting shallow from deep water. Allow the fly to sink to the bottom right at the edge of the drop-off before beginning your retrieve. This technique also works when positioning the boat in shallow water and retrieving the fly back toward the boat up and over the edge. To take advantage of any deep following fish, use the deep rip streamer technique at the end of each retrieve.

In the late fall, fishing a large streamer on an integrated sinking-head line with the bottom-bouncing technique to slowly crawl it across a sand or gravel bottom can be effective for largely dormant fish. You never know for sure exactly where the fish are holding, so it's well worth trying many different approaches.

As with all my muskie fishing, keeping several rods fully rigged in the boat is sound strategy. This

Fall Muskie Fly-Fishing Summary

Best Water Types: Shallow eutrophic-type lakes best in early fall and deeper mesotrophic and oligotrophic lakes best in the late season. Look for lakes with spawning forage such as ciscoes and whitefish. Rivers and flowages fish well the entire fall season due to reduced water levels and better clarity.

Hotspots: Early fall fish summer structure including weed and rock edges, points, and flats. Once the water begins to cool below 50°F, look for fish concentrated in basins and close to steep weed and rock edges near shallow water and forage spawning areas. Sunken timber and any remaining green weeds can also be productive. Open-water reefs and shoals are good for big fish but may be hard to fly fish effectively in the late fall due to weather conditions.

Best Flies: Large streamers and top-water patterns in the early fall. Once the water temperature drops below 50°, stick with large streamers in natural forage colors in clear water and brighter colors in stained water. Try top-water poppers on fish crashing tightly schooled bait in open water.

Best Retrieves and Triggers: Moderately fast and steady in the early fall; very slow and steady in the late fall. When water temperatures fall below 50° fish may not strike aggressively. Be prepared to strip-strike at anything.

Best Presentations: Summer-like presentations continue to work well in the early fall. Fish the prime late-fall areas with methodical fan casts either parallel or perpendicular to defined structure. Fish both shallow to deep and deep to shallow to cover the water thoroughly. In late fall try fishing deep with a streamer on a sink-tip or full-sinking line, and crawl the fly slowly across the bottom.

allows me to quickly change flies and lines depending on the structure and water type. While there are no hard-and-fast rules for which flies and lines to rig, having at least one rod ready with a streamer on a floating line and another with a fast sink-tip line allows you to cover all depths efficiently during a particular drift.

Colder water temperatures in the fall dictate the speed of your retrieve. In early fall you will most likely find fish still aggressive. A moderately fast retrieve with both streamers and top-water flies is still the way to go. Once the water temperature falls below 50°, however, the muskies' metabolism slows noticeably, and they are less likely to aggressively chase a lure or fly for a long distance.

When fly fishing in the late season, therefore, your retrieve should be steady and slightly slower with longer pauses between strips. A streamer fly with a lot of side-to-side action when it stops or one that falls rapidly such as a muskie-sized Clouser Minnow can be particularly effective to keep the fish interested. When fishing a streamer on a sink-tip or full-sinking line in the late fall season you may feel only a slight weight on or hesitation in your line when a fish hits. Although a far more subdued than a typical muskie strike, you should still be prepared to strip-strike quickly at the first sign of unusual behavior with your fly.

In the early fall, Indian summer days and gentle southwest breezes are preferred weather conditions. These days combined with a full or new moon can make for some of the best fishing of the year. In the late fall, after the first frost and big cold fronts, however, muskie fishing seems to improve the worse the weather gets. Serious muskie anglers at this time of year look specifically for raw, cold conditions with little wind and a full or new moon.

Curiously, while a warming trend in the late fall can be nice for us anglers, it actually seems to slow down the fishing, especially if combined with a warm rain instead of snow.

Wisconsin fly-fishing guides Larry Mann and Wendy Williamson with a trophy fall muskie from the famed Chippewa River. Despite challenging weather conditions, the prospect of one good fish keeps serious muskie hunters on the water until the season's end.

MUSKIE GUIDES

PROFESSIONAL MUSKIE GUIDES ARE A SPECIAL BREED. In the world of muskie fishing they are as much a part of the sport as the pine-scented Northwoods, the call of the common loon, the figure-8, and the jerk bait. In fact, many serious muskie anglers wouldn't consider spending a day on the water without a seasoned guide at their side. As you might have guessed, however, taking a client's money in return for catching a muskie is a dicey economic proposition at best. Even if you do end up seeing a fish, the probability of your client actually hooking and landing a muskie is so low that it's amazing anyone would make this a career choice. Given the elusive nature of these fish it's also no wonder there are few guides who actually specialize in just catching muskies, much less on a fly. Yet in the small world of muskie fishing—and the even smaller world of muskie fishing with a fly—there are actually some guides who do this successfully.

As a fly fisher, North American muskie guides remind me of tarpon and permit guides in the Florida Keys. Both chase big, tough, elusive fish and have to be on top of their game at all times to succeed. They also have to endure challenging weather conditions, long days in the boat, and fish that are notoriously moody. Occasionally, they have to work with clients who can't cast past their noses or have never landed anything bigger than a brook trout on a fly. Most of all, a good guide for any species is one that acts as a coach, keeps you motivated when you're down, and points out deficiencies in your approach to help you with the next cast or fish.

One major difference between saltwater and muskie guides is that there are very few muskie guides who are also fly fishers. While a quick check of tarpon fly-fishing guides will reveal dozens located between mile markers 10 and 100 in the Florida Keys, the number of muskie fly-fishing guides can be counted on one hand.

Fortunately, when considering a muskie guide for fly fishing, it isn't essential that your guide also be a fly fisher. Assuming you've read this book and mastered the basic skills, the guide's primary job is to put you on the fish so you can use the techniques I've outlined. With plenty of upfront discussion and planning, an understanding muskie guide should appreciate your special needs and spend their time positioning the boat so you can cast effectively and efficiently, pointing out likely or known fish holding structure, and even alerting you to following fish you may have missed. Your guide will also be of great assistance in telling you what lures and patterns have been working under what conditions so you can at least make an educated choice of flies and presentations. Finally, having an experienced guide in the boat is of critical importance once you hook a fish and attempt to land and release it. Ultimately, successful muskie fishing requires teamwork. Your guide should be a true partner in your quest to catch a fish.

By definition, a good guide for any fish species is one who knows the specific water you plan to fish and is wired into any subtle or not so subtle changes in the fishing patterns that you might spend hours or days trying to figure out. This highly valuable and specialized knowledge comes from years of time on the water, many fishless days and nights, and having that sixth sense about where fish are and what they want.

Before hiring any guide, ask some pointed questions about current fishing conditions, recent catches, and best times. If you have any doubts, ask for client references. Understand, however, they may not tell you exactly where they're fishing; that's what you pay them for! With a little research you should be able to determine if your guide is one who really fishes or just likes to talk about it.

Whatever the species and no matter what the price, a good guide is a valuable asset well worth the investment. When you start to consider all the wasted time fishing in the wrong place or with the wrong technique or flies, it's obvious that this is money well invested.

Listen to your guide: Whatever your experience level, a good guide's advice is worth its weight in gold. Here Canadian muskie guide Mike Lazarus points out a likely looking spot for my next cast.

While only a handful of guides today fly fish exclusively for muskies, in recent years some conventional muskie guides have seen the promise and excitement of this sport and know what it takes to guide a fly fisher successfully (see my list of recommended fly-friendly, conventional muskie guides in Chapter 12). Although these guides appreciate the challenge of fly fishing for muskies, they would not be considered fly-fishing guides in the traditional sense. No fancy picnics with your favorite wine here! They won't have the fly-fishing gear you need or teach you how to double haul—but they do know boat control, where the fish are, and how best to approach them through the season.

Among fly-fishing muskie guides, many have been taken by the unique challenges and subtleties presented when targeting this elusive predator; they are true professionals who have dedicated themselves to catching one of the hardest fish in fresh water on a fly *and* making a living doing it. Both conventional and fly-fishing muskie guides will help to make your first experience with this great fish both productive and enjoyable.

Beginning with my first muskie, I've been fortunate to fish for many years on some of the best water in

Author's Rules for Fly Fishing with a Muskie Guide

- Check your ego at the door.
- Listen to your guide; that's why you pay him!
- Respect your guide as a friend, not a slave.
- Learn to cast a big rod and big fly BEFORE you go fishing; if you can't make the right cast it's not the guide's fault.
- Always know where your guide is BEFORE you make a cast.
- If you miss or lose a fish don't blame the guide and don't pout (swearing is okay)—just "shut up and keep casting" as Wisconsin guide "Musky Joe" Flater likes to say.
- Your guide is not a mind-reader; communicate your needs while casting, retrieving, fighting, and landing a fish.
- You are not a mind reader; if your guide is the silent type, ask lots of questions anyway and make sure you understand what you're doing before you start casting.
- Your guide should not fish unless by mutual agreement, or if the guide is trying to figure out a particular spot or pattern and tells you before hand.
- If you had a good time, but still didn't manage to catch any fish, always leave a tip; muskie fishing is about the opportunity, not the catch.

North America with both conventional and fly fishing muskie guides; I am forever grateful for their infinite patience and unique knowledge they've shared with me as I spent countless hours in their boats casting a fly for muskie. The five talented guides chosen for these exclusive interviews represent well over 100 years of experience and time on the water, making their additional observations and insights unique in the world of fly fishing.

Fly Fishing Muskie Guides

GUIDE: **MARK MERITT, Victoria, Minnesota**

TOPIC: **Fishing pressured lakes in the Midwest**

BEST QUOTE: *"Muskie—the fish of 10,000 casts … So how many false casts is that?"*

Like many of us, professional muskie guide Mark Meritt got his first taste of fly fishing out West for trout. After many years of success casting and trolling for muskies in the Midwest and Canada, he started to wonder about the possibilities of fly fishing for muskies. He caught his first muskie on a fly nine years ago and has never looked back. He is also a skilled craftsman, hand carving his own lures and tying and creating his own flies that build upon his extensive knowledge of muskie behavior. Mark has guided and fished the popular muskie waters of northeast Indiana for many years. He now makes his home in Minnesota, where he can be found fly fishing whenever there's an opportunity.

Minnesota muskie guide Mark Meritt holds one of many fish we've taken together over the years.

Q: What skills does it take to become a successful muskie fly fisher?

A: There's a lot that goes into this sport but probably the most important thing in any kind of muskie fishing is a positive mental attitude. You've just got to believe you're going to catch something on each and every cast or you'll never be ready when it finally happens. Being a great caster also helps. This is hard enough work without fumbling with the casting part.

Q: What is your favorite time of year to muskie fish with a fly?

A: Depends on where you fish and what the weather is like that year. In Indiana I like the early spring but especially May and June. When the water temperatures rise above 65°F you know you'll have active fish; they just seem to really go for flies at this time. The same is true in Minnesota after the June opener. I also like the early fall when the temps are getting down around 60° and the fish are putting on the feed bag. The middle of summer can be good but where I guide there's a lot of fishing pressure and boat traffic. I find the fly fishing tough at that time since the fish are usually much deeper and hard to target. Where I fish in Indiana the late fall can also be good on the fly when the fish are chasing shad but the weather can be really nasty. It's usually a crap shoot to find them with the fly and get the cast off in time.

Q: What do you consider to be the ideal weather patterns or conditions for muskie fishing with a fly?

A: In the early season I like a sunny day to warm up the shallow water and get the fish active. Ideally I'd be fishing a warming trend with some prospect of a storm in the afternoon or evening to really turn the fish on. Later in the year I prefer cloudy conditions with just a light drizzle instead of a pounding rain. One thing I definitely don't like is an east wind … might as well tie flies when it's blowing that direction.

Q: What are some of the important factors for being a successful muskie fly-fishing guide?

A: Good question. Other than catching fish, I guess the biggest thing I focus on when I'm guiding a fly fisher is boat control and position. It's a lot different than with traditional bait casters. You've got to be on top of the wind direction and how and where your client is casting the fly at all times. You can really mess him up if you don't position the boat right for every cast…or get yourself hooked!

Another thing I do that I know may be a bit unorthodox for a fly fisher is fish behind him or her with a lure—kind of as a check and balance for what's happening. I know it sounds selfish, but it really helps me be a better guide to know what the fish are doing and how they're responding on a given day. I always ask my client first if it's okay for me to fish and tell them why I'm doing it. I also never cast until the client has a chance to cover a spot thoroughly with the fly. Of course, if a fish follows my lure I'll pull the bait away and have my client cast the fly; you'd be surprised how many fish we've caught that followed my lure first.

Finally, since fly fishing for muskies is probably one of the hardest things to do with a fly rod I always do my best to have a good time on the water and not get too stressed out. If we're lucky enough to catch a

MUSKIE ANGEL STREAMER

Originated and tied by Mark Meritt

HOOK: 2/0 to 4/0 Tiemco 811S.

THREAD: 6/0 Kevlar.

OVERWING:
Six to 10 inches of dark brown and dark blue Angel Hair extending three to six inches beyond the gape.

UNDERWING:
Six to 10 inches of chartreuse gold Angel Hair extending three to six inches beyond the gape.

HEAD: 6/0 Kevlar tied off with epoxy finish.

EYES: 3-D stick-on or Prismatic.

fish I make sure to let my clients know that any muskie on a fly, no matter how small, is a great fish.

Q: What are your favorite flies for muskie fishing?

A: Hard to say. I use a lot of different flies depending on the conditions. I guess I catch most of my fish on big streamers. It's easiest to hook a fish with them and the fish seem to like them. On the other hand, I really like fishing top water when the bite is on. Like fishing with any top-water bait, however, hooking a fish can be tough unless they totally inhale the fly and you don't pull it away first. A lot of our water is stained, so I use a lot of bright colors … chartreuse, orange, white. I also like to use a flashy, silver or gold tinsel streamer pattern of my own that gets a lot of attention when the fish are being difficult. One thing I've found when tying flies for muskies is they don't have to be fancy to work.

Q: What do you consider most critical when it comes to fly fishing gear for muskies?

A: A good rod is important if you hope to cast all day long. I like a nine-foot 9- or 10-weight graphite rod with a lot of backbone. I fish St. Croix rods but there are a lot of good ones on the market these days. Reels aren't as important, but they should be as light as possible and be able to pick up line quickly. Leaders can be pretty short, five to six feet. Muskies aren't one bit leader shy. One thing that is critical is wire of some sort to avoid bite-offs. I like to use at least 15 or 20 inches. As we know from our days together on the water, they will sometimes eat the entire rig right up to the mono.

Q: What is your most effective approach to converting a following muskie on a fly?

A: It really depends on the particular fish. In most cases, however, if I see an aggressive fish following I immediately speed up the fly and hope it hits—pretty much the same as bait casting with a lure. While I'm doing this I also like to change the direction of the fly with the rod tip, if only slightly, as an additional trigger. If the fish still doesn't eat I'll do a left or right turn and then a wide figure-8 at the boat and keep at it so long as the fish seems interested. If the fish eventually spooks I'll mark the spot and try again on the next drift or later in the day. How often I keep hitting the spot really depends on how nice the fish was and whether I think it's still catchable.

Q: What specific areas in a lake or river do you target when fly fishing for muskies?

A: Most of my fishing is on small lakes but no matter where you fish with a fly you need to spend your time on known fish-holding structure. Even if you're a great caster there's just too much water to cover if you're simply blind fishing with a big fly. I guess that's also why it's always good to hire a guide: He should know where the fish are or at least were. Depending on the season, I like a wide range of structure where I fish, everything from weed beds to boat docks. I also really like to fish isolated rock or weed structure close to steep breaks. On some of my Indiana lakes we sometimes get fish holding tight to baitfish schools in open water. This is a good way to find bigger fish but tough for the fly caster since it's usually exposed to the wind, and there's no target to shoot for.

Q: What is the biggest mistake you see anglers make when muskie fishing with a fly?

A: That's an easy one: not being able to cast! I get a lot of guys who fish for trout and want to try muskies on the fly. I'm sure it's the same with saltwater fly-fishing guides. Guys think it's just the same as trout fishing but only a bigger rod and flies. *Wrong!* This is really a demanding game. At the very least you've got to be able to cast a big, wind-resistant fly 20 to 60 feet all day long. It also helps if you can double haul. You need the line speed to make the cast, especially on an exposed lake. Line control is another area that many guys have a big problem with. I know it's not so critical in trout fishing, but when you're fishing for muskies, you've got to be on top of your cast from the moment the fly hits the water until you pull it out for the next cast … or figure-8. If you can't do any of this stuff moderately well, muskie fishing is not the place to learn it.

Q: What is your best muskie on a fly story?

A: Like most guides I've got quite a few. That time you hooked the fish on a top-water fly at the boat, lost it, and then hooked him again on a figure-8 was pretty amazing. That was one hot fish! All the other times we've had catching multiple fish in a day or even just a lot of follows are always memorable for me. As for overall best muskie story, once when my wife Lisa and I were fishing up in Canada she had a fish come after her bait as she was picking up to make the next cast. That fish came so fast and hard it jumped right in and out of the boat almost knocking her over! We were bummed we didn't get the fish but it shows just how aggressive they can be when they really want to eat. Seems like every muskie you catch is a good story one way or the other.

GUIDE: **MIKE LAZARUS, Montréal, Québec**

TOPIC: **Fishing large rivers and shield lakes in Canada**

BEST QUOTE: *"Won't be long now!"*

Mike Lazarus is without a doubt one of the greatest muskie guides. There are weeks when he accomplishes what most of us hope to do in a lifetime including boating several fish over 50 inches, some even larger. In a given season he catches and releases hundreds of muskies casting, trolling, and fly casting. Like all muskie fishing, this kind of success doesn't happen without a lot of hard work, patience, and determination. His varied fisheries are as big as his fish, and take him from Québec to Ontario to New York and back again throughout the season right up to ice-up. With his extensive knowledge, experience, and patience together, we have developed many of the important skills and techniques featured in this book.

Q: What skills does it take to be a successful muskie fly fisher?

A: The two main things, as you know from all our time together on the water, are 1) desire and 2) determination. You just don't have a prayer if you don't have these motivations to begin with. You'll always be in an underdog position with the fly rod versus the casting or trolling guys. You need to accept this fact and keep at it despite the odds. As I see it, most guys with the fly rod probably have about 20 percent of the normal muskie fishing range. Of course, a lot depends on your casting skills and most guys I fish can't cast close to the way you do … but that still leaves out roughly 80 percent of the good water using more productive conventional tactics. Still, the rewards are so great, and the hits on a fly are so totally awesome that in my mind it's always worth a shot.

Q: What is your favorite time of the year to muskie fish with a fly?

Canadian muskie guide Mike Lazarus hefts a monster muskie taken on my Tiktaalik popper.

A: I definitely like the early-season shallow-water bite right after opener. In Canada this usually falls around mid-June. If the conditions are right, with warming water temperatures, you can have some great fishing with a fly. The main thing about this time of year is that the fish are very concentrated on certain smaller spots, usually with emerging weeds, so you don't have to blind cast a huge area to move a fish. Later in the year, when the fish are more scattered, it's a lot harder to locate them, especially with a fly. Another season I like is early fall when the water starts dropping from the 70s down into the 60s. This usually happens sometime in early September when the fish move shallow again, where they're easier to target for the fly. Also, the fall bite is a great time for a real trophy muskie. The fish are putting on the feed bag and really getting fat by this time so a 45-inch fish will easily weigh 25 pounds or more.

Q: What do you consider the ideal weather patterns or conditions for muskie fishing with a fly?

A: Same as what I like for most casting situations … hot and flat! These are ideal conditions for fly casting and seem to produce the most action on any bait. At any time of year I'm also looking for that certain environmental edge to turn the fish on. Sometimes it's a period of stability in the weather followed by a big change like a storm or a cold front. Other times it's a more subtle change like a wind shift or a rise in the barometer. With most muskie fishing it's the little things that make all the difference.

Q: What are some of the important factors for being a successful muskie fly-fishing guide?

A: Putting your clients on good water all the time. No question about it, you've got to be wired and focused all the time or you're wasting your time at this game. I spend something like six months of the year fishing for muskies. I'm always learning something new. Year after year it begins to pay off. Having a positive attitude also helps a lot since this can be a tough sport physically and mentally, and things don't always go the way you expect. Even though it's impossible, you've got to try to control—or at least take advantage of—all the variables.

Q: What are your favorite flies for muskie fishing?

A: I love fishing top water! Just seeing a fish hit a fly on top is one of the best things about fly fishing, even if you don't actually get the fish. My fish also seem to respond well to a fly on top … probably because it's the only thing big and loud enough to get their attention. Your big popper patterns are killer when the top water bite is on! I also like fishing big natural-colored streamers with a lot of contrast and flash. As for overall fly choice (top-water or streamer), my personal opinion is it really doesn't matter … the fish is going to go if it's ready. I know this sounds crazy to most fly fishers, but I really think it's more about presentation and the angler's casting ability than fly choice.

Q: What do you consider the most critical when it comes to fly-fishing gear for muskies?

A: Pay attention to your knots and leaders! The same goes for keeping your hooks razor sharp. It's the little things that make all the difference in this sport. You've got to check and recheck your gear all the time if you hope to ever hook and land a fish. Rods and reels are less important so long as they can get the fly out reasonably and hold a big fish. I also wouldn't go fishing without my cradle for landing fish and a good bolt cutter to remove hooks quickly.

Q: What is your approach to converting a following muskie on a fly?

A: As you know, where I fish we don't get a lot of follows. I guess it's the lack of pressure and the fact these fish are for the most part virgin. If I do see a fish following, however, I like to pick up the speed and change the angle and direction of my fly to trigger a strike. Muskies respond well to any sudden escape-movement with a fly, especially during the last light of the day. Sometimes it's just a matter of changing the boat drift or casting angle that makes all the difference.

Q: What specific areas of a big river do you like to target when fly fishing for muskies?

A: You could write a book about that one! I cover a lot of water in a given day either casting or trolling. I guess, given the limitations of a fly rod, the best areas are those that are small and hold a lot of fish. Areas where the fish are cornered are even better because the fish don't have a choice other than to nail your fly or flee. In the early season the fish in my water will be on sand or rock bottoms that retain heat. If the area has any newly emerging weed growth close by, then you've got yourself a fish magnet.

By summer, the fish have usually moved to deep weeds edges and points which, in my case, are harder to fish with a fly since they can cover several acres. I also like current breaks and rips around structure in the summer—that's where the majority of muskie forage will be. In the fall the fish make another transition to shallow water so I fish tighter to cover but still in the open. The main thing in the fall is to follow the temperatures and baitfish schools if you can find them.

Q: What is the biggest mistake you see clients make when muskie fishing with a fly?

A: Trying to catch a muskie on a fly. *Just kidding.* Actually, I find most guys tend to lose focus after about the hundredth cast … just about when a fish finally hits. The same is true of bait casting for muskies, but your odds are better for setting the hook. You've got to expect a fish on every cast. I also think some trout fishers don't appreciate how much casting you've actually got to do to get a muskie on a fly, especially on big water like I fish. This is just like fly fishing in salt water, except you have to cast all day, whether you see any fish or not. I know I've said it already, but you've got to be physically and mentally strong to even consider chasing this fish on a fly.

Q: What is your best muskie on a fly story?

A: I've got lots of them. Once I had two guys casting top-water flies catch two different fish at the same time. That was pretty cool! The many times over the years we've caught eight, 10, 15 fish in a day on flies totally rocked, especially when the fish started pushing over 50 inches and close to the 40-pound-class. All the stuff we've learned together about how big fish respond to flies has been a real education and opened my eyes to a lot of new techniques I never thought were possible. But I guess my number one best story on any gear was the all-tackle, world-record muskie release—58½ inches by 29 inches and probably 60 pounds. Now *that's* a fish that will keep you up late at night!

GUIDE: **BRAD BOHEN, Hayward, Wisconsin**

TOPIC: **Fishing lakes, rivers, and flowages in northern Wisconsin**

BEST QUOTE: *"It takes only one fish to go from zero to hero!"*

Brad Bohen is a consummate "trout bum." In fact, he was recently recognized by a national magazine for his obsession with all fish on a fly. He's also a long-time Northwoods guide and an experienced muskie fly fisher. Growing up outside the Twin Cities he naturally took to fly fishing throughout the upper Midwest for trout, bass, and eventually muskies. Today he and his wife Jen manage an estate on the legendary Bois Brule River and operate a guide service, Afton Anglers, in Hayward, Wisconsin where he's introduced many an angler from around the country to the joys of muskie on the fly. His insights into this sport provide valuable lessons on how to do this the right way.

Q: What skills does it take to be a successful muskie fly fisher?

A: Patience, stamina, and a willingness to think outside the box are all important. The same goes for being able to focus and be in the moment when you fish. Being a competent caster is probably the number one physical skill you need to master before you even think about muskie fishing with a fly. While I've had clients who couldn't cast very well and still caught fish, they also missed one hell of a lot of opportunities through the day. Line management is also important for any fly fishing you do but especially for muskies. This really comes into play when striking and fighting a fish. It totally sucks when you finally get a fish to hit, you're standing on your line or it's wrapped around the reel seat.

Q: What is your favorite time of the year to muskie fish with a fly?

A: I personally love the fall fishing in northern Wisconsin right up to ice-up. It's a beautiful time to be on the water, and there's a lot less pressure. Most of all, however, the fish are really aggressive and seem to love flies this time of year. The spring is also great, especially if you've got a nice warm up after the late-May opener. Fish are often tightly concentrated and hungry at this time and fishing can be fantastic! Summer can be productive if it stays cool and we get enough water to keep the rivers flowing. This last summer it was pretty hot and dry all through the year, and the bite was definitely off big time until the first early frost in September.

Q: What do you consider ideal weather conditions for muskie fishing with a fly?

Guide Brad Bohen with a fine Wisconsin fish on a cold fall day.

A: Any time I can get out. I love it when you get a steady southwest wind and things first start to warm up in the spring. It seems to really turn the fish on where I fish. I also like prolonged periods of stability—three or four days—preceding a major weather change like in the summer before a front or a thunderstorm. That really puts the fish on edge and makes them hit. In the late season I enjoy fishing on those nice Indian summer days, but the fishing actually seems to get better the nastier it is. Give me a cold, cloudy day with a north wind, and I'll find you some fish.

Q: What are some of the important factors for being a successful muskie fly-fishing guide?

A: That's easy: knowing where the fish are and how to get to them. Seriously, you've got to fish a lot to be a successful muskie guide. This means being on the water solo or with clients as much as possible and really understanding what's happening through the season. These fish change preferences and locations constantly. If you're not tuned in you'll be wasting a lot of time. Good boat control is also key, especially when you've got a caster who can't hit the spots. Patience is always a virtue, for the guide and especially with a new fisherman. I'll see fish many times that my clients miss. You've got to keep things positive so they stay in the game and are ready for a strike at any time. Oh, last, but not least, I almost forgot to mention the most important thing: a good sense of humor.

Q: What are your favorite flies for muskie fishing?

A: I have a lot of patterns that work but usually stick with the same half dozen or so that I know produce. Whatever the pattern, it's got to have good "hang time" and look alive even when it's barely moving. Throughout the year I've had a lot of success with a simple natural-colored bucktail baitfish pattern I call the Angry Minnow that mimics a chub or shiner common in my water [see Chapter 5 for detailed recipe]. I also fish a large, water-pushing, chartreuse deer-hair popper I call the Beuford when the water is warmer and the fish are more aggressive. In the fall we fish a lot of black or natural large, leech-like saddle-hackle streamers slowly on the bottom with a sink-tip line. This killer fly was developed by our other resident muskie guide, Don Larsen, a.k.a. The Pond Monster. He's even had success with these flies in the late season when most muskie guides are fishing suckers on a quick-strike rig.

Wisconsin muskie guide and fly tier Don Larson, a.k.a. The Pond Monster, with yet another catch from his backyard muskie playground.

Q: What do you consider most critical when it comes to fly-fishing gear for muskies?

A: There's a ton of good equipment out there these days. I fish fast-action to medium-fast-action, nine-foot, 10-weights most of the time. Sometimes I go lighter if I'm throwing a smaller fly. The key really is to use a rod that works well for you and gets the fly to the fish. Reels are not as critical since most of your fish will be fought by hand. I particularly like the Orvis Battenkill Large Arbor: it's light-weight and reasonably priced. One thing I do that's different is fish a lot of heavy fluorocarbon for the tippet. Sixty-pound Orvis Mirage is a good one, but there are many others that do the trick. I know there's always a risk of a bite off, but I think it helps in my clear-water spots.

On the other hand, you've got me convinced to start using more coated wire with some of the monsters you've been catching! Also, as with all muskie fishing, you've got to keep your hooks real sharp and keep checking them for sharpness through the day.

Q: What is your typical approach to converting a following muskie on a fly?

A: Don't slow down! I like to keep the fly moving fast with a lot of abrupt turns back over the fish's back. If it's a hot fish—all lit-up and twitchy—usually he nails it on the first turn when he thinks it's getting away. Guess it's really more about reading the fish and then responding. Some fish will hang back out of sight and then hit just as you pull the fly for the next cast. It usually scares the hell out of the angler. You almost expect the fish to roar like a lion! Sometimes there's nothing you can do, but it sure is painful when they do this and you totally miss the fish.

THE BEUFORD

Originated and tied by Brad Bohen

HOOK:	3/0 Mustad 34011.
THREAD:	Uni Big Fly.
TAIL:	Chartreuse bucktail (length of hook shank) overlaid with eight to 10 strands of Flashabou.
LEGS:	Four long and webby grizzly saddles.
BODY:	White and chartreuse marabou, wound forward tightly, tied in tip first.
HEAD:	White, brown, black, and chartreuse deer body hair spun in alternating bands and clipped to desired shape from popper to diver.

Q: What specific areas in a lake, flowage, or river do you target when fly fishing for muskies?

A: Find the bait and you'll find the fish. If you can't find the bait, talk to a panfish angler—they usually know where the muskies are because muskies are always stealing their fish! Most of my fishing is on shallower flowages and rivers. These fish have limited options compared to lakes, so I look for any good available cover such as deadfalls, log jams, lily pads, undercut banks, and rocks. My river fish also like to hang on current seams, especially in eddies along fast-water rapids or in slow pools just below. In the fall, flowage fish move quite shallow, chasing bait right up into the reeds or rice. At this time of year I sometimes see them working and busting bait. It's a fun time to fish and a lot like bonefish or tarpon since you have to lead the fish when you cast.

Q: What is the biggest mistake you watch anglers make when muskie fishing with a fly?

A: Too much false casting! This is not like trout fishing where you have to dry the fly out before your cast. Keeping the fly in the air is a big waste of fishing time and usually gets you or your guide hooked. You've got to be able to get the fly out quickly and with a minimum of effort or you'll be worn out pretty quickly. Also, I think a lot of guys give up on a fish too quickly. Even if the fish misses the fly you can usually cast back and catch it if it hasn't spooked for some other reason.

Q: What is your best muskie-on-a-fly story?

A: The time I caught a fish from the boat landing on my first cast was pretty cool. I'm sure he was just waiting for us. He swirled on some spooked baitfish when I waded in behind the boat. I'll never forget that fish or the look on your face! The best thing was we knew right there and then it was going to be a great day, and it was. Something like 20 fish hooked and 16 landed. That was probably one of my best muskie days on a fly ever. I also just get a kick out of putting clients into their first muskie on a fly. Every time they catch one, even a small one, it's a big event.

GUIDE: **PAT EHLERS, Milwaukee, Wisconsin**

TOPIC: **Fishing lakes and rivers in Wisconsin**

BEST QUOTE: *"Muskie fishing is testosterone fishing."*

Wisconsin native Pat Ehlers guides anglers for everything from trout to bass to carp. He owns The

Fly Fishers, a full-service fly shop in Milwaukee, and fishes around the world hosting trips for sailfish, bonefish, and giant northern pike. When it comes to "toothy critters," he always jumps at the chance to do what he calls "testosterone fishing." In his many years of guiding for muskies around Wisconsin, Pat has had a chance to think long and hard about the best techniques and tackle. This knowledge has resulted in the recent development of a new line: the Teeny Pro-Series Pike and Muskie line, perfect for many muskie fly presentations. Pat is a true professional muskie fly-fishing guide. He brings a wealth of knowledge and experience to this emerging sport.

Q: What does it take to be a successful muskie fisher with a fly?

A: As in any fishing you must be able to locate fish and have the correct fly, but I think time on the water and perseverance are equally important. One thing that doesn't get enough emphasis is fly casting. Covering the water is very important in musky fishing. Too many anglers prevent themselves from being effective because their casting skills aren't what they should be.

Q: What is your favorite time of year to muskie fish with a fly?

A: One of my favorite times is the early season. Fish are coming off of the spawn and tend to be neutral to negative at this time. This is when fly gear shines. Where I do most of my guiding I also find most of my fish in shallow water, making access to them easier

Wisconsin muskie guides Pat Ehlers (right) and Steve Cervenka (left) display one of many reasons they love "testosterone fishing."

with a fly. It also may be possible to sight fish muskies early in the season and of course that takes the guesswork out of location.

Q: What do you consider ideal weather patterns or conditions for muskie fishing with a fly?

A: Windy days tend to be good days for muskies. This does create some problems with casting for the inexperienced fly angler. I'm pretty much of a "fish-when-you-get-the-chance" kind of person, but if possible I like to be on the water at moon rise and moon set. I think this is more important than the weather.

Q: What is the most important factor when it comes to being a muskie fly-fishing guide?

A: Of course there's putting your client on fish, boat control, and other guide tricks. But I think most

MUSKIE SEEKER

Originated and tied by Pat Ehlers

HOOK: 1/0 to 3/0 TMC 811S.

THREAD: UTC 140 fluorescent green.

TAIL: Fluorescent green rabbit strip (three shank lengths) over Pearl Flashabou (20 strands).

BODY: Palmered fluorescent green or orange CCT Body Fur.

LEGS: Two fluorescent orange medium round rubber legs per side.

EYES: Large plated lead eyes.

WEED GUARD:
            Twenty-pound-test hard nylon.

of all you need to be patient. And you need to keep your angler focused so if there's only one opportunity the day isn't wasted.

Q: What is your favorite fly type, color, etc. for muskie fishing?

A: Fly selection is dictated by conditions, time of year, and the fish's attitude. Early season I like relatively small flies. Black is a favored color. In tannin-stained water I like copper and gold, which show up well. Day in and day out, I do like fishing or at least trying a red and white Umpqua Swimming Baitfish. When fishing rivers, I also like to fish The Seeker, one of my own effective patterns. This fly works well on muskies, bass, and pike in chartreuse, red-and-white, purple, and fire tiger.

Q: What do you consider most important when selecting fly-fishing rods, reels, lines, and leaders for muskies?

A: High-performance fly rods are a must. You're typically throwing large flies and making lots of casts. Poor-performing, slow rods just won't cut it. Reels aren't all that important because muskies generally don't make long runs. The proper size to balance with the rod is as critical as the drag. Specialty-taper fly lines make casting large flies a lot easier. I'm prejudiced but that's why I designed my Pike and Musky taper line with the Jim Teeny Line Company: to make casting and fishing big flies easier and more productive. As for leaders I always use TyGer wire for my bite tippets. I hear anglers say I use hard Mason and don't have any problems landing fish, but I've seen these same guys lose fish after telling me the Mason was fine. The TyGer wire won't get cut.

Q: What is your typical approach to converting a following muskie with a fly?

A: The figure-8 can and should be done just like with conventional gear. In fact the extra leverage of a long fly rod makes a wide figure-8 easier to do. A lot of anglers make too tight a figure-8 and the fish, especially big ones, can't make a tight enough turn to stay with the lure. Making wider turns will help keep the fish interested. Keep in mind, however, fly rods can be tougher to hook fish with because of the extra rod length and soft tip.

Q: What specific areas on your lakes or rivers do you like to target when fly fishing for muskies?

A: In lakes, rocks are important structure to look for as well as weeds. Any place that has an edge to it is important whether it's a drop off, a weed edge, or a rock bar. In rivers I look for wood. To me it's probably the number one piece of river structure.

Q: What is the biggest mistake you see fishermen make when muskie fishing with a fly?

A: Not paying attention. It takes plenty of focus and mental toughness to be successful.

Q: What is your best muskie-on-a-fly story?

A: I was fishing at Fireside Lodge owned by my friends Alan and Audrey Brandys. They have a number of portage-accessible lakes off Little Vermillion Lake where their lodge is located. It's a prime area for fishing muskies with a fly. My son and I started out on one of the smaller portage lakes. Normally I hate catching something on the first cast of the day—it's a superstition with me, I guess. This day not only did I catch a muskie on the first cast, but I caught *three* on the first three casts. The first was 36 inches, the second 42, and the third 40. That's going to be tough to match.

GUIDE: **STEVE KUNNATH, Detroit, Michigan**

TOPIC: Fishing Lake St. Clair

BEST QUOTE: *"I am addicted to muskies!"*

Lake St. Clair muskie guide Steve Kunnath is blessed to be fishing some of the most productive water in North America. Although best known among conventional anglers for its seasonal casting and trolling opportunities, Steve has perfected fly fishing for muskies on this vast, open-water fishery with consistent success. As a warmwater fly-fishing guide for smallmouth bass, pike, and carp for the last

eight years, it was only a matter of time before he started targeting muskies on purpose with specialized flies, techniques, and presentations. Today muskies are Steve's most popular species for guiding. As he readily admits, "I am addicted!"

Q: What skills does it take to be a successful muskie fly fisher?

A: You need determination, patience, confidence, and persistence to cast all day knowing you might get only one strike or follow up. Being confident that the strike or follow up will come and always being ready for it is critical. You also need to have a vast knowledge and understanding of muskie behavior related to structure, water temperature, and weather patterns. Being able to pick out the key prime spots on any water and fish them effectively and efficiently is what my clients pay me for. And a lot of luck never hurt either!

Michigan muskie guide Steve Kunnath proudly displays one of Lake St. Clair's finest.

Q: What is your favorite time of year to muskie fish with a fly?

A: My favorite time of year to fish for muskie with a fly is September. The days are usually a nice comfortable 70°, the fish are starting to put on the fall feed, and fishing pressure is low.

Q: What do you consider ideal weather patterns or conditions for muskie fishing with a fly?

A: The ideal conditions for muskies that I dream about is when you have a stable weather pattern for three to four days straight, the wind is from the west at six miles per hour or less, barometer near or above 30, and nice clear sunny days. By the third or fourth day you need to be calling into work sick saying you have a seeing problem; you just don't imagine yourself *not* going muskie fishing. Another great condition is 30 minutes to an hour before a very big thunderstorm.

Q: What is the most important factor when it comes to being a muskie fly-fishing guide?

A: I would say that being able to communicate a muskie's behavior with your customers throughout the day is extremely important. Such as when it's five hours into a guided trip with no sign of a fish and be able to keep them confident and alert that a muskie can and will hit your fly at any time. It is also very important to educate your customer. They are paying for your time and experience. A guide is there for more then just getting you on a fish. The guide should educate you on any tactics, techniques, etc., that will make you a better muskie fly fisher and provide a great overall experience.

Q: Do you need to be an experienced fly fisher before booking a muskie trip?

A: Being experienced in fly fishing will definitely help, but the less you know, the more important it is to go with a guide. Besides putting you on fish, a guide will teach you everything you need to know to get you on the way to becoming a successful muskie angler. Everyone had to start somewhere—even the experienced guide.

Q: What are your favorite flies for muskie fishing?

A: My favorite flies for muskie are large streamers with Icelandic sheep hair in combinations of black and white with a little chartreuse. And I always have a little red on every fly.

Q: What do you consider most important when selecting fly-fishing rods, reels, lines, and leaders for muskies?

A: Rods—fast action, lightweight, stiff but loads well. Reels—exceptionally large arbor and spool diameter for fast line retrieves, built well with strong drag system. Lines—most of the top fly-line companies produce excellent fly lines and all work well. Ninety percent of the time I use very heavy sink-tips of 400 to 600 grains. If a fly line was designed that had zero stretch (comparable to Power Pro or other braided no-stretch lines) I would use it exclusively.

The hook-setting capability would be incredible. Leaders—with our clear water I now use heavy fluorocarbon bite guards exclusively, and 20-pound Maxima for the leaders.

Q: What is your most consistent approach to converting a following muskie with a fly?

A: By far my most effective method is to perform a circle instead of a figure-8. Most new guys have a tough time with the full fly-rod figure-8. This technique keeps the fly moving at close range without the learning curve. The bigger the muskie, the bigger the circle. Push the rod tip into the water and make very fast, aggressive circles. Don't EVER let the fly quit moving!

Q: What specific areas in your water do you like to target when fly fishing for muskies?

A: On Lake St. Clair we are lucky to have a shallow lake with deep-dredged shipping channels, and lots of current from the St. Clair River and Lake Huron. I always look for weed beds in eight to 16 feet of water with some current and in close proximity to the deep channels. Also, any areas with sandbars or peninsulas with dropoffs and weed beds also hold good numbers of fish. Any areas like this with lots of baitfish, good water clarity, and good numbers of bass, walleye, and pike are always worth checking out. If these conditions are all available in one spot, there will be big muskie there as well.

Q: What is the biggest mistake you see fishermen make when muskie fishing with a fly?

A: The biggest mistake is not watching for muskie behind the fly at the end of every single retrieve. They usually see the fish after it is too late to perform a circle.

Q: What is your best muskie-on-a-fly story?

A: It's pretty hard to pick out one single favorite story—just too many! One of the greatest things about muskie fishing with a fly is that almost every time you do it there is some great memory and story created. Everything from watching a customer scream when a huge lunge does a follow-up to hooking three fish in the last 35 minutes of a trip after not seeing anything all day. Or how about a muskie jumping four feet out of the water after a streamer right next to the boat? All great stories and exactly why I love muskie fishing on the fly.

GUIDE: TROY ANDERSON, Minneapolis, Minnesota

TOPIC: Fishing Metro-lakes and big water in Minnesota

BEST QUOTE: *"The guy just totally freaked out!"*

Minneapolis-based muskie guide Troy Anderson is located in the heart of what just might be the best muskie-fishing city in the country. With so many nearby Metro-lakes to choose from it's amazing he even makes it outside the city limits. When he does, he usually heads a couple of hours north to fish the legendary waters of Lake Mille Lacs, one of the best muskie fisheries in the country. With many fine muskie lakes near and far to choose from, it's no surprise he spends some serious time on the water. A lifelong fisherman, once Troy picked up a fly rod he was smitten. After his first saltwater experience seven years ago, he realized the potential for muskie on the fly and now guides exclusively for muskie and other warmwater species.

Q: What does it take to be a successful muskie fisher with a fly?

A: Time on the water—there's just no substitute for it. Hard days are just as important as the good ones. Maybe more so. Whenever I see a fish it kind of validates what I'm doing, even if I don't catch it. I also like to have a plan and stick with it. Catching a muskie on the fly is a major achievement, like running a marathon. You can't just hit the water and start casting. You've got to have a training plan before you go fishing to be successful. Each spring I make a detailed plan based on where, when, and what I want to be fishing. As the season begins, I do my best to stick to the plan but also remain flexible when things don't go as I expect. I once spent an entire season fishing shallow on a specific body of water. By mid-season, I'd kind of figured out when the fish were there and when I was wasting my time. Even though I had some tough days, sticking to this plan taught me a heck of a lot about where and how to fish this particular piece of water.

Q: What is your favorite time of year to muskie fish with a fly?

A: The Minnesota muskie opener in June is usually a great time for fly fishing. The fish are still concentrated in shallow water after the spawn, increasing your odds. The forage is also smaller which fits well with our sport. I also find that the twitch action of a fly works really well this time of year. Another thing that's important in the spring is the water is usually very clear and free of algae, allowing the fly to be seen from longer distances and increasing your strike-zone. I also like fishing in August and September. The fish at this time of year feed pretty aggressively and are often very shallow making them a good target for the fly.

Q: What do you consider ideal weather patterns or conditions through the season for muskie fishing with a fly?

A: One thing I always look for is stability, like the same weather conditions or wind direction for two or three days. A big change following stable conditions also puts the fish on edge. Give me conditions like this and I'll show you some fish. I also pay a lot of attention to major and minor moon phases and believe, like many muskie anglers, that the rise and set are key factors influencing fish behavior.

With 10,000 lakes to choose from, Minnesota guide Troy Anderson can't get enough of muskie on the fly.

Q: What is the most important factor when it comes to being a muskie fly-fishing guide?

A: Over my seven years of doing this I'd have to say that preparing the client by setting reasonable expectations is probably most important. This isn't

like trout guiding or, better yet, smallmouth-bass guiding where you can usually find and catch some fish. You've got to be totally realistic with the client and make sure he understands exactly what he's getting into. When my angler is in the boat, I also make sure to go over his tackle very carefully. If it's not right, he'll be using my stuff. Before he starts fishing I also spend a little time showing him what I like to do for retrieves, the figure-8, and setting the hook.

Q: What are your favorite flies for muskie fishing?

A: I fish a lot of big streamers throughout the season. My color preferences vary a lot depending on the body of water—natural, black, brown, and white in clear water; bright orange, red, yellow, and chartreuse for stained conditions. Honestly, though, I don't think color or pattern is nearly as critical as the size, action, and speed of the fly. As for top-water, I love to fish them, but the hook-up percentage is usually so low it's not worth it with an inexperienced client. Whatever fly I'm fishing I'm always very careful not to handle them too much after coming in contact with sunscreen, lotion, or fuel. Lindy No-Scent is a great product to use for keeping your hands clean when you fish.

Q: What do you consider most important when selecting fly-fishing rods, reels, lines, and leaders for muskies?

A: Use the best gear you can afford. I personally like a fast-action nine-foot, 9- or 10-weight rod. The Sage Xi2 is a terrific rod for muskie and will do just about anything you need it to. I fish a lot of interme-

diate, clear-tip lines in my water. They seem to work well for streamers and won't spook the fish. My leaders are pretty basic: four to six feet of heavy Maxima and a 12- to 18-inch section of 30- to 40-pound wire to the fly. I personally like TyGer wire, but there are several others that work well. I know some guys fish heavy fluorocarbon for a bite guard but I don't like it. To my thinking it's just not worth the risk.

Q: What is your most effective approach to converting a following muskie with a fly?

A: The biggest mistake I see guys make is slowing down the fly. They see a fish, forget what they're doing, and before they know it the fish is gone. If anything, you've got to pick up the speed and keep the fish interested right through the entire figure-8. I know it takes experience, but you've also got to read the fish to know what to do. If it's a hot fish I usually throw back right away. If it's "low and slow" I'll leave and come back later, like on a different moon phase, etc.

Q: What specific areas on your water do you like to target when fly fishing for muskies?

A: Depends on the lake and season but generally speaking, I fish a lot of shallow water from one to 10 feet deep. I know you can find fish deeper, but this is where I'm most effective with the fly. As for specific structure, I like shallow water cover like a weed bed, flat, or around an island. I also like covering weeds from different directions, fishing the inside and outside breaks.

Q: What is your best muskie-on-a-fly story?

A: Well, I've seen a lot of crazy stuff muskie fishing. I know you've seen it too, but it's always funny what can happen when a fish shows up. I once had a client that totally freaked out when he saw his first fish. I mean, the guy went nuts, yelling and casting the fly at the fish over and over as if he'd lost his mind. Needless to say, he didn't get the fish. That's what the sport can do to you if you don't watch out!

What it's all about: In addition to having fun on the water and caching fish, experienced muskie guides such as those featured in this chapter will teach you the proper way to release your fish to fight another day.

GREAT FLY-ROD MUSKIE WATERS

"There will be days when fishing will be better than one's most optimistic forecast, others when it is far worse. Either is a gain over just staying home."

—RODERICK HAIG-BROWN

THE NEW MILLENNIUM IS A GREAT TIME to be a muskie fisher. Thanks to the growing practice of catch-and-release fishing among most muskie anglers, enlightened fisheries management, and the hard work of dedicated organizations such as Muskies Inc., there are actually more and better opportunities for muskie fishing today than ever before—amazing when you consider how many outdoor activities have been degraded by mankind's increasing presence and impact on this earth.

In fact, despite all the negative implications of global warming, the undeniable evidence that temperatures are increasing steadily around the globe—hotter at the end of this century than any point in the last 2 million years—means that muskies will probably continue to thrive for the foreseeable future. This is also what makes the sport of fly fishing for muskies well worth pursuing, and keeps guys like me on the water casting all day and night.

It wasn't always this way. Muskies, especially giant muskies over 50 inches, were once considered a thing of the past for most anglers. As I discovered on my earliest forays into muskie country, for a long time you could only find evidence of these coveted trophies mounted on the wall of a Northwoods bar or in grainy black-and-white photos. With the advent of stricter regulations and the practice of catch-and-release, however, everything changed for the better.

Take the example of Wisconsin. As recently as the early 1980s, anglers were killing and keeping an estimated 30,000 fish over 30 inches annually. Essentially every legal fish caught was a dead fish. As Wisconsin Department of Natural Resources fisheries biologist Frank Pratt, Jr., notes, "Thirty years ago a 40-inch muskie was hard to come by in Wisconsin waters, and only 10 years ago catching a 50-inch muskie was considered quite unusual."

What changed?

By 2001 the practice of voluntary catch and release had taken hold. The number of kept fish dropped to fewer than 2,000 that year. Increasing the state size limit from 30 inches to 34 inches in 1984 also helped. Many better lakes and rivers in Wisconsin and other states have since been officially designated trophy water with higher size limits of 45 inches and even 50 inches. No doubt the fishing has improved.

As a result of this muskie renaissance around the country, some fisheries now provide good to excellent fishing close to cities such as Detroit, Minneapolis, Madison, and Buffalo. In fact, from where I sit today in downtown Chicago, I have a legitimate shot at a muskie on a fly within a three-hour drive.

Where to Go?

Choosing where to go muskie fishing is just as important as the right fly and the right guide. Many anglers spend a lifetime searching for good muskie water at considerable personal cost, despite the toll on family and friends. My hard-core muskie friends have even been known to follow the bite around the country each year in search of their own fishing Holy Grail. Given all the variables including boat access, lodging, water conditions, and fishing patterns, my advice is to do plenty of research on your own to make the right choices. Modern communication, notably the Internet, can help. But local knowledge and time on the water remain the key factors to uncovering the best fishing. Still, there are several important things to consider before you begin your quest for a muskie on the fly.

Probably the biggest question to ask is whether the water you plan to fish is action or trophy water. While not mutually exclusive, these commonly used definitions of water type will help you narrow things down and decide where to begin your quest. Action water is defined by most muskie anglers as any fishery with better than average numbers of smaller fish per acre—usually less than 40 inches. Casting a fly in action water is by no means a guarantee of fish—just

The world's largest muskie? This giant fish replica—and a vast collection of fishing memorabilia—can be found at the National Freshwater Fishing Hall of Fame in Hayward, Wisconsin, also known as the "Home of World-Record Muskies."

more opportunities. Trophy water, as the name suggests, has fewer fish per acre, but those that are there are usually larger than average due primarily to the forage base. Both offer good potential for muskies on a fly. But the odds are significantly better on action water given the overall numbers of fish and predominance of shallow-water habitat.

Another valid consideration when choosing a muskie spot is the proximity of other good muskie-water options in a given area. While most of the better regions offer at least a few good choices, some are isolated. This can result in a ruined trip if things don't go according to plan. Having fallback water to fish when the first choice doesn't pan out is always important, especially when fishing a river where water levels and clarity often dictate your success.

The historical significance or scenic beauty of a given lake or river is also well worth considering. While most muskie waters lack the traditional fly-fishing ambiance and infrastructure of popular destinations such as West Yellowstone or Islamorada, there's plenty to love when you get to know them. Better known areas such as the muskie towns of Hayward and Boulder Junction in northern Wisconsin, the numerous lakes and rivers of

Minnesota, and the vast Lake of the Woods along the Canadian border offer a long history of muskie fishing combined with spectacular beauty.

Like the better-known trout-fishing destinations around the country, these muskie Meccas are both productive and inspiring places to fish. They offer much in the way of muskie legend and lore and give the angler a real sense of the cultural influence muskie fishing has had over the years. Since ours can be a lonely and difficult sport, being in a wonderful place and fishing picturesque water adds to the experience even if the fish don't cooperate.

What follows is a regional guide to some of the best fly-fishing muskie water in North America. My list is based on both action and trophy potential. This is not intended as a comprehensive examination of exactly where to fish in each and every state or province. Rather, it is a select listing of many of the better fly-fishing waters you should seriously consider, depending on your desire for a big fish or just one fish on a fly. With muskies now present or thriving in some 35 states, the odds are you'll find yourself close to one of these prime areas. If not, you can always use this information to plan your next trip and find your own muskie hotspot.

Action Muskie Fly Water

A wise old fisherman once told me, "If you want to catch muskies, go where the fish are!" While this seems rather self-evident, like all simple truths there is more to it than just picking a muskie spot and going fishing.

Action or numbers waters fit perfectly into this category and offer what is clearly your best shot at a fish on a fly. They typically hold both natural and stocked muskies of the pure or tiger strains, or both. Although the potential for a trophy fish of 50-inches—in some places even one of 40 inches—may be limited, the potential on this kind of water to see, hook, and boat a muskie on a fly more than makes up for the size of the fish. Any fish you can see or catch builds confidence. This will make you a better overall muskie fisher. Fortunately, most action water has a mix of small and large fish. You won't be wasting your time once you've caught a few fish, and you'll be confident and prepared when the big one finally hits.

Most action waters are either natural eutrophic or mesotrophic lakes, flowages of all sizes, some man-made reservoirs, and many small- and medium-sized rivers. They are typically rich in aquatic life and provide plenty of forage for muskies to feed on throughout the year. These waters normally fish best in the spring and fall months when water clarity is ideal and most fish are shallow. Despite increased weed growth and reduced clarity as the season progresses, they also fish well in the summer months with fish most active during low-light conditions and significant weather transitions.

One of the best things about action waters is their generally manageable size and varied shallow-water structure. Such characteristics allow a fly fisher to effectively and efficiently fish specific and often visible fish-holding targets. This has a certain appeal to those used to fishing trout streams or small lakes with plenty of structure and little open-water casting.

Among the various types of action water, flowages and small- to medium-sized rivers offer some of the best fishing throughout the year. The fact that muskies tend to be concentrated and opportunistic in this type of moving water makes them especially

Near or far, action muskie water offers the best opportunity for one or more fish—and there's always the possibility of a real trophy.

The following diverse waters have historically offered better than average "catching" opportunities for fly fishers looking for one or several fish. Like all fisheries, some years are better than others so you'll need to do your own thorough investigation to determine the current status of a given piece of water.

Midwest Action Water:

Wisconsin

Boulder Chain
Chippewa Flowage
Chippewa River
Eagle River Chain
Flambeau River
Little Green Lake
Lost Land and Teal lakes
Madison Chain*
Manitowish Waters
Minocqua Chain
Pewaukee Lake
Pentwell Flowage
Presque Isle Chain
St. Croix River
Tiger Cat Flowage
Turtle-Flambeau Flowage
Yellow, Bone, and Deer lakes

Indiana

Webster Lake
Barbee Chain
Lake Tippecanoe

Minnesota

Baby Lake
Deer Lake
Forest Lake
Lake Independence
Lake Minnetonka
Little Wolf Lake
Mantrap Lake
St. Croix River
White Bear Lake

Illinois

Fox Chain of Lakes
Johnson—Sauk Trail Lake
Lake Shelbyville

Iowa

Three Mile Lake
Pleasant Creek Lake

Michigan

Budd Lake
Craig Lake
Lake Hudson
Lake St. Clair
Sanford Lake
Thornapple Lake

North Dakota

New John's Lake*

Ohio

Clear Fork Reservoir
Leesville Reservoir

Southern Action Water:

Kentucky

Cave Run Lake
Green River Lake
Cumberland River
Kentucky River
Licking River

North Carolina

New River
Nolichucky River
French Broad River

West Virginia

Buckhannon River
Elk River
Mud River
Tygart River

Virginia

Clinch River
James River
New River

Northeast Action Water:

New York

Allegheny River
Delaware River
Susquehanna River
Lake Otisco*
Canadarago Lake*
Mohawk River*

Pennsylvania

Lake Arthur
Lake Sumerset
Susquehanna River*
Woodcock Lake

Maryland

Bradford Lake*
Piney Run Reservoir*
Potomac River*

Massachusetts

Pontoosuc Reservoir*

Maine

Baker Lake
St. John River

Western Action Water:

Colorado

Quincy Reservoir*
Cherry Creek Reservoir*

Washington

Mayfield Lake*
Newman Lake*

Idaho

Hauser Lake*

Utah

Pineview Reservoir*
Newton Reservoir*

Canadian Action Water:

Ontario

Crow Lake
Canyon Lake
Indian Chain
Kawartha Chain/Stoco and
    Moira lakes
Little Vermillion Chain
Muskoka Chain

Québec

Laurentian Chain

New Brunswick

St. John River

*tiger muskie present

vulnerable to a well-placed fly, thus increasing your odds of your success. Many of my best days for muskie on a fly have come in the spring and fall on flowages and rivers when it is not uncommon to hook as many as a dozen fish or more in a single day.

Trophy Muskie Fly Water

The best trophy waters in North America have many things in common, but one thing stands out among the rest: Big water equals big fish. Most are large lakes and rivers with diverse structure and an abundance of fatty forage such as ciscoes, whitefish, smelt, trout, or various rough and game fishes that big muskies prefer. Many of the best waters also feature a lot of deep and cold environments where larger muskies often forage in search of prey. Natural oligotrophic lakes, flowages, man-made reservoirs and large rivers typically fall within this trophy-water category.

Unfortunately for the fly fisher, fishing deep water effectively can be a real challenge. Other than trolling, it's tough to keep a fly deep enough for the sustained period of time necessary to target these open water fish. However, certain times of the year such as the spring post-spawn and the early fall period when the fish and forage are concentrated and relatively shallow do offer good opportunities for large fish on the fly.

Fly-Rod Muskie Guides, Fly Shops, Outfitters and Lodges

The following is a list of recommended independent guides, fly shops with guide services, outfitters, and lodges that specialize in muskie fishing with a fly. Although very few fly fish exclusively for muskies, these dedicated professionals all share a passion for the species. They welcome anglers ready for the challenge.

Sometimes the journey is just as important as the destination: An impressive release such as this represents the culmination of time on the water, careful planning, and the right fly.

Trophy hunting is part of the natural evolution of any serious angler regardless of the species. As your muskie obsession grows, you will no doubt find yourself seeking bigger and better fish on the fly. To assist you in this search, the following better-known U.S. and Canadian trophy fisheries consistently produce large muskies—some exceeding 50 inches—and have the real potential for new fly-rod line-class, state, or world-record fish with every cast:

Wisconsin

Gile Flowage
Green Bay/Fox River
Grindstone Lake
Lac Courte Oreilles
Lac Vieux Desert*
North Twin Lake
Trout Lake
Clear Lake
Upper Wisconsin River

Michigan

Black Lake
Elk Lake
Lake Skegemog
Lake St. Clair
St. Mary's River

Minnesota

Cass Lake
Mille Lacs Lake
Lake Vermilion
Leech Lake
Lake Winnibigoshish
Upper Mississippi River
Lake Bemidji

New York

Lake Chautauqua
Lake Erie/Buffalo Harbor
St Lawrence River
Upper Niagara River

Ohio

Salt Fork Reservoir
Piedmont Lake

Pennsylvania

Pymatuning Lake
Allegheny Reservoir
Allegheny River

Illinois

Lake Carlton
Lake McMaster
Lake Kinkaid
Lake Shabbona*

Iowa

Big Spirit Lake
Clear Lake
East Okoboji Lake
West Okoboji Lake*

Missouri

Pomme De Terre
Hazel Creek Lake

Tennessee

Dale Hollow Reservoir

West Virginia

Stonecoal Lake
Stonewall Jackson Lake

Ontario

Dryberry Lake
Eagle Lake
English River
French River
Georgian Bay/Moon River Basin
Lac Seul
Lake Nipissing
Lake of the Woods
Pipestone Lake
Rainy Lake
Rowan Lake
St. Lawrence River
Wabigoon Lake

Québec

Ottawa River
St. Lawrence River

*tiger muskie present

Anything is possible when you cast a fly on trophy water. While this late season "big heavy" didn't eat a fly, it's always a possibility if you put in enough time on the right water.

This beautiful Minnesota lake is just one of many in North America offering dedicated anglers a fish of a lifetime on the fly.

Independent Guides
Specializing in Muskie Fly Fishing:

Wisconsin

Brad Bohen
Afton Anglers
Hayward, Wisconsin
Northern Wisconsin muskie fly-fishing guide
715-372-5909
www.bradbohen.com

Tom Schenk
Chippewa River Custom Rod Company
Holcombe, Wisconsin
Northern Wisconsin muskie fly-fishing guide and custom rod builder
715-312-0509

Don Larson
Hayward, Wisconsin
Northern Wisconsin muskie fly-fishing guide
715-934-2410
www.pondmonster.com

Steve Cervenka
Phillips, Wisconsin
Northern Wisconsin muskie fly-fishing guide
715-339-4261
www.flambeauguide.com

George Langley
Langley Guide Service
Eagle River, Wisconsin
Northern Wisconsin muskie fly-fishing guide service
715-479-8804
www.eaglesportcenter.com

Russ Smith
Smity Bait and Guide Service
Minocqua, Wisconsin
Northern Wisconsin muskie fly-fishing guide service
715-356-5565
www.smitybait.com

Todd Polacek
Brodhead, Wisconsin
Wisconsin muskie fly-fishing guide
608-206-4902

Illinois

Rich Brown
The Fatman Guide Services
Southern Wisconsin and northeast Illinois muskie fly-fishing guide
847-322-0881
www.fishinfatman.com

Indiana

Jay Anglin
Anglin's Guide Service
Indiana muskie fly-fishing guide service
574-210-2844
www.anglinoutdoors.com

Minnesota

Bob Bickford
Great Northern Adventures
Minnesota muskie fly-fishing guide service
White Bear Lake, Minnesota
651-426-6405

Chris Hansen
Twin Cities, Minnesota
Minnesota muskie fly-fishing guide
763-572-0717
www.wildsmallie.com

Mark Meritt
Victoria, Minnesota
Minnesota and Indiana muskie fly-fishing guide
952-797-2486

Justin Netzer
Urban Bonefishers
Egan, Minnesota
Minnesota Metro lakes muskie fly fishing guide
612-298-8141
www.urbanbonefisher.com

John Edstrom
Headwaters Guide Service
Otsego, Minnesota
Minnesota and Wisconsin muskie fly-fishing guide service
763-493-5800
www.headwatersflyfishing.com

Troy Anderson
Muskie on the Fly Guide Service
Minnetrista, Minnesota
Minneapolis Metro Lakes and northern Minnesota muskie fly- fishing guide
952-240-1022
www.muskieonthefly.com

Mike Thomas
Big Pike Mike Guide Service
Minnesota
Minnesota and Wisconsin muskie fly-fishing guide
651-485-6775
www.bigpikemike.com

Kip Vieth
Wildwood Float Trips and Outfitters LLC
Edina, Minnesota
Minnesota and Wisconsin muskie fly-fishing guide and outfitter
612-72-DRIFT
www.wildwoodfloattrips.com

Ouitdee Carson
Arrowhead Fly Angler
Duluth, Minnesota
Northern Minnesota and Wisconsin muskie fly-fishing guide
218-590-1712
www.arrowheadflyangler.com

Michigan

Captain Brian Meszaros
Great Lakes Fly Fishing, LLC
Taylor, Michigan
Lake St. Clair, Lake Erie, and inland waters muskie fly-fishing guide
734-904-FISH
www.greatlakesflyfishing.com

Captain Steve Kunnath
Lake St. Clair muskie fly-fishing guide
248-320-0688
Captainsteve1@comcast.net
www.lakestclairflyfishing.com

Canada

Québec

Mike Lazarus
Montréal, Québec
Québec muskie fly-fishing guide
514-824-6875

Ontario

Jody Mills
Georgian Bay, Ontario
Ontario muskie fly-fishing guide
705-498-1094
www.millsmuskyguideservice.com

Fly Shops, Outfitters, and Lodges Specializing in Muskie Fly Fishing:

Wisconsin

Anglers All
Ashland, Wisconsin
Roger LaPenter, guide
Northern Wisconsin fly-fishing guide service, fly shop, and outfitter
715-682-5754

Ashegon Lake Resort
Couderay, Wisconsin
Tom Greenup, owner and guide
Northern Wisconsin muskie fly-fishing guide service and lodging
715-945-2781
www.ashegonlakeresort.com

Boulder Lodge
Hayward, Wisconsin
Northern Wisconsin muskie fly-fishing guide service, outfitter, and lodging
715-462-3002
www.boulder-lodge.com

Ghost Lake Lodge
Hayward, Wisconsin
Northern Wisconsin muskie fly fishing lodge
715-462-3939
www.ghostlakelodge.com

Thanks to catch-and-release management, longer size limits, and stocking programs, many of the scenic waterways of North America are now home to growing populations of the mighty muskellunge. The unique combination of natural beauty and exhilarating fishing is an experience not to be missed.

Maine fly-fishing guide Dan Legere's client Zach Hesch proudly shows off a nice Saint John River muskie. Maine now supports a fishable muskie population well worth exploring with a fly.

Hayward Fly Fishing Company
Hayward, Wisconsin
Larry Mann and Wendy Williamson, owners and guides
Northern Wisconsin muskie fly-fishing guide service, fly shop and outfitter
715-634-8149
www.haywardflyfishingco.com

Orvis Madison
Madison, Wisconsin
Wisconsin muskie fly shop, outfitter, and casting instruction
Tony Mort, Fishing Manager
608-833-1359
www.orvis.com

Tight Lines Fly Fishing Company
De Pere, Wisconsin
Tim Landweir, owner and guide
Northeast Wisconsin muskie fly-fishing guide service, fly shop, and outfitter
920-336-4106
www.tightlinesflyfishing.com

The Fly Fishers
Milwaukee, Wisconsin
Pat Ehlers, owner and guide
Southern Wisconsin muskie fly-fishing guide service, fly shop, and outfitter
414-259-8100
www.theflyfishers.com

The Superior Fly Angler
Superior, Wisconsin
Northern Wisconsin and Minnesota muskie fly-fishing guide service, fly shop, and outfitter
715-395-9520
www.superiorflyangler.com

We Tie It Fly Shop
Boulder Junction, Wisconsin
Bill Sherer, owner and guide
Northern Wisconsin muskie fly-fishing guide service, fly shop, outfitter, and casting instruction
715-385-0171
www.wetieit.com

Maine

Maine Guide Fly Shop and Guide Services
Greenville, Maine
Dan Legere, guide
Maine muskie fly-fishing guide service, fly shop, and outfitter
207-695-2266
www.maineguideflyshop.com

Ross Lake Camps
Clayton Lake, Maine
Maine muskie fishing guide service, outfitter, and lodging
603-320-3208
www.rosslakecamps.com

Minnesota

The Fly Angler
Fridley, Minnesota
Minnesota muskie fly-fishing guide service, fly shop, and outfitter
763-572-0717
www.mnflyangler.com

Bob Mitchell's Fly Shop
Lake Elmo, Minnesota
Minnesota muskie fly-fishing guide service, fly shop, and outfitter
651-770-5854
www.bobmitchellsflyshop.com

Bentleys Outfitters
Bloomington, Minnesota
Minnesota muskie fly-fishing guide service, fly shop, and outfitter
952-828-9554
www.bentlysoutfitters.com

Great Lakes Fly Company
Duluth, Minnesota
Minnesota muskie fly-fishing guide service, fly shop, and outfitter
218-740-3040
www.greatlakesflys.com

Moose Track Adventures
Ely, Minnesota
Northern Minnesota muskie fly-fishing guide service and outfitter
800-777-7091
www.moosetrackadventures.com

Michigan

Hank's Fly Fishing Unlimited
Lake Orion, Michigan
Michigan muskie fly-fishing guide service, fly shop, and outfitter
248-393-1500
www.hanksflyfishing.com

Orvis Detroit
Royal Oak, Michigan
Michigan muskie fly-fishing guide service, fly shop, and outfitter
248-542-5700

North Carolina

Brookings
Cashiers, North Carolina
Mac Marett, guide
North Carolina muskie fly-fishing guide service and outfitter
888-544-7343
www.brookingsonline.com

Davidson River Outfitters
Pisgah Forest, North Carolina
Walker Parrot, guide
North Carolina muskie fly-fishing guide service, fly shop, and outfitter
888-861-0111
www.davidsonflyfishing.com

Elk Creek Outfitters
Boone, North Carolina
Judson Conway, guide
North Carolina muskie fly-fishing guide service and outfitter
828-264-6497
www.ecoflyfishing.com

Indiana

FlyMasters
Indianapolis, Indiana
Indiana muskie fly-fishing guide service, fly shop, and outfitter
317-570-9811
www.flymasters.com

Wildcat Creek Outfitters
Zionsville, Indiana
Indiana muskie fly-fishing guide service, fly shop, and outfitter
317-733-3014
www.wildcatcreekoutfitters.com

Illinois

Chicago Fly Fishing Outfitters
Chicago, Illinois
Muskie fly-fishing fly shop, outfitter, and casting instruction
312-944-3494
www.chifly.com

Trout & Grouse
Northfield, Illinois
Muskie fly-fishing fly shop, outfitter, and casting instruction
847-501-3111
www.troutandgrouse.com

One More Cast Fly Shop
Countryside, Illinois
Muskie fly-fishing fly shop, outfitter, and casting instruction
708-482-4990
www.onemorecast.com

Orvis Chicago
Chicago, Illinois
Muskie fly-fishing fly shop, outfitter, and casting instruction
T.J. Roy, Fishing Manager
312-440-0662
www.orvis.com

Dan's Tackle Service
Chicago, Illinois
Muskie fly-fishing fly shop, outfitter, and casting instruction
773-276-5562
www.danstackleservice.com

Pennsylvania

Clouser's Fly Shop
Middletown, Pennsylvania
Muskie fly-fishing fly shop, outfitter, and guide service
717-944-6541
www.clouserflyfishing.com

For most anglers, fly fishing out West means trout fishing on a mountain stream. Although they don't normally eat dry flies, tiger muskies, such as this gorgeous fish from Colorado, are now found in lakes and reservoirs throughout the western United States. They are highly coveted by fly fishers for their good looks and aggressive nature.

North Carolina fly-fishing guide Walker Parrot releases a nice muskie from his drift boat on the French Broad River. Although not well known as a muskie destination, North Carolina and other states in the Southeast offer some interesting opportunities for muskie on the fly.

Virginia

Murray's Fly Shop
Edinburg, Virginia
Muskie fly-fishing fly shop, outfitter, and guide service
540-984-4212
www.murraysflyshop.com

Canada

Ontario

Grand River Troutfitters
Fergus, Ontario
Southern Ontario muskie fly-fishing guide service, fly shop, and outfitter
519-787-4359
www.grandrivertroutfitters.com

The Green Drake Outfitters
Ottawa, Ontario
Canadian muskie fly-fishing fly shop, outfitter, and guide service
888-828-1915
www.greendrake.com

Fireside Lodge
Sioux Lookout
Ontario, Canada
Canadian muskie fly-fishing lodge, outfitter, and guides
800-545-0815
www.firesidelodge.com

Fly-Friendly Conventional Muskie Guides:

Wisconsin

Joe Flater
Flater's Lodge
Holcombe, Wisconsin
Northern Wisconsin muskie guide service, bar, food, and lodging
888-595-4771

Mike Mladenik
Crivitz, Wisconsin
Northeast Wisconsin muskie guide service
715-854-2055
www.mikemladenik.com

Tanner Wildes
Hayward, Wisconsin
Northern Wisconsin and Kentucky guide service
715-266-2529
www.tannerwildes.com

Ben Kueng
Guaranteed Guide Service
Southern Wisconsin muskie guide service
414-232-8459
www.benkueng.com

Illinois

Chad Cain
Chad Cain's Muskie Guide Service
Southern Illinois and northern Minnesota muskie guide service
618-549-3074
www.chadcain.com

Thad Hinshaw
Central Illinois muskie guide service
309-726-1806
www.evergreenmuskie.com

New York

Rich Clarke
Signman Fishing Charters
1000 Islands/St. Lawrence River muskie guide service
Clayton, New York
888-686-3041
www.1000islandsfishing.com

Indiana

Chae Dolsen
Webster Lake Guide Service
Northeast Indiana and Lake St. Clair muskie guide service
260-385-0623
www.websterlakeguideservice.com

Chris Walker
Indiana Fishing Adventures
Northeast Indiana muskie guide service
317-727-8432
www.indianafishingadventures.com

Minnesota

Greg Thomas
Battle the Beast Guide Service
Morehead, Kentucky
Minnesota and Kentucky muskie guide service
606-776-6729
www.battlethebeast.com

Pennsylvania

Red Childress
Allegheny Guide Service
Warren, Pennsylvania
Pennsylvania muskie guide service
814-723-5912
www.alleghenyguideservice.com

Kentucky

Crash Mullins
Cave Run Guide Service
Morehead, Kentucky
Kentucky muskie guide service, tackle shop, and outfitter
606-780-4260
www.crashslanding.com

Tennessee

Fred McClintock
Trophy Guide Service
Celina, Tennessee
Tennessee muskie guide service
931-243-2142
www.trophyguideservice.com

Fly-Friendly Canadian Muskie Lodges:

Andy Myer's Lodge
Eagle Lake
Ontario, Canada
Muskie lodge, outfitter, and guides
888-727-5865
www.andymyerslodge.com

Nielsen's Fly-In Lodge
Rowan Lake
Ontario, Canada
Muskie lodge, outfitter, and guides
800-653-5946
www.nielsensflyinlodge.com

Rough Rock Lodge
Winnipeg River system
Ontario, Canada
Muskie lodge, outfitter, and guides
807-224-3403
www.roughrocklodge.com

Northwoods muskie on a perfect fall day: In the world of fly fishing there are few things that can equal catching big fish while enjoying nature's autumnal splendor.

Red Wing Lodge
Lake of the Woods (Sabaskong Bay)
Ontario, Canada
Muskie lodge, outfitter, and guides
888-488-5601
www.redwinglodge.net

Recommended Northern Pike Fly-Fishing Lodges:

Canada

Scott Lake Lodge
Saskatchewan/Northwest Territories
888-830-9525
www.scottlakelodge.com

Wollaston Lake Lodge
Saskatchewan
800-328-0628
www.wollastonlakelodge.com

Ganglers North Seal River Lodge
Northern Manitoba
866-54-LODGE
www.ganglers.com

North Knife Lake Lodge
Webbers Lodge
Thompson, Manitoba
888-932-2377
www.webberslodges.com

Legendary Wisconsin guide "Musky Joe" Flater holds a magnificent late-season muskie just prior to release. The possibility of a monster fish is exactly what keeps anglers casting hard all day and night.

Alaska

Midnight Sun Trophy Pike Adventures
North Pole, Alaska
888-932-2377
www.mstpa.com

Fishing the Net: Helpful Internet Resources, Organizaions, and Publicaions:

Muskie Fishing Web Sites:

General muskie fishing information: www.fishinfo.com
MuskieFirst: www.muskie.outdoorsfirst.com
Muskie411: www.muskie411.com
Muskie Central: www.muskiecentral.com
Ontario Muskie fishing site: www.muskieontario.com
Ontario Muskie fishing site: www.ontariomuskiefishing.ca
Joe Bucher: www.joebucher.com
Larry Ramsell: www.larryramsell.com
Steve Heiting: www.steveheiting.com

Muskie Clubs:

Muskies Inc USA: www.muskiesinc.org
Muskies Inc. Canada: www.muskiescanada.ca

Muskie Fishing Magazines:

Musky Hunter: www.muskyhunter.com
Esox Angler: www.esoxangler.com
Muskie Magazine: www.muskiesinc.org

Fly-Fishing Publications:

Eastern Fly Fishing: www.matchthehatch.com
Fish & Fly: www.fishandflymagazine.com
Fly Fish America: www.flyfishamerica.com
Fly Fisherman: www.flyfisherman.com
Midwest Fly Fishing: www.mwfly.com
MidCurrent Flyfishing News: www.midcurrent.com
The Angling Report: www.anglingreport.com

Selected State Government Fishing Web sites:

Illinois: www.dnr.state.il.us
Iowa: www.dnr.state.ia.us
Indiana: www.in.gov/dnr
Maine: www.maine.gov/ifw
Maryland: www.dnr.state.md.us
Massachusetts: www.mass.gov/dfwele
Michigan: www.michigan.gov/dnr
Missouri: www.mdc.mo.gov
Minnesota: www.dnr.state.mn.us
Ohio: www.dnr.state.oh.us
Pennsylvania: www.fish.state.pa.us
Tennessee: www.state.tn.us/twra/fish/fishmain.html
Virginia: www.dgif.state.va.us
West Virginia: www.wvdnr.gov
Wisconsin: www.dnr.state.wi.us

Water Level Site:

USGS Web site: www.waterdata.usgs.gov

Weather Web Sites:

NOAA: www.noaa.gov
The Weather Channel: www.weather.com
Accuweather: www.accuweather.com

Muskie Records:

National Freshwater Fishing Hall of Fame:
   www.freshwater-fishing.org
International Game Fish Association:
   www.igfa.org
World Record Muskie Alliance:
   www.worldrecordmuskiealliance.com

Conventional Muskie Tackle Shops:

Rollie and Helen's Musky Shop
Minocqua, Wisconsin
715-356-6011
www.muskyshop.com

Pastika's Sport Shop
Hayward, Wisconsin
800-844-2159
www.pastikas.com

Smokey's Muskellunge Shop
Pewaukee, Wisconsin
262-691-9659
www.smokeysmuskieshop.com

Thorne Bros. Custom Rod & Tackle
Fridley, Minnesota
763-572-3782
www.thornebros.com

Recommended Muskie Books:

Complete Guide to Musky Hunting second edition (2006)
   by Steve Heiting and Jim Saric
A Compendium of Muskie Angling History third edition (2007)
   by Larry Ramsell
Moon Up–Moon Down: Story of the Solunar Theory (1972)
   by John Alden Knight
Muskie Mania (1978) by Ron Schara
Muskie! The Premier Waters of North America (2002)
   by Russ Wayre/Fishing Hot Spots
Muskies on the Shield (2001) by Dick Pearson
Muskies Suck (1997) by Pete Mania
Musky Mastery (1992) by Steve Heiting
Pike on the Fly (1993) by Barry Reynolds
Secrets of a Muskie Guide (1990) by Tony Rizzo
Time on the Water (1982) by Bill Gardner
What Fish See (1999) by Colin J. Kageyama

The Future:

In addition to becoming a member of Muskies Inc., I strongly urge you to support the following local and national organizations that work hard to protect and preserve the environment where muskies and other important game fish live:

American Rivers: www.americanrivers.org
Federation of Fly Fishers: www.fedflyfishers.org
Conservation Resource Alliance: www.rivercare.org
Nature Conservancy: www.nature.org
River Alliance of Wisconsin: www.wisconsinrivers.org
Trout Unlimited: www.tu.org

A great day with Wisconsin guide Brad Bohen: Fly fishing for muskies is really about more that just catching fish. Regardless of the destination, a day of muskie fishing is always more fun when shared with a friend.

FLY-ROD MUSKIE WORLD RECORDS*

National Freshwater Fishing Hall of Fame and International Game Fish Association (IGFA)

OFFICIAL NATIONAL FRESHWATER FISHING HALL OF FAME RECORDS

World (Kept Fish) Muskie Records

MUSKELLUNGE, Natural (*Esox masquinongy*)
Division #2—Fly Fishing

Line Class	Lbs./ozs.	Angler	Where Caught	Date
2 lb.	6-12	John Kavanaugh	Brunet River, Wisconsin, USA	6-11-94
4 lb.	12-1	Jack Giles	Middle Eau Claire, Wisconsin, USA	6-25-94
6 lb.	19-6	David Arnold	Indian Lake, Wisconsin, USA	5-29-00
8 lb.	19-8	Ronald P. Parks	North Harper Lake, Wisconsin, USA	5-27-85
10 lb.	18-9	Russell W. Fisher	Pike Lake, Wisconsin, USA	6-28-89
12 lb.	OPEN			
14 lb.	OPEN			
16 lb.	23-13	Ron Kutella	Wisconsin River, Wisconsin, USA	7-01-05
17 lb.	OPEN			
20 lb.	OPEN			
25 lb.	14-13	Glenn Kreger	Lake Tomahawk, Wisconsin, USA	6-18-95
30 lb.	OPEN			
36 lb.	OPEN			
40 lb.	OPEN			
45 lb.	OPEN			
50 lb.	OPEN			
Unlimited	OPEN			

MUSKELLUNGE, Hybrid or Tiger Muskie (Natural Muskie x Northern Pike) (*Esox masquinongy x Esox lucius*)
Division #2—Fly Fishing

Line Class	Lbs./ozs.	Angler	Where Caught	Date
2 lb.	OPEN			
4 lb.	OPEN			
6 lb.	15-8	Barry Reynolds	Quincy Reservoir, Colorado, USA	8-08-92
8 lb.	20-4	Mitch Goodrich	Quincy Reservoir, Colorado, USA	9-21-96
10 lb.	OPEN			
12 lb.	OPEN			
14 lb.	OPEN			
16 lb.	OPEN			
17 lb.	OPEN			
20 lb.	15-11	Douglas P. Radunz	Bryant Lake, Minnesota, USA	9-08-01
25 lb.	OPEN			
30 lb.	24-5	Frank Prekel	Quincy Reservoir, Colorado, USA	4-30-95
40 lb.	OPEN			
Unlimited	OPEN			

*AS OF MARCH 1, 2008

Catch-and-Release Muskie Records

MUSKELLUNGE, Natural (*Esox masquinongy*)
Division #2—Fly Fishing

Line Class	Inches	Angler	Where Caught	Date
2 lb.	39″	Donald C. Olson	Lake Superior, Minnesota, USA	9-30-00
4 lb.	48″	Donald C. Olson	Lake of the Woods, Minnesota, USA	10-11-01
6 lb.	52″	Fred J. Leisz	Nancy Lake, Wisconsin, USA	7-04-00
8 lb.	49″	Donald C. Olson	Lake of the Woods, Minnesota, USA	10-13-01
10 lb.	40″	Tom Peterson	North Twin Lake, Wisconsin, USA	5-30-07
12 lb.	49″	John R. Jezioro	Tygart River, West Virginia, USA	8-26-05
14 lb.	35″	Tom Peterson	Oneida Co. Lake, Wisconsin, USA	6-07-01
15 lb.	42″	Tom Peterson	Chippewa River, Wisconsin, USA	8-31-06
16 lb.	41″	Tom Peterson	North Twin Lake, Wisconsin, USA	5-31-06
17 lb.	47″	Derek Kuehl	Chippewa River, Wisconsin, USA	10-25-06
20 lb.	49″	Robert Tomes	Flambeau River, Wisconsin, USA	10-18-06
25 lb.	41″	Tom Peterson	Wisconsin River, Wisconsin, USA	6-03-04
30 lb.	43″	Jim Matschulat	Chippewa Flowage, Wisconsin, USA	8-14-96
36 lb.	42″	Charlie Moore	Lake Vermillion, Minnesota, USA	7-10-98
40 lb.	47″	Dave Fass	Big Fork River, Minnesota, USA	9-01-96
45 lb.	44″	Don Larson	Chippewa River, Wisconsin, USA	9-17-00
50 lb.	38″	Tom Peterson	Kentuck Lake, Wisconsin, USA	5-31-05
Unlimited	38″	Donaldson V. Lawhead	Chippewa River, Wisconsin, USA	9-30-06

MUSKELLUNGE, Hybrid or Tiger Muskie (Natural Muskie x Northern Pike) (*Esox masquinongy x Esox lucius*)
Division #2—Fly Fishing

Line Class	Inches	Angler	Where Caught	Date
16 lb.	45″	Barry Reynolds	Quincy Resorvoir, Colorado, USA	8-02-94
20 lb.	31″	Doug Cavin	Blue Water Resorvoir, New Mexico, USA	10-12-07
30 lb.	39″	Jim Matschulat	Chippewa Flowage, Wisconsin, USA	8-07-94
40 lb.	43″	James S. Matschulat	Chippewa Flowage, Wisconsin, USA	6-23-00

INTERNATIONAL GAME FISH ASSOCIATION (IGFA)

Fly-Rod Muskie World Records

MUSKELLUNGE, Natural (*Esox masquinongy*)

Line Class	Inches	Angler	Where Caught	Date
2 lb.	OPEN			
6 lb.	OPEN			
8 lb.	25-11	Rick Kraft	Grand River, Ohio, USA	4-26-02
12 lb.	29	John R. Jezioro	Tygart River, West Virginia, USA	8-26-05
16 lb.	21	Bill Sherer	Boulder Junction, Wisconsin, USA	10-17-03
20 lb.	23-8	Dr. Jerry Matlen	Rowan Lake, Ontario, Canada	6-29-04

MUSKELLUNGE, Hybrid or Tiger Muskie (Natural Muskie x Northern Pike) (*Esox masquinongy x Esox lucius*)

Line Class	Inches	Angler	Where Caught	Date
2 lb.	9-12	R. Lichtenwalner	Susquehanna River, Pennsylvania, USA	11-26-88
4 lb.	5-12	R. Lichtenwalner	Susquehanna River, Pennsylvania, USA	12-09-87
6 lb.	17-4	Paul Schmookler	Freehold, New York, USA	7-29-83
8 lb.	10-10	John Brandstatter	Horseshoe Lake, Colorado, USA	5-15-97
12 lb.	30-6	Michel Croteau	St. Lawrence River, Quebec, Canada	10-20-85
16 lb.	9	Doug Cavin	Blue Water Resorvoir, New Mexico, USA	10-12-07
18 lb.	OPEN			
20 lb.	7	Doug Cavin	Blue Water Resorvoir, New Mexico, USA	10-12-07

An Opportunity for Book Collectors

A beautiful signed and numbered limited edition volume of *Muskie on the Fly*, bound in leather with a foil-stamped slipcase, is available from Wild River Press. A premium edition featuring the book plus framed original flies tied by the author is also available. Visit www.wildriverpress.com or telephone 425-486-3638.

CREDITS

Photographs in this Book

Troy Anderson
Pages 253, 267

Brad Bohen
Pages 57, 58-59, 218, 247, 259

Dale Bowman
Page 242

Cass County Historical Society
Page 52

Steve Cervenka
Page 249

Rich Clarke
Page 39

Cliff Outdoors
Page 79

Cortland Line Company
Page 73

Marshall Cutchin
Page 16

Pat Ehlers
Page 249

Eric Engbretson
Pages 6-7, 32-33, 40, 41

Ted Fauceglia
Pages 8-9, 86, 88-89, 90, 91, 94, 98-99, 100, 101, 102, 104, 105, 106, 107, 108, 109, 110, 111, 112, 113, 114, 115, 116, 117, 118, 119, 121, 243, 248, 250

Joe Flater
Page 272

Jim Teeny
Page 70

Derek Kuehl
Page 234

Ben Kueng
Pages 82, 138

Steve Kunnath
Page 251

Mike Lazarus
Pages 28, 256-257, 263

Dan Legere
Page 268

James Linehan
Pages 20-21, 50-51, 55, 255

Larry Mann and Wendy Williamson
Page 237

Paul Melchior
Pages 61, 122-123, 133, 139, 144, 154, 155, 175, 187

Lisa Meritt
Pages 4-5, 222-223, 264-265

Mark Meritt
Page 201

Brian Meszaros
Page 221

Mike Mladenik
Jacket cover photo

Outcast Sporting Gear
Page 134

Walker Parrot
Page 270

Thomas R. Pero
Pages 23, 84-85, 87, 92, 132, 136, 176, 188-189, 193, 202-203, 206, 238-239, 241

Marc Petitjean
Page 96

Larry Ramsell
Pages 29, 210

Barry Reynolds
Pages 26, 269

Ben C. Robinson *Muskellunge Fishing* (1925)
Page 71

Rio Products
Page 69

3M Scientific Anglers
Pages 70, 73

St. Croix Rod
Page 64

Waterworks-Lamson
Page 62

Wisconsin Department of Natural Resources/John Kubisiak and Steve Timler
Pages 24, 27

INDEX

A

Action water 50-51, 260-262, 261 (sidebar)
Alaska 15, 48-49
Algae bloom 225
Anderson, Troy 253-254 (interview)
Angel streamer fly, recipe and photo 243
Angry Minnow streamer fly, recipe and
    photo 117

B

Back-set 199-192 (illustration)
Barbosa, Ed 28
Beuford fly, recipe and photo 248
Blanton, Dan 86, 110, 119
Boat control 135
    blind fishing vs. sight fishing 136-137
Boats 133-134
    casting deck 137-139
    casting from a boat 135 (sidebar)
    line management 138 (sidebar)
Boga-Grip 81, 209
Bohen, Brad 117, 246-249 (interview),
    273
Boulder Junction 12, 13, 15, 259
Bowing to the fish 204, 205 (illustration)
British Columbia 17
Bryant, Nelson 8
Bunny Twin-Tail streamer fly, recipe and
    photo 107

C

Cain, Chad 214, 270-271
Cameras 83
Carlson, Dave 53
Casting deck 137-139,
Catch and release 207-208, 258
Cave Run Lake, Kentucky 31
Cervenka, Steve 249
Chapralis, Jim 1-3, 124
Check haul 144
Chippewa Flowage, Wisconsin 28, 31
Chippewa River 237
Clouser, Bob 109, 86
Clouser Minnow streamer fly, recipe and
    photo 109, 120, 121
Commercial muskie flies 118-119
Confidence 48-52

Conomo Special streamer fly, recipe and
    photo 116
Conventional muskie guides 270-271
Conventional muskie shops 272-273
Cowgirl streamer fly, recipe and photo
    114
Cradles 210
Crayfish 38

D

Dahlberg Diver 86-87, 106
Deibel, Robert (Icthlyo-Sys Head) 100,
    103
Destinations 258-272
Determination 47-48
Double Bunny streamer fly, recipe and
    photo 108, 120, 121
Dysinger, Mark 107

E

Ehlers, Pat 70, 249-251 (interview)

F

Fall muskie fishing 231-237, 232-233
    (illustration)
Fall turnover 234
Fighting muskies 202-207
    line management 202-204
    controlling the fish 204-207
        jumps 204
        head shakes, thrashing, rolls, and
            twists 205
        runs and lunges 205-207
        final stages 207
Flater, Joe 74, 190, 272
Flash-Tail Whistler streamer fly, recipe
    and photo 110, 120, 121
Flies and fly tying 84-121
    general design characteristics 86-87,
        86 (sidebar)
    streamers 87-92
        action 91
        colors, flash, and pattern 90-91
        eyes 91
        hooks 90
        size and profile 89
        sound and vibration 91

variations 92
weight 89-90
top-water 92-93
color 93
sound and vibration 92-93
castability and wind resistance 93-94
durability 95
hooking properties 95-96
modifications 96-103
spinners and propellers 100, 103
synthetic heads 103
trailer hooks 96, 100
twister tails 100
weed guards 103
Fly patterns 103-121
Angel, recipe and photo 243
Angry Minnow, recipe and photo 117
Beuford, recipe and photo 248
Bunny Twin-Tail, recipe and photo 107
Clouser Minnow, recipe and photo
109, 120, 121
Conomo Special, recipe and photo 116
Cowgirl, recipe and photo 114
Double Bunny, recipe and photo 108,
120, 121
Flash-tail Whistler, recipe and photo
110, 120, 121
Marauder, recipe and photo 104, 120, 121
Red-Tail tube fly, recipe and photo
112-113 (spread), 115
Seeker, recipe and photo 250
Snake Slider, recipe and photo 106,
120, 121
Tiktaalik, recipe and photo 98-99
(spread), 105
Yak Attack, recipe and photo 8-9
(spread), 111
Fly fishing, advantages and limitations of
45 (sidebar)
Fly casting
practice, importance of 124
basic skills 124-126
essential casts
single and double haul 126-128,
126 (illustration)
short-line rolls cast 128, 127 (illustration)
shooting line 126-128

long-line lift 128 (illustration)
water haul 128-129, 129 (illustration)
change-of-direction 129-130, 130
(illustration)
dealing with wind 130-133
casting big flies 130 (sidebar)
Fly tackle
fly boxes 79-80
fly lines 68-72
backing 67
floating lines 68-69
sinking lines 69-72
integrated heads 69-70
mini-tip lines 70
intermediate lines 70
core 69
finish 69
care and maintenance 69
multi-tip lines 70
over lining 72
fly reels
choosing a muskie fly reel 67
arbor size 67
drag systems 67
recommended muskie fly reels 68
(sidebar)
fly rods
choosing a muskie fly rod 61-63
action 63-64
length 65-66
guides 66
multi-piece 66
fighting butt 66
handle 66, 67 (illustration)
recommended muskie fly rods 65
(sidebar)
Fly shops 267-270
Fly-tying resources 118-119
Follows
figure-8 technique 175-176
seeing fish 176-178, 177 (sidebar),
178 (sidebar)
reading follows 178-179
converting follows 179-187
streamers 179-184
lift-and-sweep technique 180,
179 (illustration)

figure-8 technique 181-184,
   180-181 (illustration spread)
   finer points 182-184
   figure-8 alternatives 184 (sidebar)
   top water 184-185, 185
      (illustration)
   changeup and finesse tactics 185-187
Fox Chain O'Lakes, Illinois 30

G
Galloup, Kelly *Modern Streamers for*
   Trophy Trout 148
Gear check list 83 (sidebar)
Georgian Bay, Ontario 30
Gierach, John 42
Global warming, impact of 214, 258
Green Bay, Wisconsin 28
Guides 240-255

H
Haig-Brown, Roderick 257
Hand landing muskies 208-209
Hartman, Len 29
Hayward, Wisconsin 258
Hesch, Zach 268
Hooking muskies 190-202
   mechanics 193
   strike zones 194 (sidebar)
   hooksets 194-202
      strip-strike 194-197, 195 (illustration)
      sweep-set 198 (illustration)
      tip-set 199 (illustration)
      figure-8 back-set 199-200, 199
         (illustration)
   top-water strikes 200-202 (sidebar)
Hook remover 81
Hook sharpener 81
Hook sharpening 192 (illustration)

I
Incidental species 231
Independent muskie guides 266-267
Injury prevention 139
International Game Fish Association
   74, 272, 275
Internet resources 272

J
Jaw spreaders 81
Jordan, Michael 48

K
Kennedy, Ray and Jim 14
Knots 72-78
   nail knot 76 (illustration)
   blood knot 76 (illustration)
   surgeon's knot 76 (illustration)
   Albright knot 76 (illustration)
   perfection loop 76 (illustration)
   surgeon's loop 77 (illustration)
   loop to loop connection 77 (illustration)
   uni knot 77 (illustration)
   non-slip knot 77 (illustration)
   figure 8 knot 77 (illustration)
Kunnath, Steve 251-253 (interview)
Kuehl, Derek 234

L
Lac Courte Oreilles 29
Lake Chautauqua, New York 30
Lake fishing hotspots 216-217 (spring
   illustration), 226-227 (summer
   illustration), 232-233 (fall illustration)
Lake of the Woods, Ontario 30, 107
Lake Shelbyville, Illinois 31
Lake St. Clair 28, 30, 251
Lake Vermilion, Minnesota 201
Larson, Don 193, 248
Landing muskies 207-211
   hand landing 208-209
   nets 209-210
   cradles 210
   live wells 210
   holding muskies 210-211
Leaders 72-79
   line to leader connection 72-73
   leader length 73-79
   leader configuration 78 (illustration)
   taper design 73-74
   IGFA rules 74
   commercial leaders 74
   fluorocarbon 74
   super lines 78
Lazarus, Mike 28, 47, 53, 210, 244-246
   (interview)

Leech Lake Rampage 52
Leech Lake, Minnesota 30,
Legere, Dan 91, 268
Line control 133
Line management 133, 138 (sidebar),
Linehan, James 55, 108
Lodges and outfitters 267-271
Long-nose pliers 81
Lures 86-87

M
Maclean, Norman 4
Magic head 96, 103
McClane, Al 44
Meszaros, Brian 221
Mann, Larry 237
Marauder streamer fly, recipe and photo
    104, 120, 121
Maximizing opportunities 54-56
Mayo, Earl 15
Meritt, Mark 48, 215, 242-244 (interview)
Mille Lacs Lake, Minnesota 28
Minocqua, Wisconsin 14
Mladenik, Mike 39, 218
Moon phases 55
Murphy, Rich 116
Muskies, Inc., 207, 273
Muskie
    age determination 27-28
        cleithrum bone 27
    behavior 31-37
    distribution 24, 26
    evolution 24
    fecundity 27
    growth rates 27-28, 27 (graphs)
    habitat preferences 29-37
    hybridization 24
    identification 22-24, 25 (illustration)
        albinism 23-24
        barred phase 25 (illustration)
        clear phase 25 (illustration)
        spotted phase (illustration)
        tiger muskie 24, 25 (illustration),
            26, 269
    flowages 30-31
    forage preferences 39-40 (sidebar)
    migration 36-37

name etymology 22
natural lakes 29-31, 30 (illustration)
    oligotrophic lakes 30
    mesotrophic lakes 30
    eutrophic lakes 30
population densities 29
records 28-29, 274-275
reservoirs 30-31
rivers 30, 31 (illustration)
schooling 35
spawning 26-27
strike behavior 37-39, 36-37 (illustration)
temperature preferences 36-37
vision 36 (sidebar)
weed preferences 31, 34 (illustration)

N
National Freshwater Fishing Hall of
    Fame 259, 272
Nets 209-210
Night fishing 225
Northern pike 23 (sidebar), 24, 25
    (illustration), 39, 51, 271-272
    (destinations)

O
O'Brian, Ken 29
O-ring 144
Oxygen levels 225

P
Parrot, Walker 270
Permit 16, 18
Pero, Tom 202-203 (photo spread)
Personal safety 134-135
Petitjean, Marc 96, 103
Photoperiods 55
Plastic fish replicas 206
Plastic gear storage box 80
Pratt, Frank, Jr. 22, 40, 258
Predator pose 143 (illustration)
Presentations 140-171
    line management 143-144
    basic retrieves 144-146
    streamer retrieves 146-151
        basic retrieve 146-147, 147
            (illustration)

variations 147-149
   jerk-and-strip retrieve 148, 149
    (illustration)
top-water retrieves 151-155
   sweep-and-strip retrieve 151-152,
    153 (illustration)
   top-water considerations 152-153
   variations 153-155
    popping 153-154
    chugging 154
   top-water problems and solutions
    154 (sidebar)
specialized presentations 155-171
   tick-and-twitch 157
   ripping 158
   jigging 159
   bulging 160
   pause-and-twitch 161
   slop fishing with streamers 164
   slop fishing with top-water flies
    165
   bump-and-run 166
   break dance 167
   deep rip 168
   bottom bouncing 169
   cast-and-blast 170
   streamer swing 171
sight fishing 148-151
   boiling or rolling fish 148-149
   laid up or sunning fish 149-151
   cruising fish 15
Pressured fish 161, 186-187, 242-244
Puglisi, Enrico 118-119

Q

R
Rainy's Flies 118
Recommended muskie resources 272-273
Red-tail tube fly, recipe and photo
   112-113 (spread), 115
Release glove 80
Releasing muskies 211
Reynolds, Barry 26, 269
River fishing techniques and hotspots
   170 (illustration), 171 (illustration),
   228-229 (illustration)

Rocks 31, 35
Rough fish 39-40
Rules for fishing with a guide 241 (sidebar)

S
Sanchez, Scott 108
Seasons 214-237
   summer fishing 221-231
    lake hotspots 226-227 (illustration)
    river hotspots 228-229 (illustration)
    fish location and patterns 221-225
    presentations, retrieves, and flies
     225-231
    summary 230 (sidebar)
   spring fishing 215-220
    lake hotspots 216-217 (illustration)
    river hotspots 228-229 (illustration)
    fish location and patterns 218-219
    presentations, retrieves, and flies
     219-220
    summary 220 (sidebar)
    influence of sun and wind 218
     (sidebar)
   fall fishing 231-237
    lake hotspots 232-233 (illustration)
    river hotspots 228-229 (illustration)
    fish location and patterns 234-235
    presentations, retrieves, and flies
     235-237
    turnover 234
    summary 236 (sidebar)
Seeker streamer fly, recipe and photo 250
Shawe, Victor 48
Sholseth, Thomas 37
Smallmouth bass 39, 231
Snake Slider diver fly, recipe and photo
   106, 120, 121
Speed trolling 39, 221
Spirit Lake, Iowa 30
Spot on a spot 156 (illustration)
Spray, Louis 28, 29
St. Lawrence River 30, 219
Steelhead 17, 18
Stripping basket 81-82
Stripping glove 80
Strip-strike 194-197, 195 (illustration)
Sun Zi 58

Sunglasses 82-83
Suspended fish 35
Sweep-set 198 (illustration)

T
Tape measure 81
    use to calculate weight of fish 81
      (sidebar)
Terminal connections 72-79
Tiktaalik popper, recipe and photo
    98-99 (spread), 105
Tip-set 199 (illustration)
Top-water flies and fishing 92-93,
    151-155, 165, 184-185
Tracy, Dwight 85
Trophy water 262, 263 (sidebar)
Trout Lake, Wisconsin 30
Tube flies 92

U
Uhlenhop, Jon 92, 107, 111
Umpqua Feather Merchants 119

V
Vermilion Lake, Minnesota 201
Visualization 56-57
Vogt, William C., 71

W
Walton, Issac 11
Wading 133-134
Weeds 31-34
Wood 35, 166
Wolf packs 35
World Records 28-29, 274-275
Wilde, Oscar 147
Webster Lake 47-48
Williamson, Wendy 237
Windows of opportunity 52-56
Wind direction 218 (sidebar)
Wire bite guard 74-79
    recommended brands 74
    length considerations 78-79
    care and maintenance 78
Wire clipper 80
Wulff, Lee 189

X

Y
Yak Attack streamer fly, recipe and
    photo 8-9 (spread), 111
Yellow perch 39, 41, 116

Z
Ziploc bags 80